Theatres of the Left 1880–1935

History Workshop Series

General Editor
Raphael Samuel, Ruskin College, Oxford

Routledge & Kegan Paul
London, Boston, Melbourne and Henley

Raphael Samuel
Ewan MacColl
Stuart Cosgrove

Theatres of the Left
1880–1935
Workers' Theatre Movements
in Britain and America

First published in 1985
by Routledge & Kegan Paul plc

14 Leicester Square, London WC2H 7PH

9 Park Street, Boston, Mass. 02108, USA

464 St Kilda Road, Melbourne,
Victoria 3004, Australia and

Broadway House, Newtown Road,
Henley-on-Thames, Oxon RG9 1EN, England

Set in Bembo 11 on 12 pt
by Input Typesetting Ltd, London
and printed in Great Britain
by The Thetford Press Ltd
Thetford, Norfolk

Library of Congress Cataloging in Publication Data

Samuel, Raphael

Theatre of the left, 1880–1935
(History workshop series)
Includes index
1. Workers' theatre. 2. Political plays. I. MacColl,
Ewan. II. Cosgrove, Stuart. III. Title. IV. Series.
PN3305.S35   1985   792'.09'043   84–4909

ISBN 0–7100–0901–1

Contents

Preface

This book began life in 1976, when I was asked to go and see Tom
Thomas in Welwyn Garden City. Tom, I was told, was dying:
He had had six heart attacks. He wanted to pass on documents of
something called the WTM – a kind of early version (I was told)
of Unity Theatre, perhaps to record some memories. I went,
partly out of duty (*History Workshop Journal* subsequently printed a
selection of the documents), but also because of memories of Unity
which had been my local theatre when I was a boy in St Pancras,
my occasional Sunday evening church (there were club performances for members) and the scene of my only contribution to
British theatrical life. (I had acted in *The Townsends*, a drama of
slum life in Westminster in which my stage mother was stabbed
to death, and a 'concerned' schoolteacher – played by a man with
crinkly hair – was simultaneously courting my elder sister and
trying to win her mind to higher things.)

The WTM, from Tom's account of it (we had three recording
sessions which form the substance of his narrative in this book)
turned out to be very different from Unity. It belonged in spirit
to the England of the General Strike (the year when Tom founded
the Hackney Labour Players) rather than that of the Popular Front.
It used revue and cabaret (Tom toured the Rhineland with a
German troupe in 1930) rather than stage plays. It was devoted to
agitation and propaganda, especially the first, rather than to 'social
significance' (Unity's watchword). Its dramaturgical location was
the factory rather than the slum (WTM was deadset against Sean
O'Casey who was one of Unity's cultural heros). Just before Tom
died we (the East London History Workshop) put on a performance of Tom's version of *The Ragged Trousered Philanthropists*,
which the Labour Publishing Company had put out in 1928. The
stage was that of the Hoxton Hall, an 1858 music hall which the
Quakers had bought up to save the people from drink. By then
Tom had had another heart attack and it was thought unwise that

he should come. But Tom did come; and so did Charlie Mann – the writer of *How to stage Meerut*, printed in this book – and four other WTM hands. At the end they sang one of their songs – frail voices, but the words – those of a Polish workers' song of the 1920s – were appropriately robust:

Whirlwinds of danger around us are swirling
Overwhelming forces of darkness and fear
Still in the sights of freedom of humanity
Red Flag of liberty shall yet prevail

Going to Ewan MacColl was quite different. He was (I thought at the time) the first real revolutionary I had ever met, terrifyingly well organised, whether engaged in tracing the etymology of a word in a Scottish tinkler's song, or one of the extra-mural theatrical activities he described to me – organising a production of Aristophenes *Frogs* from a minesweeper in the Pacific with the putative cast (after the war they formed *Theatre Workshop*) spread out in the Royal Navy halfway across the world. As a youth – a Manchester proletarian and Communist revolutionary of the 1920s – he had walked the evening streets with a 'red haze of anger' before his eyes, occasionally exalted at the thought of workers' power, then iconoclast and dreaming of the time when the slate-roofed streets would be razed to the ground. Ewan, though much younger than Tom Thomas (he was a 16 year old motor mechanic when he formed his first WTM troupe), was far more culturally ambitious and in his narrative he describes the way he and his friend, Alf Arnitt, searched the Manchester libraries for the international *avant-garde* – the lighting theory of Appia and the revolutionary theatre of Vaghtangov in particular. The recording testified to Ewan's terrifying mental efficiency. It lasted most of twelve hours; it was about a time – his early youth – on which he had no public 'line' and which, it seemed, he had not remembered aloud before. When the transcript was made, I found there was scarcely a line that could be cut, nor did I need to edit or change its order. Apart from Ewan's own compressions, the text of 'Manchester Theatre of Action' (*Part 6* of this book) is a direct transcript of this recording.

When I started research on this book, I was excited to think that I had discovered a lost tradition, and having, as I thought, found it, I decided to trace it further back, first to the Socialist Sunday

Schools and the Clarion dramatic clubs, then to Eleanor Marx and Ibsenism, to Miss Horniman and the Manchester Gaiety, to the Repertory Movement and *Hindel Wakes*. In mid-Victorian times I came across a whole crop of working-class Shakespeareans, and found indeed that the Shakespeare tercentenary committee of 1864 was a kind of radical working mens' 'front'. Chartist times were particularly rewarding. I found the London trades hiring a theatre to honour the Tolpuddle Martres; the London printers taking over theatres and performing their own scripts to provide 'friendly benefits' for the bereaved and sick of the trade; most affecting of all the stonemasons, who were engaged in building Trafalgar Square, hired the Old Vic when they came out on strike in 1841 to give a dramatised version of their case.

Sadly, though, I have concluded that there are no traditions, except those which have been broken or lost: only a series of moments such as that which furnishes the material for this book. But as anyone will know who had the privilege of visiting Joan Littlewood's theatre in Stratford East (my own real initiation to theatre), or the old Half Moon in Great Alie Street; or who has heard the melancholy of 'The rain, it raineth every day'; or even who remembers Beatie breaking out to dance in Wesker's *Roots*; it is in such moments as these that theatre is made.

Acknowledgments

This book has accumulated a number of debts in the course of a
long gestation. Hannah Mitchell was my companion at the earliest
stage of the work; we undertook the recordings with Tom Thomas
together, and discussion with her was also responsible for much
of the hidden agenda of this book – especially on the matter of the
aesthetics of realism. Clive Barker, an old theatre workshop hand
and latterly – in his improbable fastness at Warwick University – its
living archivist, was generous in the loan and copy of documents.
Richard Stourac and Kathleen McCreery, then of Broadside
Mobile Theatre and engaged on a similar project (their book on
the international WTM will shortly be published by RKP) lent
me transcripts of interviews with the Lewisham Red Players – a
generosity which seems to come more easily to the fraternity of
theatre researchers than to those engaged in more conventional
academic pursuits. Bert Hogenkamp of Amsterdam volunteered
the best text I have so far obtained on Labour Party theatre in the
1920s – an account of the Co. Durham tour of Ruth Dodd's
The Pitman's Pay. Alex McCrindle wistfully recorded his theatrical
apprenticeship with the Glasgow Clarion Players. Hetty Bower,
one of Tom Thomas's recruits in Hackney, recalled the 'coming
out' of a young Jewish girl, and her excitement at the mauve
curtains and modernity of two local Communist teachers – one of
them the redoubtable London agitator, Kath Duncan. Ray
Waterman, one of the second mothers of my childhood, introduced
me to Tom Thomas, and without her urgency this book would
not have been started. John Mason tracked Colindale references to
the WTM in the *Sunday Worker*; Alun Howkins – then at a pitch
of 'Third Period' enthusiasm supplied me with those from the
Daily Worker; David Meyer and Tony Jackson educated me in the
elements of the Repertory Theatre Movements. To these, and also
to Sally Alexander, with whom over the years I have discussed
many of the issues in this book; John Savillew, Lee James, David
Bradby, Angela Tuckett, and Malcolm Knight, my thanks.

Introduction: Theatre and politics
Raphael Samuel

Theatre, as the most public of the arts, is second cousin to politics, and even when the relationship is a forbidden one – as it was on the English stage, until recently, under the Lord Chamberlain's regulations – there is a two-way traffic between them. The earliest European theatre was a drama of government and power, law and justice, albeit allegorised in the tragedy of kings and courts; and the Athenian stage also provided an arena for comedy and satire in which the political issues and factional divisions of the day were fought out. Not the least of its functions, as so often in later times, was to offer a reverse image of chaos, an imaginary resolution of conflicts which in real life were intractable. Statecraft was of course one of the great subjects of Elizabethan drama. The stage, from the time of *Gordobuc* onwards, served as a nursery of the national idea – *Richard II* and *Henry V* can remind us both of its potency and of its novelty. The private theatres of the aristocracy (banned as subversive under legislation of 1604) were a recruiting ground of faction, and the players' scene in *Hamlet* testifies to the part played by court theatre in the rivalries, intrigues and grooming of Renaissance kingship. The direct representation of politics was prohibited on the nineteenth-century English stage, but it is not difficult to identify the presence of proto-political themes, or to hypothesise the influence of theatre in the formation of sub-political attitudes. The cult of Wellington, and the re-enactment of the battle of Waterloo, the most famous of the equestrian dramas staged at Astley's amphitheatre (an annual event from its first public performance in 1829) helped to keep the military spirit alive in the alien environment of free trade liberalism; later, in the aftermath of the Crimean War and the Indian Mutiny, English militarism was given a fresh boost by such booth theatre favourites – an early form of living newspaper – as the representation of *The Siege of Lucknow*. In radical politics, the enormously popular stage adaptation of *Uncle Tom's Cabin* helped to mobilise sentiment behind the anti-slavery cause (Eliza's escape across the ice is one of the most frequently remembered scenes in memoirs of nineteenth-century childhood); Poor Law dramas, such as *The Workhouse Girl*, helped to keep the anti-Poor Law agitation alive long after it had ceased to be an issue in national politics; Siberian escape drama, a sensationalist sub-genre which owes its origin to the Paris theatre of the Restoration, and which was still a favourite at the London suburban theatres of the 1900s, helped to sustain a strongly anti-Tsarist public opinion whatever the twists and turns of government diplomacy and foreign policy. Melodrama, the great popular art form of the period, provided a universal idiom for popular religion and politics. The moral crusades of the 1870s and 1880s – as also arguably the Salvation Army and Socialism, could be said to take their cue from it, their paradigms of rescue work, if not their words of blood and fire; while the stage representation of landlords and aristocrats – stock villains in melodrama – is possibly not the least of the reasons why, right down to 1914, land rather than capital was the popular metaphor for class oppression; and why, so late as 1909, 'Peers versus the People' could still serve as the rallying cry of English democracy.

The resemblance of politics to theatre has long been a favourite theme of parliamentary commentators, observing the ritualised combat, stylised gesture and histrionic abilities of public men, and it may be that the disappearance of high politics as a subject for stage representation had to do less with the severities of theatrical censorship than with the appearance of the hustings and, later on, the rise of the platform, as an alternative space for the dramatisation of politics. Bagehot's cynical observations in *The English Constitution* on the 'complex, august, *theatrical*' parts of the constitution – not least the 'Gothic grandeur' of monarchy – can serve to underline the dramaturgical dimensions of public authority and the awe-inspiring rituals of the Crown, the Law and the Church. Theatricality is, if anything, even more apparent – though also more impromptu, in the mobilisation of popular politics, carnivalesque at one moment, melodramatic at another, but always larger than life. The idea that Beaumarchais 'stages' the storming of the Bastille, though plausible (he was an opposition playwright, who had recently taken up living quarters in the Faubourg St Antoine, and took part in the mass assault) is no doubt a canard, but is has the merit of highlighting the dramatic character of great public events. A political demonstration is necessarily an act of street theatre, albeit one with a multitudinous cast, and a rhythm and tempo of its own. Readers of Samuel Bamford's *Passages in the Life of a Radical* will know how carefully Peterloo was stage-managed, before the proceedings were brutally interrupted by the charge of the Manchester yeomanry. Much the same ritual accompanied the processionings and appearances of the Chartist orators and leaders, including, on occasion, the use of cavalry escorts; while at the 'monster' torchlight demonstrations the impromptu firing of pistols, and brandishing of pikes, heightened the make-believe by simulating a revolutionary catastrophe. The international socialist movement of the period of the Second International (1890–1914) was a prolific source of proto-theatrical forms most memorably in the invention of workers' May Day. Dramatic pageants and festivals were the major forms of mass mobilisation, while at indoor meetings, readings and recitations, of the kind described in chapter one of this book, were as much a customary part of the proceedings as the political lecture or address. No Russian Beaumarchais has ever been hypothesised as the impresario of the storming of the Winter Palace, but the theatricality of the event made it an irresistible subject for Meyerhold when, in the following year, he staged his revolutionary mass spectacles. (By the same token, it is interesting to note that Romain Rolland, in his 1900s campaign for the establishment of a 'People's Theatre', stages *Le Quatorze Juillet*, re-enacting the storming of the Bastille as a mass spectacle, though tempering the revolutionary example with a humanist message, and making the leading protagonist an individualised heroine from humble life.)

Theatre seems to exercise a 'metaphysical' influence on politics or at any rate an influence out of all proportion to its size, or the number of its audience. Quite often it seems to prefigure or anticipate major political themes, as though a live performance on stage constituted a kind of symbolic recognition of the entry of some new issue into the arena of public debate. Thus the free woman, in the person of Ibsen's *Nora*, was walking the boards of the London stage for some years before the emancipatory movement of women forced itself on to the agenda of national politics; while at the Abbey Theatre, Dublin, the magic of Irish nationality was being proclaimed a dozen years before it was taken up by the heroes of the Easter Rising. A number of other examples suggest themselves, where the stage might be seen as *anticipating* politics rather than reflecting it, and life as imitating art. One might be the idealisation of the English gentleman, as a lovable eccentric rather than a military or playing-field hero, a stage stereotype which crystallises in *The Importance of Being Earnest* and which was enchantingly amplified (at least so far as West End audiences were concerned) by 'Mad Dogs and Englishmen' (in Noel Coward's *Cavalcade*) and the society comedies of Freddie Lonsdale. A more clearly documented case would be the extraordinary resonance of R. C. Sherriff's *Journey's End*, which inspired or released a whole series of influential anti-war writings (and anti-public school memoirs); and by bringing the trauma of the First World War to the centre of the stage helped to create the climate of opinion for the Peace Ballot and 1930s pacifism. Again, to take another familiar example, one might suggest that the protest movement associated with the Aldermaston marches and the first CND was announced, and the cultural revolution of the 1960s prefigured, in the Royal Court's production of *Look Back in Anger* both in its iconoclasm and its rediscovery of the 'good, brave causes' of the past. Lastly one might consider the possibility that experimental theatre – the abolition of the proscenium stage, the development of theatre in the round, and the notion of theatre as an open space – provided an imaginative paradigm for the campus revolt of 1968 and the anti-authoritarian movements associated with it.

The idea of propaganda theatre – the subject of this book – could be traced back to very early times, if one were to think in terms of anticipations rather than of lineage. One obvious prototype would be the late medieval morality play, a theatre of the church-yard or the street, with its ritualised combats of good and evil, its stock characters and its intense audience participation and involvement. Another would be the 'theatre of instruction' advocated by Rousseau and practised by Diderot against the 'theatre of entertainment' of the privileged. It was conceived of as a vehicle of popular enlightenment, to combat superstition and priestcraft; in a later version, championed by Michelet, theatre was conceived of as a kind of social church, a school for patriotic and republican virtue. Both these ideas were embodied in the didactic play (the *pièce à thèse*), a recognised dramatic sub-genre in later nineteenth-century France, and they were the leading idea of the 'people's theatre' experiments which, in the 1890s and 1900s, grew up on the peripheries of the socialist movement, and as auxiliaries of the Bourses de Travail. A more influential example for the socialists of the time was the 'ethical' drama which took its imaginative model from Ibsen. Like the 'theatre of instruction' of the philosophies, it was self-consciously an alternative to the 'theatre of entertainment' ('after-dinner theatre' as it was derisorily labelled) of the rich. It took 'stage realism' as its watchword, 'sociological' drama as its object. Ibsenism had an enormous influence on middle-class revolutionists, as for instance Bernard Shaw and the Avelings in Britain, Fernand Pelloutier in France, but neither ethical drama nor its naturalist offspring were popular art forms; they found their home, typically, in the burgeoning 'arts' theatres, such as Stanislavsky's theatre in Moscow, or the Royal Court in London, catering to a 'concerned' minority of the professional classes, and more artistically-inclined scions of the bourgeoisie.

The socialist movement of the period of the Second International (1890-1914) worshipped at the shrine of art; it conceived itself as a messenger of high culture, bringing education and enlightenment to the masses. But the very reverence for high culture made socialists diffident about attempting to instrumentalise it. The absolute autonomy of art was unquestioned, and the writers, painters and musicians who came into the socialist ranks were treated with exaggerated respect. 'We do not wish to domesticate them', wrote Jules Destrée, one of the architects of the very impressive cultural politics of the Belgian Workers' Party, 'but to allow them all possible liberty, Nor do we admire an artist because he is a socialist but because he is an artist and produces masterpieces.' Kautsky maintained a similarly abstentionist position in relation to the future: 'communism in material production, anarchy in intellectual production' was how he defined the socialist state. Art might carry a social message, but it was the common sense view of ideologues and aesthetes alike that it served the movement best if it remained true to itself, absorbing emancipatory ideas, but expressed, in the first place, artistically. The German SDP, despite the ambition of its educational aims, resolutely refused to embroil itself in cultural controversies, and when the issue came to a head, in 1896, refused to intervene even in matters which affected its own publication: 'equal rights in the cultural sphere', i.e. workers' access to art, was the summit of its ambition. These tendencies were reinforced by the activity of socialist cultural groups – the educational associations, arts circles, theatre groups, orchestras and choirs established in the ambit of the socialist parties. Even when launched, like the Free People's Stage in Berlin, with the aim of applying 'socialist principles' to the arts, they tended to develop enthusiasms of their own and to find their place in a wider orbit. Repertoires, typically, were diversified, and even when a nominal allegiance to the parent organisation was retained, the gravitational pull was exercised by audiences, performers and followings.

The 'People's Theatre' projects of the period were particularly liable to escape the Party orbit. They were started, typically, on the fringes of the socialist movement, by sympathisers rather than activists, and with the philanthropic aim of giving the masses access to dramatic art. They depended, for their survival, on building up an independent following: unlike the orchestras and choirs, they could not be integrated into Party cultural life (the festivals, galas and anniversaries which did so much to establish a socialist presence); unlike the writers and poets they could not be published in the columns of the Party press. Some developed into arts theatres, playing to minority audiences, and making their reputation on the performance of uncensored plays. Many foundered for want of popular support. The German *Volksbühnen*, the most successful (by the 1920s they had a mass membership of 50,000), though started with the aim of applying 'socialist principles' to the theatre, seem to have settled down, by the 1900s, to a mainly classical repertoire. The local dramatic troupes, started in association with workers' or socialist clubs, often set out with a propagandist intention, but they were peculiarly subject to the demand for entertainment, more especially when they were engaged in fund-raising: the Belgian Federation of Socialist Theatre groups, organised in 1909, made a determined attempt to put on 'message' plays (*pièces à thèse*), illustrating both socialist principles and 'rationalist morality', but the proportion of 'message' plays dwindled, and those that survived seem to have done so by their effectiveness as melodrama – the single most popular class of play. The Clarion dramatic clubs, started in 1910, made a speciality of playing Bernard Shaw but, like the Co-op drama groups of later years, most of their effort seems to have gone on the production of entertainments, or, more occasionally, of simple moralities.

Left-wing drama in these years, whether produced for the arts theatres, or for local and 'popular' performance, seems to have been socially conscious rather than politically engaged. Like other cultural initiatives of the period, it was conceived of as a form of spiritual uplift, taking on the powers of darkness, and exhibiting the light of knowledge. Realism, as in the democratic melodrama favoured in Belgium, had to be ennobling, showing tableaus of working-class misery, relieved by individual heroism: as Fernand Mercier, a leading protagonist of 'social theatre' in Belgium, and a popular playwright, put it, 'dramas . . . which describe simply all the devotion, all the self-abnegation, all the sacrifices and all the heroism of the proletariat'. As in socialist songs of the period (English readers will be familiar with the 'Red Flag') there was a strong emphasis on redemption through martyrdom and suffering. Many of the propaganda plays of the period, too, seem to have been written and performed as moralities, offering ideal characters to imitate, and celebrating the victory of virtue over vice. Thus Maurice Pottegher inaugurated his 'People's Theatre' in the Vosges with a drama directed against alcoholism (a major theme in socialist literature and drama of the time, as well as in working-class politics). The Belgian Socialist Theatre groups, in their *pièces à thèse* made anti-clericalism a major theme, alongside anti-alcoholism and anti-militarism.

The 1920s and early 1930s, the period of the theatre movements with which this book is principally concerned, opened up a whole new epoch in the socialist imagination and in the relationship of socialist movements to their theatrical auxiliaries. It was the crystallisation of a self-consciously proletarian aesthetic, of a futuristic dream in which socialism was no longer an escape from the proletarian condition but rather a realisation of workers' power. Instead of the deference to high culture, there was an iconoclastic desire to break with it, no less apparent in, say, the Plebs League – the trade union based and mainly Labour Party federation of working-class autodidacts – than among Communists. Instead of moral uplift, there was agit-prop, a self-consciously revolutionary art. There was a corresponding growth in Party-mindedness in both the Communist and Social Democratic Parties of the period, and an assertion of the Party's leading role in the arts (this was true even in Britain, where Herbert Morrison, the ambitious secretary of the London Labour Party, constituted himself as a kind of cultural impresario, forming a Labour Party Symphony Orchestra and a Labour Party Federation of Choirs and Dramatic Societies). The shyness about instrumentalising art was replaced by a determination to grasp it boldly.

Interestingly, and paradoxically, the workerist turn in socialist politics, led to, or at least was accompanied by, a remarkable openness to experimentalism. The period of this book, in fact, is one which sees, in all the arts, an alliance between communism and the *avant-garde*. The socialism of this time was exuberantly futuristic, and as in Russia, so in Germany and other parts of Europe, including to some degree Britain, communists and socialists took up, or were taken up by, modernist movements. The idea of socialist art took on a whole new configuration of meanings in which pastoral ideas of beauty, as epitomised in the work of Walter Crane and William Morris, were replaced by a machine aesthetic which celebrated factory industry as a source of workers' power. In theatre, the alliance of communism and the *avant-garde* was particularly fruitful, and it was from the Russian and German models of agit-prop that the British and American troupes described in this volume took their cue.

This book is concerned with a moment rather than a continuous historical tradition, a moment which, as the introductory chapter argues, was lost with the advent, in 1935, of the Popular Front. It was as sharply distinguished from the 'People's Theatre' projects of the pre-1914 years, as from the 'Socialist Realism' of the Popular Front and after. Yet it raises some of the enduring questions which have recurred in every phase of modernism, whatever its political hue, in particular the attempt to escape from art to anti-art, and theatre to anti-theatre. It exemplifies the difficult and, as some would argue, impossible relationship between an artistic movement and organised political parties, while at the same time showing them (if only for a relatively brief period) in tense but fruitful association. It also exemplifies the *antagonistic* relationship to popular culture which, notwithstanding its democratic ambition, has normally kept the theatre of instruction as the preserve of enlightened minorities.

There is no continuous history of socialist or alternative history to be discovered, rather a succession of moments separated from one another by rupture. Yet each of these moments, when looked at closely, appear as creative, not only for the movements concerned, but also for theatre generally. Rescuing them from oblivion, then, as numbers of scholars have been attempting to do in recent years, is not – or ought not to be – a sectarian affair of committed socialists. It may have something to say to all those who have experienced the importance of theatre in their lives.

Part 1

History

Theatre and socialism in Britain, (1880–1935)

Raphael Samuel

I

British socialism, in the formative years of its existence, seems to have had an especially strong appeal to those who, whatever their particular walk in life, regarded themselves, or were regarded by others, as 'artistic'. The term was then a great deal less exclusive in its connotations than it was to become with the advent of 'highbrows' and a self-consciously minority avant-garde. It was freely applied to certain classes of artisan, as well as to the many classes of under-labourer (e.g. engravers and copyists) engaged in the lower reaches of the cultural industries and trades. It was also widely used as a synonym for the unconventional and Bohemian, for those who (like Edward Carpenter's gardener-comrade, George Hulkin) were 'not too exact or precise about details'.[1] A house-painter could be regarded as a 'bit of an artist', like Owen, the hero of *The Ragged Trousered Philanthropists*, or Robert Tressell, his real-life original, whose frescoes have recently been retrieved.[2] The artistic impulse was particularly strong (though sometimes unacknowledged) in the more revolutionary wings of the socialist movement – nowhere more so than in the 'impossibilist' and apparently severely Marxist Socialist Labour Party, for whom, in the early 1900s, James Connolly was spouting translations of Freiligrath's poetry on the Glasgow street corners, and whose members' staple reading (when not *The Communist Manifesto*) was Eugene Sue's romantically revolutionary fictions.[3] To these one might add the thousands of scribblers who contributed verse to the socialist press (as late as the 1930s there was still a poetry-lovers' corner in *The Daily Herald*); the amateur librettists who mounted operatic and choral concert-meetings; and the open-air 'stump' orators who electrified the crowds by reciting verse as much as by preaching the socialist Word – Shelley's 'Men of England' was for decades a standard peroration in platform oratory, as it had been in that of John Bright during the 1840s.[4]

The aesthetic components of socialism were, in its early years, open and acknowledged. British Marxism, as Belfort Bax noted, was in the first place a 'literary' movement and its most famous exponent was neither a trade unionist nor an economist but the poet-artist, William Morris.[5] 'The first revolt', Sidney Webb noted in 'The Historic Basis of Socialism' (one of the *Fabian Essays* of 1889) came from the 'artistic' side, in the rejection of 'squalid commercialism' and mechanical market laws.[6] In the epoch of Walter Crane and the first May Days, it was pictorial art (of the kind lovingly gathered together in John Gorman's *Banner Bright*) which both shaped the vision of the socialistic future and provided a visual allegory for the Golden Age of the past – that processional dance of bucolic peasants and artisans which served as an emblem of the solidarity of labour and the brotherhood of man. The struggle between labour and capital was conceptualized in terms of the age-old division between rich and poor rather than that of employers and employed; it owed more to 'democratic readings' from the poets than to detailed engagement with the class system. 'Socialism' wrote Keir Hardie, 'was the poetry of the poor': it exalted the masses; it transported them from the mean conditions of their everyday existence to a state of imaginary transcendence. Like poetry, it depended for its enchantment on the willing suspension of disbelief, a self-abandonment to the power of the Word. This was certainly the leading appeal of Ramsay MacDonald, in later years Labour's first Prime Minister, who intoxicated his listeners with the spell of beautiful images. The famous oration on the death of Keir Hardie, delivered to a rapt audience of the Glasgow ILP in 1916 – the speech which made him the idol of Red Clydeside – is a representative example:

> Keir Hardie: there was your old-fashioned man. Every line, every item of his home, his own characteristic. There was your man of individuality. You saw him in the Strand in London, crowded with thousands upon thousands of feet; this great river of ordinary commonplace humanity, where even strong individuality is apt to be lost. But there he was like a great boulder of whinstone, telling of the freshness of the hills. There he was, this strong individuality, amidst men, and yet above men: human and yet separate. You sing in Scotland 'I to the hills will lift mine eyes'. There are some men who are

like the hills; when you look at them you feel that strength, that power of eternity, that solidness which does not pass with a generation, but which stands the storms and the climates, which gladdens your eyes and which your children to generations will see after you have gone and slept and been forgotten. There are some men whose personalities give you the impression of eternity and unshakeable foundations and everlastingness. Hardie was one of those men. Such a man of rugged being and massive soul, of imperturbable courage and of mystic insight, was the man who founded the I.L.P.[7]

There is no doubt that MacDonald saw himself in this light, 'a man of rugged being and massive soul', a politician who was also a poet and a singer, a mystic who carried within him the vision of the city on the hill. In his peroration – which had an extraordinary impact on listeners and was talked about in Glasgow 'for years afterwards' – the religious and aesthetic notions of transcendence are fused:

The old order passes away, and you and I, standing once more at Hardie's tomb, having lingered the past hour with his memory and thoughts of him in our minds, we go back into the world to do our duty, to reconstruct society, to rebuild the fabric that has fallen, to make good the walls that have been crushed; to put a new idea, a new beauty, a new holiness into the lives of the people of Europe.

The cult of beauty, deriving from the Pre-Raphaelites, and earlier still from Shelley, as well as from such better known sources as Ruskin and Morris, and no doubt owing much, too, to the 'aesthetic' movement of the 1880s and 1890s, formed part of the 'common sense' of the Socialist movement of the time. It was the imaginative basis both of its critique of individualism and its vision of a collectivist future. Socialism was the talismanic term for the beautiful; it represented, in the moving terms of Oscar Wilde's *Soul of Man Under Socialism*, all that was potentially 'fine'; capitalism, by contrast, was an incarnation of the 'base', the 'mean', the 'sordid'. Visually socialism was represented not by the proletarian fist, but by the flowing robes of the indeterminately medieval peasants, artisans and goddesses of Walter Crane's engravings. Beauty

comprised both *nature* and *culture*, the unspoiled and the innocent
– the simple home, the dignified work, the craft that was 'true to
materials' – but also the highest products of literature, music and
the fine arts. It was a unifying, integrative principle, a way of
restoring wholeness to the world. Hubert Manning, Ann Veronica's civil servant suitor – 'a socialist of the order of John Ruskin'
– wanted to shout when he saw beautiful things, 'or else . . . to
weep'.[8] Robert Tressell, the Hastings house-painter, was no less
ecstatic when, in the coda of his novel, he projected the 'gilded
domes and glittering pinnacles' of the beautiful cities of the future
'where men shall dwell in true brotherhood and goodwill and
joy'.[9] 'We also had a handsome "hammer man" who worked shifts
at the local steel forge', Alice Foley recalls of her Bolton Socialist
Sunday School. 'He was remarkably well read and a passionate
devotee of poesy and beauty. After separation into small groups
he introduced us to purple passages from Keats's *Eve of St Agnes*
and his lovely intonation of an *Ode on a Grecian Urn*:

> Thou still unravished bride of quietness
> Thou foster-child of silence and slow time
> still lingers in the chamber of memory.'[10]

Ethel Snowden, 'a great snob' according to the jaundiced Diary
entry of Beatrice Webb, but a very popular speaker at ILP assem-
blies, sounded a similar note in her speeches. 'There is a great deal
of truth in the words of that distinguished Frenchman who said
that we can "live without bread, but not without roses"' she told
a mass assembly of London and home counties co-operators in
1927:

> . . . What he meant was that life without music and musical
> appreciation, without art and artistic understanding, without
> books and the power to read and comprehend, without
> earnestness of spirit and spiritual devotion to the community's
> interest, is not life, but existence. Therefore we struggle to add
> something to the richness of culture not only to our own
> lives, but to the lives of everyone around us. I emphasise the
> need of culture to make us gentle and good, to banish hate
> from our hearts, and to plant therein righteousness and the
> love of humanity. A mind of culture makes good things
> possible to us, and enables us to love what is beautiful and

true. Our movement is only one of many struggling for that ideal. Co-operation is eternally and in all things the law of life. Let us take up this task eternal, this burden, and this message. Confident in the righteousness and nobility of our great cause and lofty principle of co-operation, let us go forward hand-in-hand and heart-to-heart, certain that in God's good time that cause, the eternal cause of our common humanity, will be carried to a crowning and triumphant victory.[11]

As in MacDonald's funeral oration over the body of Keir Hardie, as in that vast outpouring of ILP rhetoric, transcendental longings, aesthetic ideals of beauty and ambition for cultural attainment are fused in a single discourse.

In another, more heroic, idiom, early socialism drew heavily on literature for its imagery of struggle. Thus, for example, one finds George Edwards, the self-educated secretary of the Agricultural Workers Union (he had been taught to read by his wife), signing off an annual report in 1909 as follows:

> Courage then, my Brother,
> The day has come at last;
> The clouds are lifting quickly,
> The night is breaking fast.
> Be strong then of courage,
> Our cause is just and right.
> And he who holds by justice
> Is sure to win the fight.[12]

Shakespeare, that favourite author of the nineteenth-century working-class stage, was a frequent source of texts. *Julius Caesar* in particular – 'a mighty political drama, not just an entertainment', as the young J. R. Clynes discovered when reading it in the library of the Oldham Equitable Co-Operative Society[13] – seems to have provided some popular models of heroic achievement. Socialist funeral addresses, like that of Ramsay MacDonald on Keir Hardie, drew heavily on Mark Antony's oration in the Forum, while other famous passages served as calls to duty and service. Alfred Greenwood, the very militant secretary of the South Yorkshire glass bottlemakers, and a friend of Eleanor Marx-Aveling, fills his quarterly trade union reports with quotations from Shakespeare and the poets. Dealing with a historic lock-out, whose effects were still being experienced in 1886, he turns to:

> There is a tide in the affairs of men,
> Which taken at the flood, leads on to fortune;
> Omitted, all the voyage of their life
> Is bound in shallows, and in miseries.
> On such a full sea are we now afloat;
> And we must take the current when it serves,
> Or lose our venture.[14]

And comments: 'if this philosophy could have been realised, not only the Thornhill Lees and Conisbro disaster might have been averted; but also a great portion of its train of evils which has since marked that event.' J. R. Clynes kept his boyhood memories of *Julius Caesar* with him when he sat on the Opposition benches in the House of Commons: 'The haughty Tribune who reproved the mechanics for daring to walk abroad on a labouring day "without sign of their profession" was typical of many who sat on the benches of the House of Commons in my boyhood; and men of like spirit sit there yet.' One of the most ardent of these working-class Shakespeareans was Tom Mann, a leader of the great dock strike of 1889, the stormy petrel of industrial syndicalism in the years 1911–14, and for the last twenty years of his life the Grand Old Man of British Communism (he was chairman of the Party when he died in 1943). As a young engineer in Chiswick he had formed, with his workmates, a Shakespeare Mutual Improvement Society. Later, in his family life, he instituted 'joyous evenings' at which everyone present had to sing, recite 'or at least read' something of Shakespeare. In hospital, after his eighty-first birthday, he recited to his fellow patients. 'Indescribable fire and music would fill his tiny sitting-room in those last years as he strode about it', his biographer, Dona Torr, records, 'roaring out his favourite passages, plunging into the angry flood and emerging, a bulky symbolic figure, bearing upon his shoulder the tired Caesar':

> Well, honour is the subject of my story.
> I cannot tell what you and other men
> Think of this life; but, for my single self,
> I had as lief not be as live to be
> In awe of such a thing as I myself.

I was born free as Caesar; so were you . . .
The torrent roar'd, and we did buffet it
With lusty sinews, throwing it aside
And stemming it with hearts of controversy;
But ere we could arrive the point propos'd,
Caesar cried, "Help me Cassius, or I sink!"
I, as Aeneas, our great ancestor,
Did from the flames of Troy upon his shoulder
The old Anchises bear, so from the waves of Tiber,
Did I the tired Caesar . . .[15]

The Fabians, though less literary in their inspiration than the Marxists, or those working-class autodidacts who figure so prominently in the annals of Labour representation, drawing their idiom from *Pilgrim's Progress* and the Bible, and claiming Ruskin or Carlyle as the teachers who had set them on their path, made an outstanding contribution to British theatre in these years, and if there is one field in which the Fabian strategy of 'permeation' may be said to have triumphed – albeit not one which they would have thought to acknowledge – it was that of dramaturgy. Quite apart from inventing the 'discussion' play and initiating, with *Widower's Houses* (banned by the Lord Chamberlain in 1892, but zestfully maintained in an underground existence by the first 'fringe' theatres and by socialist drama and play-reading groups), those 'sociological dramas' in which the issues of the day were put on stage, Bernard Shaw, by his championship of Ibsen, precipitated that revulsion from Irvingite histrionics and turn to a more naturalistic 'lifelike' style of presentation which has remained the dominant mode in English acting from that time to now. Granville Barker – one of the recruits to the Fabians in the Society's 'second Spring', and a member of its Executive Committee between 1907 and 1912[16] – was hardly less influential on English theatre practice, initiating the project for a national theatre which has come to fruition in our own times. His management of the Royal Court Theatre between 1903 and 1907 brought a whole new repertoire on to the English stage – Shaw's work most notably, Ibsen and Chekhov; later, the 'social problem' plays of Galsworthy, Barrie, Drinkwater and others. Fabians, as Ian Britain notes in *Fabianism and Culture*, largely officered the Stage Society,[17] which before the Barker-Vedrenne seasons at the Court was the sounding board of the theatrical avant-garde; while in another sphere (oddly neglected by the Society's historians) Fabians played a leading role in the foundation of the Repertory movement.[18]

In general, it is difficult to overestimate the influence of socialist ideas on English theatre practice in this period. By any account it was vast, and quite out of proportion to the influence of socialist ideas in the country as a whole. Socialists had been the earliest partisans of Ibsenism, not only Shaw but the whole circle around Eleanor Marx and Edward Aveling, who had championed him in the socialist press when his works were still unknown in this country (Eleanor was taking the part of Nora in a privately staged performance of *The Doll's House* five years before it was given a public performance; she taught herself Norwegian in order to translate *An Enemy of the People* and *The Lady from the Sea*).[19] The socialist and trade-union agitations of the period found an immediate and sympathetic repercussion on the stage – as in Mrs Lyttleton's *Warp and Woof* (1904) 'with its poignant reminder of what Society clothes cost those who made them'[20] (the Women's Trade Union League used it in their efforts to organize a dress-makers' union); Cicely Hamilton's *Diana of Dobson's* (in the production of which Margaret Bondfield, then an organizer for the National Federation of Women Workers, and later a Labour Cabinet Minister, played the role of documentary adviser)[21]; and Granville Barker's *The Madras House*, which also rehearsed the plight of the shopworkers, though in a tragic rather than a comic vein. At second or third remove, translated into the language of social guilt and moral choice, the socialist propaganda of the time, and in particular the questioning of bourgeois morality – the sanctity of private property, the hypocrisies of organized religion, the 'bad faith' of bourgeois marriage – can be seen as providing the whole agenda of Edwardian 'ethical drama' (the plays of John Galsworthy in this period are paradigmatic), as also, in a lighter vein, for the 'regional' playwrights of Dublin, Glasgow and Manchester. The socialist influence at the Gaiety Theatre Manchester was, according to the testimony of those who acted there, a dominant one: Stanley Houghton, the author of *Hindle Wakes*, with its factory-girl heroine, claimed to be a socialist by conviction though a Liberal in nominal political commitment;[22] Harold Brighouse's *The Price of Coal*, if not his *Hobson's Choice*, entered into the repertory of 'social problem' drama. Indeed the

Edwardian stage, in its preoccupation with the documentary and the naturalistic, as also in its radical individualism, could be said to have prefigured what were to be some of the most abiding preoccupations of the British Left, and the major components of its unofficial culture, certainly down to the 1950s, and arguably to the present day.

It is surprising, in the light of the foregoing, how little direct part theatre played in the cultural practice of the early socialist movement. Whereas the suffragettes, for example, produced a whole theatre of propaganda, and a mass of one-act plays designed to further the cause, there was a singular deficiency in their socialist equivalent, nor did drama play a leading role in Socialist cultural life. A number of reasons might be suggested for this absence. First there was the increasing social exclusiveness of the theatre, which in the 1900s was ceasing to be a popular art and losing much of its popular following. Then there was the gentrification of the acting profession, a process which, paradoxically, the new and more 'realist' drama, though often proclaimedly anti-bourgeois, served rather to enhance than to subvert, since it excluded popular dramatic forms, such as fantasy and melodrama. Second, and closely related to the first, there was the quasi-religious fervour of socialist converts and activists which consorted uneasily with the ironies and rationalities of the discussion play. Third, there was the predominantly male character of socialist activism. Most of all perhaps there was the vitality of other art forms in which the message of socialism could be expressed, in which the transcendental longings which accompanied them could find an emotional release, and in which its aesthetics could find more appropriately dramatic forms.

The main cultural thrust of the early socialist movement was in music, the 'indispensable expression' (as an ILP journal put it) of the 'seriousness' of the Movement, 'and of the happiness there is in it'.[23] At open-air meetings brass bands and communal singing were used very much as they were by the Salvation Army, as ways of gathering a crowd. At branch meetings, the singing of socialist anthems and hymns, such as Edward Carpenter's much-loved 'England, Arise', served, like congregational singing, to express what a Clarion Club called 'the joys of fellowship' and the yearning for a better life. 'Have singing at all the meetings', ILP branches were advised in September 1903. 'A good hymn puts everybody in good humour.' 'If possible, have at every meeting a soloist, quartet or reciter.'[24] Vocal or instrumental performances were a regular feature at ILP Sunday evening lectures, the 'musical programme', as it was called in the advertisements, lasting for perhaps an hour and being followed by the 'propaganda address' (by the 1900s some ILP branches could boast their own orchestra). Choral singing was a major feature of the life of the Clarion League, with the formation, in the 1890s, of a Clarion Vocal Union 'for the performance of unaccompanied choral music, for the enjoyment of the members, and for the service of Socialism': its principal musical aim was 'to revive interest in the wealth of glees, madrigals and part songs so popular in days long ago, when England was really a musical nation'.[25] Even the Labour Party, culturally the least ambitious organization ever produced by the British Left, felt obliged in its early years to maintain a musical side. In 1925 the National Executive was sponsoring a Choral Union 'to develop the musical instinct of the people, and to render service to the Labour movement';[26] and in London there was even a Labour Party symphony orchestra.[27] Singing was if not a necessary then certainly a much-admired accomplishment of Labour leaders. Thus one finds George Lansbury in 1909 delighting his local branch with a rendering of 'Nancy Lea';[28] Herbert Morrison, as secretary of the South London Federation of the ILP, scoring a 'great success' with his rendering of a ballad 'in the musical interlude of a great political demonstration held at Lambeth baths';[29] Rosslyn Mitchell, a Labour MP of the 1920s 'who prided himself more on the fact that he was a singing member of Hugh Robertson's famous Orpheus choir than on his seat in the House of Commons'.[30] On the far Left, Willie Paul, editor of the *Sunday Worker* in the 1920s, had a long-standing reputation in the Labour and Socialist clubs as a singer and entertainer (during the First World War he had made a small living at it: in July 1926 one finds him advertised to sing a group of folk and Labour songs at a cinema in Tottenham, 'Proceeds for miners' relief fund').[31]

The place of drama in the early socialist movement was more uncertain and it served as an adjunct to other activities rather than – as in the case of 'singing for socialism' – a spearhead. In the SDF and the Socialist League – the Marxist organizations set up in the 1880s – 'dramatic entertainments' were put on as a way of raising Party funds, and livening up social occasions – 'Two Laughable

Farces, Singing and Instrumental Music' were the Sunday evening's fare when the Clerkenwell Branch of the Socialist League held a benefit for its new branch premises in May 1888.[32] When the Southwark branch of the SDF held a Grand Concert in February 1886, H. M. Hyndman (the leader of the Party) occupied the chair and recited *The Birds* of Aristophanes; John Burns sang several songs 'in a masterly style' including 'The Mikado' in costume. Miss Hanlon was 'greatly pleased' with her renderings of 'The Kerry Dance', 'The Lost Chord' and 'Come Back to Erin'. The Misses Paul, Mrs Burns, Mr Jack Cole and friends 'gave an amusing sketch'. Mr Jack Cole gave a selection from comic opera and a recitation, 'The Walrus and the Carpenter'. Mr C. Sykes 'gave an entertaining character sketch . . .'[33] The new trade unions, like their mid-Victorian predecessors, used musical, comic and dramatic entertainments as a way of raising strike funds: during the great Dublin transport workers strike of 1913 Delia Larkin, sister to the strike leader, set up a Workers Dramatic Company which went on tour to mobilize funds and support.[34] Only the Fabians, of the early socialist organizations and societies, seem to have incorporated drama as a normal part of their branch life; their repertoire was very much of a piece with the 'advanced' drama being put on by the Stage Society and the burgeoning 'little theatres'.

As in the case of the Owenite and Chartist movements of the 1830s and 1840s, the most systematic theatrical activity was among the children, those who attended the Socialist Sunday Schools. Here operetta, cantatas, fairy plays and *kinderspiel* (a kind of morality play for children) were a staple fare. Pantomimes such as *Dick Whittington*, *Ali Baba* and *Aladdin* were regularly staged for the Christmas concert;[35] recitations and sketches would be performed as the children's contribution to May Day, or in aid of branch concerts (the dramatic class at West Leeds made its debut in July 1908 with 'the jealous scene' from *Othello*).[36] Drama was also very much to the fore in class work. 'It was customary for one of the young members to recite', Alice Foley recalls of her Bolton Socialist Sunday School, 'I recall most vividly a girl student, the possessor of a deep dramatic voice, who at monthly intervals intoned scenes from Longfellow's *Songs of Hiawatha*. We delighted in Hiawatha's childhood, his later wanderings, hardships and prophetic idealism, but especially did we youngsters thrill to the brief wooing of the lovely "Laughing Water". Our reciter seemed to fling the syllables Min-ne-haha at us, instead, I thought, of gently caressing them, but we shared in the simplicity of the marriage feast: Leaving Hiawatha happy/With the night and Minnehaha.'[37] At the Bristol Socialist Sunday School – a heterodox affair since the members of the Bristol Socialist Society were of all faiths – Christian, Jews, Secularists, Spiritualists, Marxians, Fabians, Theists and Theosophists – the superintendent, R. S. Gillard, wrote a pantomime with a Socialist moral 'which was several times successfully performed by the elder children'.[38] The Parkhurst, Glasgow, Socialist Sunday School produced the expressively titled plays *The Poor House* and *Simple Life* for the anniversary concert of the local socialist Hall.[39] North Salford Socialist Sunday School in 1909 were performing 'an original Socialist musical play', *The Snow Fairy*, for their Easter concert.[40] A popular *kinderspiel* in the Scottish schools, widely staged in 1908–9, was *Brotherhood*, a dramatization by the Superintendant of the Paisley Sunday School of a story 'Joy cometh in the morning'. The principal parts were taken (as so often happens in such affairs) by 'semi-grown ups' and the choruses sung by the boys and girls.

A pleasing feature of the play which commends itself, is, that the whole school takes part in it. It is also educative; the economics and ethics of Socialism being taught right through the play, and from a propaganda standpoint, it is excellent. The play opens with a school scene, the children all singing 'We're a merry, merry band from the Socialist school', after which Modesty, the teacher, gives a beautiful lesson on 'Brotherhood'. The children then go to Brotherhood Castle, given by Lady Goodwill only to those who agree to love and serve each other. All the different characters of modern society are represented: a Bankrupt Private Trader, a Working Man and his Wife, an Ideal Philanthropist, a Minister, a School Teacher, a Bottom Dog and a Socialist Student. All these relate their troubles to each other, and show up the iniquitous system which modern society is living under; and consequently, Lady Goodwill being converted to Socialism hands over Brotherhood Castle to all those who need it. The court scene is most educative. All the children are in court, with red flags, singing 'Lift the Socialist Flag on High' and

after the Working Man has been convicted for stealing his
master's rabbits the Socialist Student's Sister interrupts the
Policeman taking the prisoner away, exclaiming, 'All this will
be at an end when we have established the Golden City'. Then
all the children sing in full chorus, with fine effect, 'Have you
heard the Golden City'. The final scene 'Brotherhood Castle',
where all the nations of the earth meet to have their anniversary
celebration of the triumph of Brotherhood, is very picturesque,
all singing in beautiful chorus.[41]

One proto-dramatic form much used in the early Socialist movement, again as in the Chartist and Owenite movements of earlier
years, was reading and recitation, which had the advantage not
only of being able to call on the pre-existing enthusiasms of
members, but also of giving the poetic impulse free rein. Thus
one reads of T. J. Hart, Chairman of the Cardiff and District
Trades Council, reading G. R. Sims' *Christmas Day in the Workhouse* 'with much feeling and in a dramatic manner' at a smoking
concert in November 1890;[42] of 'readings from favourite authors'
at the Sunday evening meetings of the Bournemouth ILP;[43] and
'A nicht with Burns' – 'the Scottish poet-dramatist' – at Scottish
branches of the ILP.[44] Recitations of Dickens's *Christmas Carol*
were a great favourite at Christmas concerts and socials of the ILP
– 'interspersed with songs' when one was given in 1908 at the Hull
branch.[45] Poetry readings were also very much a feature of open-
air propaganda, serving, in some sort, as a secular equivalent for
the reading of Biblical texts. At the Labour Churches, Sunday
service began with a hymn, a brief prayer, and 'a reading from
some Religious or Democratic book' after which there would be
an address by the pastor[46] (as late as 1927 the Gillingham branch
of the ILP was proposing that at its branch meetings, members
should give 'a speech, prayer, or simply a reading' as a way of
giving the meeting form).[47] Annie Davison, a boilermaker's
daughter in Glasgow, recalls becoming 'well-known' in Socialist
propaganda meetings as a reader 'especially of poems with a
message' and was asked everywhere in the city. 'Your wee girl
does elocution – she does readings?' 'Yes, do you want her to
come along?' Her father would say 'Oh Annie will go along'.

I went to the BSP Sunday school – British Socialist Party –

and I went to the Anarchists – they had a Sunday school for children – and of course all the other Socialist Sunday schools in Glasgow – we had a great number of them. There must have been about thirty . . . There was one poem in particular that I used to be asked to do because it was a real old rousing socialist one and my father found it in the weekly paper *Forward*. I never found out who wrote it, it had eight verses . . . real socialist propaganda, I gave it full throat.[48]

A more sophisticated 'reading', very popular in the Socialist movement down to the 1930s, was the 'lecture-recital', a kind of histrionic equivalent to the lantern slide lecture. Thus at the Birmingham Socialist Centre, in February 1909, one comes upon a notice of a dramatic recital by Hubert Humphrey ('Mrs Warren's Profession – tickets from ILP branch secretaries');[49] at the Hyde Socialist Church (June 1909) 'Cde Hobbs: dramatic reading from Shaw's Arms and the Man';[50] Accrington SDF (October 1908): 'The indoor meetings commenced last Sunday at our rooms, Bull Bridge, Comrade J. Mitchell, elocutionist of Bradford, gave a recital "The Dream of John Ball" which was interspersed with glees by the socialist choir.' In the Accrington branch of the ILP Williamson of Stockport is well remembered: 'he was elocutionist, he came pretty regular . . . he was a main educationalist and entertainer'.[51] At the Brighton branch of the Social Democratic Party, the Sunday evening lectures in December 1912 were successively 'An evening with Nietzche', 'Lessons from an Ibsen play' and 'Are Wagner's music/dramas socialistic?'[52] Daisy Halling, 'late leading actress' and author of *The Fire Witch*, was much in demand at ILP branches around 1909, with 'dramatic recitals' consisting of selections from *Widower's Houses* and *Pillars of Society* as well as readings of her own poems (in the following year she was producing a political skit, *Jumbo in Rumboland*, at the Parkhurst Hall Manchester, and a play of her own, *Pinnacles of the Future*, a four-act propaganda play 'which had been praised by Bernard Shaw').[53] A very popular turn at ILP branches in the early 1920s was 'Casey and Dolly' – Casey being a violinist who (assisted by Dolly) gave an illustrated lecture on 'music and socialism' interspersed with pithy politics: when, in 1922, his Stradivarius broke its strings, ILP branches all over the country subscribed to buy him a new one.[54]

The most sustained dramatic initiative in the movement was the
setting up of the Clarion Players. Blatchford himself, the founder
of *Clarion*, and its editor – the greatest socialist propagandist of
the epoch – was the son of an unsuccessful strolling player, the
actress daughter of a theatrical composer; he had been engaged
with theatre when he was still working as a journalist on the
Sunday Chronicle and wrote a comic opera. In the early days of
Clarion the theatrical managers of the north 'more . . . by way of
sympathy . . . than of advantage to themselves' had supported the
paper 'unstintedly' giving the *Clarion*, for a time, the appearance
of a theatrical paper.[55] No doubt dramatic readings and performances had some place in *Clarion* activities at all times (Liverpool
Clarion Players were presenting *Widower's Houses* at the Balfour
Institute in April 1909, getting Shaw's permission to produce it in
aid of the *Clarion* bread-and-soup fund: two years later they were
putting on Galsworthy's *Silver Box*)[56]; but it was in 1911 that a
major effort seems to have been made to give them the permanence
of the Clarion Vocal Union. In Glasgow, a Clarion Comedy Club
'assisted by several Professional Friends' was set up, advertising in
Clarion for scripts to make an audience 'smile' ('we are rather afraid
that those plays mentioned in the *Clarion* lately are too heavy and
serious for our purpose'); they opened their public activity by
presenting 'for the first time on any stage', *Two Up, Right* ('an
episode in Glasgow life' by Victor Maclure), and 'an old-fashioned
comedy' entitled *A Weaver in spite of himself.*[57] Stockport Clarion
players – possibly made more ambitious by the presence in the
town of a fine experimental theatre, the Stockport Garrick –
presented *Cathleen ni Houlihan* by Yeats, *Makeshifts* by Gertrude
Roninns and *A Question of Property* by M. Sackville Martin.[58]
The London Clarion Players entertained Hackney branches of the
British Socialist Party in a show at the Chandos Hall, Charing
Cross.[59] In the following year a National Association of Clarion
Dramatic Clubs was established, and set about attempting to form
a library of plays dealing with Labour and Socialist subjects, and
encouraging local authors to write for the central body. Among
the plays available to them at that time were the expressively titled
Women's Rights by Sackville Martin, *Recognition of the Union* by
Landon Ronald, and *Evolution* by Norman Tiptaft.[60]
   The most impressive of these Clarion ventures, and certainly
the most enduring, was the dramatic club established at Newcastle-

on-Tyne in the spring of 1911 (as 'The People's Theatre' Newcastle, it survives to the present day). It started life as a Clarion
Club offshoot of the British Socialist Party, running in tandem
with it, first as the BSP, and later as the Socialist Club, down to
the end of the 1920s, and then branching off on its own. The
nucleus was made up from a family called Veitch – Norman, who
was to be one of the leading actors for the next fifty years, Colin,
who was also captain of the Newcastle United football team (at
that time holders of the Football Association Cup), and his wife,
who acted as financial secretary. The theatre had been started by
the BSP (later the Newcastle Socialist Club); from 1911 to 1928 it
shared the same premises. It was originally formed to raise funds
for the BSP, but soon branched out into propaganda sketches and
full-length plays on 'advanced' subjects. Nine of the first twelve
plays were by Bernard Shaw, and it was the performance of Shaw
which made the group's local reputation, though they also put on
some of the propaganda sketches of the Clarion League, and, in
later years, the dramas of Toller and the brothers Capek, as well
as a more orthodox repertoire of amateur dramatics.[61]

The Newcastle club sustained a strong political intention,
notwithstanding their theatrical success, as, in effect, the city's
'little theatre'. After 'overworking Bernard Shaw outrageously'[62]
in the first season (Shaw was at all times the favourite dramatist
of Clarion players) they moved on to Ibsen, Galsworthy and
Synge. Their first première, Norman Tiptaft's *Cowards*, performed
in October 1912, was 'weak in dramatic merit but strong in propaganda': it was the work of a frequent writer in the columns of
Clarion.[63] When, a year later, the club scored an 'immediate success'
with Gilbert's *Pygmalion and Galatea*, they seem to have been somewhat ashamed. 'It had none of the propaganda of social betterment
we thought a play should have and was, in fact, a standard senti-
mental comedy that had been successful on the commercial stage.'[64]
They were happier with a spate of one-act plays which they put
on in the following March, drawn, it seems, from the library of
socialist plays established by the National Association.

The great surrogate for dramatic expression in the pre-1914
socialist movement was the open-air meeting, the principal means
by which the word of socialism was broadcast and by which faith
in the message was proclaimed. It called on a range of histrionic
talents – the platform artistries of gesture as much as voice – and

involved, on the part of the speaker, a non-stop and passionate performance. Style and technique were keenly savoured by audiences who approached such meetings very much in the spirit of the 'sermon-tasters' of earlier times. There were 'stars' among the stump orators as there were on the stage, and dramatic presence was as necessary as in the theatre. James Maxton, a very popular speaker in Glasgow, 'had none of the heavy forbidding economic and philosophical jargon about dialectical materialism and the like then the fashion,' Tom Johnston recalls. 'His was the merry jest and the quip, well mixed with the stuff for pathos and tears, and sauced with apt Biblical quotation and graphic description of social wrongs and injustices. His long black hair was bunched at the back à la Henry Irving. He not only preached revolution, he looked it.'[65] One of the common accomplishments of open-air speakers at this time was the recitation of poetry, as Shinwell recalls of the orators on Glasgow Green.

> Some of our well known speakers like W. C. Anderson, Dick Wallhead, Russel Williams and even the severely practical Philip Snowden rarely wound up a speech without some snatches of poetry. I remember a number of popular speakers whose orations consisted entirely of poetic excerpts which their audiences loved . . . I was not an expert in memorizing poetry . . . It seemed to me a little unfair to reel off stanza after stanza to the applause of the audience. The only extracts I could remember were those allied to the topic in which I was interested.[66]

II

The years after the First World War saw a considerable expansion in politically minded drama groups – 'Labour's auxiliaries' as they were called in the London Labour Party[67] – and the incorporation of music and drama into the collective life of an increasingly mass membership labour movement. In Glasgow there were enough local groups to hold an annual Socialist Drama Festival, an event sponsored by the Clarion scouts, in which all Glasgow's socialist troupes competed for the trophy – the Clarion Players who specialized in George Bernard Shaw; the Labour College Players who had a wide repertoire that ranged from Shaw to Strindberg and

Lady Gregory to Fenner Brockway; the St George's players (originating in the St George's Co-op, Maryhill), who took on the 'advanced' playwright, Eugene O'Neill – 'a stokehold playwright to the roots of his hair.'[68] In Bradford during the General Strike of 1926, as Vic Feather recalls 'We had to arrange cricket matches and concerts . . . and we put on Chekhov and Ibsen plays'.[69] In Battersea, the Herald League, a nursery in 1920 for both the Labour and Communist causes, offered the following programme of activities:

BRANCH MEETINGS are held on Thursday at the Labour Hall, 173 Lavender Hill. S.W. At the conclusion of Branch business, a debate, lecture or reading takes place . . .
SOCIAL GATHERINGS are held once in every month . . .
ORCHESTRA – The League runs a very flourishing orchestra, but additional players, especially of wood, wind and bass stringed instruments, will be welcomed. . . .
DRAMATIC SECTION This section is at present in course of formation, and it is expected that the early part of the winter will witness a complete performance of Shakespeare's *Midsummer Night's Dream*. The Herald League orchestra will provide the incidental music for this play written by Mendelssohn. About sixty local children will be required as fairies, and . . . other plays by Ibsen, Shaw, Zangwill, and others will follow.

A CRICKET CLUB has also been formed. . . .
DANCES are held at frequent intervals.
RAMBLING CLUB. This will be in full swing shortly, and many enjoyable outings are looked for.[70]

In the Independent Labour Party, always eager to bring culture to the service of the Cause, numbers of literary-minded members turned their hands to writing propaganda playlets – among them the Party's general secretary, Fenner Brockway. According to the *Labour Leader* (1 June 1922) there was a 'great rush' to put on plays, and the writers were urged not to let the urgency of their message make them forget the arts of dramaturgy. In Edinburgh the local ILP packed the Melbourne Hall for their propaganda sketch *This Way Out*, written by the branch secretary. In Glasgow the Shettleston ILP were no less successful with their sketch *What Tommy Fought For*. 'This makes the fifth Sunday this season that the branch propaganda party have filled the Sunday evening meeting' wrote the *Labour Leader* in February 1922. 'Branches finding difficulty in maintaining an attendance at their weekly meetings should try this method, for as much propaganda is given in the sketches as is often supplied by our ablest Socialist speakers.'[71] Some branches formed their own companies – 'ILP Amateurs', as the Halifax group called themselves when advertising for 'suitable plays . . . propagandist or other musical sketches for adults or children'.[72] In Accrington, where the secretary of the ILP dramatic company was a Miss Wrigglesworth, performances were given on Wednesdays and Saturdays and are remembered as having been 'very popular'; usually they were one- or two-act plays, some 'specially written', and a large number by Shaw[73] (like the 'little theatres', ILP groups seem to have followed the well-known adage, 'When in doubt, play Shaw'). In Gateshead the ILP dramatic club, which was established at the Westfield Hall as early as 1914, and which later was to blossom out as the town's 'little theatre', was handicapped by the hostility of the municipal authorities who refused to license the hall for dramatic performances. 'Accordingly they . . . admit the audience free and depend for finance upon dances, concerts, and collections.' The range of plays was wide – Shaw's *Candida*, Robertson's *Caste*, Shakespeare's *Much Ado About Nothing*, two medieval miracle plays, and Ibsen's *A Doll's House*. The 'greatest venture' undertaken by the Club, however, was a play written by one of its own members, Ruth Dodds' *The Pitman's Pay*, which dealt with the period of the first miners' union in 1830s County Durham. The play was performed six times in Gateshead and three in Newcastle. 'The club has received a large number of requests from neighbouring ILP branches for performances. It is not easy for workers to find time to go on tour, but three have been arranged in neighbouring villages and one has already taken place most successfully'. (The script was later published in the 'Plays for the People' series.)[74]

The ILP also supported the cause of Socialist drama nationally, forming the 'Masses Stage and Film Guild' with Fenner Brockway as Chairman. 'It produced plays and showed films on a scale never before attempted by the Socialist Movement in this country.' The Guild had the help of leading professional actors and actresses, including Sybil Thorndike, Lewis Casson, Milton Rosmer, Elsa Lanchester, and Harold Scott. Miles Malleson, then a prolific dramatist, and in later years an actor-manager, was appointed Director 'and gave most of his efforts to the establishment of amateur dramatic companies'. The Guild staged Toller's *Masses and Men*, the 'revolutionary-pacifist' drama which perhaps came closest, in theatrical terms, to representing the distinctive political ethos of the Party. It also staged, at the Apollo Theatre in the West End, the first English production of Upton Sinclair's *Singing Jailbirds*, a real-life strike melodrama, based on the 1923 Californian seamen's strike for which Sinclair had himself been jailed (*Singing Jailbirds* was to be a frequent item in the repertoire of the early Workers' Theatre Movement). Arthur Bourchier, 'a fine character actor', and manager of the Strand Theatre, was a member of the Guild and put it at the Party's disposal for 'Labour Sunday evenings', in a season which ranged from performances of *Hamlet* and *The Merchant of Venice* to the German expressionist drama *Gas* and the 'machine' play, Elmer Rice's *The Adding Machine*. Brockway refers in his autobiography to a 'remarkable series of shows, half drama, half music' organized for the Guild by Reginald Stamp. 'Bernard Shaw, John Galsworthy, Laurence Housman gave their support, allowing us to use their one-act plays. Once a month we had a film show, crowding the "Regal" Cinema at Marble Arch with members of the Guild and their friends: the star film was usually Russian, but we also ran shorts by John Grierson and others.'[75]

The Labour Party, a more electoralist organization than the ILP, was less ambitious in the cultural sphere, and its leadership, both nationally and regionally, was more apt to be recruited from organization men. Even so, in the early days of its existence as a mass-membership Party (individual membership was only introduced under the Constitution of 1918), a number of Constituency Parties formed dramatic groups. At the Town Hall, Dunstable, in 1925, the Welwyn Garden City Labour Players staged a performance of *The White Lady*, 'a serious play', written by the group secretary, H. B. Pointing, 'describing the unhappy lot of the farm labourers in the year 1830, and their struggles to break the chains that bound them.'[76] The Holborn CLP (later disaffiliated from the Party because of Communist influence) staged a 'Living Newspaper', a 'new form of workers' dramatic expression' avowedly based on the model of Russian agit-prop.[77] At Stockport, Cheshire, a Labour dramatic society put on Tom Thomas's version of *The Ragged Trousered Philanthropists*.[78] In Woolwich, the Social Committee of the Labour Party brought into being the Woolwich Labour Thespians, 'one of the best amateur dramatic societies in London',[79] which the right-wing leadership of the local Party used, during the General Strike, to 'keep people off the street' and counter Communist threats to public order. 'We used to put these things on with young Labour entertainers every afternoon at the Town Hall, about three evenings a week as well to give the men something to do', a member of the Thespians recalls. 'They brought their wives and families and so every afternoon we were full up.'[80]

In London, Herbert Morrison, the great fixer of metropolitan politics, and secretary of the London Labour Party, set in train a whole series of short-lived cultural initiatives of which he himself was, in some sort, the impresario. His model was the 'scientific intensity' of the German SDP, where the Party constituted itself as a kind of Church, or anti-State – a whole universe in which members could pass their lives.[81] In 1924 Morrison set up the London Labour Choral Union 'which aims at improving the local choirs and creating machinery for . . . massed performances',[82] and followed this up with a successful Musical Festival where he himself acted as Master of Ceremonies, and where the adjudicator was the eminent composer, Vaughan Williams.[83] Encouraged by his success, Morrison set up a London Labour Dramatic Federation and a London Labour Symphony Orchestra. The Federation grouped together some 15 Labour dramatic companies and in October 1926 hired the New Scala Theatre in the West End to put on some performances of the *Insect Play* – three evening performances and a Saturday matinee. Nine members of the Royal Arsenal Co-operative Society were involved in the production. Monica Thorne, a former actress who was the presiding genius of the very extensive dramatic activities of the Royal Arsenal Co-op, was partly responsible for the production as well as taking one of the leading parts.[84] The Labour Party's *London News* urged members to attend in the following terms:

> The Insect Play . . . portrays the lives, the cynicism and the infidelities of the insect world; it illustrates the greediness and cruelty of lower forms of life, culminating, in the ant scene, in

a great exhibition of wholesale mutual destruction. But the real purpose of the play is to show that social and domestic life under capitalism is perilously near the moral standards of the insect world. The butterfly scene shows the insincerity and fickleness of life among the idle rich. . . . The ant scene is really an exposure of militarism and war! . . . The Insect Play is probably the most effective satire on capitalism and war that has ever been staged. . . .[85]

The efforts of literary-minded branch secretaries were seconded by the publication of play-scripts intended for use in and around the Labour movement, and for the propagation of the Socialist idea. 'Plays for a People's Theatre', a series directed at the attention of 'those whose eyes are turned towards the future' began publication in 1920 – among its texts were *Captain Youth* by Ralph Fox, 'a romantic comedy for all socialist children',[86] *Touch and Go* (described as a play of 'Labour interest') by D. H. Lawrence, Hamilton Fyfe's *The Kingdom, the Power and the Glory*, ('an attack on kings, queens, and emperors, who are represented as imbeciles, and . . . therefore working-class propaganda');[87] a poetic drama by Leonid Andreieff; and three one-act plays by Margaret MacNamara, a satiric writer whose plays seem to have gone down well in public performances. Another series, issued by the Labour Publishing House, began publication in 1925 and continued until 1928, under the editorship of Monica Ewer, dramatic critic of the *Daily Herald*. It included a popular farce by Margaret MacNamara, *Mrs Jupp Obliges* (a kind of proletarian fantasy of the world turned upside down in which a charlady cheats her mistress of a week-end cottage); *Foiling the Reds* by the left-wing humourist Yaffle (later a popular columnist in the co-operative Sunday newspaper, *Reynold's News*); and *Sir George and the Dragon*, a secular-minded piece 'tilting at our sanctimonious hypocrites'.[88] But the characteristic themes, beginning with Monica Ewer's own offering, were sombre. Some idea of their flavour is conveyed by a review in *The Sunday Worker*:

Although none of the plays is exactly what one has looked for, three of them at least show that there is a growing school of proletarian dramatists. Perhaps the most satisfactory is 'The Forge' by Edwin Lewis, a young writer whose work is known to *Sunday Worker* readers. This play shows how crude and cruel industrialism crushes the life out of a sensitive Worker. The play is written with insight and power, but it is pessimistic. . . . The same criticism applies to 'The Street'. This is a drama showing how a clean-living working woman is driven to prostitution by economic conditions. . . . 'Bringing it Home' is a story of a hangman whose occupation drove his wife to suicide. The play is dramatic and introduces working class characters. It is an interesting combination of anti-capital punishment propaganda and a working class 'thriller'. It brings out the hypocrisy of religious people who believe in capital punishment, but recoil with horror from those whom they employ to do the dirty work. Horace Shipp's 'Invasion' is not, strictly speaking, a working class play, but a well constructed pacifist drama. . . . Written to show the 'futility' and 'stupidity' of national conflict, it strives to bring home the lesson that – apparently irrespective of class as well as national barriers – all men are brothers.[89]

Anti-militarism – common ground to both revolutionaries and reformists on the Left – was a central theme in the Socialist drama of this period, and the 'futility' of war a recurrent motif long before the sensational West End success of R. C. Sherriff's *Journey's End*, the play which is generally credited with having caught the mood of disenchantment with, and revulsion from, the catastrophe of the First World War. Miles Malleson's *'D' Company* and *Black 'Ell*, published in 1916 by Henderson's of Charing Cross Road, and seized by the police as a 'deliberate calumny on the British soldier', was a prototype. Malleson had joined up enthusiastically at the beginning of the war, but was invalided out and became a war resister. A later pacifist play of his, *Paddy's Pools*, was one of the few left-wing dramas to become a normal part of the amateur dramatic repertory.[90] Another early anti-war play was Douglas Goldring's *We Fight for Freedom* (1920), 'a terrible exposure of the effects of war on the sex instinct, and a splendid plea for tolerance and clear thinking on the subject'. It was the first of the scripts to be published in the 'Plays for a People's Theatre' and rehearsed a central predicament in the Socialist ethics of the time, the permissibility or otherwise of violence. Margaret Lambert, the daughter of a clergyman, is engaged to Captain Henderson, who goes out to 'fight for freedom'. On returning home after two years in the trenches he finds that Margaret loves another – or thinks she does. In a fit of passion he drugs her champagne and seduces her. There is a desperate attempt on the part of the family to get Margaret to marry her betrayer, but she insists on defying 'respectability' and maintaining her freedom. She anxiously awaits the return of the Socialist whom she thinks she loves. To her disgust he refuses to sympathize with her desire for vengeance and suggests that Captain Henderson is more an object of pity than of hate:

> The poor devils of soldiers suffer so horribly that they really are not responsible. Human nature can't stand what they are called on to go through. There must be a reaction. . . . In normal times Henderson would probably be quite a decent fellow, incapable of the grotesque blackguardism of which you were the victim. Surely you must see that? . . . Punishment for the crimes of soldiers – even for 'atrocities' – ought to be visited not on the tortured devils who actually commit them, but on the heads of those who made the war. . . . Those are the real criminals. . . .[91]

In a kindred vein it was as the writer of 'pacifist-revolutionary' plays that Ernst Toller became, in these years, a kind of cultural hero of the British Left, and that his dramas (first staged by Sybil Thorndike and Lewis Casson at the Gate Theatre, Covent Garden, in 1924) entered into the repertory of socialist troupes.[92]

The most sustained, as also the most various, of Labour initiatives in the drama came from the Co-operative Societies. The Societies were expanding rapidly both in the number of retail shops and in branches and membership (in London region the advance was spectacular: membership quadrupled in the space of 20 years), and the movement was increasingly politicised, affiliating to the Labour Party in 1927, extending the range of its educational and cultural activities, and advocating with increasing confidence the establishment of the 'Co-operative' or 'socialistic' commonwealth.[93] For thousands of what were known at the time as 'Labour families' the Co-ops provided a whole universe of social and cultural life, with the Woodcraft folk and young pioneers as an anti-militarist alternative to the Scouts, regular Sunday evening 'concert-meetings' or propaganda concerts (musical or dramatic performances, with a 'lecturette' in the interval), and carnivals such as Co-operators Day and May Day, which were the occasion for tableaux vivants, decorated lorries, etc. Light opera or, where children were concerned, 'fairy plays' were the staple fare at the concert-meetings, though scenes from Shakespeare or impersonations of Dickens's characters were sometimes put on by the dramatic classes and on separate occasions there were performances of full-length plays.[94]

Drama was closely bound up with co-operative education, and especially the education of working women. The Royal Arsenal Co-operative Society, which in 1928 was sustaining some 280 drama and music groups, took advantage of the 1918 Education Act to set up elocution classes as a training in public work.[95] These often doubled with the function of drama groups. Sometimes the accent was on utility ('Besides making students acquainted with the best literature, it is a valuable achievement to learn how to speak the "King's English" correctly');[96] sometimes it was on more general elevation, as in the case of working women: 'it introduced them to good literature, taught them to speak well, and gave them the necessary self-confidence. In addition, the acting took them out of the hum-drum of everyday affairs.'[97]

The fundamental condition of existence for these different versions of Socialist drama was the increasing class polarization of both culture and politics in the 1920s, and the formation of Labour, in some sort, as a separate estate. The Labour Party was not a majority party in the country, or even in the working class, but there were particular districts were it had become, locally at least, hegemonic, where the muncipality was normally Labour, and where there was a whole galaxy of social institutions – trade unions, co-ops, Socialist Sunday schools, rambling associations, Clarion cycling groups, women's co-operative guilds, Labour halls and clubs – which served as a kind of anti-church or cultural universe in which 'serious-minded' labour loyalists could live. The ILP constituencies of Glasgow are one example, the South Wales and Durham mining villages another, the industrial suburbs of London, such as Woolwich and West Ham, a third. Musical and dramatic performances expressed, first and foremost, the moral bonding, the sense of 'fellowship' (a word greatly in requisition in Labour Party discourse of the time). They might also serve to assert Labour's association with 'advanced' ideas – a questioning of religious orthodoxy, an eagerness to pioneer new forms of family life, and a greater equality for women among those who believed that the prevailing dogmas about marriage were wrong. What had been, in the time of Ibsen, of the Stage Society and the Royal Court, 'unconventional' attitudes, confined to a minority of the liberal intelligentsia, were now diffused as the 'new idea' of which Labour was the apostle.

The 'propaganda' in Labour Co-op drama, though proudly and frequently avowed, was for the most part ethical rather than directly political in character. Shakespeare was loved for his 'wonderful knowledge of humanity'.[98] Jerome K. Jerome's *Passing of the Third Floor Back* (a great favourite with the Co-op drama groups) was 'a great moral drama'. Sybil Thorndike appealed as a 'great spiritual actress'. Galsworthy was popular as 'drama with a purpose';[99] *The Silver Box*, it was claimed, was a play which 'probes beneath the fickle surface of society'.[100] 'So ended a very noteworthy season,' writes Veitch of the Newcastle season of 1924–5, 'a season of propaganda, of religion, of pacifism, of sociology, and of ethics preached by authors who meant what they said and could say what they meant.'[101] In the 'problem plays' of the repertoire, too – those (such as Toller's) which appealed to the more politically conscious Socialists – the ethical question was very much to the fore, and above all the balance of humanity and necessity, the idealist and the materialist, liberation and violence, 'the conflict going on in the minds of many of us', as one of Toller's English admirers put it.[102] Monica Ewer's *The Best of Two Worlds* – a 1-act play in the 'Plays for the People' series – was written in this spirit. Here is the *Sunday Worker* review of it (15 Nov. 1925).

> It presents an excellent picture of the struggle in the minds of socialistic intellectuals between the ideal of the olive branch v. force and the reality of force v. force, and the conversion of the idealists to the latter by the truth of actual events.
>
> The struggle and conversion may be said to be fully expressed by the leading character, Ruth Allison.
>
> When the play opens a committee has decided that a demonstration shall go to Whitehall 'to point out that there are two million unemployed and partly starving men.' Ruth

dislikes the committee, she fears the demonstration will lead to violence, and she 'hates fighting.'

She is the soft unpractical type of Socialist who wants to make the best of both worlds – the world of aesthetic idealism and the world of Humanity, or the world represented by the National Gallery where she goes instead of attending the meeting and the world represented by the East End where she lives with her practical Socialist husband.

Her fear is not shared by her husband, a pacifist and one of the group leaders; nor by John Grant, who has 'the fire of a Danton, the poetic outlook of a William Morris, the tender selflessness of a St. Francis.' John is really a sad case.

In spite of all the present-day evidence that Capital and Labour do not want to run in a peaceful couple, he is firmly convinced that the demonstration will go off like a Lord Mayor's Show when it does not snow. Ruth's fear is justified, and John's hope is not. John goes forth to lead the van and the 'Thugs' shoot and he is laid out.

Perhaps John's death is symbolic for it seems to say that the anti-force idealism is dead, and force must meet force in the old, old way. At any rate Ruth accepts this meaning and decides that the cause of struggling Humanity is worth fighting for. The play is all talk, by which means the characters are unfolded.

Ruth talks through three acts and is so full of epigrams that rightly the play should be called 'The Woman With a Load of Epigrams.'[103]

Labour Co-op drama sometimes invoked the term 'working-class' to describe what it was doing, but the fundamental inspiration was that of access to a higher culture, elevation to a more spiritualized plane – in brief, *emancipation from* the working class's condition of existence. Just as poetry was read for its 'beauties' (Walt Whitman was a favourite with co-operators on this score), so literature and art generally were thought of as representing transcendent values, a purer state of being: love of them was bound up with a post-Christian morality in which reading became an act of dedication.[104] Propaganda was subordinate to the more general aim of making 'great art' available to working people. Drama, wrote Philip Snowden, then national chairman of the ILP, in the manifesto of the Liverpool ILP dramatic society (1917), was 'of all

the arts supremely the one through which great moral teaching
may be done . . .'; a dramatic society should have the twin aims
of educating members in the principles of socialism, and cultivating
'a love for the higher and better dramatic art'.[105] Herbert Morrison
gave a more cockneyfied and belligerent expression to the same
sentiment. 'The modern working class is not waiting for well-to-
do people, however well-intentioned, to uplift them. We are going
to uplift ourselves. . . . We are going to force the doors open, we
are going to take our place at the feast of beauty. . . . There will
be an Art for the people, produced by the people, played by the
people, enjoyed by the people, for we will not be content with
the commercialized stuff of modern capitalist society.'[106]

Practice, as very often in movements of political theatre, seems
to have departed widely from principle. Often of course performances were staged rather as a form of 'light relief' or 'to introduce
a little colour' into politics rather than as a form of spiritual
uplift,[107] and of the published playlets of the period it seems to
have been the comic ones which took on best. At Co-operative
functions – anniversaries, festivals, and shows – such very old
favourites as *Les Cloches de Cornerville* (a comic opera first produced
in 1879) were clearly more appealing than the 'advanced' European
dramas being pioneered in the 'little theatres'. For the players
themselves, propaganda necessarily took second place to the
performance, a means of self-expression which, like public
speaking, offered a momentary release from the limitations and
conventions of everyday life. This is certainly how it was experienced by Clifford Hanley, who has left a graphic memoir of his
dramatic experiences in a Glasgow branch of the ILP when he put
on a New Year's Day revue:

> Nobody had thought of putting on intimate review in the place
> before, but that's what I decided on; a few sketches, songs, a
> bit of music, monologues and funny bits. I have hardly ever
> enjoyed anything so much, and mainly being accepted
> without question as the sole creator and master boss-man. It
> was easy to get performers and help because it was All for
> The Party, with a couple of bits of simple-minded propaganda
> among the items. These were of no propaganda value, as it
> happens, because the entire audience would be members of the
> Converted, but it would please everybody and show that we

weren't just frivolous stage types. One of the pieces was a long poem I wrote to be spoken in the person of Santa Claus all about the horror of bomber aircraft. This went down tremendously. The other was a one-act play set in an improbable cafe stuck on a Welsh mountain somewhere, perfectly terrible stuff about soldiers and pacifists with a ghost dragged feebly in to point a moral, which was that pacifism, like patriotism, is not enough. I found a drama-minded conscientious objector to play the hero, but the backstage bickering was frightful because he personally thought that pacifism *was* enough, and luckily we finally abandoned the play, which improved the standard of the show.[108]

Realism, though stoutly affirmed as an ideal – 'plays that give us truth and enlightenment on questions affecting everyday life' as the Liverpool ILP dramatic company manifesto put it – was conspicuous by its absence. In the published plays one has either the comedy or farce – the world turned upside down – or else a heavy morality play presenting existence as a Calvary of the oppressed.[109] In Shakespeare, too, either melodrama or else the lyric escapism of the woodland scenes from *Midsummer Night's Dream* and *As You Like It* seem to have had the most appeal.[110] 'Love interest' and 'the eternal triangle', so much despised when they were shown at the cinema, were apt to return by the back door in the self-styled 'serious' or 'problem' play.[111]

Like the cinema, if in a Socialist idiom, some of these perform- ances offered the enchantment of the dream world. In *A Fool and his Wisdom*, for example, a musical play composed for the Royal Arsenal Co-op by Winifred Young to music of John Rodgers, and recommended as a good example of 'footlights propaganda' ('co- operative truths . . . enforced . . . in an unobtrusive form without making it too much a problem play'):

The story . . . refers to the revolt of the populace of a kingdom who have been ground down by injustice and excessive taxation. By some magic power rich and poor are deprived of their money, but all is made right by the establishment of a co-operative commonwealth. The court jester takes a leading part in bringing about this transformation, and, of course, in the fitness of things, marries the duchess who formerly ruled over the kingdom.[112]

In *The Bruiser's Election*, a sketch by Stephen Schofield, the lumpen-proletariat (as in *Mrs Jupp*) have their revenge. 'It is election time, and three parliamentary candidates call to obtain the Bruiser's vote. The Bruiser and his wife seize the opportunity to extract money by tricks from the three to meet the election expenses of the Socialist candidate.'[113] The so-called 'sociological' comedy, Cicely Hamilton's *Diana of Dobsons*, a favourite item in the repertoire of some of the South London co-operative groups,[114] is in fact a modern Cinderella tale in which an exploited shop-girl inherits a small legacy, pretends to be rich, confronts her employer with her accusations about the conditions in which she and her sisters had been compelled to work, and eventually (after many adventures) is married to him. A kind of male version of Cinderella is at the heart of Miles Malleson's *Conflict*, a new drama produced at the 'Q' theatre in 1926 and eagerly snapped up (for reasons which bear speculation) by numbers of Labour groups. It was announced, when it was performed by the Shornell's elocution class, as 'of great propaganda value to those who foster working–class interest',[115] but one may imagine that not the least of its appeals was that it offered both class and sexual fantasy of a kind which might have been designed to flatter the young bachelor heart. The play is about an old aristocrat and his daughter, 'the usual society butterfly' and her rival lovers, one Conservative, the other Labour:

In the first act the Labour man is down and out but gradually makes good. The girl asks him to tea in order to show him the error of his ways, but ends by falling in love with him, much to the dismay of her old father. However she becomes a convert and insists on marrying her Labour lover. This is quite a 'labour' play, the author's sympathies are obvious, but he gives the other side a spirited defence. There are flaws in the characterisation here and there, especially in the girl. She is such an absolute society idiot in the first two acts, that it is difficult to find her brilliantly clever and Shavianly witty in the last act. But the hero is well drawn and also the two aristocrats. The play hangs fire a little in the second act, but the first is quite thrilling, while the third is perhaps the wittiest and most entertaining. The dialogue is natural without being studiedly clever and the construction does not exceed the bounds of probability. It is a play that should be popular among play-producing circles, as it is fairly easy to put on and the cast is not large. Moreover, it is a treat to find a play of this kind with definite Labour sympathies (hence its value as propaganda work), and with a quite plausible and pleasant hero – not like that terrible hero of Sir James Barrie's *What Every Woman Knows*.[116]

III

The Workers' Theatre Movement (1926–35) was marked off from Labour-Co-op drama in a whole number of ways, but above all, perhaps, by its emphasis on class struggle. It belonged to the Communist rather than the Labour wing of the Socialist movement. It was concerned with agitation rather than moral uplift or entertainment. It saw itself as a theatre of action, dealing with immediate issues – in 1926, at the time when the WTM was born (in the period of the miners' lock-out following the betrayal of the General Strike) 'victimisation, police persecutions; miners' stand; attack on T.U.'s; recuperation of T.U. funds; consolidation of the Workers' World'.[117] Theatrically, it turned from 'naturalistic' drama and the 'discussion' play to agit-prop, in the form of sketches, cabaret and revue. As Huntly Carter, the ideologue of the movement in its earlier phase, put it: 'Workers should edit present class-struggling experiences, episodes, stories, scenes in plays & c. The form should be episodic, not epic; short stories with punch, rapid and exciting actions, satirical revues; not big canvasses.'[118]

The rise and extension of the Workers' Theatre Movement was closely associated with – and to a degree anticipated – the 'Left' turn in the Communist International (1928–34) and its translation into terms of 'class against class' in Britain. Though developing, in many cases, out of a pre-existing tradition of Labour drama, it mirrored the sharp break which took place between Labour and Communist in these years. The WTM stepped zestfully into this breach:

It rejects decisively the role of raising the cultural level of the

workers through contact with great dramatic art which is the
aim of the dramatic organizations of the Labour Party and the
ILP. . . . the task of the WTM is the conduct of mass
working-class propaganda and agitation through the particular
method of dramatic representation.[119]

There was a parallel development in music when Rutland
Boughton (a leading composer, and for many years an indefatig-
able worker in the socialist cause, whose musical work for
Socialism can be traced back in *Clarion* as far as 1911) left the
London Labour Choral Union (one of Herbert Morrison's brain-
children) and formed a new choir devoted to revolutionary mass
singing: for too long, it was claimed, Labour choirs bearing
Socialist labels had been singing nothing but 'Annie Laurie' and
'Aberystwyth'.[120] (Christina Walshe, Boughton's ex-mistress, and
organizer with him of the Glastonbury Music Festivals, was the
first secretary of the WTM, and Ruby Boughton took part, as a
singer, in some of the early performances).[121]

The rupture was fully in line with Party feeling, and it had the
notable endorsement of two of the leading Communist intellectuals
of the day. Palme Dutt denounced ILP drama as 'reformist'[122]
while Maurice Dobb was no less scathing about the 'so-called
socialist' plays of Miles Malleson, 'whose "labour" hero is so much
at home with a baronet's daughter in a Mayfair drawing-room,
and whose *Fanatics* discuss the "sex problem" as though . . . the
class struggle did not exist.'[123] Huntly Carter, a notable propagandist for 'modernism' in the arts (as also for socialism) generalized
the attack as follows:

Existing intellectual playwrights, no matter how friendly they
may be towards the Workers, seem to be unable to put an
embargo on their own mental kinks. Moreover, they write
with an eye to the main chance. Hence their technique. They
dilute their plays with dangerous elements as follows: Cloudy
symbolism (The Beggar in Toller's 'Machine-Wreckers');
dream tricks (Toller's 'Masses and Man'); downright cowardice
and social snobbery (M. Malleson's 'Conflict'); crude pacifism
and cat-lap characterisations (M. Malleson's 'Black 'ell');
demonstrations of the superstitious fears of the author (Capek
and Kaiser's prejudices against machinery); of the ignorance

1 Meerut: the theme of this play was that of the jailed trade unionist in British India. Its dramaturgy – borrowed from one of the most successful Agit-prop groups in Germany – is described in the article by Charlie Mann on p. 106

and superstition of the masses ('Machine-Wreckers');
mysticism (O'Neill's 'Great God Brown'); revolutionary
situation expressed through the reactions of tenement
defectives (O'Casey's 'The Plough'); impossible stage
technique and dialogue (some of Sinclair's plays).[124]

The WTM was preceded by – and should be understood in the
context of – a whole series of local and national initiatives. At
Bowhill, in the Fife coalfield, a group of players formed around
Joe Corrie, the miner-poet, presenting dramas of mining life in
the pit villages which, in the 1935 election, were to return Britain's
first Communist Member of Parliament.[125] In Woolwich, Labour's
earliest citadel in South London, the Trades and Labour Council
set up a workers' theatre at the Plumstead Radical Club, to offset
the 'anti-working class dope' of press, pulpit, school, cinema and
radio, and to propagate the Co-operative Commonwealth. Tom
Mann opened the first show, which was made up of a comedy on
the housing question – *Mrs Jupp Obliges* – and a political farce on
general elections.[126] More generally, the Plebs League, and the
National Council of Labour Colleges (NCLC) – the Syndicalist
and Marxist breakaway from Ruskin College, and rival in adult
education to the Workers' Educational Association – were fostering
a propagandist drama with class struggle rather than pacifism or
social ethics as its central theme. It was from the NCLC that the
most systematic case for class struggle drama was to come – Ness
Edwards's *Workers' Theatre*. In this little book the author, a Labour
College tutor at the time, later a miners' agent, then an MP,
dismissed every species of legitimate theatre as either irretrievably
class-biased (Shakespeare was accused of dignifying royalty, and
making his plebeian characters figures of fun) or else – like West
End marriage dramas – sterile and superannuated. He pays tribute
to Ibsen and Shaw ('radical social drama'), but argues that the new
workers' drama, corresponding to the movement and the spirit of
the age, must present problems in class rather than personal terms.
'The Workers' Drama is an agitational force. It is propaganda by
a dramatisation of facts.' 'What the drama was able to do for the
Catholic Church, the Guilds and the ruling classes, it can be made
to do for the working class. . . . No longer will it be confined to a
professional clique, no longer will it be merely an entertainment.'[127]
The WTM was contemptuous of what it termed 'left centre' and

ILP drama, but this was the soil in which it was originally nourished. The Council for Proletarian Art, to which it owed its remote origins, was formed in 1924 by a joint group of Communists and ILP left-wingers, possibly as a counterbalance to the kinds of theatrical initiative being taken within the ILP by Miles Malleson and ILP sympathizers from the West End stage.[128] The actual formation of the WTM, in 1926, seems to have come about as a joint initiative of the *Sunday Worker* (then a broad Left paper, though edited by Communists) and the Central Labour College, who together put on a dramatic reading of Upton Sinclair's *Singing Jailbirds*, and then sent it on its rounds. The first public performance, at the Memorial Hall, Farringdon Road, in July 1926, was held under the auspices of the Plebs League. Frank Horrabin, the cartographer, a very well-known figure in the Plebs League, played the part of Red Adams, the IWW organizer. His wife Winifred was Nell and students from the Labour College played several parts ('some', commented the *Sunday Worker*, 'showed real dramatic talent').[129] At one of the early performances in Battersea Town Hall (a constituency where the Labour MP was Saklatavala the Communist) Ellen Wilkinson MP took the chair, William Paul, the editor of the *Sunday Worker*, sang a group of songs, and Horrabin made another appearance as Red Adams (the performance was held under the joint auspices of the Plebs League, the *Sunday Worker*, and International Class War Prisoners Aid).[130] In its early years the WTM was vigorously promoted in the columns of the *Daily Herald* by the dramatic correspondent, Monica Ewer, whose role in the promotion of Labour-Co-op drama has been referred to on previous pages. Not till 1929–30, when the Communist Party line moved sharply to the Left, and when some Labour College students were expelled for taking part in a WTM production, was there a total break between the WTM and the Labour movement's other theatrical auxiliaries.

Locally, the overlap between the WTM and other, more 'Labour', forms of drama, is no less apparent. At Levenshulme, Manchester, the WTM developed out of the dramatic section of the National Council of Labour Colleges, and performed its first play, in October 1927, under the auspices of the local Labour Party; the *Co-operative News* gave it an enthusiastic reception. 'Ultimately the theatre may become similar in outlook to the Moscow Arts Theatre, and present plays under conditions which will make community drama possible.'[131] The Lewisham Red Players grew out of a hard core of what one of them has described as 'old SDF families'. Two of them had played with the Plebs League, and also taken part in 'Red Concerts' and the Deptford Labour choir. Another was a teacher who had been recruited from the Lewisham Labour Party dramatic group.[132] Charlie Mann, the convenor of the group, attributes his interest in the theatre to a performance of Shaw's *Showing up of Blanco Posnet* – a long-time favourite in the repertoire of the *Clarion* groups. The Salford 'Red Megaphones' evolved – as Ewan MacColl points out in his narrative – from a group of Clarion Players, some of them, like the Lewisham Red Players, from 'old SDF' families, and when the group established an indoor theatre in 1934, it was at the headquarters of the South Salford SDF which also doubled for many years as the club of the local Clarion League.[133]

The Hackney People's Players, who in 1928 took charge of the Workers' Theatre Movement nationally (as Tom Thomas tells us), was originally recruited within the local Labour Party, and was formed with no more than the modest intention of livening up branch nights.[134] 'An advertisement in the *Daily Herald* produced a good response from members of the Labour Party, ILP and CP, and the first gathering took place in the premises rented by the Central Hackney Labour Party in Dalston Lane.' At this gathering Kath and Sandy Duncan, two elementary school teachers, then members of the ILP, though later well-known Communists, offered the use of their flat in North Hackney for further meetings. Two prominent members of the Hackney Labour Party were in the group – Herbert Butler, later MP for Hackney, and Albert Cullington, later a Labour mayor. 'From Stoke Newington George Jeger (later MP for Goole) and his sister joined the group.'[135]

One unifying thread which connected the WTM in its early years with the broad Labour movement was a kind of free-floating 'proletarianism' – the belief that workers were the 'coming class' and that the future would be made in their image. Its most vigorous proponent in Britain, interestingly, was not the Communist Party – a rather uneasy alliance in the 1920s of upper-middle class Bohemians, skilled engineers and unemployed miners – but rather the trade-union-based and largely Labour Party-oriented National Council of Labour Colleges. The NCLC and the Plebs League, locked in bitter conflict with the university-led Workers' Educa-

2 Daily Suppress: a photograph from the Workers' Theatre Movement archive in Warwick University theatre studies department. No information about the players

tional Association, stood for what they called 'Independent Working Class Education'. Philosophically and methodologically they propounded a kind of vernacular Marxism, in which 'MCH' (the Materialist Conception of History) was combined with a thoroughgoing Darwinism, and cultural proletarianism: work was the entire edifice on which civilization rested and in the new era those who performed it would come into their own.[136] Internationally, the 1920s saw the brief hegemony, in the international Labour movement, of a kind of non-denominational proletarianism which transcended the very real divisions of organization, strategy and tactics which separated Communists, Social Democrats and Anarchists. (The world-wide mobilization of protest – in which Communists took the lead – to save the anarchists Saccho and Vanzetti is indicative of the ecumenical solidarity which still prevailed.) In Britain, the Labour Party, though subject to strong cross-currents, came momentarily close to adopting Proletkult in the year of the General Strike: Annual Conference in 1926 called for an investigation into how far a Labour government of the future – 'a worker's administration' as the resolution called it – might cultivate 'a proletarian outlook on life'.[137] The WTM, like the Communist Party of the late 1920s and early 1930s, was in some sort a residuary legatee of a 'proletarianism' which, in the years up to the defeat of the General Strike, had been close to being the 'common sense' of the Labour movement as a whole. In Britain, whether in its conceptualization of the industrial struggle, or the artistic celebration of workers' strength, it owed more to syndicalism than to Communism, and if it had an international point of reference it was to be found not in the Red International of Trade Unions in Moscow, but rather in the US Wobblies – the self-styled 'Industrial Workers of the World'. The idea of a 'Theatre of Action', a leading inspiration of the WTM (it was originally going to be called 'The Workers' Council of Theatrical Action'), seems to have been borrowed directly from the syndicalist notion of 'Direct Action' (the term used by Huntly Carter in 1926 to describe it as a school of drama).[138] It is perhaps indicative of this that the first major WTM production was Upton Sinclair's *Singing Jailbirds*, a real-life drama about a Wobblies strike, with many songs from the Wobblies *Little Red Song Book*; that the early performances should have been staged in support of International Class War Prisoners Aid; that the second major production should have had an American strike play as one of its main items; and that another Upton Sinclair play, *Bill Porter*, should have been proposed as a third. 'Let us hope that the Workers' Theatre Movement will be able to make this play one more link between the Workers of England and America', wrote Christina Walshe in her *Sunday Worker* column, 'between Saccho and Vanzetti and the brave Communist fighters who have recently demonstrated the similarity between the foundations of "injustice" in both countries.'[139]

The early WTM was very clearly an exercise in 'Proletkult'. So far from desiring an emancipation from the proletarian condition – the leading inspiration behind the Socialism of the school of William Morris, and the aesthetic of Truth and Beauty, as also, more generally, of international Socialism in the years before the First World War – it could be said rather to have revelled in it. It looked forward to a universal 'Workers' World' of which the Russian Revolution was the harbinger. It saw itself as first and foremost enacting the class struggle on stage. It aimed to promote the writings of worker-playwrights, and its notion of 'real workers' drama' gave a privileged place to the strike. *Singing Jailbirds*, the WTM's first production, told the story of an IWW leader, beginning with his arrest during a strike and his examination by the District Attorney; going on to his imprisonment; recounting his dreams while he lay in prison, with flashbacks to his earlier life; and concluding with his death after a hunger-strike. As *Plebs* commented when the text was first made available. 'It doesn't talk around and about the class struggle . . . it *is* the class struggle, dramatised and made vivid for us.'[140] The WTM's second big initiative – first performed at the North Camberwell Progressive Club in February 1927 and then (like *Singing Jailbirds*) sent on tour – had two short strike plays as its centre (with a satirical sketch about Mr Baldwin to offset them). The first, 'specially written for the Workers' Theatre Movement' by the miner-poet Joe Corrie, was called *In Time of Strife* and was based on real-life experience during the miners' lock-out:

> This dramatised, very vividly, what happened to a miner's family during a struggle with the mineowners. All the types seen during a lockout or strike were brought upon the stage, and their attitude towards Labour expounded. Corrie's play gave the dramatic side of the domestic problem that confronts all Workers' families in attempting to resist the employers' attack on their wages and standards of living. This is real Labour drama, and is just the type of play that a Workers' Theatre Group can perform with real enthusiasm and feeling.

The second play dealt with the great American textile workers' strike at Passaic, New Jersey, and was described as a 'mass play' showing 'the open conflict between capital and Labour'. It had been written by two students at Brookwood, the American Labour College, and performed by Brookwood students. The play was based on real-life incidents (its hero, Frank Pitto, was a striker who had been clubbed down by the police on the picket line and died the next day), but it was also experimental, transposing its message into one of those dream-sequences popularized by German expressionism. Christina Walshe commented:

This play is a very striking experiment in the new technique
of revolutionary drama and will be worth taking a little
trouble to see for the sheer vigour and reality of its
expressionism. There is a scene in purgatory, where the soul
of the dead striker 'has a few words' with the soul of the dead
capitalist, and where Peter allots to each his appropriate
reward. The fat man is to have his weight 'reduced' in the
time-honoured manner known to cooks, and the striker has
his choice of going to heaven 'the nicest place you've ever
dreamed about' – or going back to help in the fight. He is
greatly tempted to feast and enjoy, but hears his old pals singing
the 'international' outside and decides to go back and carry
on. The Brookwood students actually gave this play at Passaic
the day after fifty strikers had been beaten up, and with the
audience well peppered with 'plain clothes dicks'.

Aesthetically, the Workers' Theatre Movement proclaimed itself
modernist, envisaging a total break with conventional dramaturgy,
and a turn from realistic to symbolic representation. It proposed
to dispense with traditional staging techniques and, like the revolutionary theatre in Russia, to abolish the curtain, 'that symbol of
mystery which had hitherto separated the world of the stage from
that of the auditorium';[142] to replace the 'social problem' play with
a futuristic repertoire – 'plays interpreting the New Machine Age
from a proletarian point of view';[143] and to transcend the written
word – as in Meyerhold's 'bio-mechanics' and Eisenstein's circus
acrobatics – by a theatre of swirling physical movement. A new
breed of proletarian Thespians, as Huntly Carter envisaged them,
would emerge from the factory floor, capitalizing on their experience of industrial life to produce plays which dealt 'with their own
world of scientific industrialism', and developing a technique of
acting which followed machine movements, acrobatics and
athletics.[144] From the Russians came not only the idea of agit-prop
but also, it seems, that intoxication with machinery which was the
hallmark both of the revolutionary period and later of the Five Year
plans. 'What the workman, when he thought himself oppressed,
regarded as a symbol of his slavery seems to become, at the
moment of his freedom, a symbol of his deliverance and even
more a sign of his power.'[145] From the Russians, too, came the
celebration of the rhythm and pace of the City, no longer seen, as

3 A scene from the original New York production of Clifford Odets's play, *Waiting for Lefty*, with Elia Kazan as Agate, 1935

in early Socialism, as the City of Dreadful Night, but rather as pulsating with energy and life. 'The direct action play is the kind that the Workers want to start with. . . . It can be got by very simple means, such as are used in the Left Front theatre in Russia to-day. The general idea of the Russian method is the use of the form, motor and other, and sounds and movement that you find in the city to-day.'[146] From the Russians, too, in a more obvious sense, came the idea of making the audience take the part of the players, and become, in some sort, participants in the drama, though the tiny halls where the early WTM performances were staged were remote indeed from the sensational settings of revolutionary mass spectacle in Moscow or Petrograd.

A less tangible, though perhaps more potent, influence on the early WTM aesthetic was that of post-war German expressionism, with its predilection for montage and mass spectacle, and its violent rejection of bourgeois and 'naturalistic' art-forms. This was the movement to which Brecht owed his artistic formation, and was the cradle of German agit-prop. It came to England via the experimental 'little' theatres, like the Everyman, Hampstead, and the 'Gate', Covent Garden, but it was immediately adopted by the cultural Left in the Labour movement. Ernst Toller's dramas made by far the greatest impact on the Labour movement, to judge by their reception in the socialist press, and their effect was heightened by the fact that when the first translations appeared the author was still serving time in jail for his support of the Bavarian Soviet in 1918. As early as 1922 the *Labour Leader* was hailing Toller's work as the most brilliant poetic product of 'revolutionary pacifism', and in 1924 *Plebs* was producing a special cheap edition of *Masses and Men* for its readers. Ness Edwards had this to say about *Machine Wreckers*, Toller's verse-drama about the Nottinghamshire Luddites:[147]

> This play is a real workers' drama. It depicts the class struggle, the class problem; it exposes working class weaknesses, arouses class emotions, and endeavours to carry its audience with it to make Lud's prophecy become a living fact.

Another play to have a big impact, as an attack on machine civilization, was Karel Capek's *R.U.R.*, first produced in 1926. It is a kind of stage equivalent of *Metropolis*, a nightmare vision of Capitalism in which cheap work machines, or robots, replace the working class. Capek's *R.U.R.* was one of the first WTM productions, and Toller's *Masses and Man* and his *Machine Wreckers* were among the very few full-length plays to keep their place in the WTM repertoire when it had turned, for the most part, to cabaret and revue. (Another to survive was an earlier German play, Hauptmann's *The Weavers*; Kaiser's expressionist drama *Gas* also enjoyed a high reputation among Socialist theatre workers in these years.)[148] The turn to street theatre, which from about 1931 dominated the WTM's self-conception, also owed its inspiration to German theatrical practice, as the narrative of Tom Thomas makes clear. On the other hand the idea of breaking with the discussion play, and exploring the genre of sketches and revue, was with the WTM from the start, and owed its popularity perhaps as much to the indigenous tradition of the music hall and the concert-party as to the more highly disciplined European examples.

The WTM linked its work, wherever possible, to specific agitations. The sketch 'Gas Masks', for instance, served as a prologue to anti-war meetings; those on the Means Tests to rallies of the unemployed. In Sheffield, the WTM was reformed by a group of younger members who wanted to pursue a more activist course: during a local strike of newspaper sellers they wrote a sketch about it and played it on the streets, while the strike was proceeding, 'with very great success'. The Becontree Reds, at Dagenham, East London, wrote a sketch about an eviction and were able to perform it outside the house where the actual eviction was threatening, 'thus contributing very effectively to the fight to defend the workers' homes.'[149] 'Grim drama', as the *Daily Worker* rightly remarked, marked a WTM performance of *Murder in the Coalfields* in the Rhondda: the troupe had hardly finished putting on the first performance of the play, at Treherbert, when news was brought to the hall that eleven miners had been killed in a terrible pit explosion at Llwynypia.[150] The WTM also played an active part in raising funds for strikes. One of their early efforts was in support of the 12-week strike for union recognition at Rego's, a tailoring factory in North London. In the course of it seven students from the Central Labour College were expelled for singing for the Rego girls at a WTM strike benefit.[151] In Lancashire, during the 'more looms' agitation of 1931–2 (a series of rolling strikes in which hundreds of thousands of workers were involved), the WTM members – mostly unemployed young workers – made fund-raising their central activity. As Ewan MacColl, a member at the time of the Salford 'Red Megaphones', recalls:[152]

It became a question of going and performing on every street of a town, putting on a show lasting about four minutes, collecting contributions, and then moving on to the next street. You took a barrow with you, or a hand-cart, and collected food, and bundles of clothing, and money, and it all went into the strikers' relief fund.

The WTM also came to occupy a definite place in Communist Party life. They would be used as crowd-drawers at street-corner meetings, or to hold the fort until the speaker had arrived. They would perform from the back of lorries at the larger demonstrations, or in street-corner work, with planks and trestles as the stage. They were also widely used on social occasions, as cultural shock brigades, very much as the Clarion Players had served the ILP. Harry Pollitt found their May Day Show in 1931 very impressive, but 'got the impression that the comrades were apt to be concentrating on getting too much propaganda across of rather heavy character'. Characteristically he called for more wit and colour. 'In all their shows they should remember that there are many humorous incidents both in the workers' lives and the capitalist class social life that can most effectively be portrayed, and, at the same time, a political message can be conveyed.'[153] The most hazardous work was in the open air. Like other Communist activity at that time it involved a cat-and-mouse relationship with the police. Ewan MacColl recalls:

> If we were due, say, to go to Wigan, in the bus on the way we'd write the sketch and we'd try it out for about half-an-hour, and then put it on at the market place by the stalls. We'd maybe be there for ten minutes before the police arrived in a van, and we'd scarper, say, to the steps of the public baths, and put it on there. Or we'd go to a factory, and occasionally we'd manage to get through a few satirical songs outside the factory gate before the police came and moved us on.[154]

The WTM had an ideology – a definite theory of what theatre was about. All art was propaganda and the theatre itself a splendid weapon of struggle, both as a means of consciousness-raising and of dramatizing specific issues. They rejected what they called the 'theatre of illusion' and instead put forward a theatre of ideas. They were equally opposed to 'naturalism' ('a mere photographic view of things as they appear on the surface') and counterposed to this what Tom Thomas called 'Dialectic Realism' – 'the X-ray picture of society and social forces'.[155] They performed not full-length plays, but sketches and satires, or montages of mime and song. Instead of individualistic characterization ('the basis of the bourgeois stage')[156] they concentrated on types, and employed the simplest possible devices as signifiers. 'If you wanted to represent the boss you put a top hat on, and if you wanted to be a worker you put a cloth cap on.' The WTM used no costumes, except for dungarees, and no make-up: when 'Proltet', the WTM's Yiddish-speaking group in East London, used a judge's wig in one of their sketches, a heated controversy followed and a special meeting was

4 A scene from the WPA living newspaper *Triple A Plowed Under*, 1936

called at which they were threatened with expulsion for making use of props.[157] Words were kept deliberately simple, partly to cut down on the need for elaborate rehearsals, partly to avoid 'individualistic self-boosting', but chiefly in order to get the message across. Charlie Mann, of the Lewisham Red Players, devised a particular method of choral speaking, and made his actors clip their words so as to avoid the risk of any of them being slurred. He also went in for half-repetition (suitably disguised), to heighten audience concentration, and make sure that nothing was lost.[158]

WTM troupes had nothing in the way of a stage beyond a bare platform. They built up their visual effects not by scenery, but by rhythm, gesture, and pace. In the *Meerut* sketch, a short piece about the jailed trade union agitators in India, the sketch opened with the statement: 'In every state in British India, troops and police are out to crush the rising tide of revolt.' But the tension was built up not so much by words as by a tightly disciplined choreography. The actors came on with broomsticks – three vertical, two horizontal – which they clasped together to indicate a prison. Each of the prisoners then told his story and ended by stretching his arms through the bars. 'The secret was to start on a sombre note and then intensify,' Charlie Mann recalls, and his directions (reprinted on pp. 106–8) show how meticulously the gestures were planned. In *Rationalisation*, a sketch about unemployment in industry, the players were introduced with a song ('Speed up, speed up, watch your step / Hold on tight and show some pep') but the drama of the action lay in the mime. 'The speed up was introduced and then one [worker] dropped, and another dropped out, until only one was left.'[159]

Many of these techniques were adapted from the agit-prop theatre in Germany, then in the most brilliant, if tragic, phase of its development, on the eve of Fascist power. They made an enormous impact on the WTM troupe who toured the Rhineland in 1931, as Tom Thomas testifies, and the impact was enhanced by the German 'contacts' who were sent to England to give advice and instruction to the WTM.[160] Nevertheless the evolution in the direction of sketches and cabaret was an indigenous British development, which preceded the movement's contact with Germany, and so too were such sketches as the Hackney Dialogue, reprinted on p. 112–13, with their peculiar mixture of the colloquial and the didactic, the music hall and Shaw. The rejection of 'slice-of-life' or naturalistic drama also seems to have preceded the WTM's German visit. Gorky's *Lower Depths* and Sean O'Casey's *Juno and the Paycock* were being dismissed as 'pessimistic' by English Communists in 1926, while Upton Sinclair's *Singing Jailbirds* was expelled from the early WTM repertory as 'defeatist'.[161] The idea of a street theatre seems to have been mainly due to the German example, though the Hammersmith WTM troupe had already adopted it in the spring of 1931,[162] and so too was the extremely disciplined choreography exemplified in the 'Meerut' sketch. Montage too may have been adopted from Germany, though *Their Theatre and Ours* – the script reprinted on p. 138–46 – shows that it was possible to naturalize it in a thoroughly English setting.

The WTM was uninhibitedly – even one might say exuberantly – sectarian. Parliament was 'the gashouse show' and the three main parties were treated as one and the same. The troupes sported the hammer and sickle, and their message was openly revolutionist. As the Lewisham troupe put it in their group chorus:[163]

There is a word you mustn't say – revo-lution
All the same it's on the way – the workers' revolution
Every day the world turns round – revo-lution
A few more turns, it will resound, to the workers' revolution.
It's coming here, it's coming there – revo-lution
The ground is tumbling everywhere – the workers' revolution.

How then, in a country where Communism was comparatively weak, did the WTM win a following in the Labour movement? How, even more problematically, did they get a hearing on the streets? In some cases it was because of their association with particular agitations. In others it was because their sketches were speaking to central and familiar experiences. In the case of the 'War Memorial' sketch, for instance (see p. 118) it did not require any particular Communist sympathies to respond with anger at the memory of the First World War generals who had sent millions of soldiers to their death;[164] nor, in the Hackney dialogue reproduced on pp. 112–13, to see that pallor and undernourishment were associated with low pay. 'The whole thing was to get down to the audience familiarity', Charlie Mann says, recalling his troupe's performances in Lewisham High Street; he speaks too of the invisible support of class feeling:[165]

> At that time – it doesn't apply today – there was a sort of working-class loyalty against the powers that be. It wasn't exactly socialist, but there was this feeling of brotherhood among working people. We'd get more than 50% of the audience with us – some just looking because it was something to watch. Sometimes 10% would be hostile, but these would be generally shouted down by others. We always got respect from the audience – on the whole they were sympathetic and prepared to listen.

The WTM, like other theatres of its kind, depended on real-life agitation for its sustenance, and was peculiarly susceptible to changes in the political climate. It owed its origins to the General Strike, the miners' lock-out which followed it, and the widespread anger at what was conceived on the Left as a betrayal of the miners' cause; more generally it can be situated in that tremendous upsurge of working-class political consciousness which followed, on the one hand, the Russian Revolution of 1917, and, on the other, the terrible experience of the First World War. The movement was at its height in the period of the Third National Hunger March – the largest mobilization of the unemployed in inter-war Britain. The one time in which it found an industrial base was in the 'more looms' agitation in Lancashire, of which Ewan MacColl writes in later pages. It was brought to an end in 1936 as a result of a radical realignment in both national and international politics with, on the one hand, a remarkable quiescence in specifically working-class agitation, and, on the other, a rising international threat of Fascism and a turn in Communist politics from 'revolutionism' and 'proletarianism' to the politics of a broad 'democratic' alliance. 'Proletkult', which in the years following the First World War had been the 'commonsense' outlook of the international labour movement, disappeared from both the cultural and the political stage.

The term 'Workers' Theatre Movement' – like the term 'people's theatre' frequently invoked in these years, often by high-minded philanthropists – represents an aspiration rather than an achievement. The first Workers' Theatre Movement (1926–8), certainly did stick closely to what were regarded as 'working-class' subjects (principally strikes), and it helped to encourage one interesting worker-dramatist, Joe Corrie. But the presiding spirits of the movement – Christina Walshe and Huntly Carter – seem to have been a kind of upper-middle class Bohemians, passionate advocates of modernism in the arts – and 'advanced' ways of living – as well as of revolutionary Socialism. Among the early committee were Rutland Boughton – remembered in Street variously as being 'very aristacratickle' and 'up to his neck in money and down to his ass in long hair' ('We didn't have to wait for hippies for long hair');[166] Eden and Cedar Paul, two notable literary Bohemians, translators of Marx's *Capital* and amongst the rare intellectuals whom Harry Pollitt, General Secretary of the Communist Party in later years, could abide; and Havelock Ellis. Christina Walshe, the organizer of the first WTM, who worked sometimes from the *Sunday Worker* offices and sometimes from West Kensington, was a notable artist in her own right, who had worked with Yeats before the First World War, and took a leading part in promoting a Festival Theatre for Music at Glastonbury some fifty years before Benjamin Britten succeeded in doing something similar at Aldeburgh.[167] The second WTM (1928–1935) was altogether more plebeian. The upper-

5 *The Fall of the House of Shusher*

middle-class Bohemians withdrew from participation, and it is perhaps indicative of the distance from anything to do with the professional or legitimate stage that when, in 1933, a professional actor offered to work in a WTM group, no one knew what to do with him. But the WTM seems to have been almost equally distanced from the organized working class. With the exception of the 'more looms' agitation, they did not take part in any official trade union activities. In London, the centre of the WTM, and the place where its groups were most frequent, the troupes seem to have been drawn largely from the lower professions, clerks and out-of-work young people, together with a substantial complement of East End Jewish proletarians in revolt (it may be) as much against the Orthodoxy of their parents as against the conditions of industrial life. Like the metropolitan Communist Party the members seem to have been drawn together more as a cultural stratum – or as upholders of a common politics – than as members of a class. In the Lewisham Red Players, Charlie Mann, the initial convenor – one of Tom Mann's sons – was an advertising agent 'mainly unemployed'. Philip Harker, his cousin, was an unemployed book-keeper. Alice Jones – remembered as 'very dominant' – was 'very busy' with the Unemployed Workers Movement. John Loveman, whom she married, was an engineer, possibly working at Stone's factory, Deptford. Charles Loveman his brother was a milkman. John Brown from Bermondsey was unemployed. 'A man named Hawkins' was a teacher who had been recruited from the Woolwich Labour Party Thespians.[168] The Hackney People's Players were more petit bourgeois than proletarian. Tom Thomas, the convenor, was a stockbroker's clerk, often unemployed. Kath and Sandy Duncan were elementary school teachers – remembered (by one who had been brought up in a traditional Jewish family) for their modernity. Herbert Butler, later to be a local MP, was the shop manager of Galinsky–Hyman, a Whitechapel High Street linoleum shop. Hetty Bower came from 'a large Jewish lower middle-class family' in a home of 'solid' comfort 'and very little aesthetic taste'. She remembers the devastating effect upon her of the Duncans' home: 'They had *mauve* curtains, I'll never forget that, and a settee covered in black repp, with brightly-coloured cushions.'[169]

The provincial WTM troupes may have been more working class. Ewan MacColl remembers the Salford 'Red Megaphones' as being made up of two weavers, a miner, a motor mechanic (himself) 'and the rest were unemployed'.[170] The Bowhill Players, an autonomous troupe, were indeed proletarians – miners, it seems, mostly drawn from a single street. But one's general sense of the movement, as of kindred Communist Party cultural initiatives of this period – such as the Workers' Film and Photo League, or the Workers' Music Association – is of, on the one hand, young working-class Bohemians, such as Ewan MacColl, in full revolt not only against capitalism but also against restrictive conventions of all kinds; and on the other hand, clerks and people from the lower professions (school teachers played a very important part in the Communist Party of the 1930s and 1940s) who enjoyed a second and less respectable identity by their life in revolutionary theatre, as also by their activity in a revolutionary cause.

Despite the proclaimed attachment to street theatre, the majority of WTM productions, to judge by the advertisements which appear in *New Red Stage* and the *Daily Worker*, were in fact *indoor* performances. Audiences – as in the 'fringe' political theatre of recent years – seem to have been made up largely of the 'converted', albeit of a very different provenance to those who have supported left-wing theatre in recent years. The WTM felt itself to be 'modern', 'dynamic', moving – as Charlie Mann put it – 'with the times'; it certainly did try to stage productions to the rhythm of the machine age, and to make a choreography of contemporary life. But it also called upon a much more traditional dramaturgy, on a satirical tradition which owed more to Gilbert and Sullivan – or sometimes, as in the Hackney 'Market Quack Dialogue' printed on pp. 112–13 of this volume, to British music hall – than to Berlin cabaret. Audience participation, too – evidently limited in street theatre where the actors were shouting through megaphones – seems to have been more akin to the venerable British tradition of melodrama (or to the Band of Hope) than to the revolutionary theatre in Russia. A story published in the *Sunday Worker* in February 1928 seems to be notably self-deceived:[171]

AUDIENCE AS PLAYERS
Workers' Theatre Groups working out new idea
To make the audience take the part of players, after the example of the Russian Workers' Theatre, is an idea being worked out by W.T.M. groups in Glasgow and London. In a little hall in

the Cowlairs districts of Glasgow I listened (writes J.P.) to a
workers' play, 'Get on with the Funeral' read by the author,
William McKinnon. Briefly, the theme is that the chief
characters, a man and his wife, utterly down and out in their
single-end with the dead body of the woman's mother
requiring burial, have their hopes raised high by visions of a
big prize. There appears every likelihood they have won. But
they have been poor fools. They sink deeper into the cistern
of foulness surrounding them. It is then night. The woman
sleeps. The man contemplates murder and suicide, and is about
to strike when a voice in the audience shouts 'Stop!' So the
audience enters in from this point. The opportunity is then
great for propaganda. The lesson is driven home that not by
such murders and suicides, nor by individual means, but by
concerted action will the workers find a way out of their
poverty and degradation.

Another distinctive feature of the WTM which seems to have
been an indigenous British growth (though in the 1930s, under the
name of 'Socialist realism', it was adopted as the canon of the
international Communist movement) was the insistence upon a
'positive' message. It was being vehemently championed in the
early days of the WTM, apparently in the name of a 'new' and
even 'futurist' drama, though in fact – one might suggest – from
a desire to make theatre serve the purposes of moral uplift, albeit
in a revolutionary cause. Thus one finds Chekhov, Gorky and
Sean O'Casey being rebuked in the *Sunday Worker* (by Huntly
Carter) for showing 'man purposeless and on the drift', and it may
be indicative of this that O'Casey never found a place in the WTM
repertoire.[172] T. A. Jackson (*Sunday Worker*, 24 June 1928) wrote
of O'Casey's 'pessimism' as a 'fault which will disappear from the
proletarian art of the future',[173] while Carter referred to his *dramatis
personae* as 'tenement defectives'. O'Neill's *All God's Chillun* was
condemned for presenting a problem, but leaving it.[174] As the
Party line hardened, towards the close of the 1920s, even Toller
and Upton Sinclair were condemned for being 'defeatist'.[175] Eric
Duthie, one of a crop of worker-dramatists who made their appearance in the year of the General Strike, was praised for a play
about the workhouse, but another of his plays, *Coward Love*, was
impatiently dismissed. '*Coward Love* deals with the emotions of a

boy and girl of nineteen. There are people like them, but if they
are healthy, they grow out of it. Duthie can do better things than
this, and one hopes that he will stick to working–class stuff. He
seems to know something about that.'[176] Tom Thomas, who in
1928 took over the organization of the WTM, was particularly
insistent on the positive message. He condemned 'Sham-Left'
drama which, while 'critical of capitalist society', and even showing
workers in revolt against it, never depicted them 'as being strong
and self-reliant enough to be victorious in the struggle'. He singled
out Gorky's *Lower Depths* as 'a classic example of bourgeois pessimism'. ('While it shows the terrible degradation of the Russian
working class under the Tsar, no hint is given of the revolutionary
forces which, even while it was being written, were preparing and
organizing to overthrow the system.') He was no less severe on
Sean O'Casey:

> O'Casey is perhaps the Irish equivalent of the Gorky of 'The
> Lower Depths' with the difference that pessimism plus
> humour instead of pessimism plus religion are the ingredients
> of his work. . . . There is no hint of final victory, nor is any
> weapon forged in the fight. Just the failure of the individual,
> which is brought to its logical conclusion in his latest play 'The
> Silver Tassie'.[177]

Tom Thomas adapted the *Ragged Trousered Philanthropists* for the
stage – much the most successful of the productions of the Hackney
People's Players. The 'pessimistic finish' of Tressell's novel (in the
only version of it then available) which had Owen the socialist
coughing up blood from his tubercular lungs and resolving that
he would kill his wife and boy rather than leave them to suffer the
life of hunger and misery which would be their fate after his death'
was turned into something altogether different. As the *Sunday
Worker* wrote:

> . . . The stand made by Owen, the hero, on behalf of Bert
> White, a badly used apprentice, wins the respect of his mates,
> who take his part against Crass the foreman, and insist upon
> his being heard. Finally, Harlow moves a resolution that
> 'Socialism is the only remedy for unemployment and poverty'
> and turns to the audience with 'What d'you say, mates?'

North St. Pancras Independent Labour Party

PUBLIC BATHS HALL
PRINCE OF WALES ROAD, N.W.5

On Friday, December 3rd, at 7.45 p.m.

A THREE ACT PLAY entitled:

"TOLPUDDLE"

By REGINALD SORENSEN, E.C.C.

(Prospective Parliamentary Candidate for West Leyton)

This Play has met with considerable interest and enthusiasm in each of the score or more of Districts in which it has been given. The main incidents are authentic history concerning the now famous and inspiring story of the Dorchester Martyrs, who in 1834 were savagely sentenced and deported for daring to form a Farm Labourers' Trade Union. It is an illuminating glimpse of the workers' struggle in the early days of the Industrial Revolution, and is particularly appropriate at the present period of industrial unrest, when one considers the proposed restrictions of Trade Unionism which are being contemplated by the most disastrous Government of modern times.

MAKE SURE YOU GET A TICKET, WHICH WILL RESERVE YOU A SEAT UNTIL 8.30 p.m.
PRICE 6d. EACH (Children half price.)

Obtainable at door, and from A. DIXON, 37 Islip Street, N.W.5 also at 67 Camden Road, N.W.1

Proceeds will be given to the Miners' Relief Fund

300 FREE SEATS **DOORS OPEN AT 7.30 p.m.**

Blackfriars Press Ltd., London, E.C.1

6 *Tolpuddle*

TOTTENHAM PLAYGOERS' CLUB

Manager & Secretary ... W. J. IRVING.

Monday, November 21st, 1932

At 8 p.m. prompt.

THE WALTHAMSTOW PLAYERS

PRESENT

"1848."

A Democratic Episode by REGINALD SORENSEN.

JOHN FINCH (Governor of Harmony Hall)		ERNEST HOUGHTON
MARTIN FOSTER		REGINALD SORENSEN
FRANK OLIVER		WILL AYLOT
BOB WARREN	Settlers	STANLEY BENNET
ROSE WARREN		DORIS BENNET
JOSEPH PILKINGTON		ARTHUR FAIRMANER
PHOEBE SCOTT (a Village girl)		BESSIE WILES
AGNES HOOKER		ELSIE PRACY
MARY JORDAN		

ACT 1. Scene 1.—Interior of Harmony Hall, Hampshire, 1839.
Scene 2.—The same in 1844.

ACT 2. Scene 1.—A Coffee House near Kennington Common,
April 10th, 1848.
Scene 2.—A room in Paris, June 28th, 1848.

The main theme of the play is founded on fact.

NEXT WEEK.—Edmonton Dramatic Group presents
"HAY FEVER," *By Noel Coward.*

HUNNINGS, PRINTER (T.U.) 564 HIGH ROAD, TOTTENHAM, N.17.

7 *1848*

Easton seconds it, and old Philpot as chairman puts the
resolution: 'Those in favour shout "Ay!"' (To audience). 'Let
it go now! One, two, three, ay!' The success of this device is
unquestionable, and the curtain is rung down upon a
tremendous shout of 'Ay!' from the audience.[178]

There is no doubt that WTM people were genuinely excited by
modernist techniques, adopting enthusiastically those which they
came upon from Germany, America and Russia, and Ewan
MacColl's account of Alf Armitt's enthusiasm for revolutionary
modes of stage lighting, and of MacColl's own youthful fascination
with Vandenhoff, is eloquent testimony to the direction in which
the international avant-garde could flow. But, as the instrumental
character of the WTM shows, the restriction either to audiences
of the converted or else to a heterogeneous mass of passers-by,
does not seem to have been a fruitful context for genuine experiment, and though the WTM nourished two theatrical people of
genius – Ewan MacColl and Joan Littlewood – it was in the
very different setting of Theatre Workshop that their distinctive
contributions began to take shape. One restriction on experiment,
which the WTM shared with its Labour-Co-op predecessors, was
a thoroughgoing suspicion of popular culture. Even dialect plays
seem to have been viewed with suspicion, as insufficiently dignified
for the revolutionary cause. Sean O'Casey, though a bricklayer's
assistant by trade, a revolutionary socialist and later a Communist,
was never performed by any WTM group. Satire was restricted
by the need to convey the urgency of the political message. Thus
one finds the Bureau of the Central Committee of the WTM
condemning groups in 1933 for 'playing for laughs' – the Castle-
ford, Yorkshire, WTM for 'presenting the police in a humorous
way' and so destroying 'the value of our propaganda', the Rebel
Players of East London, for 'paying all their attention to getting
laughs instead of mainly trying to get the political message
across'.[179] Only, it seems, at the level of melodrama did the requirements of theatre and those of political urgency converge.

IV

The demise, or virtual demise, of the WTM in 1936, after a
vigorous life of some seven or eight years, corresponds to a much

more general change in the cultural and political climate. Very summarily and crudely, one may suggest that the WTM was a casualty of the Popular Front, and the change in the Communist Party line from 'class against class' to that of the broad 'progressive' alliance – the eventual response of British Communists, like those in other lands, to the rise of Hitler's Germany. The Popular Front marked the end, or the partial end, of the revolutionary epoch in European Communism; artistically it was associated with the rise of 'socialist realism' in the Soviet Union and a decisive rupture between communism and experimental art. In theatre it was accompanied by the destruction of agit-prop, along with every other species of socialist and communist activity, in Nazi Germany. At home the WTM was irretrievably associated with what now came to be regarded as sectarianism; its exuberant revolutionism was an embarrassment, its attacks on the Labour Left out of place, while its very name was an obstacle to building the broad alliance. It is possible that there were other less immediately political causes at work, sapping its cultural energies and undermining its appeal – the partial stabilization of British capitalism in the mid-1930s, the falling off in the industrial struggle, at least in the old manufacturing areas, and the decline in the number and even more strikingly the mass activity of the unemployed.

Another tendency, closely related to the rise of Fascism, was the quite widespread recruitment of professional people – among them actors – to the ranks of the British Left, a phenomenon which was to find its apotheosis in the mass membership of the Left Book Club. As early as December 1933 one or two theatre people were beginning to take an interest in the WTM and to offer their professional services. There was, it seems, consternation when the first of them – a well-known London producer – appeared, and after much discussion it was decided to assign him to the 'Rebel Players', 'a troublesome and difficult group in East London'.[180] But by 1935 at least four WTM groups were under professional producers, and when Unity Theatre was founded in March 1936, the leadership of professional directors was accepted without question. Outside the WTM the Westminster Theatre was putting on plays of 'social significance' (among them were two by 'the well-known revolutionary poet' W. H. Auden)[181] while the Embassy, Swiss Cottage, was experimenting with mass spectacle, notably in the anti-war play *Miracle at Verdun* (Andre Van Gyseghem made his reputation there as one of the most brilliant directors in London, before moving on to Unity Theatre in 1936). The appearance of a 'West End' theatre Left was also marked by the formation, in April 1934, of an organization called 'Left Theatre', which put on Sunday performances at the Phoenix Theatre, and took its shows to Labour and Co-operative halls. It was composed exclusively of professional actors and actresses, and among those who appeared for it were Ina de la Haye, an artiste 'frequently heard on the wireless', and Anita Sharpe-Bolster, who gave entertaining sketches of village ladies.[182]

Within the WTM there seems to have been a growing demand for more professional standards of performance, and there were also a number of moves towards the establishment of indoor theatres. The West Ham United Front troupe were proudly announcing in March 1935 that they now had their own hall ('with a properly equipped stage, and an electric light outside').[183] Theatre of Action in Manchester set up in a permanent home, and they were followed by the Rebel Players in London, who in 1936 established themselves, as Unity Theatre, in a converted mission hall in Goldington Square. In Manchester (from the occasional snippets which appear in the *Daily Worker*), there seems to have been a deliberate attempt to break out of WTM's theatrical isolation. In February 1935 it was pleased to record that the Rusholme Repertory company had called on it for assistance in providing a crowd of workers who actually looked like workers ('this sort of operation means a big step forward for the WTM and it should become universal', the *Daily Worker* approvingly commented); and it followed this up by sending out a questionnaire to actors, critics and authors with a view to forming a 'united front' of theatre progressives.[184]

In art as in politics the epoch of the Popular Front made revolutionary perspectives an embarrassment.[185] Unity was the watchword of the day, and in the theatre it found its most extreme expression in the formation of the New Theatre League. The League was intended to subsume the Workers Theatre Movement in a larger, umbrella organization, which would link all amateur dramatic groups with 'progressive' ideas and also obtain the co-operation of professional artists. At the inaugural meeting there were performances by the Dance Drama Group, the Labour Choral Union, Theatre Action of Manchester, and the Battersea Players, and the speakers included Gillian Scaife of the Westminster Theatre, William Armstrong of British Actors Equity, and the Earl of Kinoull, who spoke on 'Peace Plays'.[186] No WTM names appear among the speakers, and when Unity Theatre was opened some three months later, the opening ceremony was performed not by an agit-prop troupe, but by Dr Edith Summerskill, the victorious peace candidate in the Fulham East by-election and in later years a well-known cabinet minister.[187]

The founding of Unity in 1936 marked a partial breakaway from agit-prop, and a return to legitimate, conventional theatre. It was under the firm direction of professional producers, even though its actors were part-time, and amongst the actors themselves there was a good deal of traffic with the West End stage (Alfie Bass, Bill Owen and Ted Willis are three of the well-known theatre people who first made their name at Goldington Square). Unity Theatre productions were widely reviewed in the capitalist press, and the notices pinned up for members to see in the club-room. It also won favourable notice in the world of amateur dramatics, and in 1939 carried off the prizes at the annual festival of the British Drama League (the WTM, by contrast, confined its competitive efforts to the international Olympiad of revolutionary theatre groups in Moscow). Artistically Unity made few innovations, and for the most part was content with a fairly simple naturalism. Politically, too, its aims were comparatively modest, and though it prided itself on the 'social significance' of its plays ('Sing me a Song of Social Significance' was a pre-war Unity hit tune), the main thrust of its work lay in the direction of finished staging and accomplished performances.

The WTM was dead set against the entire paraphernalia of the theatre, whether in its West End, repertory or amateur dramatic forms. Unity, on the other hand, was much more ambiguously placed, and on many of the artistic issues of the time found itself facing both ways. Yet one should not exaggerate the rupture. *Waiting for Lefty* – the play which made Unity's reputation – is a play which breathes a revolutionary spirit, and dates from an earlier period (it had already been performed by two WTM groups in 1935). The trade union leaders are the villains of the piece (the play is about a taxi-drivers' strike in New York), and it ends with a tremendous appeal to the 'stormbirds of the working class' which has not lost its theatrical, or political, force today. The 'mass-

RAUNDS LABOUR PARTY

Programme of

ENTERTAINMENT

TO BE GIVEN BY

THE WALTHAMSTOW PLAYERS

ON

Saturday, February 2nd, 1935

To commence at 7-30 p.m.

PROGRAMME - ONE SHILLING

F. W. March & Co., Manor Shining Works Raunds.

8 Entertainment by the Walthamstow Players, 1935

1. SUNDAY EVENING

A COCKNEY EPISODE

Joe Wilkes	Reginald Sorensen
Annie Wilkes	Muriel Sorensen

2. FAILURE

Scene—Hammerton's Private Office

Richard Hammerton ...	Reginald Sorensen
Joan, his wife	Elsie Pracy
Ross, an elderly clerk ...	Ernest Houghton
Thompson, a warehouse clerk	Stanley Bennet

3. TOLPUDDLE, Act II

Scene 1—Interior of an Inn, Tolpuddle, 1834.

Margaret Stanfield ...	Doris Bennet
Jennie, a maid	Kathleen Marter
George Loveless ⎱ farm	William Aylott
James Loveless ⎰ labourers	Stanley Bennet
Thomas Stanfield ⎰	Arthur Fairmainer
Harry Courtney ...	Reginald Sorensen
(A strange visitor from London)	

Scene 2—Corridor at the Dorchester Assizes,
   March 20th, 1834. As above.

Gailor	Ernest Houghton

4. COMPETITION

Scene—A Small Garage.

Philip Dunning	...	Stanley Bennet
Eddie Squires	...	Arthur Fairmainer
Ben Jackson	...	Ernest Houghton
Robert Brownlow ...	...	Reginald Sorensen

5. THE RULING CLASS

A MORAL FARCE

Scene—The Hall of Myopia Villa.

King	...	Reginald Sorensen
Queen	...	Elsie Pracy
Lizzie	...	Muriel Sorensen
Jack	...	Stanley Bennet

speaking' by the audience which follows – a minor theatrical sensation in its day – was precisely the same device as the Hackney
Labour Players had used to conclude their 1928 production of the
Ragged Trousered Philanthropists. The 'Living Newspaper', another
of Unity's early theatrical coups, had been widely used by the
Proletkult groups in early 1920s Russia, and was staged in England
by the Holborn Labour Party players as early as 1926.[188]

The relationship of Left theatre in the later 1930s to its predecessors is difficult to characterize, and awaits a critical and historical
account both of the Unity Theatre movement (there were Unity
Theatres in the provinces, as well as the London one in Goldington
Square) and of the Left Book Club Theatre Guild, which in 1938
had some 250 different groups.[189] It is clear, though, that the spirit
of the WTM was very far from dead. Many of the new groups
played the Labour and Co-operative halls, very much as the WTM
had done, and the pageants they took part in had much in common
with the mass speaking which the WTM had pioneered. In Manchester, the Theatre of Action, led by Joan Littlewood and Ewan
MacColl, was developing a combination of theatre and song and
mime which, like many of the WTM sketches, was to draw heavily
on popular idiom. Unity Theatre itself, at least in its early years,
kept strictly to group ideals, and until the war, the actors' names
did not even appear on the programme.

Notes

1 Sheila Rowbotham, 'Edward Carpenter' in Sheila Rowbotham and
  Jeffrey Weeks, *Socialism and the New Life*, London, 1977, pp. 50–1.
2 Robert Tressell, *The Ragged Trousered Philanthropists*, Panther ed.,
  London, 1965.
3 For an autobiographical memoir, Jean McCrindle and Sheila
  Rowbotham, *Dutiful Daughters*, Harmondsworth, 1979.
4 George Barnett Smith (ed.), *The Life and Speeches of John Bright M.P.*,
  London, 1881, vol. 1, p. 84.
5 E. Belfort Bax,
6 Sidney Webb, 'The Historic Basis of Socialism' in *Fabian Essays in
  Socialism*, London, 1889, p. 45.
7 L. MacNeill Weir M.P., *The Tragedy of Ramsay Macdonald*, London,
  n.d., p. 77.
8 H. G. Wells, *Ann Veronica*, Everyman Ed., pp. 38–40.

9 Tressell, *Ragged Trousered Philanthropists*, p. 584.

10 Alice Foley, *A Bolton Childhood*, Manchester, 1973.

11 *The Co-operative News*, 8 Oct. 1927, p. 6.

12 George Edwards, *From Crow Scaring to Westminster*, London, 1922, p. 114.

13 J. R. Clynes, *Memoirs*, London, 1937, vol. 1, pp. 49–50.

14 London School of Economics, Webb TU Coll., *Glass Bottle Makers of Yorkshire, Quarterly Reports*, 1886, p. 363.

15 Dona Torr, *Tom Mann and his Times*, London, 1956, pp. 67–8.

16 E. Pease, *The History of the Fabian Society*, London, 1916, p. 186.

17 Ian Britain, *Fabianism and Culture*, Cambridge, 1982, p. 173.

18 Elizabeth Sprigge, *Casson*, London, 1971, p. 73; Basil Dean, *Seven Ages: an autobiography*, London, 1970, pp. 54–5; Rex Pogson, *Miss Horniman and the Gaiety Theatre*, London, 1952, p. 59.

19 Yvonne Kapp, *Eleanor Marx*, vol II, London, 1979.

20 Mary Agnes Hamilton, *Mary Macarthur*, London, 1925, p. 48.

21 Margaret Bondfield, *A Life's Work*, London, 1949, pp. 72–3.

22 Harold Brighouse (ed.), *The Works of Stanley Houghton*, London, 1914, p. xiii.

23 *New Leader*, 28 Sept. 1923, p. 12.

24 *I.L.P. News*, Sept. 1903, p. 6. The 'hymns' referred to are Labour anthems.

25 *Clarion*, 21 May 1926, p. 9; for an early Clarion choir, *Clarion*, 9 Nov. 1895, p. 356.

26 *Clarion*, 21 Aug. 1925, p. 7; cf. also *Sunday Worker*, 31 May 1925, p. 10; 1 Nov. 1925, p. 8; 6 Dec. 1925, p. 8.

27 B. Donoghue and G. W. Jones, *Herbert Morrison*, London, 1973, pp. 70–3.

28 *Labour Leader*, 8 January 1909, p. 23.

29 Lord Morrison of Lambeth, *Herbert Morrison*, London, 1960, p. 53.

30 Mary Agnes Hamilton, *Remembering My Good Friends*, London, 1944, p. 183.

31 *Sunday Worker*, 4 July 1926, p. 8.

32 *Commonweal*, 28 April 1888, p. 136.

33 *Justice*, 5 March 1886, p. 4.

34 Emmett Larkin, *James Larkin*, London, 1965, pp. 161–2. James Sexton, the Liverpool dockers' leader, had been a member of the Boucicault Amateur Dramatic Society before beginning his union activities (*Sir James Sexton, Agitator: The Life of the Dockers' MP*, London 1936, p. 55). In 1909 he was helping the Liverpool Clarion players to perform Shaw. In 1913 he wrote and had produced in Liverpool a play on the 1911 Liverpool Dock Strike vindicating the 'responsible' stand which he had taken against the rank and file. In the dénouement – a possibly

unique example of right-wing trade union self-pity – the union leader (i.e. Sexton himself) is carried lifeless off stage. There is a copy of the play (*The Riot Act*) in the British Museum.

35 Cf. *Young Socialist*, November 1907, February 1908.

36 *Ibid.*, August 1908.

37 Foley, *Bolton Childhood*, p. 68.

38 S. Bryher, *The Labour and Socialist Movement in Bristol*, Bristol, n.d., Pt. II, p. 54.

39 *Young Socialist*, December 1908.

40 *Labour Leader*, 2 April 1909, p. 2.

41 *Young Socialist*, June 1907, March, April 1908, November 1908.

42 *The Labour Pioneer* (Cardiff), December 1890, p. 6.

43 *Labour Leader*, 16 February 1922, p. 8.

44 *Bradford Labour Echo*, 18 June 1898; *Labour Leader*, 19 February 1909, 5 March 1909; Foreword, 22 January 1921, p. 8.

45 *Labour Leader*, 1 January 1909.

46 Henry Pelling, *The Origins of the Labour Party*, London, 1954, p. 135.

47 LSE., Coll. Misc. 464, Gillingham ILP Minute Book, 10 March 1927.

48 *Dutiful Daughters*, pp. 62–3.

49 *Labour Leader*, 12 February 1909, p. 112.

50 *Ibid.*, 4 June 1909, p. 368.

51 Oral testimony, int. of Eric Jones with W. M. Sproull, May 1978; *Justice*, 8 February, 10 October 1909. I am grateful to Eric Jones for undertaking this interview for me.

52 Information from Andy Durr based on Brighton SDP minutes. I am grateful to Andy Durr for this information.

53 *Labour Leader*, 29 January, 5 February; 2 April; 21 May 1909.

54 *Comradeship*, May 1920, December 1922; *Labour Leader*, 19, 26 January, 12 February, 13 April, 31 August 1922.

55 'Dangle' (Alexander Thompson) *Here I Lie: The Memorial of an Old Journalist*, London, 1957, p. 116; Laurence Thompson, *Robert Blatchford: Portrait of an Englishman*, London, 1951, p. 67; Robert Blatchford, *My Eighty Years*, London, 1931.

56 *Sir James Sexton, Agitator: The Life of the Dockers' MP*; *Labour Leader*, 23 April 1909; *Clarion*, 24 February 1911.

57 *Clarion*, 13 January, 24 February 1911.

58 *Clarion*, 24 March 1911.

59 *Clarion*, 31 March 1911. In the women's column of *Clarion* Julia Dawson was projecting a scheme for the 'Clarion Strolling Players' to go out in the summer with the 'Clarion Vans'.

60 Norman Veitch, *The People's, being a history of the People's Theatre, Newcastle-upon-Tyne, 1911–1939*, Gateshead, 1950, pp. 14–15.

61 Veitch, *The People's*, for an excellent chronicle. For the foundation of

the players, *Clarion*, 31 March 1911; for an autobiographical account by one of them, Bonar Thompson, *Hyde Park Orator*, London, 1934, pp. 216–17; for a visitor's account, J. B. Priestley, *English Journey*, London 1934, pp. 278–80, 286–9.

62 Veitch, *The People's*, p. 9.

63 *Ibid.*, pp. 10–11.

64 *Ibid.*, p. 13.

65 Tom Johnston, *Memories*, London, 1952, p. 229.

66 Emanuel Shinwell, *Conflict without Malice*, London, 1955, pp. 44–5.

67 Cf. *The London News* (journal of the London Labour Party) December 1925 and *passim*.

68 *Daily Herald*, 28 January 1928, p. 9; Douglas Allen, 'The Glasgow Workers' Theatre Group', *New Edinburgh Review*, no. 40, p. 13.

69 Margaret Morris (ed.), *The General Strike*, Harmondsworth, 1976, p. 90.

70 *Battersea and Wandsworth Labour and Social History Newsletter*, no. 9, October 1979, pp. 1–2. For an account of the Herald League see Ken Weller, *Anti-War Movements in London during the First World War*, London History Workshop Pamphlet (forthcoming). Tom Thomas was converted to Socialism by the Herald League, see this volume, p. 78.

71 *Labour Leader*, 16 February, 6 April, 19 May, 1 June 1922.

72 *Ibid.*, 18 May 1922, p. 8.

73 Eric Jones, interview with Wallace Haines, 11 June 1978. I am grateful to Eric Jones for carrying out this interview.

74 Veitch, *The People's*, p. 22; *New Leader*, 22 December 1922; *The Labour Magazine*, vol. 11, no. 3, July 1923. I am very grateful to Bert Hogenkampf of Amsterdam for this last reference, an extended account of the Gateshead group and its productions.

75 Miles Malleson, *The ILP Arts Guild*, London, 1925, p. 3; *Socialist Reviews*, 1925, pp. 44–5, 164, 276–7; Huntly Carter, *The New Spirit in the European Theatre*, London, 1925, pp. 255, 273; *Sunday Worker*, 27 March, 31 May 1925; 21 March 1926; *Clarion*, 20 February 1925.

76 *Clarion*, 23 January 1925.

77 *Sunday Worker*, 14 March 1926, p. 9.

78 Fred Ball, *One of the Damned*, London, 1973, p. 215.

79 W. Barefoot, *Twenty-Five Years Woolwich Labour Party*, Woolwich, 1928, p. 40.

80 Deborah Thom, *Woolwich. The General Strike*, London n.d. (1976?), pp. 3–4.

81 Donoghue and Jones, *Morrison*, p. 71.

82 *Co-Operative News*, 9 May 1925, p. 11.

83 *Clarion*, 25 December 1925, p. 2.

84 *Comradeship*, October 1926, p. xiii; May 1926, p.v.

85 *The London News*, October 1926, p. 3.

86 There is a copy of *Captain Youth* in the British Museum.

87 *Sunday Worker*, 7 January 1925.

88 For some contemporary comments, *The London News*, July 1925; *Sunday Worker*, 15 November 1925, 14 November 1926; *Plebs*, XVIII, November 1926, p. 424; August 1926, p. 8.

89 *Sunday Worker*, 14 November 1926, p. 11.

90 *Clarion*, 13 February 1925, *Sunday Worker*, 7 June 1926; R. M. Fox, *Smoky Crusade*, London, 1937, p. 220; *Daily Herald*, 8 February 1928.

91 *The Worker* (Huddersfield), 3 January 1920, p. 4. For Goldring's part in the cultural politics of the period, Douglas Goldring, *The Nineteen-Twenties*, London, 1945.

92 *Labour Leader*, 15 June 1922; Veitch, *The People's*, p. 74; *Sunday Worker*, 7 March 1926; 16 June 1929; *Clarion*, 30 May 1924, p. 3; *Plebs*, September 1924, p. 353, October 1924, pp. 394–5. When Toller became a refugee in England in the 1930s, he set up a theatre in Welwyn Garden City and campaigned for a theatre in Welwyn Garden City, see Nicholas Hern, 'The Theatre of Ernst Toller', *Theatre Quarterly*, vol. 2(5) January–March 1972.

93 For the expansion of Co-op membership, G. D. H. Cole, *A Century of Co-operation*, London 1944.

94 John Attfield, *With Light of Knowledge: a hundred years of Education in the Royal Arsenal Co-operative Society*, London, 1981, is a valuable account of the educational activities of the Royal Arsenal Co-operative Society; *Comradeship*, its monthly journal, gives a mass of document-ation; the *Co-operative News* gives full descriptions of the pageantry of Co-operators' Day.

95 Among those who were introduced to drama at these Co-op drama classes was André van Gyseghem (then known, before his studentship at RADA, as Stanley Gyseghem) later a founder of Unity Theatre.

96 *Comradeship*, June 1923.

97 *Ibid.*, July 1923.

98 *Ibid.*, March 1926, pp. iv–v.

99 *Ibid.*, May 1926, p. ii.

100 *Clarion*, 16 January 1925, p. 8; *Co-op News*, 6 March 1926, p. 9; *Clarion*, 7 August 1925, p. 3.

101 Veitch, *The People's*, p. 70.

102 T. Ashcroft, 'Socialism and the Drama', *Plebs*, September 1924, pp. 334–7. Ashcroft was Principal of the Central Labour College at Earl's Court and father of Dame Peggy Ashcroft, the West End actress.

103 *Sunday Worker*, 15 November 1925. Monica Ewer was dramatic critic of the *Daily Herald*, and editor of 'Plays for the People'.

104 'Real Spiritual in Co-operation', *Co-Op News*, 14 February 1925, is a fine statement of the ideal.

105 Len Jones, 'The Workers' Theatre Movement', pp. 29–30. A copy of the thesis is deposited with the Warwick University theatre collection and I am grateful to Clive Barker for letting me consult it.

106 Donoghue and Jones, *Morrison*, p. 71.

107 H. M. Watkins, *Life Has Kept Me Young*, London, 1951, pp. 145–6 for an account of such an initiative in the Cardiff Labour Party.

108 Clifford Hanley, *Dancing in the Streets*, London, 1958, pp. 132–4.

109 *Oration on the Death of a Miner*, 'an item for a workers' revue' was a dramatic piece produced in the aftermath of the General Strike.

110 Very popular at Shornells, the country house settlement of the RACS where the grounds provided a sylvan setting for Shakespearean productions.

111 The point is well made in *Sunday Worker*, 20 March 1927, p. 8.

112 *Comradeship*, December 1923, January, February 1924.

113 *Sunday Worker*, 15 November 1925.

114 *Comradeship*, 27 October 1926.

115 *Comradeship*, December 1926.

116 *Clarion*, 25 December 1925. For more critical accounts of Malleson's plays of this period, *Sunday Worker*, 20 March 1927, p. 8; 8 August 1926, p. 8; 20 March 1927, p. 8.

117 Huntly Carter, 'Workers and the Theatre', *Sunday Worker*, 18 July 1926, p. 8.

118 *Ibid.*

119 Tom Thomas Papers, memorandum of resolutions dated July 1930.

120 *Sunday Worker*, 14 July, 1 December 1929.

121 *Sunday Worker*, 20 March 1927, p. 8, for Ruby Boughton. Her fellow singer, at a Camberwell performance of the WTM, was the well-known tenor – a singer on Communist Party occasions for some thirty years – John Goss. Boughton's complex love-life – he left his first wife Florence to live with Christina Walshe and Christina Walshe to live with someone else – was, according to Ray Burrows of Street, Somerset, who has collected reminiscences of fellow-villagers, a cause of considerable disquiet, somewhat negating the effect of his having gone to live in a labourer's cottage. For an account of these complexities, or 'scandals' as they were called in the rather strict idiom of the time, Percy Lovell, *Quaker Inheritance 1871–1961*, based on the correspondence of Roger Clark of Street, the patron of the Glastonbury festivals. Both Boughton and Christina, whose relationship dated back to before 1914, seem to have been radicalized by the war; and they kept up a working relationship after they had separated as lovers, though Bernard Shaw claimed in 1934 that Christina 'bored'

Rutland with her Communism. There is an appreciation of him by a fellow-composer, Bernard Stevens, in *The New Reasoner*, Spring 1959.

122   R. Palme Dutt, 'Notes of the Month', *Labour Monthly*, August 1926.

123   Maurice Dobb, 'The Theatres', *Plebs*, March 1929, p. 54.

124   Huntly Carter, *loc. cit.* Like Boughton, Huntly Carter's activity for Socialism – as also his championship of 'modernism' – stretched back to the years before 1911.

125   Corrie, a prolific dramatist, began writing verse while working in the coal-mines in Fife and had his first plays – *The Shillin'-a-Week-Man* and *The Poacher* – performed by the Bowhill Village Players during the General Strike. 'This group of actor-miners, of which Corrie himself was one, toured the music-halls of Scotland and the north of England with Corrie's plays during 1929–30'. Phyllis Hartnoll, *Oxford Companion to the Theatre*, London, 1951, p. 157. *Sunday Worker*, 8, 29 January 1928; *Daily Herald*, 3 January 1928. Corrie, who continued publication until the 1960s, was a prolific playwright on Scottish subjects; his plays were much in demand by amateur dramatic groups in the 1930s.

126   *Sunday Worker*, 10 January, 11 July 1926; 2 February 1927; Sean O'Casey was one of those who sent good wishes for the opening show.

127   Ness Edwards, *The Workers' Theatre*, Cardiff, 1930, pp. 39–52, 79, 27–31.

128   Tom Thomas, article in 'Arbeitbühne und Film', June 1930, pp. 11–14, quoted in Jones thesis, p. 34.

129   *Sunday Worker*, 4 July 1926, p. 8.

130   *Ibid.*, 25 July 1926, p. 8. The play was also being performed in the same month by the St Pancras Women's Committee at the Memorial Hall, Hawley Rd (*ibid.*, 25 July 1926). Jack and Alice Loveman, who played with the Greenwich 'Red Blouses' and the Streatham 'Red Front' WTM groups, remember performing *Singing Jailbirds* with a 'Plebs' group about 1924 or 1925, using Wobbly songs to heighten the drama of the readings (interview with Richard Stourac and Kathleen McReery, July 1977). For Tom Thomas's account of the Hackney People's Players production of *Singing Jailbirds*, see his narrative on pp. 86–7 of this volume.

131   *Co-operative News*, 29 October 1927, p. 9. The Labour Club had been opened in December 1925, with William Paul, editor of the *Sunday Worker*, giving a song-recital on 'Music and the Masses'. *Sunday Worker*, 6 December 1925, p. 8.

132   Raphael Samuel, interview with Charlie Mann, 30 June 1977.

133   Raphael Samuel, interview with Ewan MacColl, 13 August 1977;

Ewan MacColl, 'Grass Roots of Theatre Workshop', *Theatre Quarterly*, vol. 111, 58–61, January–March 1973; Eddie and Ruth Frow, 'Manchester WTM', typescript article, 1977.

134 For some press notices of the Hackney group, *Daily Herald*, 26 January 1928, p. 9; *Sunday Worker*, 8 August 1926, p. 8; 23 December 1928, p. 6; 14 July 1929, p. 7.

135 Raphael Samuel, interview with Hetty Bower, 31 March 1978. Letters from Hetty Bower, 14 March 1978, 29 April 1978, 29 June 1978.

136 For an excellent account of 'Plebs' ideology, Stuart MacIntyre, *A Proletarian Science: Marxism in Britain 1917–1933*, Cambridge, 1980.

137 Quoted in Carolyn Steedman, 'Battlegrounds: the struggle for curriculum control in the primary school', *History Workshop Journal*, vol. 17, Spring 1984.

138 Carter, 'Workers and the Theatre', *Sunday Worker*, 18 July 1926.

139 *Sunday Worker*, 5 December 1926, p. 8.

140 *Plebs*, vol. XVI, p. 406, October 1924. The writer is J. F. Horrabin.

141 *Sunday Worker*, 30 January; 13, 20 March 1927.

142 René Fuelloep-Miller, *The Russian Theatre*, London, 1930, p. 67.

143 *Sunday Worker*, 7 June 1925.

144 *Sunday Worker*, 10 January 1926, p. 8.

145 Fuelloep-Miller, p. 127.

146 *Sunday Worker*, 18 July 1926, p. 8. In later years, the Soviet Airman's song, sung as a lusty chorus in WTM productions around 1934, and the Soviet Young Communist Song ('The voice of the City is sleepless/The factories whistle and sound') were sung in the same spirit.

147 Edwards, *Workers' Theatre*.

148 Tom Thomas Papers, 'List of Plays now Available' (1934?).

149 Tom Thomas, 'The Workers' Theatre in Britain', *International Theatre*, 1934, pp. 23–4.

150 *Daily Worker*, 29 January 1932, p. 6; for the disaster, *ibid.*, 27 January 1932, p. 1.

151 *Sunday Worker*, 23 December 1928, p. 1. Three of the expelled students were from the South Wales Miners' Federation, two from the National Union of Railwaymen, and two were on TUC scholarship.

152 Ewan MacColl, 'The Grass Roots of Theatre Workshop'.

153 *Daily Worker*, 5 May 1931, p. 11.

154 Ewan MacColl, 'The Grass Roots of Theatre Workshop'.

155 *Daily Worker*, 8 February 1930, p. 11.

156 *Ibid.*, 3 January 1931, p. 4.

157 Ray Waterman, 'Proltet' (see this volume, p. 149). Richard Stourac and Kathleen McCreery, interview with Philip Poole.

158 Raphael Samuel, interview with Charlie Mann.

159 *Ibid.*
160 The first German 'contact' spoke at a WTM weekend school in June 1930. He spoke of the 'brilliant work' of the Hamburg 'Riveters' and criticized 'the mistaken attempt' of the WTM 'to wed decadent and erotic jazz tunes to the revolutionary message'. *Daily Worker*, 11 June 1930, p. 5.
161 *Sunday Worker*, 1 December 1929, p. 4; 24 June 1928, p. 8; *Daily Worker*, 8 February 1930, p. 11.
162 *Ibid.*, 17 March 1931, p. 3.
163 Raphael Samuel, interview with Charlie Mann.
164 A copy of the War Memorial sketch is in Tom Thomas's papers.
165 Raphael Samuel, interview with Charlie Mann.
166 Interviewed by Ray Burrows to whom my thanks. Boughton, 'for professional reasons' (according to Alan Bush, *Morning Star*, 23 January 1978) felt obliged to withdraw from Communist Party membership in 1929 when he also resigned from the London Labour Choral Union. His interest revived when he attended a World Peace conference in 1947 and he rejoined the Party, but left it again in 1956. 'His interest in Communism however never failed to the last day of his life' (*ibid.*).
167 The *Sunday Worker* (27 September 1925) describes her as 'one of the most brilliant stage artists in the country'. Archie Ziegler, her fellow organizer in the early days of the WTM, is variously described as a 'seaman' and a 'painter'.
168 Raphael Samuel, interview with Charlie Mann, and Richard Stourac and Kathleen McCreery, interview with the Lovemans.
169 Raphael Samuel, interview with and correspondence from Hetty Bower.
170 Raphael Samuel, interview with Ewan MacColl.
171 *Sunday Worker*, 26 February 1928, p. 8.
172 *Ibid.*, 4 July 1926, p. 8.
173 *Ibid.*, 24 June 1928, p. 8.
174 *Ibid.*, 25 November 1928, p. 7.
175 Tom Thomas, 'The Workers' Theatre in Britain', *International Theatre*, 1934, p. 22.
176 *Sunday Worker*, 5 December 1926, p. 8.
177 *Ibid.*, 1 December 1929, p. 4.
178 *Ibid.*, 28 February 1928, p. 8.
179 Workers' Theatre Movement *Bulletin*, January and February 1933, quoted in Jones, thesis, p. 114.
180 Richard Stourac and Kathleen McCreery, interview with Phil Poole.
181 *Daily Worker*, 27 April 1935, p. 8.
182 *Ibid.*, 9 April 1934, p. 4.

183 *Ibid.*, 26 March 1935, p. 4.
184 *Ibid.*, 19 February, p. 4, 14 April, p. 4, 1935.
185 '. . . Although it is not possible to draw many actors together on a pro-socialist basis, it is possible to get them on an anti-Fascist basis,' John Allen, 'The Socialist Theatre', *Left Review*, vol. III, 418, August 1937.
186 *Daily Worker*, 31 January 1936, p. 7.
187 *Ibid.*, 22 February 1936, p. 6.
188 *Sunday Worker*, 14 March 1936, p. 9.
189 'A Real Worker's Theatre Movement', *Discussion*, March 1938, p. 42.

Part 2

The Workers' Theatre Movement (1926–1935)

A propertyless theatre for
the propertyless class
Tom Thomas (1977)

I was born on 18 June 1902 in Gayhurst Road, Dalston, East London, a road which was a typical mix of comfortable respect-ability and hand-to-mouth poverty. My father was a basketmaker, a very ancient craft: he told me that my brother and I were the first males in the family who had not followed the trade. He was a staunch trade unionist but politically he was a Liberal. The only political words I ever heard from him were when he recounted how a work-mate had been so bitterly disappointed at the failure of the German workers to oppose the Kaiser's government on the question of war. After all their undertakings at conferences to have a General Strike, there was nothing. My father was quite happy about that because it showed that his work-mate, who was a keen socialist, was wrong.

I became a socialist, an emotional and ill-formed one, quite early in life because of the influence of my grandmother who was an Ulster Unionist, and of her *Daily Mail*, which was the only news-paper that came into our house. I read it each day from the age of seven or eight. Disgust turned to loathing as I read the campaigns which it ran against the reforms which the Liberal government of Mr Asquith was introducing. 'Ninepence for fourpence' shrieked the *Mail*, in horror at the new National Insurance scheme. The proposal to pay a pension of 5s a week to persons of seventy who had actually not contributed a single penny to the cost of providing it, was an almost criminal act in the *Mail*'s eyes, a loosening of the moral fibre of the nation. In the same issue I would read fulsome descriptions of country house parties, presentation parties, etc. The clothes worn and the meals eaten received the full flunkey treat-ment. I was nauseated by such selfishness. When I sang in the church choir, 'He hath put down the mighty from their seats and exalted the humble and meek. He hath filled the hungry with good things and the rich He hath sent empty away', I looked at the occupants of the pews, and it was clear to me that He hadn't done any of these things and it was about time somebody else did.

On the way back home from school one drenching, wet day, I passed a house where something unusual was taking place. Beds, bedding, furniture, clothing had been thrown out in the front garden and were getting soaked and probably ruined. I asked my mother why this was happening and was told, 'They haven't paid their rent.' This made a deep impression on me, that people and their poor belongings could be treated like this.

At school, at church and at home these things were never discussed, so I resorted to books. I was already a voracious reader, and by the time I was fourteen I had read Shaw, Wells and Galsworthy. I had also come across Blatchford's *Merrie England*, and having read about evolution I had left the church. Then I read the Hammonds' *Town Labourer* and *Village Labourer* and learned how the underdogs had been treated in the past.

My own family situation taught me much. My father was a craftsman, a basketmaker, and for some years the president of the London Society of Basketmakers. He earned around 30s a week. We lived in a small, reasonably comfortable house in a district which had large gardens. But the rent was crippling, and we only paid it by taking in a lodger who got meals at week-ends. Even with this extra my mother had to pinch and scrape to provide food. New clothes were very rare indeed. My mother, the family financier, gave my father every morning his sandwiches and his tram fare for the day and that was that until the weekend when he was given a shilling or so to go to the pub to meet his friends. That seemed a lousy existence for an intelligent and hard-working man.

But it was the War which really educated me politically. First, the tragic absurdity of the bishops on both sides praying for victory to the self-same God. Seeking the real cause of that ghastly blood-bath, I heard of meetings at Finsbury Park on Sunday mornings. At these, which were organized by the *Herald* League,[1] I listened to anti-war speakers who sometimes received quite a rough handling from some of the crowd. Here I bought the *New Leader*, the paper of the Independent Labour Party (ILP), and other literature and learned how the war, in their opinion, was caused. It was here that I bought my first copy of *The Ragged Trousered Philanthropists* which was to me, as to many others, both a revelation and an inspiration. I joined the *Herald* League, but apart from attending their meetings, there was little I could do. Then came the Russian Revolution with the overthrow of the Tsar. I had read translations of the Russian novelists and knew that all that was best in Russia had fought for the destruction of this tyranny. I followed the events from March 1917 onwards with the greatest interest and when in November the Bolsheviks took power in what at the outset was practically a bloodless revolution, I, with socialists everywhere, felt that a new era had dawned in the tragic history of mankind and of the oppression of the masses by their owners and masters. Right from the Spartacus revolt in Rome and earlier, through peasant risings and in our own Civil War in the seventeenth century, the hungry and oppressed had risen against their masters, only to fail. But now, a real workers' republic had been born. Within a few weeks, many decrees, including the nationalization of the land, the banks and large enterprises, without compensation, showed that this was a revolution aimed at the destruction of capitalism, root and branch. An immediate peace without annexations and without indemnities was called to stop the horrors of the war. Henceforward I was a socialist, I joined the ILP and later, when individuals were admitted, the Labour Party, playing an active part particularly at elections. I was active in the Labour Party for a number of years but in 1926 I left it because of the way the General Strike had been betrayed. I could not continue under the MacDonald leadership which I was convinced would commit fresh betrayals, so I joined the only other socialist organization, the Communist Party, and remained in it for many years, though after the Second World War I rejoined the Labour Party, of which I am a member today.

So by 1926 I had a firm political commitment and by then I had also developed a deep interest in the theatre and music. After leaving school at fourteen and getting a job as a clerk in a stockbroker's office, I studied a course of commercial subjects at a London County Council evening institute. This course included a leavening of non-commercial subjects, English and Drama. I very much enjoyed these subjects but when I was seventeen or eighteen I had to make a decision; it was clear that to study for a degree or equivalent in the commercial subjects I should have to put in another three or four years and of necessity abandon literature and drama, there was no time for both. I decided to follow the studies which would teach me how to live and not merely how to get a higher level of pay in capitalist society, which seemed likely to collapse of its own rottenness within my lifetime. So I threw myself wholeheartedly into the drama group, the Queen's Players, which was run by a brilliant young man, A. C. Ward, who afterwards published a string of books for literature and drama studies. He produced very effectively Shakespeare (*Romeo and Juliet, Macbeth, Twelfth Night*) and many modern plays, chiefly Shaw, in which I earned myself leading roles to my very great enjoyment. I also started going up to the theatres in the West End with a friend of mine. I got into the habit of going every week, and got a very good view of the triviality of it, the unpleasant outlook of the West End stage at the time – all Oxford accents except for the funny servants.

I was also interested in music. As soon as I began work at the age of fourteen, I went to the concerts at South Place[2] every Sunday night. And that was the most wonderful privilege. We heard the current leading soloists and quartets. My only musical education was as a choir boy till about the age of eleven, when I left the church. When I was nineteen years old, I joined the London Philharmonic Choir. I also applied for membership of the Madrigal Society, but I hadn't read music for so many years since leaving church and choir that they failed me on sight reading. I was with the Philharmonic Society for eight years. It was really quite a wonderful experience. Singing with the orchestra gives one a wonderful insight into the whole mechanism.

In the mid-1920s my two main interests came together in a quite unexpected way. In the winter months the Hackney Labour Party invited Labour supporters and their neighbours to free 'socials' on occasional Saturday nights. There was usually a good attendance, for then there was no TV and radio was in its infancy, but what could be offered but speeches and then tea and biscuits. The school halls that we used were at least warm compared with the homes that many people came from. But they were rather dull occasions enlivened by the rare good speech. Just to brighten things up I put on *Sealing the Compact*, a one-act play by Gwen John I found in the library of the British Drama League. It was a one-act play dealing with a pit tragedy. There was no stage, not even a platform, but somehow we established a playing area, rigged up a couple of screens and some props. With a minimum of furniture we managed to suggest a miner's cottage. And the lift up! The interest! The applause! It was most enthusiastically received and we repeated it several times at other socials.

Then it struck me, here was something people really enjoyed coming to, which was also a way of spreading the message. So in 1926 I started the Hackney Labour Dramatic Group. I got hold of two of the brightest people in the Labour Party, Herbert Butler and Albert Cullington. I disagreed with them politically, but they were used to public speaking and once you're a public speaker you're not very far from being an actor. Butler afterwards became one of the Members of Parliament for Hackney. He was for many years the manager of a furniture business in Whitechapel Road. He had come into the Labour Party after the First World War, when he became active in the NUX – a militant, left-wing version of the British Legion, called the National Union of ex-Servicemen. I don't know what Cullington did. Like Butler he was a very capable person, used to street-corner work and public speaking. They were the younger generation in the Labour Party, both very active. Neither of them stayed beyond the first show, but it was a tremendous help to have the leavening of people who could learn their lines and speak with a minimum of producing. Then in the same show we had Kath Duncan, who became a well-known member of the Communist Party. She was a very strong personality with a Scottish background. She and her husband had a house in Upper Clapton and my wife and I went to live in an upstairs flat there.

The Hackney Labour Dramatic Group gave its first performance on 24 April 1926 at the Library Hall, Stoke Newington. We were supported by the Hackney Trades Council and included – we claimed – 'all shades of working-class opinion'. Later we changed our name to the Hackney People's Players, and then in 1928 we became a branch of the Workers' Theatre Movement.

We started off with one-act plays. The first programme of the Hackney Labour Dramatic Group had four plays – *Augustus Does His Bit*, by Bernard Shaw, *A Woman's Honour*, by Susan Glassville, *The Man on the Street*, by Sutro, and *Twelve Pound Look*, by Barrie.

I spent many hours in the library of the British Drama League, searching for plays which dealt with the realities of the lives of the working class in Britain, and which analysed or dissected the social system which had failed to prevent the war, had completely failed to deliver the 'homes for heroes' promised during the war, and maintained a class system in which the wealthy flourished, and the great majority of the people were their wage slaves. But I could find no such plays. So it was clear that if the People's Players was to fulfill its aim of exposing the evils of the capitalist system, and the oppression of the people, then the plays had to be written. By whom? At that juncture there was only one answer – by me. And by anyone else whom I could persuade to attempt the task. But until the plays were written, the group had to be kept in being and trained, putting on whatever plays I could find which had some modicum of 'social significance'.

Capek's *R.U.R.* was an obvious choice. It had had a run in the West End. Its theme was the manufacture of mechanical men and women who would carry out all the work previously performed by the working class, with no food or other requirements, except fuel. These robots were clearly the ideal solution for the capitalist class, and promised an immense reduction in costs, and a subservient class of slaves. But the robots developed human feelings, and became what their masters called 'unreliable'. Untimately they overthrew their masters, the human race. It was a clear and unique parable of the workers' revolution we were hoping for.[3]

After *R.U.R.*, in the next few months we put on single performances of Shaw's *Mrs. Warren's Profession*, and *The Adding Machine* by Elmer Rice. They were well received but in subsequent discussions we came to two important realizations. We were still performing plays which in our view added nothing of real value to the people's struggle. And secondly, we were performing them to an audience of friends and supporters and not breaking through to the vast majority who were yet to hear the socialist message.

By the middle of 1927 the Hackney People's Players, as we now called ourselves, was an organization of about twenty members. We played mainly at working men's clubs and we also had one or two requests from Labour and Communist Parties. Most of the members of the group came from Hackney but some from other parts of the East End. We were a success. We were able to buy ourselves a nice lighting set, for example, with dimmers and floods and spots. We had successfully tackled several modern plays. What was more significant, a number of workers were finding that there was a group who would perform their efforts and they began to write for us. *Lady Betty's Husband*, an election playlet by Bernard Woolf, was one of them. I wrote a play about Chiang Kai Shek –

at the time he seemed to be leading a people's movement against the old regime. Then I wrote a play called *Betty Burton's Father*. It was about a father who had been in jail because of his activities in the General Strike and what happened to Betty at school when the other children learned about it. I wrote it for the Hackney Young Pioneers.[4]

The first full-length play I wrote – we produced it in 1927 – was *The Ragged Trousered Philanthropists*. It was a book which cried out to be made into a play and when I re-read it I realized that it had the material not just for one play but a dozen. The book depicted the life of working people with tragic realism. It criticized the capitalist order of society in new and striking ways. And it showed the utter emptiness of the catch-phrases by which the 'philanthropists' who slaved their lives away in misery, for the benefit of their masters, were bamboozled into voting for their oppressors at elections. The plight of the working class had been depicted in many novels, but this was almost the first novel to be written by a victim of the system who had himself suffered from hunger, unemployment and the personal humiliation of a gifted man at the hands of ignorant but all-powerful employers.

I decided that the play should be as unashamedly propagandist as the novel, and should not depart from Tressell's words except as demanded by dramatic effectiveness. The final scene in the novel was omitted – i.e., of Owen bringing up blood from his tubercular lungs and resolving that he would kill his wife and child and then himself rather than leave them to suffer the life of hunger and misery which would be their fate if they survived him. After the abounding confidence in the socialist future of mankind in Owen's great oration, it would have been wrong for the audience to be plunged into Owen's final tragedy. By bringing down the curtain on a great shout of 'Aye!' to the resolution 'That socialism is the only remedy for unemployment and poverty' (and this invariably occurred) – the audience participated in the triumph of Owen and his ideals.

It would be difficult to say who enjoyed it more, the audience or the players. From the moment the curtain went up and Bert White, the starveling tea-boy, was told 'I don't think much of this bloody tea', a roar of laughter at such a commonplace but unexpected phrase being heard on the stage, in people's own language, spurred the actors to get a laugh out of every appropriate line, and of course treat the serious scenes with the full emotion which they demanded. It was clear that there was a real rapport between the audience and the play. It was about a world they recognized and understood. The cast that night, fourteen in all, included two electricians, two clerks, a book-keeper, a former able-seaman, a tailor, a haberdashery salesman, two housewives, and two cabinet-makers.

The play went down very well. The best evidence of that was at the Mildmay Radical Club. It was the biggest and best working man's club in North London, I was told.[5] It certainly had a very fine hall and a very fine stage. They paid us £8 for a single show. When I got there the chap at the bar said, 'Who's the guv'nor here?' and I said, 'Well I'm not the guv'nor, but I'll answer for the group.' And he said to me, 'Well, I always tell people who are putting on shows that they *must* finish by quarter to ten because we have to close the bar at ten and they must have their drinking time. So I'm telling you that at a quarter to ten I'll ring a loud bell and if you haven't finished then they'll all walk out on you.' I said, 'I'm sorry, but this is a play and we can't leave it in the middle.' Well, the house was pretty full and sure enough at quarter to ten the bell rang out but not a single soul got up to leave – the best tribute.

After several performances had been given to Labour Parties in their halls in various parts of London we had to apply for a licence for a public performance in the Edmonton Town Hall. The Lord Chamberlain objected to the number of 'bloodys' in the text – 31. I pointed out that Shaw had broken the ice with a single and celebrated 'bloody' in *Pygmalion* and that I had already been guilty of misrepresenting the vocabulary of the building workers by leaving out all the numerous and then completely unprintable words with which their language was embellished. We finally compromised: 15 'bloodys' would be licensed, 16 or over, not. I agreed but left an all important question unanswered because unasked – namely – who would count the 'bloodys'?

After the Mildmay shows we were booked by clubs in many parts of London, even one as far out as Braintree, Essex, which we reached by motor car. One of our best performances was at the Manor Hall, Hackney. We were interrupted by the arrival of a column of Hunger Marchers from the North who received a rousing reception from audience and players alike, after which the play was continued to a super-packed audience and tumultuous applause.

We received as much as £1 for some of these shows, which covered the fares of the cast and left an income for the group with which in time we were able to build a stage lighting set (two floods, two spots, switchboard and a dimmer). Normally our members, leaving their jobs at, say, 6 p.m., found their own way by bus, tram or tube to the club at which we were performing, carrying their own props and even additional props which were not personal but had to be brought for the show. We gave 30 performances in the first year, which placed a considerable burden on all taking part, but for each it was a memorable experience, a living contact with working-class audiences – audiences who perhaps for the first time were seeing their own lives, their sufferings, their problems portrayed on the stage.

We had now achieved both our original aims. We were able to play to new audiences and not only to the Labour supporters, presenting to them the socialist message in Tressell's uniquely effective words. We still needed new plays, *The Ragged Trousered Philanthropists* included only two parts for women and new plays were necessary for other members of the group who we were not then using. I would have liked to organize a second group to undertake this while keeping the *RTP* for as long as there was a demand from a club, which might have been for years. But this would have strained our human resources (all unpaid); besides we all felt we had a duty to reflect the world-shaking events which had occurred since Tressell wrote his masterpiece in the early years of the century. So in 1928 I wrote *Women of Kirbinsk*, a one-act play which took place in a remote Russian village in the period 1917–18. With most of the men called up for the war the women have to face the problems of the village. Driven desperate by hunger they decide to take over the estate of the local landowner; there is confrontation but despite his threats they hold on to the land. Then a man comes back from the army with the news of the revolution and that the land question has been solved by a decree of the socialist government authorizing the peasants to take over the land.

The second of our new plays was *The Fight Goes On*. It was set in a mining village during the months of lock-out which followed the betrayal of the General Strike. I contrived a situation in which the local coal-owner visits a family whose man is in prison for the part he has played during the General Strike. Catastrophe has struck the family with the death of the baby son whom the father has never seen. There are bitter exchanges between the young wife, her parents, and the coal-owner, interrupted by the marching and singing of a large demonstration come to express solidarity and sympathy. A speech is made (off-stage) to the marchers by one of the leaders, expressing their determination to fight until victory is won. I was able to arrange a most effective crescendo for the marchers by putting the singers in a lavatory adjoining the back of the stage and opening the door very gradually as the marchers approached the house.

A third new show was made up of Russian songs. 'The Funeral Song for a Dead Comrade', 'The Prison Song', several songs of the Red Army, etc. While each one was being sung, an appropriate scene was enacted on stage. The first performance took place at the Ladies Tailors' Trade Union Hall, Whitechapel, on Monday 17 December 1928. Monica Ewer wrote an enthusiastic review of it in the *Daily Herald*:

> There were seven little scenes illustrating the Russian workers' rise from slavery to freedom and each was accompanied by a song; they were most artistically produced and were a striking example of what brains and taste can do without any great expenditure except for time and trouble.

Our next venture was *Singing Jailbirds* by Upton Sinclair. It dealt with the imprisoned Wobblies (Industrial Workers of the World) in the United States. We rehearsed it at a garage on the corner of Well Street, Hackney; this was the first time we had met for rehearsals anywhere except in private houses. We booked a church hall for the performance: the hall of St Bartholomew's in Dalston Lane. When we gathered for the dress rehearsal the Saturday before the show was due to open, we found the vicar was there. I realized we had two alternatives: a dress rehearsal and no show – as the vicar would certainly object to what he heard – or no dress rehearsal and a show. So I passed the word for a props, lights and movements run-through, but no words.

The show went on to a packed house. But we realized that in spite of its powerful appeal, the effect of the play was profoundly pessimistic. In the play, the Wobblies are not released from their cells. They suffer as martyrs in their cause. The play was in effect a glorification of martyrdom. Was this the message we wanted to give our audiences? After a discussion in the group it was decided there would be no repeat performance.

Sometime in 1928 I attended a committee meeting of the Workers' Theatre Movement – a group which was run in association with the Caxton Hall, Westminster. The Movement was almost moribund. I formed the opinion that while we could do little to help them as an acting group (they were far away in West London), we should at least combine forces. At the next meeting of the Hackney People's Players I proposed that we should become part of the Workers' Theatre Movement, and this was agreed. I sent Christina Walshe, who was the convenor of the WTM, the draft constitution which I had drawn up for the Hackney group, hoping that it could serve as a model for other groups which might come into existence by our example. But I learned that the WTM had now collapsed. In this way our group became the nucleus of what was to be an entirely new movement.[6]

After the Upton Sinclair play we started searching around for a new dramatic form. We were fumbling towards the idea of an Agit-Prop theatre – a theatre without a stage, a theatre which would use music and song and cabaret, and which could improvise its own material instead of going in for full-length set pieces, a theatre in which the audience could take part. *The Ragged Trousered Philanthropists* demanded a stage, many rehearsals, people who would give up a lot of time. I realized we needed shorter things.

Two developments seemed to point possible ways forward. The Manchester group we heard had put on a show *Still Talking* for which the setting was an ordinary public meeting with 'planted' actors in the audience interrupting and finally making speeches. It had no props whatever, and contained a number of different sketches with a direct political message put on at area conferences of political parties.

I had long thought we could put on a revue, a collection of items with singing, dances, sketches and individual items all making pungent comments on some aspects of the political scene. Such a show could be taken apart whenever required – we could use monologue, a couple of scenes, or one or more of the sketches. It would be infinitely flexible. But how to provide the music for the songs? It happened to be just the period of the new 'all talking' films of which songs were the main ingredient. So 'The Wedding of the Dancing Doll' became for us the opening of 'The Talking Doll', a satire on Parliament, and Al Jolson's 'Sonny Boy' became 'Money Boy'. In the autumn of 1929 we put on *Strike Up* at the Conway Hall in Red Lion Square, an evening of mixed items: of songs accompanied by dancing and an orchestra, sketches and monologues. It was an important breakthrough for us: for the first time there was plenty of laughter as well as indignation. It was entitled *Strike Up* because of the number of strikes which were then occurring all over the country and also because we were striking out on a new style of show. In *Strike Up* there was a kind of antiphony between the group on stage and another group we sprinkled in the hall. At the appropriate moment they responded to what was happening on stage by saying 'Yes, strike!' so that it sounded as if the whole audience in the hall was calling for a strike (Clifford Odets used the same device a few years later, in *Waiting For Lefty*).[7]

In 1931 we went to Germany.[8] We learned that there was an International Workers' Theatre Movement based on Moscow and we had written to German comrades in the Arbeitertheaterbund Deutschlands, sending them some of our material and telling them what we were doing. They invited us to bring our group over and do a tour of the Rhineland at Easter. We started at Cologne where there was an enormous meeting in the Exhibition Hall. We were greeted with great enthusiasm up on the platform though there wasn't much we could put on – we had no material in German. We were able to take part in a special section written for 'Die Engländer' and learned one or two of their songs. And then we toured the Rhineland up to Koblenz.

The Arbeitertheaterbund (ATB)[9] had originally been part of the Social Democrats. The Social Democrats had provided a life within the state, really: they had Social Democratic organizations in practically everything, including music and theatre. The ATB had a very large organization all over Germany with highly artistic and technically competent people, but they were coming more under the influence of the Communists. The people now in control of the Arbeitertheaterbund were against the naturalistic theatre. They were convinced that the propaganda theatre could be a spearhead of the whole movement. They faced considerable opposition, and you can see that for groups who were used to the tradition of amateur theatre, working under good conditions, and having their own audience organized for them by the Social Democrats and good stages and all the rest of it, the idea of coming on the streets wasn't very inviting. But the Agit-Prop tendency seemed to be winning the day. Their shows were very flexible. If there was any sort of interruption they would stop the play and say, 'Well come on, we'll argue it out, that's what we want you to do.' There was no illusion about it. The people were dressed up in dungarees and the audience could interrupt. It didn't matter. It added to the theatre. Their performances were absolutely smashing. We could see that. They were all very fine actors. They didn't change their clothes though they appeared physically different in each scene. They used a lot of music and song, drawing on the tradition of German cabaret. I said to Arthur Pieck who was the organizer, 'You must have some wonderful people who write this music for you.' He replied, to my astonishment, 'We do it ourselves' and convinced me that given some natural aptitude, writing tunes for songs could be just as effective as the amateurs who wrote plays and sketches.

We could not hope to emulate the brilliance of the German performances. But by adopting the revue style – which we had already been working towards – we could, almost at once, achieve the freedom of the streets, however crude our initial material and performances might be.

When we got back to England we decided to try it, building up a show from different items, and working to break down the barriers between players and audience. We were full of enthusiasm for the idea of groups who could create their own repertoire, and talk to the people directly on the streets. We rejected the idea of playing to friends and relatives, which was the basis of most amateur dramatics, or of asking people to come and pay money, which was the basis of the commercial theatre. We didn't call ourselves Agit-Prop, but we adopted the same basic idea. Instead of a theatre of illusion ours was to be a theatre of ideas, with people dressed up in ordinary working clothes. No costumes, no props, no special stage. 'A propertyless theatre for the propertyless class' we called it.

From that point on we had a most tremendous growth, abandoning the closed theatre and going to where the people were, on the streets. Before then – although we called ourselves the Workers' Theatre Movement – we had just been one main group in London. Very soon we had some ten groups in London, and all over the country from Bristol to Dundee, from Rochdale to Reading, new groups were formed. The groups' titles proclaimed their political allegiance to the revolutionary left – Dundee Red Front Troupe, Woolwich Red Magnets, Greenwich Red Blouses, etc. The Hackney group became Red Radio, opening their show with a song:

> We are Red Radio,
> Workers' Red Radio,
> We show you how you're robbed and bled:
> The old world's crashing,
> Let's help to smash it,
> And build a workers' world instead.

Not great verse, but sung to a rousing tune, it said something and meant something.

We had weekly meetings of our Central Committee and a monthly all-London Show. This was held in a trade union hall in Blackfriars Bridge Road, a small hall holding two or three hundred people.[10] The groups came to try out their pieces and to learn from each other. They took our material but if they found it unacceptable they wrote their own. Most of the people who joined the groups were youngsters, but the Streatham group had a man in his fifties, Bill Woodward, a taxi-driver, a splendid comrade. Phil Poole, who became the secretary, was working almost full time with us. So was Charlie Mann (Tom Mann's son) who wrote some of our sketches and who produced our paper *Red Stage* (later *New Red Stage*). John Horrocks, who was later active in the Workers' Music Association, ran our music side, issuing song sheets and song books.

A lot of our material was satirical, about the press, about the ILP and about the Labour Party, though we were a bit happier after 1931, when we were attacking a National Government instead of a Labour Government. One of our earliest sketches, written in 1929 I think, was about war memorials – there was a spate of them at the time.

They're building war memorials yet
And honouring the graves of the dead.
The generals, bare-headed, earnestly pray
For the souls of the men they arranged to slay
And quietly curse that they're on half-pay
While the next war brews from day to day
 . . .
While the men who were 'lucky enough', shall we say,
To bring back their bodies intact
Are tramping the streets with the unemployed.

Our ideal was that groups should write their own material. A letter from the group at Edinburgh told the committee that 'we realise that to get a sketch suitable for local needs requires that we provide one ourselves.'

1931 and 1932 was a period of intense activity and growth. We heard of new groups being formed when they wrote in for copies of sketches and songs. In the London area I could visit and help new groups with the techniques of performance, but I could not afford to pay the costs of going further afield, as I was by then unemployed. The publication of *Red Stage* was a big step forward. Charlie Mann, in addition to producing and performing in the Red Players group (small in numbers but immense in enthusiasm and activity), undertook to produce this journal. It served many functions, publishing reports of the activities of groups, and new sketches as they became available, stating our criticism of the bourgeois theatre and setting out our views. Charlie did a magnificent job. Such numbers as survive are very readable and admirably laid out.

The National (Tory) Government became our main target and our repertoire grew rapidly as some of the new groups joined in the task of writing new sketches to meet new situations as they arose. For example, the Hammer and Sickle group of North-West London produced a very effective sketch, *Meerut*, dealing with the imprisonment in India of what later became known in a much wider context as 'freedom fighters'. By the use of six broomsticks a prison was suggested from which the prisoners told their story and appealed to our audiences for help in their fight for freedom. When they finished up with 'Break the Chains, Break the Bars', that was marvellous. On one occasion at a street performance, police seized these six broomsticks as being offensive weapons!

I hadn't heard of the existence of the group before they put it on. All over the country people were writing their own stuff. It was the most amazing outburst of creativity.

Our organization was transformed when we could afford to rent a room in Parton Street, Southampton Row, above the bookshop there.[11] Workers could come during the day (if they were unemployed), and others joined them in the evening to help with correspondence and to duplicate sketches and circulars.

At the 1931 election, Bill Woodward of the Red Front Group, suggested a tour of Scotland in an old Ford-T van, with three of their members: Bill, his comrade-wife and Phil, an interpreter of many languages. He asked if we could find two more to make up their usual numbers and fill the van to capacity. The purpose was to help the Communist candidates.[12] Bill Savage of the Islington group volunteered to join the tour; his experience of street-corner oratory in London over many years made him a very valuable addition. With myself, the team was complete. We played in 'the backs' of the miners' cottages in most of the miners' villages in West Fife, and in the streets of Kirkcaldy, also every evening at election meetings, and received a warm welcome and hospitality. One of our main items was 'The Crisis' in which we turned ourselves into MacDonald, Snowden & Co. and exposed their plans to make the workers and the three million unemployed bear the brunt of the crisis by imposing a 10 per cent cut all round. The various characters sang many of their lines to the tunes of well-known songs. Another main item was the 'PAC' (Public Assistance Committee), about the local committees of well-to-do people who decided which claims for assistance made by hungry families should be passed and which rejected. These proceedings regularly turned into a pitiless inquisition on the incomes and possible assets of each member of a family who had committed the most criminal act in the eyes of the PAC – of failing to get a job, in a situation where the capitalist system had broken down and had sacked millions of its workers. The sketch simply showed proceedings at a PAC inquisition which many among our audience had experienced in person. We then did the same for a couple of days in Dundee before heading for Edinburgh to perform at a monster rally on the Mound, in the open space between the two art galleries. There was an enormous crowd, at least 25,000 we were told, which packed this large area. We performed on a flat dray which raised us above the level of the crowd and we had to shout to be heard. Our show had a terrific reception and people crowded round to thank us and shake our hands when we finished. One elderly man was in tears when he said, 'That's just what they done to me, the swine.'

Half a dozen street shows filled a day in Glasgow and Greenock. The next day, we made for Liverpool and Birkenhead, where we put on our last shows of the tour. I think we could claim to be the first-ever political theatre to have made a tour through Scotland and parts of England, performing on the streets as well as to indoor meetings. The welcome and hospitality which we received from comrades everywhere, and the tremendous enthusiasm of the crowds, made this a most memorable tour, and it helped to establish new groups in Dundee and Edinburgh.

In the spring of 1932 we were able to send to South Wales, in the same old Ford-T van, a group consisting of three members of the Red Players and three others. Our street performances were fewer than in Scotland the previous year as there were no election meetings at that time. But every evening we performed at meetings and socials up and down the valleys.

May Day was a big day in our calendar and we would prepare a new sketch or rather a declamation to honour it. Band parts were also prepared by the music group so that demonstrators could march to appropriate tunes and sing songs from the new songbooks which John Horrocks and his music group circulated to all groups by mid-April. Reports of 1932 May Day show that our groups were well received everywhere and led the singing most effectively. Large sales of *Red Stage* and song books were achieved.

At our national conference in June 1932, twenty-two groups were represented; another ten could not be for financial reasons. In the evenings after the conference proceedings we held shows at which as many sketches as possible were performed to help the newer groups. There was always a steady stream of inquiries for the sketches, which were being written and duplicated and were available at cheap rates. No royalties on performances of course!

In 1933 twenty members of quite a number of groups were sent to Moscow to take part in the International Workers' Theatre

Olympiad and to see the performances of groups from the many countries which were attending this great event.

There was, in this period, a hiving-off of certain special activities. For instance, two members of one group found that they could hire out films and the projection apparatus to individuals and organizations who wanted to see celebrated Russian films like *Battleship Potemkin.*[13] Once this had been established it ran very successfully for several years. Then John Horrocks got together members of London groups who were in the musical side of our work and established the Workers' Music League, which is still flourishing as the Workers' Music Association.

About 1934 there began a movement of opinion inside the Workers' Theatre Movement towards having indoor theatres. You might say that Joan Littlewood and Ewan MacColll in the Manchester WTM had already effected that transformation. In London the 'Rebel Players' group of East London received a great deal of assistance from the professional producer André van Gyseghem, who in later years was to be a leading figure at Unity Theatre.[14] Under his leadership this group reverted in time to plays requiring a curtained stage, and after a while they launched Unity Theatre, with indoor premises at a converted mission hall in Goldington Crescent. This, from 1936 onwards, became the best-known socialist theatre group in Britain.

In 1934 there was a gradual change in the political direction of the WTM. It became clear that in Germany the political warfare waged between socialists and communists had been tantamount to mutual suicide, and that in the rest of Europe survival would depend on alliance of everybody threatened by Fascism. This wise attitude, when generally accepted, brought problems for the WTM. The whole of our work had been against the Labour Party and the ILP as well as against the National Government. MacDonald, Snowden, Jimmy Thomas and their ilk had been sitting ducks for our attacks even before they joined the National (Tory) Government. We had lampooned Jimmy Maxton and George Lansbury, and treated Labour and Tory as the same. The new Popular Front line didn't lend itself as easily to popular theatre. In theatre terms, it's much more difficult to present an argument for a constructive line, like building a united front against Fascism, than to write satires and attacks on the class enemy.

I was very surprised when it was put to me in 1935 or 1936 that

as the organizer of the WTM and as the author of so many
lampoons upon the Labour Party my continued leadership might
be considered in some quarters a minor obstacle to the development of the Popular Front. If my resignation would remove even
a minor obstacle I could not allow my personal regret to stand in
the way. So I resigned after nearly ten years' hard, but extremely
interesting and enjoyable, work. I then took up activities in the
Communist Party in Welwyn Garden City and was soon busy
getting signatures for the peace petition, an activity in which all
progressive people in the town were working together.

The Workers' Theatre Movement continued for some time, but
it didn't really fit in with the Popular Front campaign, and though
it took a new name – the New Theatre – by 1938 it was, I believe,
dead.

I am convinced that Agit-Prop – for want of a better term – is
a far more effective method for conducting propaganda and the
workers' struggle than the closed theatre selling tickets to members
and friends. Indoor work is much more comfortable than playing
out on the streets. You put on make-up. You have character parts
and all the rest of it. You can be a bit of an exhibitionist.

Agit-Prop is quite different. Unlike the 'theatre of illusion' it
has no stage, no curtains, no props. Instead of creating illusions,
it can speak to people's own experiences of life, dramatize their
troubles, present them with ideas. It is mobile – it can be taken to
the people instead of waiting for them to come to you. And it is
a theatre of attack. 'Naturalistic' theatre gives you the appearance
of reality, but it does not show what lies beneath it.

The strength of the revue format is that it can be put on with a
minimum of props, a maximum of audience participation, and
a lot of group discussion and creative work by the performers
themselves. Individual items – songs, sketches, monologues – can
be improvised, can be shuffled and reshuffled according to
particular local needs. Gaiety and indignation can be combined.
The Germans carried this furthest, stripping a show down to its
barest essentials and reaching the point of having the simplest
kind of performance, but very pungent, attacking personalities,
commenting on the social system and so on. Based on the cabaret
form that had been developed in Germany, with its satirical
sketches, songs and bitter commentary on events and personalities,
it was given a more definite turn to the left by the adoption of

a uniform for the performance, namely, workers' overalls. The brilliance of acting and characterization was such that by the addition of hats or other simple changes, the actors could transform themselves into easily recognizable types.

But Agit-Prop theatre is difficult to maintain without a political movement to carry it forward. This was the experience of the People's Theatre in Newcastle-upon-Tyne. It was set up in 1911, as an offshoot of the Clarion League, with the idea of putting on socialistic plays. Within a few years it had turned into an amateur dramatic group. I know that theatre very well because when I lived in Newcastle I was its treasurer. They had started out as socialist missionaries, but by the 1940s, when I worked for them, they were just an amateur theatre – of very high standing but no political significance whatever. A propaganda theatre cannot stand still. Once it stops making converts for the cause, it is finished.

Looking back over my nine years' hard but absorbing work I think that the most significant experience was the surge forward when we turned to street theatre. From one group performing in halls, rapidly there were thirty groups all over the country giving shows on the streets with material they had mostly written themselves. It may be urged that this could be accounted for by the exceptional period in which it occurred and the deep sense of injustice which long-term unemployment and heavy wage cuts had created. This certainly made people more interested in what we had to say, but undoubtedly we had discovered a way of taking theatre to the mass of people and communicating with them and so getting through the clouds of lies and deceptions which were created by the mass media.

Notes

1 The *Daily Herald* was the Labour paper, edited for many years by George Lansbury, which had been founded by the striking Fleet Street printers in 1912. It was later sold by the Trades Union Congress to Oldham's Press, and enjoys a miserable after-life today as the *Sun*.

2 South Place Ethical Society, whose concerts are now held on Sunday evenings at Conway Hall, Red Lion Square. For a brief history, see Rosemary Hughes, 'South Place – a Home of Chamber Music', *Musical Times*, February 1953.

3 The brothers Capek's *The Insect Play* – a parable about militarism and

capitalism – had been staged by the London Labour Dramatic Federation at both the Strand and the Scala theatres in 1926. *Clarion*, 13 August, p. 2, 29 October, p. 1, 1926.

4 An article on the Hackney Labour Dramatic Group in the *Sunday Worker* (8 August 1926) gives the following as their autumn repertoire: *R.U.R.*, four-act play by Karel Capek (seven men, four women); *Sealing the Compact*, one-act play by Gwen John dealing with the miners' strike; *Lady Betty's Husband*, by B. Woolf, 'the first play to be written for the group'; *A Night at the Inn*, one-act thriller by Dunsany; *The Night Shift*, a mining play; and 'one or two other mining plays that are promised from various people'.

5 For Hackney working men's clubs in an earlier period, and the part played by drama in their activities, John Taylor, *From Self-Help to Glamour: the Working Man's Club 1860–1972*, History Workshop pamphlet, 1972.

6 The earlier abortive Workers' Theatre Movement referred to here can be followed in the socialist press of the time. It seems to have been founded by Christina Walshe of the Glastonbury Players, with strong support from William Paul of the *Sunday Worker* and Monica Ewer, drama critic of the *Daily Herald*. The committee included Huntly Carter, author of *The New Theatre and Cinema of Soviet Russia* (London, 1927) and a frequent correspondent in the socialist press, Eden and Cedar Paul, the translators, Rutland Boughton, and Havelock Ellis. Among the plays produced by this group were Upton Sinclair's *Singing Jailbirds*; a play about the Passaic strike written by two students at Brookwood (the American Labour College); and *In Time of Strife*, a play by Joe Corrie, the Fife miner-poet. See *Sunday Worker*, 4 October 1925; 25 July, 3 October, 14 November, 5 December 1926; 30 January, 27 February, 13 March 1927. Christina Walshe had worked with Rutland Boughton and they may have been the original nucleus of the Movement. One of the last performances by the group was given at the Caxton Hall under the auspices of the Westminster Labour Party, and it is possibly this which made Tom Thomas associate it with West London. (For a storm of disagreement about this show, *Sunday Worker*, 8 and 15 January 1928.)

7 For a critical review of *Strike Up*, *Daily Worker*, 10 February 1930, p. 5.

8 Tom Thomas was not certain of the date of the Rhineland tour. A WTM group certainly did go to the Rhineland in 1931 (*Daily Worker*, 17 January 1931, p. 4) but there seems to have been some contact with the ATB conference at Dortmund in the previous year (*Daily Worker*, 10 May 1930, p. 5; 3 January 1931, p. 4).

9 For documentation of the ATB, Ludwig and Daniel Hoffman,

Deutsches Arbeitertheater, 1918–33, 2 vols, Berlin, 1972, and the forthcoming Bristol University thesis of Richard Stourac.

10 Friar's Hall, Blackfriars Road. I think this is the same as the Builders' Labourers' Hall at no. 84.

11 The previous committee room of the WTM had been in Manningtree Street, Commercial Road, E1. 2 Parton Street was the bookshop of Central Books (now in Gray's Inn Road), and in the later 1930s provided the offices of the Student Labour Federation and *Left Review*.

12 The Communist candidates polled remarkably high votes in Scotland compared with other parts of the country; Bob Stewart got 10,000 votes at Dundee, William Gallagher 6,000 in West Fife, A. Ferguson 6,000 at Greenock.

13 *Battleship Potemkin* was for a number of years banned by the London County Council (LCC), ostensibly on the grounds that the film was in breach of its fire regulations. The showing of Russian films – and the making of workers' films in Britain – was a major form of Communist cultural work in these years, which in many ways parallels the WTM.

14 André van Gyseghem, born 1906, had worked as an office-boy with a London music publishers; he joined an LCC night-school drama class and worked with a South London troupe of Co-operative players. At the age of 19 he won an LCC scholarship to RADA (Royal Academy of Dramatic Art). In 1930, when the Embassy Theatre, Swiss Cottage, was founded as a metropolitan repertory theatre, he worked there under Ronald Adam; he had a reputation in these years as one of the most brilliant young producers in London. He is remembered by Charlie Mann as 'ultra professional' and was shocked at the sergeant-major techniques which Charlie used to drill his troupe. There is a portrait of him in *International Theatre*, 2, p. 50, 1934, and there are references to his earliest dramatic performances in *Co-operative News*, 22 August 1925, p. 5.

Documents

The basis and development of the Workers' Theatre Movement (1932)

Workers' Theatre Movement first National Conference, Charter Hall, 59 Cromer Street, London, 25–26 June 1932

The Workers' Theatre Movement has been in existence now for just over six years. Four years of patient laying of foundations have been succeeded by two years of very rapid expansion, until during the past winter as many as thirty groups have been at work.

This rapid growth has two main causes. First, the stiffening of the workers' resistance to the evergrowing attacks on their standard of life, and second, the complete change in the methods of the Workers' Theatre Movement, by which it has been able to respond to this and play an active part in the struggles.

The Central Committee considers it necessary to put forward a statement at the first National Conference on the nature of the movement, its development and future activities, in order to provide a basis for discussion at the Conference.

The capitalist theatre
The theatre and cinema, like the press and wireless, serve to blind the workers to the existence of the class struggle, while particularly in times of war, they are used to drive the workers of the different countries to slaughter each other for the benefit of their exploiters.

The contributions that capitalism has made to the art of the theatre share, with the rest of bourgeois culture, in the general decline of capitalism. Nine-tenths of life, as the mass of the people know it, is taboo at the theatres and cinemas today, and they attempt to cover up their bankruptcy of ideas by means of extravagant and meaningless display.

The left-wing theatres
The revolt of the intellectuals against the triviality of the large-scale capitalist theatre finds its expression in the rise of the 'little'

and repertory theatres, and, also in the advanced section of the amateur dramatic movement. However, such theatres do not realize that the capitalist basis of the bourgeois theatre is the cause of this triviality, and, proclaiming themselves to be 'above the battle', lose themselves in ingenious but sterile technicalities and experiments.

Labour Party, ILP and Co-op groups

Within such groups two main tendencies exist. First, the belief that it is their mission to bring the working class into contact with 'great' art (i.e. capitalist art) and second, the tendency to produce plays which may deal with the misery of the workers, may even deal with the class struggle, but which show no way out, and which therefore spread a feeling of defeat and despair.

The Workers' Theatre

But the Workers' Theatre does not pretend to be above the struggle. It is an expression of the workers' struggle in dramatic form. It is consciously a weapon of the workers' revolution, which is the only solution of the present crisis. It not only unmasks the capitalist system but organizes the workers to fight their way out.

Because it deals with realities it escapes from the emptiness of bourgeois drama and becomes the first step in the development of proletarian drama.

Abroad

In other countries the Workers' Theatre, having passed through the early stages of development, has already become a powerful factor in the workers' struggle. For example, in Germany its value has been attested by the Fascist Government by a decree of practical illegality – but performances are carried out in spite of this. In Japan, it is an important part of the proletarian cultural movement, which alone of the workers' organization is permitted to exist legally. Two monthly papers are issued, and in Tokyo alone there are 40,000 organized spectators around one workers' theatre.

In the Soviet Union the workers, having overcome capitalism, are faced with different problems. This is reflected in the theatre, which is becoming a leading force in building up socialism, while even capitalist observers are compelled to admit the great artistic achievements of the theatres and cinemas of the Soviet working class.

In Britain
In Britain the Workers' Theatre Movement, while profiting from the experience of the more advanced organizations abroad, must learn to adapt itself to the particular conditions which exist here. Every strike, every wage-cut, every attack on the workers' conditions must find its expression on the platform of the Workers' Theatre and no exclusive attention to general political events can be a substitute for this.

Methods of work
In most countries there has been a parallel line of development, in spite of many local differences. First has come the conception of using the theatre form as a propaganda weapon. Plays borrowed or adapted from the bourgeois stage were given a new emphasis and played in the traditional manner. Next, new plays were written, still based on the curtained stage and the traditional style of acting, but with revolutionary themes. In England a beginning was made in 1926 with some of the plays of Shaw, Capek, Elmer Rice, etc., until in 1928 sufficient technical experience had been gained to construct plays for ourselves, with a working-class content. The dramatic adaptation of *The Ragged Trousered Philanthropists*, *The Fight Goes On* are typical productions of this period, which came to its close by the end of 1930.

The naturalistic method
The experience gained with these plays shows:
1 that the naturalistic form, namely that form which endeavours to show a picture on the stage as near to life as possible, is suitable for showing things as they appear on the surface, but does not lend itself to disclosing the reality which lies beneath. And it is just this reality existing beneath the polite surface of capitalist society that the Workers' Theatre must reveal.
2 That the unities of space and time, which are one of its main features, greatly hinder the portrayal of the class struggle in dramatic form (consider, for instance, the difficulty in bringing together in a reasonable, naturalistic way, an ordinary worker and an important capitalist).

3 That the audiences reached by such plays which demanded a
well-equipped stage were insignificant compared to the mass of
workers who could not be brought to the theatre or hall to
witness them.

'Agit-Prop' style

So to enable the message of the Workers' Theatre to reach wide
masses of the workers, and to give a much more flexible and
dynamic picture of society than is possible on the curtained stage,
a new form is being evolved. This form, which is known in
Germany as the 'Agit-Prop' style needs no elaborate stage, but an
open platform. No scenery that is not easily carried about by
hand; no make-up; and a minimum of costume. In a word, the
propertyless class is developing the 'property'-less theatre.

Wherever this form has been adopted it has led to a great expansion of the movement. No longer does the Workers' Theatre play
– as do the amateur dramatic societies – to a circle of friends and
relatives. It goes out to the workers wherever they may be, at
meetings, on the street corners, in the parks; and now has the
immediate task facing it of taking their performances to where the
workers are actually waging the class struggle, at the factories, the
labour exchanges, etc.

There are other advantages of the 'Agit-Prop' style:

1 Its flexible, and usually short, form is quickly adapted to meet
local and topical situations. The preparation of special items
dealing with events as they arise, should be a matter of days
only.

2 Instead of emphasizing the ability to portray characters, a
difficult job for workers with very little spare time, it uses
instead the class experience of the worker-player, which
convinces a worker audience much more than the studied effects
of the professional actor.

3 The direct approach to the audience, together with the fact that
the performance is surrounded by and part of the crowd, is of
great value in making the worker audience feel that the players
are part of them, share their problems and their difficulties, and
are pointing a direct, reasonable way out.

Nevertheless it may be that the naturalistic method should not
be entirely ruled out from the workers' theatre, and this question
must be thoroughly discussed at the Conference.

It must be said that up to the present even the best performances given have not touched a hundredth part of the possibilities of this new style, and the struggle for a higher level of technique (a higher level of effectiveness) is one that every group must undertake very seriously. To tolerate a low standard of performance is one of the worst forms of sabotage. Strict self-criticism and criticism from the audiences must be developed. Finally, the effectiveness with which our sketches are presented depends to a large extent upon the political consciousness and conviction of the players, which can only be heightened by systematically raising their political level.

Our repertoire
As the Workers' Theatre expresses itself by means of the sketches and other material which it produces, it is clear that the nature of this material determines the whole line of the movement. During the past two years over fifty items have been issued.

Most of these items have aroused great interest amongst the workers wherever they have been played, but their success must not conceal certain important shortcomings. The most dangerous of these faults, because it strikes at the very purpose of the Workers' Theatre, is the narrowness of outlook, which assumes, in one way or another, that the audience is already familiar with the revolutionary point of view. This can only repel the vast majority of workers who are not yet convinced. The acid test of a sketch is whether it starts on a basis which is common to a non-political working-class audience and leads them step by step to agreeing with its revolutionary conclusion. Without this all is merely preaching to the converted.

In choice of subject, too, this sectarianism has often been apparent. It is the job of the Workers' Theatre to deal in a dramatic way, not only with the events of the workers' everyday lives, the struggles in the workshops, the problems of the working women in the market-place and at home, and the current political question, but, in addition, the scandals, sensations, and injustices of capitalist society, and in every case show them as part of the class struggle.

These are the most dangerous tendencies, which, if not corrected, lead to a divorce from the working masses and complete sterility. On the other hand, there has been an occasional tendency

to revert to the plays of the 'Left' bourgeois theatre because of a
desire to produce a naturalistic play.

Collective writing

How is the repertoire to be developed on the broad lines which
have been indicated? While continuing to use the services of the
present writers there must be drawn into this productive work a
much larger number of those taking part in the groups, by means
of collective writing. As a regular activity, independently undertaken by each group, it can have great results, not only in the
material produced, but by way of political and technical training.
Every member of a group can help in some way. The most
important method is to organize the collection of facts and information upon which the sketch can be based. First a theme is
chosen, and then every member of the group endeavours to get
information about it by talking to those workers it concerns. Then,
at a subsequent meeting, the information is collectively discussed,
the line of the sketch determined, and, if necessary, it can be left
to one or two members to write it up.

The questions involved in improving the technical level of the
Workers' Theatre Groups and in broadening and transforming the
repertoire on these lines need very detailed consideration. A special
report will be made to the Conference embodying the experience
of the past two years and of our brother organizations abroad.

Organization

The chief need is for all groups to widen their basis by bringing
in new elements from the working class. It is not sufficient to sit
still and be ready to welcome these new elements. They must be
sought at every possible opportunity amongst the ranks of the
militant workers, and also amongst those workers whose class
consciousness is not yet developed, but whose desire to take part
in dramatic activities of a working-class type attracts them to us
because of the virility, originality and effectiveness of our
performances.

All groups should endeavour to make friendly contact with
workers in other dramatic organizations, particularly those of the
ILP, Labour Party and Co-operative Guilds.

These tasks are as important as those of technique and repertoire.
Only with a broad basis among the workers can we hope to

withstand the attacks which are bound to be made upon us as our effectiveness in the struggles of the working class grows with our numbers and efficiency.

How to produce Meerut (1933)

It should not be necessary to give reasons advocating the desirability of performing the *Meerut* sketch wherever practicable during the campaign for the release of the prisoners, and the new revised version brings out the class message directly and powerfully.

Four, five or preferably six members can perform this sketch excellently; but despite the sameness of position throughout, an unusually high degree of emotional intensity is necessary. All the members should be strong, vibrant and capable of expressing intense feeling, because of the limits placed on them in regard to lack of movement, change of position, etc. This means that the whole of the response must be obtained by sheer power of emotional appeal through the voice and facial expression – a task calling for the highest degree of acting ability. The sketch is not an easy one and should be tackled only by experienced troupes.

You cannot convey the impression of rigid resistance to imperialist oppression by a weak-kneed effort, however sympathetic the actors may feel. Pretty girlish voices must be cut right out, but a strong feminine voice vibrating with the conviction of the message can be just as effective as a masculine one.

It is important to erect the 'prison bars' in the least possible time. Rehearse this part thoroughly. Let every member have his bar and all line up off stage in single file. When they come on, each takes up his position immediately and knows exactly where to place his pole – so, 1, 2, 3, 4, 5, 6, and the bars are up. And the bars must not be moved from position one inch until the time comes. Wobbling bars look like a prison that is as farcical as the trial. It doesn't matter about the space between the bars being large, as long as the effect is symmetrical. You are not portraying a jail, but symbolizing imprisonment.

Make an effective 'picture' by grouping properly – two kneeling, one half lying, perhaps two standing, but all close together and bursting to get the message through. The mass speaking where it occurs must be as perfect as possible. The sketch opens with the word 'murder' repeated four times. Don't blare this raggedly. Let the leader count four in whispers, then all come in together – softly at first then in crescendo until the last 'MURDER!' really sounds like it. Do this well and you will grip the audience from the beginning, and if this sketch is done properly you won't hear a breath from the audience all through it.

Inflection of the voice is most important. Bitterness, oppression, resistance, triumph of class solidarity, and nearly every emotion is called for in the right place. This sketch offers most unusual opportunities for voice-acting. Take the first speech for instance. Mere statement of fact is not enough. The voice must be pent up with repressed emotion so that the audience *feels* what is being described. And the bitter sarcasm of 'in India – the brightest jewel in Britain's crown' must be made the most of . . . but not overdone.

The tempo all through the sketch must be quick. As each player finishes his speech the next comes in at once – there is no time to waste – act – act – act – is the message. Mass speaking, as nearly always, must be staccato and clear. Clip the syllables short and the aggregate effect will be words that can be understood.

Get the utmost out of the words – these and your faces are your only means of expression. Understand the full political meaning behind every passage. Mean it. Get it over. Not just by speaking loudly, but by intensity, conviction. If this makes you speak loudly – and it probably will – that's all right in this sketch. But remember contrasts and inflections are much more powerful than one long shout.

When it comes to the mass-speaking line 'and thrown into Meerut Jail' the bars should actually tremble under the bitter emotion of the actors. But don't obviously shake them. Grip them hard and the very intensity of your feelings will do the trick. The same at the finish. 'Comrades – comrades – comrades – comrades – SMASH THE BARS'. As the word is repeated (half an appeal, half a demand) the bars sway ever so slightly from side to side till at the word 'smash' they are flung down. (All the same way, please.) It is a bad mistake to sweep several feet to the left and then to the right. The audience then guesses what's coming and half the dramatic effect of the ending is lost. Just a slight inclination one way and then the other, hardly inches, is all that is needed. If you are tense the effect of *strain* is conveyed much better this way than by giving an impression that you can do what you like with the bars anyhow. As the bars crash, stand up in a straight line shoulder to shoulder for two or three seconds before going off.

A good effect at 'Comrades – hands across the sea; comrades – solidarity' is to release one hand and put it appealingly through the bars towards the audience. But do be careful to rehearse this sufficiently so that the bars don't topple down when you let one hand go.

All through the sketch, which is quite short, the main things are tempo and emotional intensity. Remember your two media are words and faces. Facial expression is just as important as the words. While one prisoner is speaking, the others must be acting all the time – reflecting the words. Tense, haggard, anxious, determined and other expressions suggest themselves, as the lines progress. Feel the sketch, mean it, and you will convey the message of it in a way that will strike home to the class-consciousness that is latent in even the most reactionary member of your worker-audience.

CHARLIE MANN

Solidarity appeal from the Proletarian Theatre Union of Japan (1932)

To the American and English comrades   Tokio
                                                      12 April 1932

The Japanese bourgeoisie has started since the end of March new preparations for the Imperialistic war. The latest mass-arresting of the revolutionary workers and peasants and the destroying of the proletarian revolutionary organizations are a menace to Japan.

During the Parliament Elections in February 1932, the only legal workers' candidate in Tokio District who stood under the leadership of the illegal Communist Party of Japan was arrested. At the same time, not only were five members of the Central Committee of the Japanese Section of the Young Communist League arrested, but also the revolutionary workers who voted for the workers' candidate were persecuted.

The same thing is happening now in Japan that happened in Europe before the outbreak of and during the World War from 1914 to 18. In Japan, where the most important proletarian organizations (Communist Party of Japan, Young Communist League, Red Trade Union, Japanese Sections of the League against Imperialism and the International Red Aid) are illegal, at the moment, the only legal proletarian mass organization, namely KOPFJ (Federation of Proletarian Cultural Organizations in Japan), the united proletarian cultural organization corresponding to the IFA (Interessengemeinschaft für Arbeiterkultur) in Germany, plays an inestimably important role in the class struggle. And since the outbreak of the present war, or more correctly, since the beginning of the first step towards Imperialistic war and the intervention against the Soviet Union and Soviet China, the KOPFJ has carried out important activities for the class struggle against the war and intervention's danger, on the lines of the Bolshevistic tactic of the Communist Party of Japan.

The KOPFJ was founded first in November of last year as the united Japanese cultural organization. It consists of fifteen up-tillthen isolated organizations. The KOPFJ and its affiliated organizations give out monthly various mass periodicals (*Proletarian Culture*,

Friends of the Masses, Working Women, Young Pioneers, Workers' Illustrated News, Proletarian Literature, Proletarian Theatre, Proletarian Science, Our Science, Proletarian Art, Proletarian Cinema, Proletarian Poetry, Kamarado, Militant Atheists, New Pedagogy), and fortnightly mass papers (*Literary News, Theatre News, Art News, Kino-Graph, Musical News*). These periodicals and newspapers play a very important role in the revolutionary education and mobilization of the masses.

Further, meetings have been held as part of the battle against the war for the annexation of China and the Soviet Union.

The more important the part played by the KOPFJ in the present difficult time, the more brutal and systematic is the persecution on the part of the ruling class of Japan. The Japanese Government which is every day getting more Fascist has lately forbidden nearly all the periodicals of the KOPFJ and has broken up all its meetings.

Between 24 March and 12 April, altogether twenty-six comrades of the Central Committees of various organizations of the KOPFJ were arrested.

The Japanese Government announced in all its bourgeois papers on 12 April its purpose not only to take action against the party fraction in the KOPFJ but to completely destroy the whole KOPFJ organization, because the Japanese ruling class has clearly seen during this robber-war the important and successful part played by the KOPFJ for the Proletarian Revolution.

The KOPFJ is threatened with prohibition. That means that the only legal revolutionary mass organization in Japan will be destroyed. If this were to happen, it would be a terrible loss for the revolutionary proletarian movement in Japan. The prohibition of the KOPFJ is nothing less than a preparation for Imperialistic war and the intervention against the Soviet Union.

We must organize a mass-protest against the prohibition of the KOPFJ and we must organize the KOPFJ as a real mass organization. We begin this battle with the following slogans:

Down with the oppression of the proletarian culture movement!

For the liberation of the revolutionary fighters of the proletarian cultural movement!

Build 'Culture-circles' in the big factories and in the important industries!

Strengthen the local bodies of the various cultural organizations and provincial councils of the KOPFJ in the most important provinces!

Down with the Fascistic and social-Fascistic culture of the bourgeois!

Defend the KOPFJ!

Down with the white terror!

Down with the Fascism and social-Fascism!

Down with the Imperialistic war!

Against the dividing-up of China!

Down with the intervention against the Soviet Union!

It is further absolutely necessary that the protest should [be made] internationally through Proletarian Solidarity [text damaged and illegible . . .] will help us with your advice for the reorganization of [. . .]

With revolutionary greetings
Central Council of the KOPFJ
Proletarian Theatre Union of Japan

Scripts

'The Market Quack' in Hackney – a monologue (1930?)

I've stood in this market-place for 25 years, and don't forget it, 1906 I first come 'ere on Sat'day night, of course none of you ladies would remember that, you must have been kids then – some of the gents might be older and wiser, so to speak. And my old Dad said to me 'Look 'Orace, look at all them people with *ill 'ealth* written all over them,' he said, 'ill 'ealth, that's what it is, ill 'ealth.' It's well-known the length and breadth of the medical profession that the people of Hackney is chronic sufferers. *Chronic* sufferers, that's the word, all sorts of ill health and ailments from the A's – asthma, acidity, alopecia, ancenia, arthritis – what you get from drinking too much port – some of you would like a chance to get it wouldn't you? – apoplexy, appendicitis, allcrotic poisoning. You can go right down the list – boils, biliousness, deafness, headache, fistula, gangrene, hiccoughs, locomotantax (which is *nothing* to do with railways or taxicabs, though you might think it has), right down to zymotic fever. You can find them all in 'Ackney, including the common cold, which is the most dangerous of the lot. So for 25 years I've stood in this market-place putting the people of Hackney right. And what do I see? Do I see any improvement? No. If my dear old Dad, Gowd bless 'im, were to come back 'ere tonight and look around at yer pasty faces, yer thin bodies with 'ardly enough flesh on 'em to cover your osteopath or bony frame, and listen to yer coughing and yer sneezing and your corns and your 'eadaches, and the common cold that all of you are cursed with, he'd say as he said on that night 25 years ago, 'Horace, Horace, ill health, that's what it is, ill-health.' Now, I've never been to a doctor in my life, except once – I wanted to get a day off work – now mind you, I don't say a word against doctors, they don't do you much 'arm and they're nice men usually, except when you're a panel patient. But if a man or a woman got any common sense, they'd work it out for themselves – now *you*, guv'nor, you excuse me I hope – just by looking at you – you work in a factory all day long, sweating your guts out, and you eat that cheap and nasty at a cookshop, breathing polluted air, and you come home at night fair worn out, and when the missus puts a nice two-eyed steak in front of you, you can't touch it. The missus gets upset because you can't eat, the kids get on your nerves, everything goes wrong and all you can think of is to go out and 'ave one just to put things right. Now what's wrong with you? It's your blood. You're overworked and overstrained, same as the Prince of Wales when 'e's been shaking 'ands all day, and what will put you right as rain? – why the identical treatment as is given to his Royal 'Ighness – one week of complete rest and nourishment – can you? No? Well one bottle of my blood mixture will make you feel a new man, now this is not a patent medicine . . . I believe in helping those who can't help themselves – the working class who work so hard for the boss, they've never got time to work for themselves, and so my blood mixture, what's worth as they say a guinea a box, is sold for less than that, far less than that. Yes if you wanted this stuff up West, done up with tissue paper with gold lettering on the cork and sold by a young lady assistant with a voice like a countess, you'd pay ten and sixpence for it, no less. But my price ain't ten and six, it ain't even five bob or 'arf a dollar, yes, my famous blood mixture, which is guaranteed to make you feel a new man, to cure all the ill health, all the ailments which I specified a few minutes ago, is sold for the strictly working-class price of six pence per bottle, or one shilling for two.

 * [Editor's note: A *Daily Worker* review (10 February 1930, p. 5) of the production *Strike Up* criticises it for (among other things) an impersonation of a London coster which smacked of the music hall. Presumably it referred to this monologue, though Tom Thomas could not say when it was first performed. R.E.S.]

Meerut (1933)

Notes
The players use six poles to make prison bars, and between them support
these in such a way that three are held vertically and three horizontally.
The 'cell' should be made quickly, after running on. This needs much
rehearsal. This is a highly dramatic sketch, and the intensity must not be
lost for a moment. Those players not actually speaking must look dejected,
indignant, as occasion demands, but never relax.

ALL: Murder! Murder! MURDER! MURDER!

FIRST: In every state in British India, police and troops are out,
to crush the rising tide of revolt against our vile conditions
– long hours in the mines and mills! Exhausted by our
labours! Our British taskmasters stand over us with whips
to drive us harder – and for what? The average wage for all
workers and peasants is less than a shilling a day in India –
the brightest jewel in Britain's crown.

SECOND: In Bengal mines are 35,000 women, working
UNDERGROUND – forced to take their children with
them from their hovels of sun-baked mud – to die by their
sides as they work. Their parents are forced to sell their
children into marriage – to sell them into prostitution to
contract venereal disease – to sell them into death! In British
India 10,000,000 workers and peasants die yearly of forced
famine, forced starvation, forced disease. The race is dying
under British rule.

ALL: MUST WE NOT REVOLT?

THIRD: The Government denies us education, and when, as in
England, in Germany and France, in America – in every
capitalist state in the world – they sought to drive us harder
by wage-cuts and speed-up, throwing more and more of
us on to the streets –

ALL: WE REVOLTED!

FOURTH: They foster our religious differences in order to divide
us, so that they can extract their millions yearly in profits
and taxation.

SECOND: They send you here with arms, saying it is to stop us from flying at each other's throats.

FIFTH: They tell you we are religious maniacs.

ALL: COMRADES, THEY ARE LIARS!

THIRD: In Peshawar they brought out our HINDU brothers, the Gharwali Riflemen, armed to shoot us down – a peaceful MAHOMMEDAN demonstration. They refused to be used to butcher us. THEY WOULD NOT SHOOT! They showed their class solidarity with their brothers of another religion. They handed their rifles over to us – and the hypocrite Macdonald has jailed them for refusing to fly at our throats.

ALL: ALL HONOUR TO THE GHARWALI RIFLEMEN – MORE POWER TO THEIR REVOLT!

FIRST: June 1928, 20,000 workers struck on the East Indian Railway for six shillings a week and the simple right to organize into trade unions. They shot at us as we lay across the lines to stop their blackleg trains. They broke our strike.

ALL: IN BLOOD AND TERROR!

SECOND: Order was maintained for His Majesty the King Emperor, and the strikers went back to even greater misery.

FIFTH: 150,000 workers in Bombay, against a 7½ per cent wage-cut and the speed-up, April 1928. . . .

ALL: A STRIKE!

FIFTH: 150,000, and only 6,000 organized in a trade union, whose leaders tried to betray them. But they built in struggle their *own* Union, the GIRNI KAMGAR – the RED FLAG UNION, 60,000 strong.

FIRST: The police shot at them, their brothers in the Indian Army were forced to shoot them – *your brothers*, your HUSBANDS – YOUR SONS – were sent from England to shoot them, to massacre them, to break their strike.

ALL: IN BLOOD AND TERROR!

FIRST: Comrades, YOU let them go. Comrades, THEY ARE STILL GOING. COMRADES, STOP THEM!

ALL: (*straining one hand each through the bars*) COMRADES, HANDS ACROSS THE SEA! COMRADES, SOLIDARITY!

SECOND: Against the terror they stood out for six months. The Government saw they could not be beaten *that* way. To gain time the Government set up a Commission to enquire into their conditions. In March 1929, three days before the Commission reported, the workers' leaders all over India were arrested

ALL: AND THROWN INTO MEERUT JAIL.

THIRD: No bail allowed; filthy food in the stifling heat of the Indian summer. Cholera broke out, and two of their fellow-prisoners died before their trial had commenced. In Indian jails, bar fetters are used. In Indian jails, ball chains are used. In Indian jails are 60,000 political prisoners, rotting under British rule.

FIFTH: In Meerut jails were the *real* leaders of the Indian workers and peasants.

FOURTH: Fighters for the freedom of the Indian masses – not hypocrites like Ghandi, who tells us to be patient, for God is watching!

SECOND: Not like Ghandi, who led us in peaceful demonstrations to be shot at and butchered; but comrades who showed us how to fight, how to organize, how to break the bonds of British tyranny.

FIRST: Charged with 'Conspiracy against the King' they were flung into jail by a Conservative Government. The Labour Government kept them there – refused passports to witnesses for the defence. The National Government prolonged their agony. For nearly four years their trial was dragged out.

FIFTH: Comrades, their trial was a mockery – their trial was a farce – to perpetuate the reign of

ALL: BLOOD AND TERROR!

THIRD: Their torture is now crowned with the most revolting sentences. Transportation for ten years – for twelve years! Transportation for life! What does this mean?

ALL: A LIVING DEATH!

FIRST: All the horrors of Devil's Island, all the brutalities of the American chain gang – are as nothing compared with the horrors of India's penal settlements.

SECOND: Thus do the bosses hope to terrify India into submission. Just as the Tsar tried to crush the Russian workers and peasants.

ALL: THE TSAR FAILED – AND THEY TOO WILL FAIL.

FOURTH: Bombay textile workers have already taken their stand, and the workers of Seven Mills have struck –

FIRST: Without strike pay, without support of any kind, the heroic Bombay mill workers have struck – to demand

ALL: THE RELEASE OF THE MEERUT PRISONERS.

THIRD: Workers of Britain, unite *your* power with the Indian toilers. This is your fight. Those who have jailed the workers in India are the men who cut wages and enforce the Means Test in Britain.

FIFTH: Factory workers

SECOND: Housewives

FOURTH: Trade unionists

FIRST: By resolutions

THIRD: Demonstrations

FIRST: By strikes.

ALL: FORCE THE RELEASE OF THE MEERUT PRISONERS (*With hands through the bars*) – COMRADES, HANDS ACROSS THE SEA! COMRADES, SOLIDARITY!

(*Swaying from left to right with the rhythm of the appeal*)

COMRADES— COMRADES— COMRADES—
COMRADES—
SMASH THE BARS!

(*As they say this, they fling the bars down*)

War (1932)

Collectively planned. Written by J. L. and P. J. P.

Section 1 Armistice Day

General Bulldozer is making a speech. In the forefront of the crowd on his left, a working man; on his right, a poorly-clad woman.

BULLDOZER: Ladies, Gentlemen, Britons! Today, the fourteenth anniversary of the signing of the Armistice, we assemble to commemorate an event which brought fourteen years of peace to the world; which gave succour to the bleeding nations, and which witnessed the victory of right, the downfall of iniquity. Let us bare our heads in grateful honour of those men who fell fighting the great fight of Liberty, Democracy and Civilization . . .

(*A whistle blows. Short silence*)

Having thus rendered heartfelt thanks to our glorious dead, let us return to our appointed daily tasks, resolved that there shall be no more grumbling or shirking or discontent, but that each shall carry on with the same devotedness that these lads displayed.

(*As he turns to go, he is approached by the worker*)

WORKER: A fine speech that was, General . . . You wouldn't remember me of course, but once you pinned this (*indicates medal*) on my tunic.
BULLDOZER: Not remember you! How can I ever forget that wonderful action by which you . . . when you . . . Now let me see . . .
WORKER: I wasn't no hero, General. But I liked that part of your speech when you talked of us going back to our jobs.
BULLDOZER: (*gratified*) Ah! I struck the right note *there*, did I? Yes, yes, we must all do our jobs.
WORKER: Then could you help me to get one?
BULLDOZER: Not *unemployed*? Dear, dear, you have my sympathy.

WORKER: But I thought perhaps . . .

(*the General shows signs of restiveness*)

Please! I've got to do something. Unemployed now for these
two years. My wife expects another baby – she needs food!
And there are two other kiddies, they must be cared for.
And because we owe for rent, they mean to chuck us out
– this week, (*pleading*) can't you help us?

BULLDOZER: My dear fellow, I wish I could, but I've thousands
of applications from people like you. Really, I'm afraid I
cannot assist. You should apply to the labour exchange, I
believe that is the right place.

(*He turns and walks in the opposite direction, where he is stopped by the
woman*)

WOMAN: Thank you for that speech, it made me feel that my Bill
did not die for nothing after all.

BULLDOZER: (*nobly*) He died for his country, Madam. 'This earth,
this realm, this England.' Had he not laid down his life at
the Call, we should not now enjoy security of freedom.

WOMAN: You know about such things, of course, I'm tired of
trying to understand. When I mope through being lonely,
I just search round to see what I can do for somebody. It's
a comfort to be a friend. It's true I'm not much use to
anyone. But why can't they leave me in my home, our
home, that Bill went to defend? Why are they trying to
send me to the Workhouse?

BULLDOZER: Madam – My good woman, I appeal to your
commonsense. It is an axiom of good Government that the
rates must be kept low. You are a charge on the rates. It is
quite conceivable that you object to the poorhouse. But
you may console yourself by remembering that there are
others far worse off. These are difficult times, Ma'am. We
must cut public expenditure, we must economize.

(*During Bulldozer's speech, another worker has entered*)

2ND WORKER: You said that well! Only it is not *you* – it is the
war widow and the unemployed man that have to
economize. You take care of that. But as you are at such

pains, General, to tell us we *must* go short, why not also tell us the reason?

BULLDOZER: That I've already explained. Times are hard.

2ND WORKER: Hard? Not for *you*. Our best times were hard enough. Today it's Hell.

1ST WORKER: (*to 2nd*) Don't trouble to argue with him, mate. I asked him to help me get a job. As soon as he spoke I realized what a fool I was. I see that the likes of him only want us for their dirty work and fighting.

2ND WORKER: Well, if they can't offer you work nowadays, they're doing their best to provide fighting. Talk of economy! They spend every possible penny on war and still say its not enough. They cannot give you food but they are producing some beautiful submarines. They cannot give your children boots, clothes or houses. But they *are* building some fine bombers and really good battleships. First things first, you know!

BULLDOZER: Quite right. They are necessary to guard our colonial possessions.

2ND WORKER: 'Our' colonial possessions!!!

WOMAN: You reckon you need an army to guard your colonial possessions. All I say is, Gawd help the PAC if they try to take my home possessions. (*Turning to 2nd worker*) But you say that they – the rich folks – are preparing for war. Is it true? Haven't they stopped munitions going to the East?

2ND WORKER: That they haven't, missus. I'll agree the Cabinet made a great row about it, to stop the real fight against war, and then they called it off. For remember (*with quiet emphasis*), Manchuria borders on Russia. Russia is a country where they've abolished unemployment, stopped evicting workers, thrown out the bosses or made them work, and are building socialism. (*Sarcastically*) So you see, we must support Japan. The General agrees!

BULLDOZER: I suspect you of sarcasm, Sir.

2ND WORKER: However, you do not deny my conclusions.

WOMAN: But how can there be war, when most people want peace?

Section 2 Official Lies

2nd worker strides to centre of stage and addresses audience, while the others stand behind, also facing front. As the players speak, they must suit the word to the action and the action to the word, in order to bring out the irony of the situation.

2ND WORKER: You see! That is what they *(indicates Bulldozer)* say today. They are not planning war against the Soviet Union. They are not backing Japan in China. Oh dear no! Perish the thought! Precisely the same as in 1914. Listen to the truthful Asquith in 1913.

(He steps back, as the 1st worker comes forward with the dignified air of a politician about to put across some bluff, slowly, emphatically)

1ST WORKER: 'As has been repeatedly stated, *this country is not under any obligation*, not public and known to Parliament, *which compels it to take part in any war.*'
2ND WORKER: But, after they had organized the wholesale slaughter of workers they blurted out the truth. Lloyd George, 1918 . . .
3RD WORKER: We had a compact with France, that if she were wantonly attacked, the United Kingdom would go to her support.
2ND WORKER: In 1914 the British bosses claimed to have been caught unawares, but listen to what the British General, Lord French, said when all was over . . .
GENERAL: 'The British and French general staffs had for years been in close consultation with one another. The area of concentration for the British had been fixed' . . .
2ND WORKER: Less than a year before the war they spoke of the Kaiser as
3RD WORKER: *(very pleasantly)* 'A very gallant gentleman whose word is better than many another's bond; a guest who we are always glad to welcome and sorry to lose, a ruler whose ambitions are founded on as good a right as our own.'
1ST WORKER: But when the war started . . .
3RD WORKER: 'The madman is piling up the logs of his own pyre. We can have no terror of the monster; we shall clench our teeth in determination that if we die to the last man, this

modern Judas and his hell-begotten brood shall be wiped out.'

1ST WORKER: And they manufactured stories of incredible atrocities. They told how Germans hung priests upside-down in bells to act as clappers; how corpses were boiled in order to make margarine . . .

2ND WORKER: Lies, all of them. Because of such vile stories the flower of the world's youth fought one another and died. And the chemicals sold by Germany to its opponents were used to send their own men to a ghastly death. And the munitions sold by English armament firms to the Turks were used to mow down English boys as they advanced to a certain death – 'according to plan'. They died, – for what? Bonar Law said

1ST WORKER: 'We are not fighting for territory.'

2ND WORKER: And Lloyd George . . .

3RD WORKER: 'We are not fighting a war of conquest.'

ALL: LIES, ALL OF THEM.

(*All players drop back except Bulldozer, who struts complacently across the front of stage*)

BULLDOZER: It was . . . the reward of patriotism. And patriotism is something that pays – that pays most decidedly. The proof is that those patriotic gentlemen who lent their money to the Government during the war now get a cool million a day interest. A patriotic capitalist is a good business man.

2ND WORKER: (*advancing*) And a patriotic worker is a fool. We perished in millions. Our reward is lower wages, unemployment, starvation, the threat of further war.

BULLDOZER: What are you worrying about? In case of another war, you'd not be unemployed but well-off.

2ND WORKER: 'Well-off' be blowed! We're in a different world from 1914.

1ST WORKER: Oh, I don't know, there'd be plenty of work during the war. Last time there was work in plenty. Factories were running day and night and no nonsense about Sunday being a holy day. People were working like devils making stuff to blow others to hell.

2ND WORKER: How lovely! Well that was *last* time. *Today* we've three millions out of work at the lowest reckoning. What with new machinery, sweating, and skilled men being replaced by girls, will they want us to do work that girls can do cheaper?

WOMAN: (*bitterly*) Might want you for cannon-fodder, though.

1ST WORKER: It's a lie to say we'd be better off. War means not work but death. The air fleet of the great powers are waiting at the moment to raid the big cities and unloose plague and fire and slaughter on young and old. 'One single bomb,' says Lord Halsbury, 'filled with modern asphyxiant gas, would kill everybody from Regent's Park to the Thames.' (*Turning on Bulldozer*) And what hope does your class offer? What says Stanley Baldwin, your *great man*? 'Our only defence is to kill *more women and children quicker than the enemy.*'

1ST WORKER: Seems the only safe place in this war will be in the Air Force! But of course, all the nobs are *there*.

WOMAN: Gas doesn't distinguish between the sexes. Perhaps I'd better join up too. But I'm not a very good shot. Might shoot you by mistake, General.

1ST WORKER: Bloody good mistake too.

BULLDOZER: I'll not stop to be laughed at! (*Makes to go*)

2ND WORKER: (*barring way*) No, you'll stop to hear a few straight words from us.

BULLDOZER: Let me pass, I say.

(*raises hand to strike. But it is seized and held by 1st worker.*)

1ST WORKER: Easy, old sport. And stop cursing. You're not on the parade ground now. (*to 2nd worker*) Go on, mate. Wrap it up for him.

2ND WORKER: Surely you've enjoyed our little talk, General? After the humbug you've been spouting the truth must come as a breath of fresh air. What is more odious than a capitalist talking peace – today. . . .

2ND WORKER: (*continuing*) Your press does its damnedest to make hatred for Russia. You are preparing to break all relations with her. You praise Japan for her anti-Soviet war moves. At any moment mass murder may devour us like a tidal wave . . . But the last word is with the workers!

BULLDOZER: (*with icy sarcasm*) Is that all, sir?

2ND WORKER: That's all for you.

BULLDOZER: Then I'll thank you to get out of my way.

2ND WORKER: Oh, no trouble at all, I assure you.

1ST WORKER: In fact, the sooner you go, the better.

BULLDOZER: I think so, too. I won't stop another moment.

(*He walks away. Just before disappearing he turns, and exclaims with patriotic fervour, removing his hat*)

    Rule Britannia!

WOMAN: Yes, and Britons never shall be slaves!

(*Exit Bulldozer. The others face the audience.*)

1ST WORKER: Our sketch is finished, but before we go
        We want to point the lesson of our show.
        What way can we fight war? Can it be done
        By prayers for peace?

WOMAN: Prayer never spiked a gun!
        No, we must act.

1ST WORKER: What, in our sense of Right,
        Merely as pacifists, refuse to fight?

2ND WORKER: That gets us nowhere. We need action now,
        Before the storm breaks we must act – but how?

1ST WORKER: The organized resistance of our class
        Is requisite *before* war comes to pass.

WOMAN: In Amsterdam and then in Bermondsey,
        The workers' voices spoke in unity:

ALL: 'Workers against war, unite, in common strife
    For work and wages, freedom and for life!'

A note on production

It will be seen that in this sketch there is a blending of the naturalistic and Agit-Prop styles, the central passages exposing war 'stories' etc., being in sharp contrast to the opening and following scenes. Where troupe numbers permit it may be felt better to keep the General out of the Agit-Prop passages and give the speeches marked for him to another player.

The Rail Revolt (1932)

Meeting of railway men. Tramp in soft hat (labelled) mounts chair to right of stage.

TRAMP: Brothers, again we are faced with a serious situation in which our sanest and most statesmanlike consideration is undoubtedly essential. The companies, as you are aware, are asking for a reduction of 10 per cent in your wages . . . THIS IS *TOO* MUCH . . . What are we to do? Are we to strike as our hot-heads would suggest, at a time when our funds are so low? We must face facts. (*Hear! Hear!*) Hard solid facts. To fight is useless. The railways are not paying . . . receipts are down . . . there is less goods traffic . . . as Mr Thomas said at Pontypool, we can't get more out of an industry than we put in it . . . we can't get a quart out of a pint pot (*voice – The bosses are getting their profits all right!*) Dear Brothers, we have to be diplomatic, we have to be statesmanlike, level-headed . . . we must not let our natural anger spoil our judgement . . . The railways are in difficulties . . . we must give the companies a fair chance . . .

1ST WORKER: Do they give us a fair chance?

2ND WORKER: They cut our wages year after year.

3RD WORKER: They get their profits, while our wives and kiddies live on bread and margarine.

4TH WORKER: Yes, and they're taking our food and still want further wage-cuts.

1ST WORKER: (*turning and pointing to Tramp*) Aye, and what's more you're HELPING THEM, you want us to take it lying down, just like Jimmie Thomas did. (*Turning to men*) Brothers, I move we refuse to accept any further wage-cuts, and that we fight for the return of the 1919 agreement.

3RD WORKER: I second that.

3RD AND 4TH: Hear! Hear!

TRAMP: I'm sorry, we are not here to pass resolutions. . . . I'm very sorry. Nevertheless, I note the feelings of the men, and as the executive have left me to get the best possible terms I promise you I will fight the companies as never before on behalf of the bottom dog. The meeting is now closed.

(*Tramp makes his exit with such alacrity that the men can only stare at one another too amazed to swear . . . At Arbitration Board. 3 Directors in Top Hats, labelled 'Wagewood', 'Joss', 'Damp' etc.*)

(*Enter T.U. officials, Tramp and Robley*)

DIRECTORS: Good morning, gentlemen, Good morning . . . delighted to meet you. . . . Yes, er – have a cigar. Yes, a cigar, a cigar.

ROBLEY: Oh, you are *so* kind. . . .

1ST DIRECTOR: About this reduction. . . . We are demanding a 10 per cent cut in wages in order to give you a chance. We are prepared to – er, er – climb down, ahem – to 7½ per cent so that you can inform the men that you have won another great victory. What do you say to a 7½ per cent cut?

ROBLEY: No, No, that's too much to ask for. . . .

2ND DIRECTOR: Oh, have a cigar. . . .

ROBLEY: Dear, dear, this is *SO* touching. . . . As I said at the banquet of the Industrial Alliance in April of this year (1932) . . . as I said, the capitalists are such *decent* fellows that I have great difficulty in frightening them . . .

DIRECTORS (ALL): Ha, Ha, well done . . .

TRAMP: Yes, yes, dear Mr Thomas trained us to respect our betters, . . . oh thanks, (*taking a cigar*) I'll smoke it after lunch. . . . Now gentlemen, you must realize you are giving us a difficult job . . . the men are damned obstinate. . . .

3RD DIRECTOR: Oh have a cigar Mr Tramp . . . er . . . have a drink of champagne . . .

TRAMP: Yes, thanks, er – as I was saying . . .

ROBLEY: No, no, . . . its more than we *dare* do. . . .

1ST DIRECTOR: (*hurriedly*) Have a cigar . . . have two cigars . . . have a drink Mister Robley . . . a drink. . . .

(*Robley and Tramp now have two or three cigars in mouths, others behind ears etc.*)

TRAMP: We realize your difficulties, gentlemen, and we hope to

face them as Britishers . . . but our men are very
awkward. . . . It's the Communist element you know. . . .
(*pleading*) Can't you really make it 5 per cent?

ROBLEY: We have *our* difficulties too, remember gentlemen, er,
keeping the men quiet . . . calm . . . passive.

2ND DIRECTOR: We realize that too. . . . Our difficulties are
mutual. . . . We're both in the same boat, as you say. . . . The
Reds make it so awkward . . . but I'm sorry, we are sticking
to our demand of 7½ per cent.

1ST DIRECTOR: Stand by us . . . and . . . we'll stand by you.

3RD DIRECTOR: We didn't let Thomas down. . . . He's got a good
job . . . his sons are pushed into fat jobs . . . his daughters
are married to DECENT people. . . . We stood by Jimmie
and we'll stand by you . . . if you do our bidding.

1ST DIRECTOR: Have a cigar. . . .

2ND DIRECTOR: Yes, a cigar.

3RD DIRECTOR: Here, take the box!

ROBLEY AND TRAMP (together): Right oh!, gentlemen, we'll do our
best to put it across. . . .

DIRECTORS (together): And may you get away with it!

Meeting of Railwaymen

MEN: Here he comes! Here's Tramp. . . . Wonder what he's done
for us?

TRAMP: (*Mounts stool. Applause*) Er, fellow railwaymen, brothers,
I know you are all anxious to know what transpired as a
result of our meeting with the directors. . . . (*mops his brow*)
We've had a hard fight. . . . My colleague, Mr Robley and
myself, came away from the meeting exhausted from our
labours on your behalf. . . . The Reds who call us traitors
. . . who say we have sold out . . . and all the rest of their
PERNICIOUS paraphernalia . . . should know a little of
the difficulties and hardships of your leaders in these days of
strife and stress and crisis. . . .

We met the employers . . . they were hard as steel. . . .
They care nothing for the lives of men . . . and women
. . . and little children. . . . They demanded a full 10 per
cent off your wages and threatened they would fight for

more if we entered into argument. They pointed out the bad
state of the industry, and men, we have to recognize that
they HAVE A CASE. . . . They showed figures to prove
the .esperate plight of the shareholders . . . and so on.

With all due modesty I must say we fought the employers
tooth and nail. . . . We pointed out your hardships. . . .
We said with all emphasis . . . that LIVES MUST COME
BEFORE PROFITS . . . that was our clarion cry. . . . We
fought inch by inch (*mops his brow*) . . . all along the line. . . .
No leaders ever fought harder for their men. . . . At last
we forced them to give way . . . just a small point, but a
point nevertheless. We pressed home for all we were
worth. . . . Remember, these men have a college education
. . . they are skilled in diplomacy and arbitration. . . .
Nevertheless, we battled until our tremendous labours
simply compelled them to concede our case . . . and to
reduce their demand to one of only 7½ per cent.

Think of it, men, instead of losing two shillings in the
pound as a result of our, may I say er – gallant fight, you
will now lose only one and six. This is a VICTORY . . . a
GREAT VICTORY. . . . We have forced the employers
to concede the point that they don't have the right to
dominate our lives. . . . That we are NOT slaves . . . but
that we will march from this VICTORY to even greater
victories. (*mops brow*) I will thank you for a motion of
confidence in your trusted representatives . . . agreed? . . .
AGREED.

(*He leaves hurriedly – Murmurs and growls of disapproval*)

1ST RAILMAN: So *that's* a blinking victory, eh?
2ND RAILMAN: It's a trick. . . . How can a wage-cut be a victory?
3RD RAILMAN: It might have been worse.
1ST RAILMAN: There you go . . . every wage-cut might have been
  bigger. . . . That's what they said about the first 2½ per
  cent cut, that's what they said about the 5 per cent cut . . .
  so it goes on. Why when they take your last ha-penny
  you'll say – 'Oh well, we have got fresh air and sunshine to
  be thankful for . . .'
4TH RAILMAN: That's it, a few crumbs from the bosses' table are

better than no bread at all. . . . Thank the Lord for a few crumbs . . . that's the blasted theory of the lesser evil.

3RD RAILMAN: But the profits are going down. . . . The industry can't pay.

2ND RAILMAN: What comes first, our lives or their profit?

1ST RAILMAN: What are we going to do about it?

2ND RAILMAN: Fellow-workers, we have lost over three hundred million in wages in five years. . . . These are Tramp's own words. . . .

ALL (placard): *Three hundred million pounds in five years.*

2ND RAILMAN: Every year the shareholders demand 50 million pounds profits.

ALL (placard): (*slowly*) 50 million pounds profit every year.

1ST RAILMAN: They have introduced rationalization . . . speeding up methods . . . to cut down wages . . . to cut down staffs. . . . THEY HAVE REDUCED STAFFS BY 120,000. . . . These are Tramp's own words . . .

ALL (placard): THEY HAVE REDUCED RAILWAY STAFFS BY ONE HUNDRED AND TWENTY THOUSAND.

3RD RAILMAN: They are degrading men by the hundreds, reducing our wages . . . more and more are becoming redundant.

4TH RAILMAN: They are driving us down . . . down . . . DOWN

ALL: AND ALL THIS TO KEEP UP PROFITS.

1ST RAILMAN: They cut down the size of the gangs . . . less men have to do more work.

2ND RAILMAN: They have introduced more and more powerful locomotives . . . which pull double the load . . . and loco-men are being degraded.

3RD RAILMAN: They build coal-hoppers to sack hundreds of coalies. . . .

4TH RAILMAN: They are introducing automatic carriage-washers . . . and sacking cleaners.

5TH RAILMAN: They are cutting down meal-times . . . taking away our privileges . . . forcing us to keep hard at work all the time. . . .

1ST RAILMAN: They are sacking vanboys, and making the carmen do more work.

5TH RAILMAN: This is what the Companies are doing. . . . What are WE to do?

2ND RAILMAN: We railwaymen must struggle against every wage-

cut. . . . We must fight against every attack on our
standards. . . .

3RD RAILMAN: Aye, and more . . . we must fight to get back the
conditions of the 1919 agreement.

ALL: HOW CAN WE FIGHT?

4TH RAILMAN: Can we trust Robley and Tramp?

ALL: NO.

4TH RAILMAN: Who can we trust?

ALL: OURSELVES.

1ST RAILMAN: Comrades, is this not true? How can we trust the
Tramps and Robleys who already have inflicted wage-cuts
upon us? Did not Tramp agree to cut the wages of the textile
workers by 6¼ per cent? Did not Robley and Tramp both
recommend the last wage-cut? You *know* they did.
Comrades, we must recognize our enemies including both the
company directors and their lackeys, the reformist union
leaders. . . . We must fight to defend our conditions by
building up rank-and-file depot and station committees
everywhere. We must build our *own* leadership. . . . THE
ALL-IN DEPOT COMMITTEE.

ALL: Long live the all-in Depot Committees of Action. Fight for
the 1919 agreement.

W.S.

The First of May (1932)

A mass speaking scene by Tom Thomas

If possible groups should march through hall to platform singing a revolutionary song, and stop just as they get to platform and shout:

ALL: THE FIRST OF MAY – THE WORKERS' DAY
1ST GROUP: Throughout the world.
2ND GROUP: With flags unfurled,
3RD GROUP: Workers of every race and land,
4TH GROUP: Workers who toil by marchine or hand,
5TH GROUP: March! (*Begin to march on to platform singing softly*
    WHIRLWINDS OF DANGER)
1ST GROUP: (*Join in*) March.
2ND GROUP: (*Join in*) March.
3RD GROUP: (*Join in*) March.
4TH GROUP: (*Join in*) March.

(*Speaker runs forward*)

SPEAKER: March. (*Keeping time to the rhythm of the marching*)
    Out of their slums and their hovels –
GROUPS: March.
SPEAKER: Out of the sweatshops and factories –
GROUPS: March.
SPEAKER: Out of the darkness of the mines, and the stench of the
    mills –
GROUPS: March.
SPEAKER: On to the streets to the *light* –
GROUPS: March.
SPEAKER: To unite in the struggle for *life*.
ALL GROUPS: FOR LIFE

(*Groups arrange themselves in a semicircle behind speaker. Marching or
    marking time stops.*)

SPEAKER: In 1889 the Socialist International called on the workers
    of the world to demonstrate.
ALL GROUPS: For a universal 8-hour day. Against capitalist war.

For international solidarity between the workers of all countries.

SPEAKER: And every year since 1889 –

1ST GROUP: A spectre has haunted Europe.

2ND GROUP: A spectre has haunted the capitalist rulers of the world.

3RD GROUP: The spectre of the working masses refusing any longer to toil for the profits of the rich.

4TH GROUP: The spectre of the growing solidarity of the working masses of the world.

5TH GROUP: The spectre of the working men and women of the world organizing to overthrow the system of profits and mass murder.

ALL: THE SPECTRE OF COMMUNISM.

SPEAKER: And on one day in the year at least, as they dine and wine, or read the reports of their ever growing profits, the bourgeoisie of the world have shuddered and grown alarmed –

1ST GROUP: Have called out their police –

2ND GROUP: Have arrested and batoned –

3RD GROUP: Have warned their armies –

4TH GROUP: Have charged and murdered –

ALL: *But* have failed to stop the advance of the working class.

SPEAKER: In 1889 there were May Day demonstrations –

1ST GROUP: In Germany –

2ND GROUP: In France –

3RD GROUP: In England –

4TH GROUP: In America –

5TH GROUP: In Belgium –

SPEAKER: By 1899 there were *more* May Day demonstrations –

1ST GROUP: In Norway and Sweden –

2ND GROUP: In Switzerland –

3RD GROUP: In Italy –

1ST GROUP: In Canada –

2ND GROUP: In China and Australia –

3RD GROUP: In Mexico –

4TH GROUP: In South Africa –

5TH GROUP: In Argentine, Brazil, and Chile –

SPEAKER: But by this time capitalism had its agents firmly established within the ranks of the working class, and when

on the first of May, 1914, the Labour leaders in every country
spoke of the international solidarity of the working class
the capitalists could afford to smile. THEY KNEW THEIR
MEN. And when in August 1914 the guns were fired, the
mass murder started –

1ST GROUP: The workers were led –

2ND GROUP: The workers were driven to the slaughter –

3RD GROUP: *By their own leaders.*

4TH GROUP: By Renaudel and Longuet in France –

5TH GROUP: By Scheideman and Kautsky in Germany –

1ST GROUP: By Plekhanov and Martov in Russia –

2ND GROUP: By Renner and Adler in Austria –

3RD GROUP: By Macdonald, Henderson and Clynes in England.

ALL: By the trade unions, Labour Party and ILP in England.

SPEAKER: And May Day became a day in all countries for inciting
the working class to fiercer hatred, and to a more bitter
struggle against their brothers. Only Lenin's word sounding
across the battlefields gave hope and direction to the
working masses slaughtering each other for their masters.

(*A large portrait of Lenin is held up, and three players group round it
with megaphones, and deliver the following, emphatically*)

The only way out for the working masses in every country
is to turn the Imperialist war into a Civil War against their
oppressors. Peace, Land and Bread.

SPEAKER: And on May Day 1917 –

ALL: The working class of the world was rejoicing in the
overthrow of the Tsar. (*Exultant*)

SPEAKER: While the Russian workers were organizing to gain
power, to take over the factories and land, and to drive out
their capitalists and landowners. Under the leadership of
Lenin and the Communist Party they succeeded, and on
May Day 1918 there had been established for seven
months –

ALL: THE FIRST WORKERS' STATE. THE RUSSIAN
SOCIALIST SOVIET REPUBLIC. (*Triumphantly*)

(*The 1ST GROUP unfurls Red Flags and waves*)

ONE VOICE IN 1ST GROUP: The land for the peasants –

2ND VOICE: The factories for the workers –

3RD VOICE: Complete equality for women –

4TH VOICE: Freedom for all the enslaved races –

ALL 1ST GROUP: Culture, Art, Science, LIFE, for the working
     people.

SPEAKER: And now the spectre has become a *grim reality* to the
     capitalists of the world.

1ST GROUP: And for the workers –

2ND GROUP: A HOPE

3RD GROUP: A PROMISE

4TH GROUP: A G U A R A N T E E –

5TH GROUP: The guarantee that capitalism can be overthrown –

ALL: AND WILL BE OVERTHROWN.

SPEAKER: Hundreds and millions of pounds and thousands of lives
     were spent by the capitalists of the world in attacking the

2ND GROUP: We fought and struggled in Germany –

3RD GROUP: In France –

4TH GROUP: In England –

5TH GROUP: EVERYWHERE

ALL: To defend the First WORKERS' STATE.

SPEAKER: And every May Day since has been proclaimed – in the
     Soviet Union –

1ST GROUP: A step further forward in the building up of socialism.

SPEAKER: And in the capitalist world –

2ND GROUP: Solidarity with the Soviet Union!

3RD GROUP: Hands off the Workers' Country!

4TH GROUP: Down with the decaying capitalist system!

5TH GROUP: Defend wages and hours!

SPEAKER: The class struggle in the capitalist countries grows
     fiercer.

2ND GROUP: Every May Day, Paris is an armed camp –

3RD GROUP: Police and Army mobilized –

SPEAKER: By whom?

4TH GROUP: Socialists and Conservatives alike.

5TH GROUP: Hundreds of arrests.

SPEAKER: BERLIN, May Day 1929 –

2ND GROUP: Demonstrations forbidden –

SPEAKER: BUT –

3RD GROUP: Demonstrations took place (*raises flags*)

4TH GROUP: Hundreds of workers murdered

SPEAKER: By

5TH GROUP: The SOCIAL DEMOCRATIC POLICE.

SPEAKER: England, May Day, 1926 –

2ND GROUP: The first General Strike – (*Raises Red Flag*)

3RD GROUP: Betrayed!

SPEAKER: BY WHOM?

4TH GROUP: The Labour party –

5TH GROUP: The trade union leaders –

SPEAKER: MAY DAY, 1932! The crisis of capitalism grows more and more acute. In England –

2ND GROUP: 3 million unemployed.

SPEAKER: In Germany –

3RD GROUP: 6 million unemployed.

SPEAKER: In the United States –

4TH GROUP: 12 million unemployed.

SPEAKER: IN THE WORLD –

5TH GROUP: 40 million unemployed.

ALL: Hundreds of millions starving.

SPEAKER: But in the Soviet Union –

1ST GROUP: No unemployment. 2 million more in industry. The Five Year Plan of socialist construction.

SPEAKER: And the starving millions are demanding from decaying capitalism

ALL GROUPS: BREAD AND LIFE (*low and grim*)

SPEAKER: Capitalism can no longer give them –

ALL GROUPS: BREAD AND LIFE! BREAD AND LIFE!! (*fierce*)

SPEAKER: Capitalism in every country can only give them –

1ST GROUP: Unemployment –

1ST AND 2ND GROUPS: Lower wages – (*with increasing anger and bitterness*)

1ST, 2ND, and 3RD GROUPS: Longer hours – (*with increasing anger and bitterness*)

1ST, 2ND, 3RD AND 4TH GROUPS: Starvation – (*with increasing anger and bitterness*)

ALL: MISERY! (*with increasing anger and bitterness*)

SPEAKER: And in every country of the world, the workers are breaking loose from the shackles that tied them to the will of their masters! (*exultantly*)

SPEAKER: In the United States

2ND GROUP: Hunger Riots – Strikes

SPEAKER: In France –

SPEAKER: In SPAIN
ALL GROUPS: REVOLUTION!
SPEAKER: In Austria
ALL GROUPS: Armed Revolt!
SPEAKER: In China
ALL GROUPS: 60 million people in Soviet China!
SPEAKER: Everywhere – demanding
ALL GROUPS: BREAD and LIFE! BREAD AND LIFE!! (*fierce and urgent*)
SPEAKER: Everywhere the workers' May Day demonstrations are threatened by –
2ND GROUP: Police –
3RD GROUP: Rifles –
4TH GROUP: Machine-guns – (*Threatening*)
5TH GROUP: Armoured Cars –
SPEAKER: EXCEPT –
1ST GROUP: Only in the Soviet Union. WE MARCH *with* rifles, *with* Machine–guns, *with* Armoured Cars, *with* Aeroplanes.

(*while all other groups sing softly Soviet Airmen's song, shouting at finish with 1st Group*)

ALL GROUPS: DEFENDING THE USSR.
SPEAKER: (*with tremendous emphasis and enthusiasm*) Millions and millions of workers and peasants, men and women alike, Tartars, Russians, Georgians, and Kirghiz, demonstrating freely on the streets their implacable hatred of capitalism and their determination to defend the workers' country.
2ND GROUP: Millions of workers

(*begin emphatically, but not too loudly – from here build up to final climax*)

2ND AND 3RD GROUPS: In the capitalist world,
2ND, 3RD AND 4TH GROUPS: Marching!

(*all begin to mark time*)

2ND, 3RD, 4TH AND 5TH GROUPS: Demonstrating!!!
SPEAKER: Demanding!!!!

(*The voices must keep to rhythm of foot-beats*)

2ND, 3RD, 4TH AND 5TH GROUPS: BREAD AND LIFE!!

SPEAKER: All the workers of the world united in the common
    struggle –

1ST AND 2ND GROUPS: Against Capitalism!

3RD, 4TH AND 5TH GROUPS: Against Imperialism!

(*cease to mark time*)

ALL GROUPS: IN DEFENCE OF THE SOVIET UNION!! FOR
    THE INTERNATIONAL SOLIDARITY OF THE
    WORKING CLASS! UNITED . . . IN . . . THE . . .
    COMMON . . . STRUGGLE . . .

(*converging forward to centre behind speaker with flags raised*)

1ST GROUP: FOR THE WORLD

1ST AND 2ND GROUPS: FEDERATION

1ST, 2ND AND 3RD GROUPS: OF SOCIALIST

1ST, 2ND, 3RD AND 4TH GROUPS: SOVIET

ALL GROUPS: REPUBLICS!!

(*All sing 'the Internationale'.*)

Notes

The group passages must be made as clear to the audience as the
solo passages. By careful rehearsal and attention to consonants each
group can be made into one mass voice. But this mass voice does
not grind out the phrases mechanically with equal emphasis on
each syllable. It deals with them like an orator would, with well-
marked changes of rhythm, emphasis and intensity, reinforcing
the message of the words by appropriate 'tone-colours' of the
voice. The Groups stand on stage alert, in a uniform posture,
giving an impression of eagerness and proletarian discipline.

    Particular attention must be paid to the crescendo of volume and
intensity that so frequently occurs, each group building up to the
climaxes where all speak together. A steady shout throughout is
the very opposite of what is intended. The scene can be made
thrilling and dramatic, holding the interest of the audience at every
turn.

Their Theatre and Ours (1932)

Note
It is vital that the strongest contrast in style be made between the burlesque inset scenes of the capitalist theatre and films, and the serious passages.

(The sketch is planned for six performers but can be adapted to either more or less. The troupe marches on well-disciplined, singing enthusiastically and in well-marked rhythm the following song, with each word well brought out and distinct. The refrain '*We're Worker Players*' should be adapted to the name of the group if it can be fitted in. For instance '*We are Red Radio, Workers' Red Radio*'. The march-on and song should receive particular care in rehearsal, and if possible should be accompanied by a portable musical instrument. The first impression the audience gets is very important.)

(All players march on, singing resolutely. The tune is given in sol-fa notation.)

| .s |:d.r. |m   :m |.s :d.r. | m. :m | .s:d.   r.
From mills and workshops we march before you to raise the
|m :s |
workers'
 f :m| r:| .s   :s s.| t   :t | .s :s   s. | t   :t|
voice a–gain Thro' age-long hardships at last they're wak–ing
  .s :t. l. |s   :f |m   :r | d
to boldly smash their slav'ry's chain.
        |.s   :d .r | m :m | .s   :d r.| m :m |
(*Refrain*) We're Worker Players, Red Worker Players . . . etc.

> From shop and factory
> We march before you,
> To raise the workers' voice again.
> Through age-long hardships
> At last they're waking
> To boldly smash their slavery's chain.
> (*Refrain*)
> We are the Red Front,

The Worker Red Front,
We show you how you're robbed and bled.
The old world's crashing,
Let's help to smash it,
And build a workers' world instead.
Speed-up and wage-cuts
And unemployment,
Have brought starvation to our door.
With stage and film show,
They're always striving,
To hide from you the real class-war.
(*Repeat refrain*)

ALL: (*in line*) WORKERS' THEATRE! WORKERS' THEATRE!
    WORKERS' THEATRE!
1ST: The theatre of workers like yourselves
2ND: Who play in every town and country
3RD: To workers like yourselves
ALL: WORKERS' THEATRE! WORKERS' THEATRE!
    WORKERS' THEATRE!
4TH: We show the life of working men and women
5TH: Their hardships and their hunger
6TH: Their struggles to exist
1ST: We are robbed at work for the profits of the rich!
2ND: They speed us up, and throw millions out of work!
3RD: Three millions of us and more are out of work!
4TH: They cut the dole and put us on the Means Test
5TH: But the landlord gets his rent, or throws us out on the ear.
6TH: The bondholders get their hundreds of millions in interest
    every year.
WOMAN PLAYER: Workers' children are robbed of their milk
ANOTHER WOMAN: And the death rate of the workers' children
    rises.
3RD: (*to audience*) Why don't we workers unite and end this
    misery, this starvation, this mass-murder?
1ST: *Because* many workers are still satisfied with their rotten
    conditions.
2ND: *Because* others think that the workers have always been poor
    and oppressed and always *will* be.

4TH: *Because* thousands more think that the rich class are too powerful for us to overthrow.

5TH: And why do they think like this?

6TH: Because the capitalist class make you think just exactly what they want you to think.

1ST: The press

2ND: The schools

3RD: The theatres

4TH: The cinemas

ALL: Are controlled by the capitalist class.

2ND: When things get bad, they sing to you at the pictures –

(*The group gather round like a chorus on stage or film 'plugging' a 'cheer-up' song. A satirical picture of the way this stuff is put across. Faces ghastly with forced happiness. 2nd leads them in the song:*)

'Happy days are here again, The skies above are clear again'. (*Straight on to:*) 'There's a good time coming, So keep your sunny side up, up' –

(*All break off singing suddenly and become a worker audience coming out of a show.*)

1ST: (*enthusiastic*) Good show, that!

3RD: (*wearily*) Not bad.

1ST: Nice and cheerful!

3RD: It's about the only thing that is!

4TH: Don't I know it? I've been out nearly two years. Just lost one of my little ones – couldn't feed her properly.

5TH: And we're all working short time – and speeded up like mad while we're there.

6TH: Yes, and by the time you've paid the landlord and the clubs there's nothing left to live on.

4TH: What we want is a revolution!

1ST: (*still cheerful*) Cheer up, mate. There's a good time coming!

3RD: (*laughing sourly*) So keep your sunny side up – eh?

1ST: (*sings softly to himself*) Sing Hallelujah, Hallelujah, and you'll shoo your blues away.

2ND: (*breaks into scene; the others go off quickly*) And that's how they do it on you. There's always a good time coming – but the workers never get it.

3RD: And when in 1914 the bosses drove us to fight their bloody war for them, to increase their profits – their theatres and cinemas did the dirty work.

GIRL: (*enters and sings to audience in heavily emphasized music-hall style*) For we don't want to lose you, but we think you ought to go, for your king and your country both need you so.

ANOTHER GIRL: And one million men who were caught like this never came back but died ghastly tortured deaths for the profits of the capitalist class.

MAN: And thousands who did come back are tramping the streets – unemployed – unwanted – outcasts – And what do the king and the country care? (*to the music-hall star*) Our miserable disablement pensions are stolen by the Means Test.

MUSIC-HALL STAR: (*starts to dance [if possible] and sings in sloppy style*) I'm singing in the rain, yes singing in the rain, What a glorious feeling, I'm happy again.

MAN: (*continuing ignoring the interruption*) While the royal parasites draw their half a million pounds a year for doing nothing – and are *not* put on the Means Test!

(*One of the players in straw hat or bowler walks round in affected style shaking hands, mumbling and grinning sheepishly*)

VOICE: (*from back through megaphone – as in News Film*) The Prince has a busy day. In the morning he reviewed the Puddleton Boy Scouts and opened the new bridge, which 500 men have been building for two years. We see him being welcomed by the mayor and corporation.

(*Player who plays the mayor sticks his stomach out at this – and gravely shakes hands*)

We see him receiving the cheers of the 500 men who finished up today

(*Mayor claps his hands faintly*)

who thus express their appreciation of the splendid work he is doing.

(*The players representing the workers blow raspberries.*)

VOICE: (*continues*) The Prince, though naturally fatigued by his exertions, after a sumptuous lunch provided by the Town Council, reviews a parade of the police force

(*rest of players line up while he 'reviews' them*)

who have distinguished themselves recently by a baton charge against unemployed demonstrating to the Town Council against the Means Test.

(*On this they draw imaginary batons and use them.*)

His day finishes with a ball organized by Lady Thistlethought in aid of unemployed opera singers. (*Dances round*) And thus he sets an example of devotion to duty to the whole nation.

2ND: (*interrupting fiercely*) And many workers are still taken in by this nonsense, and don't see that we're poor because these others are rich and suck our life-blood. When have you seen the workers' life, as you know it – on the stage, music-halls or films?

3RD: They show us palaces, hotels, cabarets, evening dress, bedrooms, bathrooms – a life of luxury and ease where nobody works or is hungry . . .

2ND: Or poverty shown as something beautiful and noble – played by actors and actresses who are getting up to £1,000 a week – more than an unemployed worker would get in 25 years.

GIRL: (*as film actress, runs in and flings her arms round 4th's neck*) (*in languishing tones*) Oh, I want to get away from this terrible wealth and luxury.

HE: (*nobly*) Money's never brought anyone *real* happiness.

GIRL: Oh, to be poor once more, and happy, to get away from the burden of money . . .

HE: How well you understand! Let us go away together!

SHE: (*naïvely*) Do you think my husband would mind – much?

FILM DIRECTOR: (*enters*) That'll do for now, Miss Greater Garbage. And here's the cheque I promised you.

SHE: (*looks at cheque in disgust*) You're a mean skate, Mr Griffiths. Ten thousand bucks is no good to me. I'm having a midnight supper party tonight!!

(*They go off.*)

2ND: They show us the murder, the mystery or the gangster play
or film . . .

(*One player comes on, stands with his back to crowd, with his hands
extended. Another comes on and hangs his hat on the extended hand.*)

3RD: I'm the gunman they can't catch! The criminal they can't
bump off. I'm known to the police on 500 continents, as
Dandy Dick, or Footling Philip, or Chicken-Fits. But my
most dreaded name is – The Squirt!

GIRL: (*runs on screaming*) Oh! So it's you, the Squirt! Alias the
Slosher! Alias Charlie Chaplin! Alias the Archbishop of
Canterbury! Give me back my jewels and my honour!

3RD: Say, Cutie, you want a lot. You can't have both!

GIRL: Make it the jewels then. (*He hands over big rope of 'pearls'.*)

6TH: (*jumps up with revolver*) Hey there, stick 'em up! (*They do
so.*)

3RD: Snakes and ladders! Inspector Fishface!

6TH: Hah, you didn't know me did you! I've been disguised as a
hat-rack.

GIRL: Say, buddy, I'll have the honour too, now the inspector's
arrived.

(*She puts her arms round the inspector's neck and pulls his obviously false
beard. 6th raises his hand to put back beard, and 3rd takes advantage
of this to whip out a revolver and 'shoot' him*)

3RD: That's not Fishface. It's the Snorter himself from Cincinatti!

6TH: (*reeling around dying*) I know who you are. Only one man
could shoot as straight as that. You're not the Squirt, or
Chicken-Fits. You're the man I've dreaded most all along.
And now you've got me – Inspector Fishface! (*dies*)

3RD: I'm sure glad he knew me before he skidded! Fishface! That's
a name to be proud of! (*Picks up the jewels.*)

GIRL: You lie, you foul brute. Leave them jools alone! You're not
Inspector Fishface.

3RD: How do you know?

GIRL: (*shoots him, as he falls she says*) Because I AM! (*Pulls an idiotic
face*) DON'T I LOOK IT?

2ND: All this sort of stuff that is put across to you on stage and
film has only one purpose. To take your attention away

from the drudgery of your existence, and above all, away from any thought of struggling against your rotten conditions.

(*All run on*)

1ST: Murder and blackmail!

2ND: Patriotism and piousness!

3RD: Revolvers and machine-guns!

4TH: Sex-appeal and slop!

5TH: War!

6TH: All those the boss-class theatre and cinema will show you,

ALL: BUT NOT

1ST: The lives, hunger and degradation of the workers in all countries,

2ND: The struggles of the workers against worsened conditions,

ALL: BUT NOT

6TH: The struggle the workers are waging in all countries to overthrow the system that condemns them to poverty and starvation.

1ST: Without stage effects,

2ND: Without curtains,

3RD: Without make-up and costumes,

4TH: Without everything that the boss-class theatre has got,

ALL: THE WORKERS' THEATRE plays to you in every town.

5TH: And we've got something that the boss-class theatre hasn't got,

6TH: And cannot buy.

1ST: The spirit of the working class that is changing the world

2ND: The support of the working class who realize that we are fighting in their battles

1ST: Our Workers' Theatre is YOUR Theatre!

2ND: Worker players

3RD: Worker playwrights and musicians

4TH: Worker producers

5TH: We labour for the cause of the workers –

6TH: Against the capitalists, landlords, exploiters, and their political puppets.

1ST: We show the life of the workers,

2ND: Their struggles in factory, mine and workshop.

(*Here insert a few lines of the most dramatic part of a factory, or similar sketch the group has played*)

3RD: We show the rotten conditions under which they have to live.

(*Here play a few lines from a housing sketch – example from 'Timber Sketch'*)

2 PLAYERS – MAN AND GIRL: (*declaim together*) We've got a house, a nice little house, right in the middle of a slum,
We pay heavy rent, and none of it is spent in keeping out the weather, so we're glum,
We're miserable, so damn miserable, living in a tumble-down house,
The roof is leaking and the walls are creeping, and the landlord tells us not to grouse,
The floors fall in, the doors fall out, it's all of a rattle if we sing or shout,
We're miserable, so damn miserable, living in a tumble-down house. (*This can be sung to the tune of 'Misery Farm'.*)

4TH: We showed the truth about the sailors' strike at Invergordon, which struck a mighty blow against the national starvation government.

(*a few telling lines from the 'Sailors Strike' are played*)

5TH: We've shown what the Means Test has meant to thousands of workers

(*short passage from the 'M.U.W.M. sketch'*)

Note: The above are put in as examples. Each group should introduce and play short scenes from some of the sketches they have played.

2ND: The WORKERS' THEATRE in Britain has grown rapidly in the past two years.
1ST: This is the work we are doing in thirty towns and districts throughout Britain.
3RD: And this is only a beginning!
4TH: And now we are organizing –
ALL: A WORLD OLYMPIAD OF WORKERS' THEATRES!

1st: From Germany, France and Belgium

2nd: From Holland, Denmark and Sweden

3rd: From Czechoslovakia and Switzerland

all: WORKERS' THEATRE GROUPS ARE COMING –

4th: From China, Japan and Mongolia

5th: America, Canada and Argentine

6th: And also from London, Manchester, Edinburgh and Dundee!

all: WORKERS' THEATRE GROUPS ARE GOING –

1st: To the capital of the first working-class country in the world

all: TO WORKING-CLASS MOSCOW

2nd: There we will learn from our brother organizations in these other countries

3rd: And see the victories of the Soviet working people in the building up of socialism

4th: And the development of working-class dramatic Art.

2nd: *But* for ten British Worker Players to go to Moscow we need money

3rd: Money that only the working-class will give us!

4th: Working men and women! We devote our time and energy without pay to the workers' cause – to *your* cause.

5th: We are building a weapon!

6th: A weapon in the struggle . . .

1st: For the freedom of our class!

2nd: A weapon in the fight against poverty, starvation and war.

all: HELP THE FIGHT OF THE WORKING CLASS BY HELPING THE WORKERS' THEATRE!! SUPPORT THE OLYMPIAD.
We're Worker Players
Red Worker Players
We show you how you're robbed and bled.
The old world's crashing,
Let's help to smash it,
And build a workers' world instead!
WORKERS' THEATRE!! WORKERS' THEATRE!!
WORKERS' THEATRE!!

TOM THOMAS

Part 3

The Yiddish-speaking WTM

Memories of Proltet
Ray Waterman (1978)

When I asked Fegel Firestein, a founder member of Proltet, how it began, she said it grew out of a Yiddish Drama Group already in existence in the East End Jewish Workers' Circle. And how did *that* begin? O that, she said, grew out of a literary group there; and *that* was formed by the Progressive Youth Circle within the Jewish Workers' Circle, which began . . .

It seems that there is never a beginning, strictly speaking. One simply draws an arbitrary line and says, start here.

Fegel Firestein, Alf Holland and my late husband Alec Waterman were among a small group of young Polish-Yiddish immigrants who arrived in London in 1927 or 1928. Fifty years later Mrs Firestein still speaks with a sense of outrage at the cultural desert in which they found the Jewish youth of the East End and, to some extent, their parents also. The older people were members of the mass migrations of the late nineteenth and early twentieth centuries; long hours of sweated labour or the demands of one-man businesses hampered or entirely precluded their efforts at self-development and education. They spoke a strange mixture of Yiddish and English and their children hardly spoke Yiddish at all, and knew little or nothing of the rich cultural heritage created in Eastern Europe. The Whitechapel Theatre gave Yiddish performances but the productions were poor; it came to life only when the lively Vilna Theatre came from Poland for a season, or Morris Schwartz or other well-known actors came from America to perform there. The Jewish Workers' Circle, then in its heyday, played a great role as a cultural and social venue for the immigrant population. But it did not attract the youth.

It was this situation that these newly-arrived immigrants, with a number of like-minded others, set out to remedy by forming the Progressive Youth Circle* inside the Workers' Circle. All were

★ For a lively account of the Progressive Youth Circle in a fictional setting see Ray Waterman's novel of East End life in the 1920s: *A Family of Shopkeepers*, published by W. H. Allen, 1972, pp. 191–213. [Ed.]

young workers earning a living as skilled or semi-skilled tailors and dressmakers, cabinet-makers, hairdressers and shop assistants. Politically they were a mixed bunch representing left- and right-wing Zionist, Labour, Communist or Anarchist views; a few were non-political; but on the whole they were orientated towards the left-wing of the labour and progressive movement. Their speeches and activities reflected a passionate desire to improve and eventually to change the existing social order for a more just form of society.

The cultural development of Jewish youth through the medium of the Yiddish language was seen by the Progressive Youth Circle as an essential element of these strivings. Its leaders and membership, while struggling with the new language, were still in love with the mother-tongue and hoped for its revival.

Starting off with lectures and discussions on political and sociological topics such as women's rights, free love, Zionism, Communism, etc., the PYC was an immediate success, attracting not only the youth but often their elders to the crowded room they occupied at the top of the Workers' Circle in Great Alie Street. Among those who came to speak for the PYC or to take part in discussions were Simon Blumenfeld (author of *Jew Boy*), Professor Hyman Levy, who spoke on the Jewish question, Aron Rollin and Jacob Fine, trade union leaders in the garment industry, who spoke on the history of British trade unions, Moishe Ovid the antique dealer, Sam Alexander, who spoke on the history of the Jewish people, and many others. Some of the lecturers were at home in both languages, some only in English.

With an eye to the future, Alf Holland re-activated a defunct school for Yiddish that had at one time been run in the Workers' Circle. He and Alec Waterman both taught these Sunday morning classes until the need for a more professional teacher brought Dr Natanyi from Poland. The school flourished for about three years in the early 1930s until support fell off.

The Progressive Youth Circle also set up a Literary Section which arranged talks on the work not only of Yiddish writers such as Sholem Aleichem and Peretz, but also on English-language writers and dramatists such as Bernard Shaw, Theodore Dreiser and others. Occasionally scenes from a book were dramatized and the characters put 'on trial' as a way of studying the writer in depth. From such beginnings grew the Dramatic Group. (There had once been a Children's Yiddish Drama Group in the Workers' Circle. I saw them perform to a good professional standard in the Whitechapel Theatre in the late 1920s. It was a charming political fantasy with music and songs called *Children of Tomorrow* by S. Palme, an immigrant poet.)

The new Dramatic Group was intended to attract young Jewish people whose knowledge of Yiddish was limited, and to give expression to the ideas motivating the Progressive Youth Circle. They performed scenes from the work of established dramatists and also wrote their own. These performances were given in the Tailor & Garment Workers' Hall in Great Garden Street, Whitechapel (which held about 350 people), the Workers' Circle Large Hall (about 200), and the Notting Hill Branch of the Circle (about 60–80). The Yiddish Drama Group were lively and inventive in their productions and at a public performance of amateur dramatic groups they attracted the attention of the Workers' Theatre Movement, who invited them to join as a Yiddish-speaking group of the WTM.

And that is how Proltet began.

I hope to be forgiven a digression at this point. I myself was a member of an English-speaking group of the WTM in the East End (it was called either Red Radio or Red Players, I don't remember). We performed sometimes near the London Hospital in Whitechapel in a side street whose two levels offered a convenient platform, and sometimes in London Fields, Hackney, where we were once pelted with over-ripe tomatoes (not then in the luxury class). We retired in disarray to clean up, deciding that the young workers we had hoped to inspire were not yet ready for our message.

To return to Proltet, it was the only WTM group performing exclusively indoors. Although the East End of those days was immigrant Jewry's *shtetl,*★ only a fraction of a street audience would have understood Yiddish. This distinction apart, Proltet modelled itself entirely on the Agit-Prop style of the English-speaking groups. Both sexes wore the navy bib-and-brace overalls and white shirt to symbolize their sense of identity and solidarity with the working class, and also the concept referred to by Tom

---

★ *shtetl* – Yiddish name for the small towns of Jewish settlement in Russia and Poland.

Thomas in *History Workshop* 4 of the 'Propertyless Theatre for the Propertyless Class'. The slogan was adopted for practical reasons (think how costumes and props would have hampered our quick get-away in London Fields). But like other useful and pithy slogans it hardened into a dogmatic principle. Proltet's performances being given indoors, where lighting and furniture were available, touches of naturalism inevitably crept in, and there was heated argument over a sketch, collectively written, where the judge was given a wig, the prisoner a bloodied bandage, and the policeman a helmet. Incidentally, Philip Firestein, Mrs Firestein's husband, who was Proltet's secretary, acted as the policeman. He knew no Yiddish but was a great success; he had only to raise and lower his magnificent George Robey-like eyebrows for the audience to fall about helplessly.

Proltet's first production was *Strike!* by Michael Gold (author of that little masterpiece of the Jewish immigration to America, *Jews Without Money*). One idle Sunday Alf Holland conceived the idea of translating it into Yiddish and it was performed with great verve to enthusiastic audiences. As in the English production of the same play mentioned by Tom Thomas, actors were dispersed among the audience to shout *Strike! Strike!* rhythmically to those on stage, and were often indignantly shushed by those not in the know. Mr Holland tells me that *Strike!* in the original English was criticized by someone who saw it in both languages as being a poor translation from the Yiddish . . . Proltet's production of *Strike!* was also performed at one of the monthly performances staged by the London WTM groups, and so impressed Andre van Gyseghem, the professional producer, that he offered his services (free of course) to produce Proltet's *Finf-Yor Plan* (*Five-Year Plan*) which they had collectively written for a national competition of all WTM groups. The collaboration bore fruit, Proltet being awarded first prize.

Other sketches were written collectively, among them *Birobijan*, about the Jewish settlement in the USSR, once intended as a Republic. The writing sessions were often stormy. Politics were simpler then, the issues more clear-cut, or perhaps they seemed so to us because we were young, and the young in every period are usually confident in their opinions. In 1854 Tolstoy wrote in *Boyhood*:

In those days the reformation of mankind, the abolition of all the vices and miseries, seemed possible, and it seemed such a simple, easy matter to improve oneself, acquire easy virtue and be happy. Incidentally, God alone knows whether those lofty aspirations of our youth were actually ridiculous, and whose fault it is that they were not fulfilled . . .

We in the Proltet and other WTM groups also had lofty aspirations. We saw ourselves as part of the movement towards socialism, and our responsibility for what was publicly said in its name was keenly felt. Every bit of dialogue, every nuance, was scrutinized for departure from the general line that 'the people' embodied all virtue, the capitalists all evil, and that socialism would provide the solution to all problems. But what writer can bear to see his words altered? All fought fiercely to keep them unchanged.

We worked as hard at the preparation and performance of these sketches as any professional, and perhaps even harder because they were intended not as a means to earn a living or for mere self-expression, but for what we saw as a noble cause, and if it so happened that we hugely enjoyed ourselves in the process, that was an unsought bonus.

Proltet functioned for approximately three years from 1932 to 1934, when it was found impossible to continue. Its members were dispersing, some to other countries; some, through marriage and the setting up of new homes, to distant parts of London; and some, through pressure of other political tasks as Fascism grew more threatening. Moreover, the group of immigrants who were its core was too small to compete with or resist the natural process of absorption into the all-pervasive culture of the host country.

The Progressive Youth Circle itself continued until the outbreak of war caused the final dispersal. It organized support for various causes including the Botwin Brigade, the Jewish section of the International Brigade to Spain. Alec Waterman was the secretary of this Committee.

I started off by saying – what cannot be news to students of history – that strictly speaking there is no beginning to anything. Nor, strictly speaking, is there any end. The gallant attempt at a Yiddish-speaking revival failed, but the Progressive Youth Circle, by fathering Proltet and other offspring, raised the political and cultural level of its audiences. In those busy years in that crowded

room at the top of the Workers' Circle I and many others first had
our sensibilities quickened to the changing ills that afflict society
and to the unchanging need for struggle to overcome them. . . .

In preparing this little piece, I came upon the following letter from
F. Le Grass ('Bill') Clark which may help to convey to younger
readers something of the spirit of the time.

13 May 1934

Dear Ray,
　Now with regard to your article, on which I want to write
an appreciation.
　. . . What is this stuff about a revolution of content and form
only being realised in a classless society or under communism
or what not? Is it not clear that by the time we are advancing
into the classless society or towards communism, the category
of 'revolution' ceases in great part to apply. No, a revolution
is the actual seizure of State power and of factories, land,
banks etc. by a hitherto submerged and exploited class. The
revolutionary class smashes the old governmental forms and
establishes its own in their place. But it *does* and *must* have a
state, a code of laws, an administrative apparatus, an army
and so on, just as the old ruling class had. Yet it is most
emphatically a revolution and in fact this is just what a
revolution is; and you and others have no right to employ the
term as loosely as you do. You will all be losing yourselves
in a maze of false dialectics.
　Take the phrase, 'a revolution in content demands a
revolution in form'. What on earth does this mean? If I put
oil into a bowl instead of water does it demand a revolution
in the form of the bowl? Wordsworth wrote some very loyal
sonnets. Milton wrote some very revolutionary ones. But both
keep the precise sonnet form; and yet there is no doubting
that they wrote under very different inspirations. Certainly
after a while a fresh set of ideas will start to mould its own
form of expression and after some long time a completely new
form may have been evolved. But this does not imply that
anyone can state categorically that a change in content demands

a change in form. Let us wait and see patiently whether it does.

Who invented this term 'agitprop' drama? It appears to me that a certain style of presentation, reminiscent entirely to me of the decadent style of bourgeois drama called expressionism, was selected (heaven knows why) as to the style to be used in the WTM. And that then this style was sanctified and hallowed, as it were, by giving it the name 'agitprop' and daring anyone to dare to question it. *You* say, I think, that naturalistic drama is the usual drama of the bourgeois stage. This is not true entirely. Many plays and sketches put on today are certainly not naturalistic either in text or production or both. If you want 'naturalism' in its simple form, you must listen to a lively worker telling his mates the story of what the foreman said to him and what he replied to the foreman and what the manager said and so on. It is simple acted narrative with one man taking all the parts – as of necessity on this occasion he must. A little permissible exaggeration of gesture or tone of voice may be given, as it is *always* given on the stage, for otherwise the effect would not get across. Remember that. There is no such thing as pure naturalism and never could be.

Most of the argument is going on in the air. Neither form is at all satisfactory, as they at present stand. We must come down closer to the workers and begin to work hard. Don't say 'close to the masses'. The phrase can be used to excuse one from coming close to anyone at all. One trouble is that much of the stuff done is done without taking any trouble to find out what workers really say to one another and in various situations. That is a scientific task for a WTM group to perform very patiently and painstakingly.

But chiefly, as regards your article, I think the term 'revolution' must be dropped out of this loose way of handling it.

But now, when that has all been said so decidedly, the fact remains that I highly approve of the underlying tenor of your article and that you quote Lenin above all. We can never have too much of that.

Yours ever,
Bill

Proltet: reply to critics (1933)

Proltet has discussed the January issue of the *Bulletin* closely, and here are some of our conclusions. We whole-heartedly agree with and support the line in 'Our tasks in the New Year' and 'To the factories and unions'.

ALL-LONDON SHOW. We will deal with comrade B. Woodward's criticism point by point.

Point 1: 'The playing of two sketches in Jewish was bad, in fact, speaking in Jewish is unnecessary. I have had several complaints about this, some from Jewish comrades. They say that only some very old Jews do not understand English, and as our object is to reach as many workers as possible, we defeat our purpose by presenting Yiddish sketches.'

Comrade Woodward and his Jewish friends need to learn a little more about the Jewish question before dismissing so lightly the need for a Jewish revolutionary force, of which Proltet is but a nucleus. First of all it is untrue that only old Jews do not understand English. We have ourselves seen that our audiences are composed of young and middle-aged as well as old Jews. Even if we played to old people only, isn't it a fact that parents to a certain extent influence their children? However, that is by the way. Here are some real facts:

In every capitalist country exist reactionary Jewish agencies which exercise great influence on the Jewish masses. In London alone, where there are 150,000 Jews of whom the majority are workers, two Jewish reactionary newspapers have a joint daily circulation of about 100,000. This seems to prove that at least 100,000 Jews are sufficiently interested in their own language as to read a Jewish newspaper every day. These papers play the same part in influencing the minds of their Jewish readers as the English capitalist press, pouring out streams of anti-working-class propaganda in general, and national chauvinist sentiments in particular.

It must be realized that the Jewish people are more liable to be attracted by this nationalist propaganda, because of their position as a national minority.

In addition, there is in Britain a powerful Zionist movement, which, by pretending that all our troubles will be over if we only go to Palestine (under the protection of British guns) prevents Jewish workers from realizing their fundamental unity with their non-Jewish class brothers, and that the solution of their particular problem will come with the solving of the workers' problems as in Russia today, after a working-class revolution.

It is interesting in this connection to note that the Chief Rabbi, Dr Hertz, at a recent meeting in Shoreditch Town Hall, stated that the Jews under the Soviet Government were worse off than under the Spanish Inquisition, because under the latter regime in spite of their bodies being tortured, their faith was kept alive, whilst under the former, although they had physical freedom, their faith was being destroyed. Thereby implying that the Chief Rabbi would rather see the Jews programmed and suppressed than playing their part in industry and culture, as in the Soviet Union. Thus does the Jewish reaction play its part in the general campaign against the Soviet Union.

To be brief, wherever there is reaction, it needs to be fought, and fought in its own language. Except for our comrades in the unions (reformist and revolutionary) and the Committee in Aid of Jewish Colonization in USSR, there is at present no Jewish revolutionary movement in existence.

We think the above remarks prove not only the justification but the crying need for Proltet's existence. Our future work is going to be concentrated on sketches to combat this reaction.

Point 2: 'Has WTM absorbed Proltet or has Proltet absorbed WTM?' This phrase is very ambiguous. Is Comrade Woodward chastising us for absorbing WTM, or is he chastising WTM for allowing itself to be absorbed by us?

Point 3: 'The sketch *Strike!* should be banished from WTM repertoire . . . a greatly over-rated sketch . . . production full of faults . . .' Indeed, Comrade Woodward! This is the first we've heard of it! As a production it has been acclaimed by all, including the CC (Central Committee) of WTM – see December issue of WTM

Monthly Bulletin (*MB*). Its tremendous dramatic appeal, coupled with its attractive form (audience feeling itself part of play), make it (in our opinion) one of the most valuable of WTM sketches. We are all agreed that its political line needs altering, and this we are now engaged in doing.

Point 4: 'If the producer can do no better than this, he had better stick to Elstree, and leave WTM alone.' Shame, Comrade Woodward, and on you, Comrade Editor, for allowing such a remark to appear in the *Bulletin*! Is this the way to attract into our movement the talent and sympathies of people not yet politically with us? It happens that our producer couldn't take his medicine, and is no longer in our group, but when those lines were written he was still with us. Would those words have encouraged him to overcome his conventional ideas and habits? Our attitude is rather: 'Don't send 'em back to Elstree. Try to keep them in the movement and make 'em toe the line.'

Point 5: 'Red Players in *Meerut* were mis-cast . . . Cockney accent of one player very bad'. In our opinion Red Players in *Meerut* were very good. It is ridiculous to object to a Cockney accent. Don't we want the workers to join the WTM? If so, are we to send them to an elocution school before we allow them to play in our sketches? And doesn't it appeal to a working-class audience to hear the players speaking to them in their own 'lingo'?

(Proltet invites all comrades interested, and particularly the CC, to give an opinion on the above remarks, especially Point 1. Proltet also wishes to say that one comrade as Editor is insufficient, and that the *MB* should have an Editorial Committee of at least three comrades.)

Editor's explanation
Point 4 is not given correctly: the producer resigned from Proltet on 22 December. At a show on 24 December this individual tried to persuade members of the Proltet group to leave and form another society. The bulletin was not composed till 1 January. There is no question here of attracting people *in* but of preventing one person from using influence to pull people *out* of the WTM.

Consequently we decided to publish this remark of Comrade Woodward's in order that it should receive the criticism and condemnation it deserves. This is a concrete example of what is meant by using the *Bulletin* as a method of thrashing out our various ideas so that we can see the way forward, with all doubts and misunderstandings cleared up.

Proltet's letter proves this point when it says that 100,000 people read daily papers in Yiddish. There is now no room for the doubts which some comrades entertained about the usefulness of a Yiddish group. If this criticism of Woodward's had not been put in who would have known of the valuable facts given above?

(Source: WTM *Bulletin*, February 1933, pp. 6–9)

The debated question of Yiddish (1933)

Readers will remember the correspondence which has appeared in the *Bulletin* on the subject of the Proltet group. Some contributors were of the opinion that it was wrong for this group to perform in Yiddish. Others said that it was very necessary to have such a group.

The Central Committee reviewed the correspondence at a meeting recently and decided that as there are thousands of Jewish workers in the East End who speak and understand Yiddish, it is important that we should have such a group active among this section of workers.

Criticism has been levelled at those responsible for the *Bulletin* to the effect that they should have made a statement on their attitude and not allowed this question to be debated.

We disagree entirely with this view: the columns of this *Bulletin* are free to all members and workers in our audiences to express their opinions of the sketches we produce. It is by criticism of our sketches that we can improve our technique and material.

On questions such as that of the performances of sketches in Yiddish, we believe we are fully justified in listening to the opinion of our audiences before coming to a decision.

(Source: WTM *Bulletin*, September–October 1933, p. 15)

Do we overcrowd our sketches? (1934)

Comrades, how often have we heard the criticism, 'The WTM tries to crowd the whole policy of the Comintern into each sketch?' And, theoretically, all of us agree it is a mistake to say too much and try to explain too many problems at once. Yet in practice we go on making the same mistake. I will give one or two concrete examples:

EXAMPLE 1   Our group translated into Yiddish *The Great Deception*, a sketch showing how Fascism came to power in Germany. You will remember that, in the English version, the sketch ends with the German revolutionary (after being clubbed into unconsciousness by the Fascists) picking himself up and delivering a long speech warning the British workers to learn from the fate of their German brothers, and to stop Fascism before it is too late. Our group was unanimous in the opinion that this ending was bad, that long speeches of this character were utterly boring and valueless. But the question then arose – how then to end the sketch? And at this point opinion was divided. I (in a minority of one) thought that the sketch should close at the point where the German revolutionary lies beaten into insensibility; the erstwhile Fascist is led off under arrest shouting (of Hitler) 'Swindler, murderer, betrayer!'; and the stage is swamped by a torrent of anti-Fascist leaflets (the latter being a happy inspiration of one of our lads to show that the revolutionary workers were alive and kicking).

The majority of the group, however, maintained that we dared not leave the sketch at this point. They said we must not leave the sketch without a definite lead; we must explain to our audience that what happened in Germany could happen in England if they were not warned in time; and we must explain to them *how* to fight the danger of Fascism. Also, said the comrades, the action at the opening commenced in England, therefore it must finish in England. (Apparently their sense of harmony was outraged by the suggestion that a sketch could begin in England and finish in Germany.)

Now, the reasons I wanted to close the sketch at the point

mentioned were: First, the sketch was intended to convey what its title implied – the great deception – how the workers of Germany were tricked into Fascism. This alone would tell such a different story to that found in the popular press, that the audience could not but gain a lesson from the mere telling of it. Second, I agreed that we needed to tell the workers of Britain concretely *how* to fight against Fascism, but for this a new and separate sketch was necessary, we could not plant this important political lesson on to the tail-end of *The Great Deception*, a sketch constructed to last about twenty-five minutes in all. Such treatment could not possibly be effective, either politically or artistically.

I could not convince the group that I was right, but curiously enough, *The Great Deception* was presented at the All-London Show in the form *I* had suggested, not because they agreed with me, but because they could not think, in time for the Show, of an ending which they considered suitable. And at the very moment I write these lines, my poor comrades of the Writing Committee are meeting somewhere in London, puzzling their heads over this very question.

EXAMPLE 2   You all remember *The Fight Goes On*, a sketch dealing with a domestic incident in the 1926 General Strike. This, in my opinion, is a good example of the type of sketch we should be presenting more frequently. The characters are true to life, the situation convincing, the lead to action inspiring: the audience is inevitably drawn into sympathy with our arguments. And the scene itself, the home of a worker, is of vital interest to the worker-audience, and one we have sadly neglected in the past. In this opinion I am in good company. Comrade Diament, of the International Union of Revolutionary Theatres, in his lecture on the Olympiad in May 1933, said:

> When we analyse different productions of the Olympiad, staring us in the face is the almost complete absence of historical problems and questions of domestic life. For instance, domestic problems of workers' everyday existence, the unemployed at home, of conflicts arising within the workers' family, the influence on such a family of the present capitalist crisis, all these have not been really expressed, hardly even shown. And such rightly presented would considerably help

the organization of the workers in the struggle against capitalism, against fascism, against exploitation, of which so much has been said in slogans, shouted by agitprop groups from the stage.

But during a discussion with a member of my group, he said that *The Fight Goes On* was not a good sketch, because it did not show the organization of the General Strike, its political and economic aspect. He said that to present a picture of any strike which gave only its domestic aspect was giving a one-sided, and therefore false picture of the strike.

Again, I quite agree it would be a fine thing if we could in one sketch view the strike from its various angles, – the causes, demands of the strikers, committee-room discussions, the picket-line, and so on. But does any serious-minded person really believe we can do this convincingly in half an hour? Such a broad canvas needs a full-length three act play.

In concluding, I want to emphasize my opinion that we of the WTM do infinitely overcrowd our sketches: that while we can allow ourselves only twenty to forty minutes we would gain far better results (politically and artistically) by presenting our problem from only one aspect, instead of attempting, as we do at present, every aspect . . . and failing miserably.

Ray Waterman

(Source: WTM *Bulletin*, March 1934, pp. 20–2)

Part 4

The debate on naturalism

A Look at the Workers' Theatre Movement (1933)

By one who is not a member

It seems to me that the WTM may be reflecting the whole transition stage of the movement towards united-front work, towards closer and unbreakable relations with the masses. This means that the WTM is coming through its infancy, but has not yet discovered how to advance to a more mature stage.

The solution lies in at once relaxing and strengthening the 'Agit-Prop' character of the WTM. This may sound strange, but I will explain what I mean. I mean that on the one side the WTM must relax its artificial limitations. It is not yet by any means a true 'Agit-Prop' vehicle. It is rather a development of what is called 'expressionism', and 'expressionism' is less a type of revolutionary and proletarian drama, than a type of decadent and pessimistic bourgeois drama. Expressionism tickles the palates of the bourgeoisie and helps them to escape the painful force of the representational and personal drama, when this latter deals with certain subjects painful to the bourgeoisie, i.e., with the class struggle and with the forcible ending of the present property relationships.

So let us visualize on the one hand a return to very simple realism, and on the other hand an expansion of the 'Agit-Prop' idea into fresh channels and with fresh inspiration behind it. I will deal with these two aspects separately.

1 Return to realism and representationism on a simple basis. We find that there are a fairly large number of working-class dramatic organizations in the country associated with the Labour party, Co-op, etc., as well as a number of semi-working-class and petit-bourgeois groups, amateur dramatic associations, and so forth. Even when these groups are middle-class in composition, they sometimes contain, or are capable of being captured by, radical thinking persons of semi-revolutionary or advanced views. Naturally most of the plays they select are fairly realistic and straightforward. Yet many are waiting, even if unconsciously, for a new

lead. Many would welcome plays expressing a definite anti-war, anti-Fascist, socialistic point of view. Any organization that could bring such plays to their notice would gain a reputation. Also, it would be beneficial to the broad Movement that such plays should be put about and performed by amateur societies of ability.

How then to set about it? We have first to consider whether such plays exist already. Probably there are a few; and it would be as well to think in terms mostly of one-acters at this stage. Then we must consider the large number of writers of reputation that have associated themselves with the anti-war movement, the German Relief Committee, etc. Correct approach to these might in time achieve unexpectedly good results. It is even possible for us to think in terms of getting a sympathetic publisher to put out a series of new one-acters, etc., called 'Plays for the Moment', or something of that kind. It has not, I think, been tried. I do not suggest that it can be done in a moment, but it will enable the WTM to influence certain writers towards us and to have a fine basis for approaching and forming a united front with any kind of amateur dramatic groups that might come under our influence.

In my opinion the WTM should itself consider working up a certain number of simple realistic sketches. In these the central figure would be a worker, etc. who is not so much a typical 'symbol' of the working class as an actual worker with whom any member of the audience can emotionally identify himself. The drama would consist of a real problem put to that worker, as, ᵉ g., something about a strike or war; and it would be necessary to observe him in mental conflict, so that the audience would feel its own mental conflicts being worked out in that man on the stage. The plays would, of course, be short and in ordinary clothes without properties (or, anyhow, the minimum of properties). The audience could be shown a young worker invited to join the army and see his emotional conflict in his argument with the recruiting agent. He will waver to and fro and the audience will be emotionally stirred with a feverish interest in him, until finally his revolutionary consciousness wakes up to the full and he sees his way clear and expresses himself in definite terms to his 'tempter'. Many such simple scenes could be worked out; but one must note that they would need to be carefully acted by workers who took the trouble to study the parts carefully, so as to get the maximum effect across. Little scenes with two, three or four characters would

be quite enough. I feel certain that if the WTM could get together
a small experimental group for this purpose and consider carefully
one or two such sketches, the result would be most successful.

2 Fresh advances along the 'Agit-Prop' lines. I would like to
note that as a movement grows to maturity, so it becomes on the
one side more sober and painstaking and on the other side more
daring and dramatic. Think what the German workers, for
example, achieved in daring dramatic effects in the last years of
legality – the 'tapping' of Hindenburg's wireless speech is a good
instance. Another striking example in this country is the way in
which a little group of workers splashed Hitler's waxwork figure
with red paint. These incidents are staggering; they get into all the
papers, they are widely discussed. They are the dramatic aspect of
the broad 'Agit-Prop' work of the Movement.

To invent and carry out these ideas into effect is *not* the task of
the WTM. But it is the task of the WTM to excite, shock, and
impress the minds of working-class audiences by its dramatic
effects and methods. The WTM must get its wits to work and
contrive ever fresh dramatic effects, that will thrill its audiences
and fix the incidents in the mind of every member of that audience.
The WTM must get closer and closer to its audiences.

It has already achieved something in this way, of course, but
more can be done. For example, plays should start directly from
the audience. The special WTM kit should be used but sparingly
and only in street work, where it is necessary to attract attention
and draw a crowd. Indoors ordinary clothes should be used. Everything possible should be done to surprise the audience (within
limits of course). For example, one member of the cast, dressed
as a burlesque Fascist, could be dragged in by others with much
shouting, and a trial could then take place, in which the audience
is the jury. I stress the word 'burlesque' because there must be no
practical jokes on the audience. The audience must be surprised
and excited, but not alarmed and not feel that it has been hoaxed.
Another idea is appropriate for week-end schools, etc. The
members of the school would be attracted by the spectacle of some
workers apparently digging a trench or the like in a neighbouring
field; and when their attention has been attracted, the men in
question would suddenly down tools and go on strike, hold a
strike meeting, etc. The audience would rapidly grasp that it was

a bit of drama, but (if it were well done) would enter into the thrill of the idea.

It is my belief that scores of such effects could be contrived and that they would have great 'Agit-Prop' value when well carried out.

3 I will add further points that occur to me. I do not think the WTM makes enough use of humour. In this we must remember that the typical humour of the workers is often shown on the music halls. I think that much could be done by having simple back-chat comedians, two only, coming on with a series of comic comments on the political happenings of the day. Of course for this we require those who can both write and do the comic turns. Nevertheless, if we *could* do it, it would be exceedingly popular. Why not ask Bejay to write a comic back-chat turn of this kind? We must look out for humorists – men who can make the workers laugh at the reformists in a mild but destructive way. We take ourselves too seriously. Most of the WTM humour so far has been all on the anti-religious lines, and this is bad in my opinion. It is infantile.

I think that many of the WTM shows I have seen suffer from being overburdened. Too much is got in to any one sketch. It seems as though the writers were dreadfully afraid of leaving out any aspect of the class struggles and therefore all had to come in. Some propagandists are like that on the platform.

I should like to mention the idea of parodies of music hall songs popular at the moment. These should be real parodies, capable of being picked up and sung by every worker on the streets. In this they cease in a sense to be merely 'parodies' and become an effort to give the workers *our* words in place of the words he learns from the music hall and the song sheets. Especially should we achieve a success if we could get the children of a district singing *our* words in place of the words of the bourgeois song.

(Source: WTM *Bulletin*, September–October 1933, pp. 19–23)

The New Stage Group (1933)

We now give the extremely important resolution on the question of the group set up to give short and full-length plays in the ordinary style with curtains, lights, etc. The opening remarks are written by Tom Thomas, the national organizer.

In the first discussions which took place on the return of the Olympiad delegation, one fact soon became exceedingly clear: that there was no clearness whatever about the delegation as to the future work of the WTM and how the lessons of the Olympiad should be applied.

The only idea expressed was that the line of the WTM had to be changed, but why or how did not seem to be generally known. Those comrades who permitted themselves to be a little more explicit spoke of changing the open-platform work which had been carried on for three years and of the Movement reverting to the stage dramatic group.

This was all the more surprising in view of the fact that those performances at the Olympiad of which a coherent report was given – and most of the reports at the London discussion meeting were anything but coherent, though some were excellent – these performances were open-platform performances of an extremely high level of effectiveness.

These excellent shows were not, however, to be taken as our aim, but, on the contrary, the naturalistic play as typified only by the very poor Norwegian group, and, of course, by the Soviet theatres with all the advantages which the Revolution has won for them. A rather strange conclusion to draw!

I think it is probable that the explanation will be found in a misunderstanding of the many criticisms levelled against the open-platform groups at the Olympiad on the ground of 'schematism', lack of convincing characters, etc. These seem to have been taken as a criticism of the form itself, rather than the way it was being handled by many of the groups (ourselves included.)

A very full discussion took place at the London meeting when the delegates reported (or didn't, as the case may be). I pointed out that to abandon the street performance and the shows at meetings would be to abandon the greater part cf our attempts to get to the mass of the workers, which had been strikingly successful in the past.

After an excellent discussion, the following resolution was proposed and carried unanimously. It was afterwards discussed by the London groups and carried by the Central Committee:

Resolution – 2 July 1933

1 In accordance with our conference decisions and the decisions of the 1st Congress of IURT,★ we reiterate our conviction that the chief work of the WTM in Britain at the present time must be the development of groups of worker-players who will perform to the workers wherever the workers may be, and will use for this purpose the most effective method, the open-platform method.

We realize that this method has been handled in many instances very badly indeed, and undertake to improve the quality of the sketches and the standard of performance to make them equal to their task of winning the working masses to the support of the revolutionary line.

2 The plan for developing the work within the professional theatre must be carried out, drawing those elements who are won to the revolutionary line into the work of assisting the worker-players with their technical experience. We aim at developing a 'left' play-producing society which will be of great value, and an important step on the road of building a mass revolutionary permanent theatre when the time is ripe for such a step.

3 In order to utilize the services of workers who will not take part in 'open-platform' work, to win workers from other dramatic organizations and in some cases the organizations themselves, and as a further step in the development of a revolutionary theatre, it is necessary, when the possibility arises (in the opinion of the Central Committee) to develop groups

★ International Union of Revolutionary Theatres, set up in Moscow in the early 1930s. It organized an Olympiad in Moscow in August 1933 which was attended by a group from Britain. It published the magazine *International Theatre.*

of workers performing plays written for the curtained stage. These groups will play an important part in solving the financial problem of the WTM and in the development of a repertoire to win other dramatic groups to the revolutionary line.

In London, a recent addition to our forces has enabled a stage group to be formed, on the decision of the CC, the character of whose leadership guarantees an extremely successful and useful group. In other areas, where there is an experienced producer and a group of comrades unable or unwilling to undertake open-platform work, a similar step should be taken *in consultation with the local open-platform group and the CC.*

Every WTM member should study this resolution, and become completely familiar with the line of action it expresses. The statements of the first paragraph must not be allowed to remain pious aspirations. We must get down to the job of improving the sketches we use, and the way we perform them, and make our troupes the most popular and best propaganda force in the whole of the workers' movement.

This is the chief lesson of the Olympiad.

(Source: WTM *Bulletin*, September–October 1933)
TOM THOMAS

The London Show (1934)

I think it is necessary to go to basic principles and to ask ourselves '*Why* have plays at all and what is the intent of them?' Of course one has them for entertainment. That is obvious. If they were not entertaining, nobody would listen to them. But in any case entertainment, trivial, passing entertainment, is never the only thing about a play, or very rarely. The play makes an impression on one that remains to some degree after many weeks or months or years. Seeing any play of deep meaning or reading any book of great significance changes one's whole outlook to a slight degree. So it must be with the WTM plays as far as the effect on the working-class audiences are concerned. The thing to ask oneself, then, is – 'What effect is left upon me by such and such a play after several weeks or months have passed?' Not merely, – 'What do I superficially remember of it?' but rather 'What emotional effect did it leave upon me after the lapse of time?'

Applying this criterion to the sketches performed last in Bermondsey, I should give the following opinion. And note that I am trying to identify myself with the simplest worker in the audience.

Gas is still merely an allegory with symbolic figures in it, but it is good in some degree within those limits. It gives the sense of a wide destruction like a Day of Judgment in which *my* class is finally triumphant and the only thing that *is* triumphant. That is all right. It is good to sear into the heart of every worker that *he* is the real fellow – *he* is the class that counts. But, of course, *Gas* alone would be inadequate. One wants other plays of the same kind showing the same lesson from different angles. I would not call it realistic except in so far as the stage is set and the characters dressed and made-up for the parts. But that does not alone make realism or 'representationalism'. The characters are, as I say, typified. They symbolize great social forces – even the drunk and the prostitute.

I think, as others have thought, that *The Great Deception* was in any case overcrowded and confused. The business of getting everything in is fatal. Even in a speech, it is better to err on the side of simplification than of over-elaboration. It is certainly so of a play. The writer must, in imagination, sit in the audience and see what the effect will be. There was a mixture of symbolism and realism that is most confusing. You can't do it like that. You cannot mix up a realistic Hitler and Blackshirt with a symbolic capitalist and journalist. And especially one must not, in such a case, duplicate the parts, since it tends to leave the audience in utter confusion as to who is who. The scene with the capitalist etc. ought to be cut out, I think. The rest simplified and humanized.

The best moment of the whole evening was the scene where the unemployed man puts the revolver to his head. I am not talking about the acting or the style. That may or may not have been as good as it might be. The point is, that first you had a man filling the same part throughout the piece, thus breeding no confusion, and second, and most important of all, the writer had hit upon a real dramatic moment of fundamental conflict and had handled it not too badly. Now the point is this. I spoke in the beginning of the *effect* left by a play on the mind. What effect does one want to produce? You have numbers and numbers of men and women nowadays, whose minds are in profound conflict. What conflict? The conflict between the growing working-class consciousness and courage and determination, that is everywhere striving to break through the husk of individualism, timidity, despair, suspicion that has been built up about the mind by capitalism and by reformism. This conflict goes on in every worker all the time, if in a sense unconsciously and not clearly seen for long periods. But what effect one has to produce by the play is now plainly seen. One has to strengthen the true working-class side of the conflict, and so undermine and break down more and more the crust and husk of capitalist thought that still keeps it in check.

How to do this on the stage? By showing each member of the audience 'himself' on the stage – 'himself' in one of those moments of great emotional conflict that come or may come to any man. Here in the scene with the revolver was one such case. Shall I give way to despair and take the utterly individualist way out by shooting myself? Or shall I take the path of boldness and by common struggle with my fellows win through? The problem is at times a most desperate one. But what we have to do is to show the worker *himself*, i.e., some character with whom he can identify himself – and to let him *feel* the conflict working itself out before him.

I say, this question of presenting in simple realistic terms the varying forms of *conflict* in the worker's mind, should be one of the absolutely basic types of WTM drama. The WTM must become quite conscious of this and must take up the task quite systematically. First of all, our dramas must be very simple with few characters, and these carefully trained and realistic in method. Then later, when we have trained ourselves to write and play the simple 'bones' of the conflict-drama, we shall find that we can handle the form more and more capably and elaborations will begin to suggest themselves.

But first we must become primitive in our approach.

What is the precise form of this conflict-drama? The basic form is this. That a human being is shown on the stage in the first stages of a great emotional struggle between 'good' and 'evil', if you like to phrase it like that. Slowly the conflict deepens. The audience begins to hold its breath, as the conflict on the stage more and more represents the conflict in the heart of each man there. Then at last 'good' triumphs. The 'temptation' is hurled backward and the man rises to fresh determination, courage and consciousness. The effect on each member of the audience can be very profound. It can mean that, in a sense, his own problem has been solved for him by the resolution of the conflict on the stage. It can mean that he never completely forgets the lesson he has had scorched into him that evening, – even if only in a drama. That is what actually is meant by 'propaganda.' Observe any of the great Russian films, and see whether the conflict and the resolution of it is not in every case present and is the soul of that film. The significance of every one of the films, or almost every one, is the final triumph of working-class consciousness and courage after a struggle against the old bourgeois doubts, moralities, fears, selfishnesses and so forth.

Now as to some suggestions of the subject for a few simple dramas of this kind. They should in every case be worked out with great care.

1 An unemployed worker. His wife is miserable and cannot understand. She leaves him. He turns away. The foreman from a factory enters. 'Hullo, you want a job, Jack?' 'Yes, mate.' 'There's a job going at Smith's Works.' 'How's that?' 'There's a strike on.' He is being tempted to blackleg. Subtly, bit by bit every argument is brought up to him by the foreman. The audience begins to feel

his mental agony. He almost yields. Then suddenly his consciousness reasserts itself. He defies the tempter. The true reasons why he will *not* blackleg, why he *must not* blackleg, become clear to him. He states them clearly, 'You'll never get a job again, Jack,' says the foreman. 'Well,' says he, 'I can't help that. I can't let the boys down . . .', and so on.

2 A young unemployed worker is tempted to join the army. All the usual arguments are subtly and cunningly brought forward and once again the audience feel the genuine struggle in the mind of the worker.

3 The problem in the mind of an employed worker as to unity between employed and unemployed. This is a very vital matter at the moment, when the question of a strike of employed workers in defence of the unemployed against the new Bill is very much under discussion. Here it must be a matter of visualizing the unemployed workers being actually sent off to labour camps and the question of strike being brought up to the employed workers.

4 A worker is arrested and tempted to say that he will give up active agitation and that then he will probably get off, whereas he may get a year for the offence.

5 The problem of the two ways out, suicide or mass struggle, can probably be dealt with under various circumstances and in various ways.

Other suggestions and subjects will occur; but these are a few. I think the costume should be quite realistic and simple – none of the get-up worn by various of the troupes. There is no reason why the plays should not be performed anywhere or almost anywhere. But they do require most careful writing and rehearsing. Here it will be extremely valuable to have professional coaching, so that every word and gesture gets across the audience.

(Source: WTM *Bulletin*, April 1934, pp. 12–16)
F. CLARK

Agit-Prop or Naturalism – which? (1934)

Foreword
There is much confusion, I find, as to the meaning of the terms
– 'Agit-Prop' and 'naturalism'. Before commencing my article,
therefore, it would perhaps be helpful if I defined what I mean
when I use these terms in the following pages:

> *Agit-Prop*: The form of sketch which can be used as effectively
> on the street corner as in the meeting hall or theatre; dispenses
> with props, lighting effects, costume, make-up, etc.; has no
> subtle characterizations, but mainly symbolic types; and
> makes extensive use of the mass chorus.

> *Naturalism*: The conventional, straight, 'true-to-life' method.
> The method mainly used by the bourgeois theatre.

'The mistake you WTM people make', said a member of the
professional stage to me, in arguing against Agit-Prop, 'is to try
to accomplish two revolutions at once, a revolution in form and
a revolution in content.' He went on to explain that because the
ideas we present are new, and therefore difficult to grasp, the form
in which we present these ideas should be one to which the audience was accustomed, i.e., the naturalistic form. Later I repeated
this idea to the WTM organizer. He retorted, 'Don't you realize
that a revolution in content *demands* a revolution in form?'
    Since then I have given a good deal of thought to this question,
and have decided that although the views expressed above are
diametrically opposed to one another, neither is correct; and for
the following reasons:
    Under capitalism, the Workers' Theatre can achieve neither a
revolution in content nor a revolution in form. A different slant
on life is presented, yes; different conclusions drawn; a different
direction given – the working-class point of view, conclusions and
directions as against the bourgeois view of life, conclusions and
directions. Under capitalism there can be a change only in the
character of the content, but no *revolution* in content. When the
working class has seized power, culture in general, including

drama, will become increasingly and rapidly the medium of work-ing-class expression. Quantitative changes will leap forward, changes in dramatic, scenic and productive forms will take place. But only after the last vestiges of capitalism have disappeared for ever can there be a *qualitative* change in content or in form, or will there be a *revolution* in content and dramatic and productive forms.

Let us also undeceive ourselves of the notion that Agit-Prop is a revolutionary form, or a new form at all. The method we know under the name of Agit-Prop was used extensively in the ancient, earliest days of the theatre; and more recently, in our own time, by the bourgeois theatres, Bluebird and Chauve Souris. These theatres have, however, developed Agit-Prop to a much higher level than we have. I quote from a friend's description:

> These theatres present in song, in verse, in dance and in drama not only 'slices of Russian life' – pre-Revolution – but also episodes in Russian history – also pre-Revolution: naturally from the bourgeois point of view and also from the ultra-modern artistic. Latterly they added to their repertoire many non-Russian subjects and have become increasingly non-realistic. None of their presentations take longer than fifteen to twenty minutes.

Next let us glance at some of the best examples of our own Agit-Prop work: *Aufruf* (Yiddish), *Meerut*, *Strike! Aufruf*, a mass recitation with action calling on the workers to defend the Soviet Union, always won an enthusiastic reception. *Meerut*, the story of the infamous trial of English and Indian trade unionists, never failed to hold its audience spell-bound. But perhaps the most stri-king instance of the value of Agit-Prop, from the point of view both of propaganda and entertainment, can be found in our experi-ence of Michael Gold's *Strike!* During one performance, at the point where players, mingled in the audience, cry in unison, 'We are hungry. Give us bread!', members of the audience were turning to each other and asking, 'Do we have to join in? Do we have to cry out also?' It is obvious that although the ideas expressed in these sketches were unusual, the fact that the form in which they were presented was also unusual did not make the ideas any more difficult to grasp.

I have heard opponents of the Agit-Prop method, in arguing for its abolition, describe Agit-Prop as 'a set of young people in a row shouting meaningless slogans at an indifferent audience.' This argument proves only that both the people who use it and the groups they refer to have failed as yet to understand the meaning of Agit-Prop and its vast possibilities.

And now we come to the other side of the shield – the aversion that exists in the WTM to the naturalistic method. This aversion seems to me to be based on two facts:

First, that this form cannot be used in the street. What of it? Only part of our work is done on the street. The rest lies in meeting-places, and concert halls. The good work of the Rebel Players (naturalistic group) in *Gas, The Fight Goes On, People's Court*, etc., has proved that a naturalistic sketch can be produced with a minimum of props etc., so there can be no objection of expense.

Second, that the naturalistic is not a revolutionary form. Of course it isn't. Neither is Agit-Prop. Neither is symbolism. Neither is any other form we may name. Not until we have a revolution in content can we have a revolution in form. But for goodness sake don't let us worry our heads about that. At the present stage of our development *there need be no difference between the bourgeois theatre and ours, except the difference in content.*

The revolutionary theatre does not evolve a revolutionary form out of nowhere. *The revolutionary theatre grows out of and develops from the bourgeois theatre.* I will support myself in this attitude by quoting from the writings of a person whose ideas we all respect (*Lenin*: Draft Resolution on Proletarian Culture and Address to the Youth):

> Unless we clearly understand that only by studying the culture created by the whole development of humanity can we build a proletarian culture . . . Proletarian culture is not something that has leaped out of nowhere; it is not an invention of those who call themselves experts in proletarian culture. That is all nonsense. Proletarian culture should be the systematic development of all the stock of knowledge which humanity has accumulated amidst the oppression of capitalist landlords and bureaucratic society . . . Marxism won its world-wide significance as the ideology of the revolutionary proletariat, because it did not reject out and out the most valuable

achievements of the bourgeois epoch, but on the contrary, made its own and worked over anew all that was of value in the more than 2,000 years of development of human thought.

Many comrades spend a good deal of time arguing on what has become an ancient theme: *Agit-Prop* or *naturalism*?

To those comrades I say: Stop wasting your time! You are creating imaginary difficulties. You are chasing imaginary bogeys. There is room in our movement for both these forms as well as others we have not yet explored. We must use all the forms at our disposal. Variety will obviate staleness in the players. Variety will maintain the interest of the audience, which in turn will spur on WTM writers and players.

When we have experimented a little further with the tremendous possibilities of Agit-Prop; when we have assimilated a little more of the rich experience of the bourgeois theatre; only then will the WTM be on the road to becoming an effective weapon in the hands of the workers with which to combat the powerful propaganda of the ruling class.

(Source: WTM *Bulletin*, April–May 1934, pp. 9–12)
RAY WATERMAN

Part 5

Proletkult: a view from the Plebs League

Documents

From Ness Edwards, *The Workers' Theatre* (1930)

[Introductory Note: The Plebs League, an organisation devoted to Independent Working Class Education, was a mainly non-Communist organisation of British working-class Marxists. Founded under syndicalist and revolutionary influences before the First World War, it reached its major strength in the 1920s, with a Central Labour College in London, and strong trade union support, notably among the railwaymen and the South Wales miners. Ness Edwards was a Plebs League lecturer and writer (he wrote a pioneering history of the industrial revolution in South Wales), and in later years a Labour member of parliament and a government minister in the Attlee adminstration. Reprinted here are two chapters from his book on *Workers' Theatre*. R.E.S.]

The theatres are still encumbered with the rubbish of the old regime, feeble copies of the masters, wherein art and taste are set at nought, of ideas and interests which are nothing to us, and of customs and manners foreign to us. We must sweep this chaotic mess out of our theatres.

Joseph Payan

The emergence of working-class consciousness in the domain of social life has created a new set of materials for the drama. The struggle between the classes in the form of strikes, lock-outs, political and social conflicts, has also quickened the mentality of the workers. Oppression in industry, the social blackmail of trusts, the smashing of petty industry by large-scale industry, the economic insecurity of the workers and the petty middle class, the commercialization of art and the thwarting of artistic expression, the creation of industrial grime and ugliness – all these manifestations directly affect the human instincts of the sensitive artist. They mould his thoughts and focus his hatreds. An individual can hardly exist within capitalist society without being affected by the struggles arising out of the above manifestations. He cannot be indifferent; he must declare either for or against capitalism.

In these circumstances the question revolves round the retention of power by the capitalists or the conquest of that power by the workers. The majority of society are unaware of the inner meaning of this struggle. Steadily, greater and greater numbers are declaring for one or the other side. Precursors of the workers' drama are projecting their consciousness of this struggle on to the stage. They are leading the way to a workers' drama.

An example of this type of drama is *R.U.R.* ('Rossum's Universal Robots'), written by a Czech, Karel Capek. The robots are machine-made men, produced by the thousands, and sold in all parts of the world to perform the work of the world. They are made on the principle that they have no feelings, or desires. They have no souls, the author puts it. As cheap work machines, they replace the working class. In a remarkably short space of time, the world's birth rate declines in accordance to the economic need of people. A birth during the week becomes a newspaper item; it is so rare. Mankind threatens to disappear through lack of fertility.

Then robots are bought by the various governments to build up the armies. These cheap robots are used to wipe out the larger portion of humanity. But as these robots lack national distinctions, and national hatreds, they combine throughout the world. They are the producers of the world's goods, and the distributors. They have been taught to run the world by the humans. Then they revolt against their masters, and exterminate humanity. The robot revolution is triumphant.

It is interesting to note the views of the different classes upon this play. Each class agrees that the robots are the world workers. The bourgeoisie take it as a lecture on the necessity of not grinding the workers' faces into the dust. Middle-class humanists immediately use it as a text from which they argue that such an international catastrophe can only be avoided by making the workers co-partners in industry. Many workers think of it as a dramatization of revolutionary propaganda.

The problem of the play is not a personal one; it is a class problem in that it marks a great advance on previous drama. It is not the family or the individual which has to be saved, neither is it only a national section. The robots of the world are made to save themselves by a world-wide revolution. Individual revolts of the robots are punished by destruction. There was no individual salvation without general salvation. That in itself is a valuable dramatic lesson for the workers.

But the play, despite its excellent points, has a number of shortcomings from our point of view. Its end is exceedingly disappointing. If it had sounded on a note of revolutionary triumph, say a speech from the leading robot, or a massed declamation, promising the regeneration of the world in a condition of economic freedom, its message to the workers would have been more real and powerful. While the form of the play stresses the revolutionary side of the robots, it does not provide any justification for revolution. Like the robot, the revolution is mechanical. No one with any aversion for revolution would come from the play with that aversion lessened. Again, the revolution seems quite meaningless except for the saying of one robot who declares that he wants to be a master over others. That is not a characteristic of the proletarian revolution. However, this play assists in developing the workers' drama, provided its mistakes are avoided, and its deficiencies repaired.

Ernst Toller, the German revolutionary poet, while in prison after taking part in the Bavarian revolt, wrote the play called *Masses and Man*. This play has considerable interest for the workers, not only for its subject matter, but for its method of presentation. Here again the problem is one of the struggle for the conquest of power by the workers. So little is it a personal problem that the author labels his characters as types: 'The Nameless One', 'An Officer', 'A Priest', 'The Woman', 'Her Husband', working men and working women, bankers, and the 'People's Sentries'. Here the problem is a class problem, and the characters are personifications of class types.

Representatives of the ruling class are placed upon the stage and exposed most bitterly. War finance is the subject of a most cruel satire, and the morality of the financiers is placed on the lowest order.

Throughout this part, the revolutionary spirit is growing. Revolt is decided upon, and a middle-class woman is put in to show the weakness of the middle class in such situations. The revolt is crushed and the rebels are thrown into prison, and gloom and despair grips the rest of the play.

Then arises the mental conflict within the artist. He has not squared his philosophy with the facts of working-class life. Toller projects this unripeness into the mouths of two characters – 'The Nameless One' and 'The Woman'. They debate the right of the workers to use force. The woman revolts against freedom at the price of killing the guard. She is ultimately shot by the officers of the rulers. 'The Nameless One' disappears. This psychological conflict continues without finality, no solution being offered to the points raised. The message of the play is weakened thereby, and indicates that the author has not saturated himself with a truly working-class spirit.

But this dramatization of the doubts within the working class is all very well in its way if it would help the workers to decisions. The hall mark of a real worker dramatist's play is that he has been able to square the action with the conscience. His intellect, his actions, and feelings are then at peace with each other.

Masses and Man is the dramatic projection, through the genius of Toller, of the experiences of the workers in the Bavarian revolt of 1919. This revolt, as elsewhere in Germany, failed largely because the doubtings and indecision of 'The Woman' character in the play possessed the consciousness of the social democrats who held the leading positions. This failing in 'The Woman' however, has been regarded as a matter which troubles many individuals. Rather we should ascribe these weaknesses to the middle-class humanitarians who want to help the workers, but are not prepared to go the length of revolution. If the duel between 'The Nameless One' and 'The Woman' is a dramatization of individual emotions, perhaps the end of 'The Woman' will clear away any doubt as to which is the right point of view. In this sense the play shows up a serious weakness, and assists in its dispersion.

The other play by Toller which has considerable significance for the new movement is *The Machine Wreckers*. It opens with a prologue in which Lord Byron attacks a Bill which is before the House of Lords, which makes the destruction of machinery punishable by death. His attack upon the Bill was a defence of those workers who, in the early 1880s, regarded the machines as destroyers of their livelihood. These workers, known to history as the Luddites, saw the machines discarding adult labour and increasing the employment of child and female labour. Suppleness of fingers took the place of the craftsmanship of men.

The revolt of the workers against this innovation is brilliantly portrayed, and one gathers the general impression that the workers faced a problem too large for their understanding and experience. The follies and ignorance of the workers is explained in terms of bestial oppression and callous conditions.

The overriding theme of the play is indicated in the following lines, put in the mouth of Jimmy Cobbett, who is the only character in the play who possesses any understanding of the role of machines in human society:

> A rich man – Golden Belly was his name –
> With several castles all as big and fine
> As Mr Ure's new house up on the hill,
> Lived with an only daughter he called Joy.
> She wore a golden frock, and played all day
> With golden playthings in a golden garden.
>
> The man was rich, his child called Joy.
> And not far from their castle lived a weaver
> Who also had an only child, called Sorrow,
> A meagre boy with puny chest and legs
> Like sally-rods – a starveling such as thou.

This Jimmy Cobbett, an out-of-work mechanic, was the precursor of the modern class-conscious worker, and Toller makes him the purveyor of a message that only in modern times is being appreciated. Referring to the machines, he declares to the weavers:

It seemed a vampire stretching out its bloody claws to clutch your souls. A god, a devil, chaining you to drudgery. A monster made to lame your bodies, blunt your minds, and foul your honourable trade . . .
   Dreams of the world of justice, dreams of towns and countries and continents linked in common labour, each for all and all for each . . . And the tyrant of machinery, conquered by your own creative spirit, will be your tool and your servant.

In Ned Lud is expressed the faithfulness and sense of loyalty possessed by the whole working class. But the limitations of the workers are not spared exposure, though most of these limitations are shown in conjunction with the conditions in which they have their roots.

By the incitement of John Wibley, another true-to-life type of worker, the tale bearer, posing as an extremist in the pay of the employer, the workers wreck the engine and slay Jimmy Cobbett. Wibley disappears, and Ned Lud, typifying the best that is in the working class, sees through the deception, just as the soldiers hammer on the factory door. And Toller, ending on a note of optimism, prophesying ultimate victory, makes Lud declare the following lines:

> Imprison us! We know what we have done.
> We will pay forfeit for the man we slew!
> But after us will come men better school'd,
> More faithful, braver, to take up the fight
> Against the rightful foe – and they will conquer!
> Your kingdom totters, masters of the world!

This play is real workers' drama. It depicts the class struggle, the class problem; it exposes working-class weaknesses, arouses class emotions, and endeavours to carry its audience with it to make Lud's prophecy become a living fact. The dramatic problem is a class one, and not an individual problem. Class action is indicated for the solution of the problem. The nobility of such action, and the self-sacrifice that will be needed are aptly projected into the character of Lud. More than any other play of Toller's, *The Machine Wreckers* passes the test of real workers' drama.

Of an entirely different character is the play of the Capek brothers, entitled *And So Ad Infinitum*, generally known as *The Insect Play*. The form of its social criticism is both novel and arresting. The peculiarities of types of the social classes are projected into the activities of butterflies, beetles, and ants. These activities are made to pass before the eyes of a tramp, who happens to be resting in a wood.

In the first act, the follies of my 'Lord Alf' and 'Lady Rose' are typified in the activities of butterflies. The foibles and decadent affectations of 'high society' are pilloried in no uncertain manner, and are made objects fit only for spanking. Constantly in search of novelty, bored with their flimsy pleasures, insincere to the core, the society butterflies appear the least excusable ornament in society.

The second act, called 'Creepers and Crawlers', is an exposure of the folly of the capital misers. Two diligent beetles are made to roll about with them a heap of muck, which they call their capital. This ball of dirt is viewed with delicious awe by both of them; it had been the dream of their lives to own such a stock. But alas, some other beetle comes along and steals the precious capital, and leaves them to wail about their loss for the rest of the play.

The folly of war is the theme of the third act. One ant heap is made to do battle with another over the possession of a yard of mud between two blades of grass. The patriotic speeches usually made in human wars are placed in the mouths of the ant leaders. How familiar sounds the following dialogue, and equally how false:

2ND ENGINEER (ANT): Ha, ha! Lords of creation!
CHIEF ENGINEER (ANT): We are the Lords of creation!
2ND E: Ha, ha! Masters of the World!
CHIEF E: We're the Masters of the World.
2ND E: The Ant Realm!
CHIEF E: The largest Ant State!
2ND E: A World Power!
CHIEF E: The largest democracy!
CHIEF E: Against all.
2ND E: We are surrounded by enemies.
CHIEF E: We defeated the Black Ants –
2ND E: And starved out the Brown –
CHIEF E: And subjugated the Greys, and only the Yellows are left; we must starve out the Yellows –
2ND E: We must starve them all out.
TRAMP: Why?
CHIEF E: In the interests of the whole.
2ND E: The interests of the whole are the highest.
CHIEF E: Interests of race –
2ND E: Industrial interests –
CHIEF E: Colonial interests –
2ND E: World interests –

Then comes the justification of this war with the Yellows. This yard of mud is the only road to the south. It is a question of prestige and trade, and the rights of nationality. The projected war is made an honourable duty; everything is prepared, only a *casus belli* is required to commence operations. This arrives in the usual way, and the ants rush to fight to the accompanying noise of the speeches of their patriotic leaders. During this running fight the commanders pray to their beetle god for help, and the Chief Engineer even makes the ant god an honorary colonel when victory is in the air. But the promotion of the ant god is a little premature, for immediately comes the news of the all-conquering Yellows. The Yellows' commander takes the stage, the others are driven off or killed, and this commander then proclaims himself ruler of the universe. Then on his knees he goes and prays to his god:

> Most righteous god of the Ants – thou knowest that we fight only for justice, our victory, our national honour, our commercial interests.

The tramp is so disgusted that he crushes them under his heel, exterminating them. Thus ends the struggle for the path between two blades of grass.

In the epilogue, all this stinging social criticism is brought together. The tramp is dying; the butterfly still chases his love; the beetle still wails about his muck heap, his capital; the wounded soldier-ants groan for water; the chrysalis, who prated of the power of re-birth, leaves his sheath and flies into a flame and dies; and two snails pass philosophically on their way.

In this brilliant fashion the comedy and tragedy of life is placed upon the stage. It will be gathered that this play does not dramatize the class struggle, but deals rather with the struggle between persons and between nations. The dissipated society habitué, the wealth-hungry persons, and the war mongers all look as foolish as in truth they may look. But despite this brilliancy of the play it has little to offer to the worker dramatists. It criticizes types in society; it exposes human weaknesses, and seems to stress a moral that struggle is not worth while. Though it is essentially critical, it is not creative. Problems of society are not even indicated, and the play in its ultimate effect is inclined to be depressing. While an old biblical character referred to this world as a vale of tears, the Capeks seem to regard it as a vale of petty frivolity and foolishness. Emancipation and effort do not lie along such a road, and for that reason alone this Capek play cannot find a place in the Workers' Theatre.

★   ★   ★

Away with wreckage of past nations!
Enslaved crowd, rise at the call!
The world shall change from its foundations;
We that are nothing, shall be all.

The International

Briefly we have traced the evolution of dramatic art, and indicated the trend of modern drama. We have contended that this art is, and has been, mainly class art and class propaganda. Consciously or unconsciously, the dramatist has propagated the cultural point of view of a class. In that sense the drama has been propaganda. Further, it has been noted that the theme of the drama has changed in conformity with the changes in the class relations of society. As social power has changed from one class to another, so, too, has the drama found its heroes among the new class. In this way the drama has been an expression of social feeling and thought used by the classes whose relations have been determined by economic conditions. Thus it has been a function related to economic development. There remains for us to state our conception of the Workers' Theatre.

For the workers, the external condition of the theatre is entirely secondary. It is the matter of the plays that has chief importance. Just as workers will attend propaganda meetings in any old hall or on any street corner, we feel that they will attend at any place, providing the play has the right message. While tip-up seats at low prices are desirable, the workers have had to huddle in hard-benched, draughty galleries. If the many workers will wait hours in queues to see the type of play that is now being acted in the capitalist theatre, how many discomforts will they endure to see plays that have some concern with their own lives? In any case, in our opinion, the workers will not develop their drama through the commercial theatre; it will develop mainly through the many amateur workers' societies, doing their drama in labour halls, club rooms, hired concert halls, and in the open air. To us, the bourgeois considerations of cheap comfortable seats, all bookable, are merely reforms for the bourgeois theatre, and do not concern the Workers' Theatre.

Because of its theme and object, the workers' drama will be left entirely to the workers.

Romain Rolland says that the first condition of the new theatre is 'that it must be a recreation'. But a re-creation of what? If its first condition is that it must entertain or amuse, we say it will fail as a workers' theatre. If it re-creates the enthusiasm for carrying on the workers' fight, it will succeed. Enough it is that in the main the commercialized theatre has been degraded to a form of neurotic amusement. The workers' drama must have the workers' cause at heart; it must be the battleground of new ideas; in this way it enters the workers' struggle for life, and becomes alive, pulsating with the battle of life. *It must be a source of energy. It must borrow social energy by dramatizing the social struggle; it will then supply energy to carry through the social struggle.*

To consciously place the social struggle upon the stage does not necessitate that the plays shall be tales of woe and sad despair. Seriousness should be distinguished from sorrowful dirges. Exalt-ation can be achieved through laughter. Shakespeare and Shaw have achieved so much; so that the workers' theatre ought to be a place of healthy joy and working-class confidence. The workers' drama should be such as to make the workers glow with creative hope in exactly the same way as they do when listening to the best workers' leaders.

The effect, of course, is determined by the object of this drama. And the effect can be discerned more in the matter than in the housing of the drama. This little work started off by pointing out that the social function of the drama was to organize the feelings of society for a more vigorous attack upon the social problems. It did this by dramatizing these problems. The problem was placed upon the crude stage and practised. This was participated in by the whole of the people. Later it became the cultural justification of class rule, and instilled confidence in the ruling class to maintain their rule. The subject classes were 'warned off' by the exaggerated dramatized powers that were placed before them. How to make this art function in the interest of a rising class is our problem. We must aim to produce drama that will have an effect upon the workers just as such a patriotic play as *Seven Days' Leave* had upon the war-mad population. In other words, how are we to make the drama part and parcel of the class-struggle?

In the first place it must dramatize our problems and place them before our eyes upon the stage. The problem is then clearly seen. More than that, it must express our attitude towards that problem, and show the justification for that attitude. For instance, at a public meeting some time ago, a worker asked the speaker if a dramatist put a bourgeois happy family upon the stage, would not the dramatist be portraying the truth? To this we reply that it is only a half truth. To give the whole truth it would be necessary to place opposite the joyous bourgeois family the misery of the working-class family which is the reason for the bourgeois joy. Then we get back to the old definition that the drama must hold up the mirror to society. But the way the mirror is held is determined by the holder, and we want it held so as to show the whole truth. Our drama, then, must mirror the class struggle, the injustices, the oppressions and miseries of society. To merely reflect these things, however, is not enough. We are not sentimentalists. The cause of these struggles must be exposed to the light of day, with the view of creating and organizing that enthusiasm and knowledge which will work for its removal. In other words, the workers' drama must be a means of organizing the working class. It must be continually putting clear-cut pictures before them of the problems of their own lives. This will not only enthuse them, but will show them the cause of their troubles; it will make them realize their economic brotherhood, and will indicate common action for common troubles. But it should go one step further and indicate upon the stage the solution to the problems. In this sense it would give a lead to the working-class movement, and would dramatize the leads that exist. Thus the cause, the effect, and the solution, would be placed clearly before the workers, providing an object lesson in working-class tactics. In this way the workers' drama would be a means of education, a mental stimulant.

The Workers' Drama is an agitational force. It is propaganda by a dramatization of facts; only the projected solutions are debatable or represent opinions.

The object of the workers' drama is to organize the working class for the conquest of power, to justify this conquest of power, and arouse the feelings of the workers to intensify this struggle. In addition, it has to make plain that this struggle is being carried on for the purpose of saving the working class, and consequently humanity. Its object is to abolish wars, misery, poverty, and the many evils that stand over the working class like thousands of Damoclesian swords. Whilst recognizing the economic force behind the movement, the movement must be spiritualized and idealized. It must be dramatized as the world's greatest mission; it is the finest movement the world has ever known. That is the object of the workers' drama.

In fulfilling this function, the worker-dramatists have not only to select material which is suitable to the general theme, but have to present these materials in a very simple manner. In contrast with capitalist drama, the settings and scenic effects have to be entirely subordinated to the theme. No reliance can be placed upon beautiful costumes and sensuous females. The simplicity of the scenes will not only allow all attention to be centred on the play, but will make local production much easier.

The concern of the play should not be so much with personal problems as class problems; not so much with idealizing leaders as idealizing the rank and file. The differences inside the working class should be subordinated to the general unity of the workers. All the points of degradation should be subordinated to bringing forth the wonderful potentialities of the workers. Each failure which is dramatized should end with a note of optimism presaging ultimate victory. To explain what we mean – there is a certain Welsh play which ends with the singing of a funeral hymn. The character's hopes and ideals of the play had come to the grave, and the theme ended in dust.

Workers' drama must hold out the hope of ultimate victory; each defeat should be dramatized as a necessary experience to achieve ultimate victory. The conscious worker dramatist will be judged from the standpoint of how far he has dramatized those tendencies which exist inside capitalism, which make for the destruction of capitalism, and the creation of a workers' republic. These simple, direct situations need no enveloping in misty dreams or superstitious wrappings. The more simple this drama is the more easily will its message be understood.

The recommendation of his appeal by the worker dramatist is discerned and accepted by the way he clothes it. The appeal will recommend itself the better for coming from the mouths of worker characters who do not possess the characteristics of slum defectives.

The dramatized worker should represent all that is best in the workers. He must command the respect of his worker audience. He must not be a Shakespearian Bottom nor a Galsworthian Lemmy.

All that quiet unnoticed heroism which exists among the working class must be placed in the limelight; that heroism where hundreds of workers risk the petty vengeance of their employers in seeking to make their comrades' lives happier and easier. This form of heroism has not yet been realized by the workers themselves. This form of drama is bound to help in the great adventure of building up the new order of society.

The subject matter of this new drama can be divided into (1) Historical drama; and (2) Social drama.

On the historical side, a great deal of work awaits the worker dramatist. Just as history itself figures largely in working-class education, so, too, can historical drama be of great help in assisting to teach the lessons of the past struggles. Of course, it is understood that historical drama is recommended not out of regard for the past, but rather that those old struggles of the workers shall help to make plain the path of the development of the workers, and to arouse the moral indignation which helps to drive the movement forward.

Such incidents as 'The Peasants' Revolt', the 'Land Enclosures', the 'Chartist Revolt', the 'Miners' '98 Struggle' and all the historical Black and Red Fridays are of great dramatic importance, and would form splendid rallying points for the workers' enthusiasm. In dealing with these incidents, the sacrifice of the workers should be stressed; the pioneers should be held up with admiration; the justification of their actions should be portrayed; and while these revolts failed it should be shown that they were the springs which started the modern movement. This would be propaganda by example, by deed.

Let us take a concrete example. Take the Chartist Rising of 1839. First show the condition of the miners. Then the clamour for political power on the part of the employers. This could be related to the economic discontent of the miners. The use and creation of the workers' discontent by the employers to frighten the landlords. The divergence of the workers from capitalist political tutelage. The rise of the Chartists, the march on Newport and the defeat. End with an optimistic note, say by making a working-class widow charge her young son's mind with bitter reflections upon the capitalists and military. The son, with youthful vigour, swears to carry forward the task of the workers' emancipation. That seems to us to be the right way to end these historical incidents; they must not be used to damp the workers' ardour.

Regarding the second mass of material which has been incorporated under the heading of Social drama, this relates to the huge mass of material existing in modern social life. If Toller's *Masses and Man* were robbed of its mysticism, and the last picture soul searchings and doubtings were changed to messages of hope, it would form a real workers' drama. Or if Capek's *Robots* only had some justification of revolution, if their revolution had as its object the establishment of an economic democracy, that, too, would be suitable as an indication of what the workers' drama should be.

For the workers' drama, the workers' lives are the best material for conveying the new ideas. The unfamiliar thing is always best explained in terms of familiar things. Strike incidents, unemployment, war, workshop incidents, workers' solidarity, the folly of conservative workmen, the crime of blacklegging, the use of the police and Fascists, the use of universities against the workers' culture, the function of governments, the conquest of power, political trickery, blind leaders, and a hundred and one things, are awaiting the attention of the worker dramatist.

These plays can take the form of satirical comedy, farce, revue of a new type, tragedy and melodrama.

Mr Huntly Carter has made some indicative suggestions of how to construct the new type of drama. He has been considerably struck with the despondency and decadence of the pre-Revolution drama of Russia, and contrasts it with the vigour of life in Russia today. To bring out this contrast, he suggests the following arrangement:

(*Scene: A dismal room in a gloomy farmhouse somewhere in a bleak part of Russia. Outside a variety of noises, suggesting an earthquake, hurricane, blizzard, a snow, hail, and rain storm, etc., all happening at once. Odd rattle of chains to suggest a gibbet, and a howling dog. The room is in semi-darkness, which is increased by the dim light of an oil lamp. Several people sit shivering at a bare table. The door opens with a crash. Enter a small procession of characters representing the Playwrights of Gloom of the pre-war period in Russia. They include Chekhov, Andreyev,*

Dostoevsky, and Tolstoy. Each of the four wears an identity label in the form of the title of a gloomy work: Chekhov, The Cherry Orchard; *Andreyev,* The Seven Who Were Hanged; *Dostoevsky,* The Idiot; *Tolstoy,* Resurrection. *Each carries gloomy properties belonging to their plays. Chekhov, a pistol and hatchet; Dostoevsky, guns, a bottle of prussic acid, and another labelled Dreams and Death; Andreyev, a gibbet and ropes; Tolstoy has a carving knife, and wears a map of Siberia, and so on. They march solemnly round the room and deposit the properties in various places.*)

ALL: (*solemnly and slowly*) We are the Playwrights of Gloom. (*Moving towards the door*) Of gloom! Of gloom! Of gloom! Our Grand Guignol of plays reflects the soul of Russia as it was in the days of the Tsars. (*They strike attitudes of intense melancholy. Pointing to the other characters*) Here are samples of our work.

(*They exit listlessly. Terrific sounds off*)

FIRST CHARACTER AT TABLE: (*drearily*) I'm tired of waiting for breakfast. (*Takes pistol and shoots himself*)

SERVANT: (*enters hurriedly*) The canary has committed suicide in the soup. (*Takes poison and dies*)

SECOND CHARACTER AT TABLE: (*mournfully*) The soup is spoilt. (*Stabs himself with carving-knife*)

THIRD CHARACTER: Dead, and he owes me money. I will hang myself. (*Takes rope*)

FOURTH CHARACTER: Not here, in the shed. (*Third character exits*)

FIFTH CHARACTER: Where's Peter?

FOURTH CHARACTER: In the river.

FIFTH CHARACTER: He must be lonely. I'll join him. (*Exits*)

THIRD CHARACTER: (*re-entering, carrying rope*) The shed's full. (*Throws rope down*)

FOURTH CHARACTER: Try the well.

THIRD CHARACTER: The well's full. It's drier here. (*Puts his head in the gas stove*)

Mr Carter suggests that this principle could be worked out to the necessary length. He then suggests the following for Scene Two:

(*The deck of a Soviet steamer. A rope ladder, a covered hatchway, a circular piece of metal, suggesting a funnel, and a square box with a hole in it to suggest stairs to lower deck. Men seated on hatch playing chess. Another group with musical instruments. A third group surrounds the box on which is seated a commissar, who leads a discussion, in which the mean eagerly join, on the class struggle and how it is entering social life. The discussion over, there is music, songs, and dancing. The scene ends with an assertion of vigorous life in contrast to the death-like atmosphere of the first scene.)*

Whether or not the revue, *Riverside Nights*, has helped to suggest the foregoing, we would not like to hazard an opinion, but the worker-dramatist can learn quite a lot about method from that revue and the suggestions of Mr Carter. We might suggest that a dividing of the stage into two, using the one half first for the gloom, an immediate dropping of a curtain over it as soon as ended, then an instantaneous acting of the second scene would bring the audience tight up against the contrast. This suggestion might be made use of, too, in showing the home conditions of the toilers on the one hand, and the capitalists on the other. It would certainly be an effective contrast, and would indicate the dependence of the capitalist upon the workers. However, these are merely suggestions. The workers' drama will hammer out its own dramatic technique as it develops.

We now see that the drama has functioned in the struggle between the classes. In its most modern phase – the workers' drama – it returns to its ancient function of helping to solve the problems of society. Just as it assisted the primitive communists in conquering the problems that arose between man and nature, it now assists in conquering the problems between man and man. In its primal form it was a social function, a function in which the whole of society participated. Its present tendency indicates a similar participation by the whole of the workers. It is becoming part and parcel of the life of the people, not merely an entertainment for the privileged ruling class.

What the drama was able to do for the Catholic Church, the Guilds, and the ruling classes, it can be made to do for the working class. In doing this it becomes the instrument of the mass of society, it becomes the active expression of every worker. No longer will it be confined to a professional clique, no longer will it be merely an entertainment. It ceases to be the plaything of a ruling class, and takes its place in the class struggle. In this way the drama becomes an agent in the building up of the new order of society.

The Archbishop of Wales has well said that the socialist movement, particularly its Sunday Schools, fails to attract the attention of the young mind because it lacks pageants, colour, and music. In particular has the Catholic Church learned the 'holding' value of the 'deed done', as against that of the 'spoken word'. For this reason have they their masses, processions in church, symbols, and images. And in these dramatic acts each member of the church takes an active part.

Workers, too, can express themselves better in action than in talk; in action (in work) their brotherhood arises; in action they feel the effects of capitalist society; in action they will best appreciate the new ideas.

Therefore, the worker dramatists will march at the head of the workers. They will use their art as a means of instruction and agitation. On the stage they will give the workers' life, and nourish the workers with the heroic quality of their comrades. The theatre, then, becomes a most potent agent in knitting the workers together, and assisting them to understand their problems. This drama will find an echo in the meanest hamlet or village, and will appeal and encourage in whatever place the workers may be found. The energy, talent, and virgin imagination of the workers will create new dramatic forms and expressions. More and more will it intensify our enthusiasm and organize our feelings. In this creative form, egotism and aggrandizement will assume a higher role. The zeal of the individual will inflame the mass; the courage of the one will be transmuted into the courage of the mass of the workers. The individual problem will be seen as part of a class problem; the miner, or other craftsman will see himself as a unit of his class; the oneness of the working class is made triumphant. In this new theatre the workers will find their souls, and their salvation, in the ultimate victory of their class.

Can we afford to ignore this cultural weapon?

(FROM CHAPTER 6)

Part 6

Some origins of Theatre Workshop

Theatre of Action, Manchester
Ewan MacColl

I

As early as I can remember, my mother and father were involved in politics. Specifically they were involved in the politics of the Communist Party, and for my father the politics of trade union struggle. He was a member of the Iron Founders Union which at that time was a craft union; the metal trades were divided into hundreds of different crafts. My father was stomping the country with John Maclean when he was eighteen. He believed in the concept of one big union, not in the idea of the craft union at all. And so he spent pretty well all his working life agitating for the Moulders to become part of a bigger union, which was later to be the Iron Founders Union. And, consequently, he found himself involved in strikes pretty much all the time. At one period he was blacklisted throughout the whole of Great Britain, couldn't get a job in any foundry. They just told him, quite categorically, 'You're on the blacklist!' So he went to Australia to find work there. He worked on a government installation on Cockatoo Island, and organized a strike there during the First World War. He was deported from Australia, and came back to Scotland.

My father was one of that great army of iron-founders who came out of Smith and Wellstood's at the Carron Ironworks in Falkirk. They looked upon themselves as the cream of the world's moulders. And perhaps they were. And although he believed passionately in the idea of one union for all people connected with iron-working, he still had all the kind of hang-ups that you got from somebody who was a craftsman. For example, my mother's sister married a moulder too, but he was a pipe-moulder, and pipe-moulding, according to my old man, was the simplest form of moulding, 'a job for idiots'. And for the whole of my childhood, he never showed any real feelings of friendship for my uncle because he was of a lower status in the craft business. There were all those kinds of contradictions.

Our house in Salford was always filled with political people. It was a two-up and a two-down and it didn't take much to fill it, but there were always people staying there – IRA blokes on the run, fellows who had been distributing leaflets among the armed forces, and the *Soldier's Voice*, this kind of thing. That was in the early 1920s.

My mother joined the Communist Party as well, possibly because my father did, but no – probably out of conviction. She certainly remained in the Communist Party long after he died, for some twenty years after. She was never active in the sense that he was, because she didn't have the same opportunities – she wasn't working in a factory, or in a foundry – she was going out cleaning; office cleaning, cleaning people's houses, taking in washing, and all the things you do when you're hungry.

My father was blacklisted from the whole of the Manchester area after a strike in the moulding shop at Metro-Vickers. Before that he worked for a firm in Pendleton called Hodgkinson's, an old-time iron foundry – dealt with casting, moulding and all the rest of it.

I can remember the time just before 1926 very clearly, when my father was out on strike for eleven months, which is a long time to be on strike. And then the General Strike started, so he was still on strike through the General Strike, and afterwards. I can remember the absolute passion with which that strike was fought. I can remember going as a boy, and taking his lunch to the picket line and I remember being brushed aside, and the shrieks and howls of the pickets and the fighting with police and scabs. And I can remember once, in that same strike, blokes actually breaking into the foundry and me going in with them. I remember my father putting me on a metal gantry, to be out of the way of the fighting; they were throwing things all over the place, all over the moulding shop, you know. Very exciting, and very frightening too, for a small boy. And there was the experience of being taken by my old man to demonstrations. I remember going to the Victoria Cinema in Salford, during the General Strike, to hear A. J. Cook. I remember sitting up there in the gods, with an audience made up completely of trade unionists. I remember the people shouting out to continue the strike. I can remember going on the Sacco and Vanzetti demonstrations in Stephenson Square; I must have been quite young then, because I was born in 1915. That would be, what, 1926 or 1927?

I remember early hunger marches when I was very small; regional hunger marches, with maybe eighty or ninety people on them. And at home there'd be people coming to the house, and my old lady having to find food, although my old man was on the dole. And then the quarrels that would arise afterwards, you know: 'We can't go on like this.' Not because she wasn't sympathetic, but through sheer desperation; she was the one who had to find some way of meeting the situation in a way that he didn't.

I went to a school called Grecian Street elementary school. It had two parts: the central school for the brighter kids, and an elementary school for kids like me. In my part of the school there were eight or nine hundred kids. About 50 per cent were Jewish. The Jewish kids were mostly from the ghetto – at that time in Manchester there still was a ghetto. They were distinctly poverty-stricken Jews; they were the children of families who worked in the waterproof trade, as smearers and all the rest of it. Their living conditions were very little different to ours, their culture was a bit different because their parents were generally refugees from Russia, Poland, Hungary and Romania. Yiddish would be spoken in the homes. Because there were so many Jews in the school, because we shared the same kinds of living conditions, the same kind of economic conditions generally, I don't ever remember any anti-semitism, I don't remember any 'natural', so to speak, segregation of the different groupings at all. I can remember times when the cock of the school would be a Jewish lad, and times when he would be a Gentile lad. I suppose it really didn't matter to us because very few of us ever went to church, or synagogue, or anything like that. We were tough kids, and despised the notion. Anybody who went to church usually went because they were Catholics, and their parents forced them to go.

As a small child I can remember doing plays in the summer months, particularly in rainy weather. One of the kids would say, 'Come into our house, we'll have a play.' And you all collected bits of broken pottery off the croft, and used this as money for admission. If you had a nice bit of glazed pottery where the edges had got worn off through being in contact with a lot of other stones, that got you in the front seats. If you had a piece of white pottery that was still jagged, that got you in the back. There were no seats, really, we sat on the floor in somebody's front room. So you went in, and you made up a play. All I can remember of those plays is running down the stairs of a house with a metal rod, presumably an old stair-carpet rod, picked out of a dustbin probably. And rushing down and fencing with another bloke, and then this other bloke saying, 'Strike, Trelawny, strike true!' I think that was the only line in the play; the only dialogue.

We had a play-reading class at school, which was rather good. Terrible plays we used to read: *The Monkey's Paw* by W. W. Jacobs, a play by J. A. Ferguson called *Campbell of Kilmohr.* I can only remember the titles – can't remember what they were about. This was a tremendous innovation because our school was looked on as a school for the very dull kids, and for a teacher to take the initiative to start a play-reading class was absolutely fantastic. I remember only two occasions in the whole of my school life where a teacher showed that he cared about us as people. One was the fellow who organized that class, he was a professional footballer, played for Bury United, and was the hero of the kids, naturally. He was at school the year Bury got the cup, and you can imagine what that would mean in school. The other was a fellow called Mr Rushworth, and he did something that was unprecedented in my circle, he invited groups of kids to his home once a month. You were introduced to his wife, you had a meal and then talked – he talked to you as though you were grown up. And it was an incredible experience. I only went once, but I've never forgotten. Looking back on it now, he must have been a mild kind of socialist. I remember he lent me a book called *The World of William Clissold* by H. G. Wells.

This guy, he talked to you and made you feel good. Everybody else at school seemed to want to make you feel trash, they really did. Beatings went on all the time. The trick was to show that you weren't hurt, even though you were screaming in agony inside. If you could do that, if you could take massive punishment from the teachers and still not show it, you became the idol of the school. For the last two years that I was at school the cock of the school was a fellow called Isidor Schneider – very tough guy, very brilliant, you know, got a county scholarship to Oxford. Couldn't afford to go, of course, working-class parents, his father was an unemployed smearer who worked in the waterproof trade. But he used to take six on each hand – with a big, hefty teacher laying it on – and his hands would be numb for the whole day, so that he could hardly use them, but he'd smile right through it. And this was how it was.

I was unfortunate from the time I was in standard 3, that was when I was about nine. My father was on strike for a very long period and the teacher I had that year was a woman who hated working-class people. She particularly hated me because my old man was a well-known agitator. So she took it out on me, all the time – ridiculed me in front of the class. We'd been told to bring a piece of fruit for the drawing lesson and I brought an onion, which was all I could get hold of – I whipped it from a greengrocers. She never let me forget it for the whole year. Little things like that can breed a tremendous sense of humiliation.

I was a poor scholar, never passed any exams or anything like that – I was always within third or fourth from the bottom of any class I was in. But I did read all the time. And I'd read a hell of a lot by the time I was fourteen. I'd read Darwin's *Descent of Man* and *The Origin of Species*. I'd read things on the calculus, although I couldn't even do simple arithmetic. I'd read Gogol in the local library, and Dostoevsky, I'd started on Balzac, and by the time I was fifteen I'd finished *The Human Comedy*, all forty-eight volumes. I'd read it so well that when I first went to Paris I could find my way round the city.

My great dream was to become a writer, you know – a playwright, of all things. I suppose it was the influence of my father, who always believed in the power of books. My father – as I've told you before – belonged to the generation who believed that books were tools that could open a lock which would free people. He really did believe that. He wasn't a great reader himself, though he'd read a fair amount, but he was a romantic in many respects, you know, a revolutionary romantic. When he was working, he'd come from the foundry on a Saturday lunchtime, and he'd always stop at the book barrows in Pendleton market and buy me a book. They were the most extraordinary books for a kid! *The Descent of Man* was the first he ever bought me. I was eight. Then he picked up *The Origin of Species* about six months later. Well, I was too young to read them – but by the time I was thirteen I'd read them. In fact I was thrashed for reading one at school by a schoolmaster called Small; he found me reading it under the desk when I should have been reading something else!

Books for me weren't tools, they were a refuge. They were a refuge from the horrors of the life around us. Unemployment is bad enough now; unemployment in the 1930s was unbelievable, you really felt you'd never escape. I lived with the dream of escaping from the poverty, from the greyness, the blackness of everything, from the despair all around (and there was real despair), but never really believing it could happen.

So books for me were a kind of fantasy life. Books, however abstruse their theories were, were an escape. For me to go at the age of fourteen, to drop into the library and discover a book like Kant's *Critique of Pure Reason* or *The Mistaken Subtlety of the Four-Sided Figure* . . . the titles alone produced a kind of happiness in me.

I fell in love with books. When I discovered Gogol in that abominable translation of Constance Garnett with those light-blue bindings (I can remember them to this day), I can remember the marvellous sensation of sitting in the library and opening the volume, and going into that world of Akaky Akakievich Bashmachkin in *The Overcoat* or in *The Nose*, or *The Madman's Diary*. I thought I'd never read anything so marvellous, and through books I was living in many worlds simultaneously, I was living in St Petersburg, and Paris with Balzac, I really was. And I knew all the characters, Lucien de Rubempre and Rastignac as though they were my own friends, and the same with all the others. And then when George Poole introduced me to Engels, to *The Peasant War in Germany*, I thought, 'Christ, here it is, this is what I've dreamed all my life', but put clearly, explicitly, so that one could follow the arguments with ease. And then from there to the *Origin of the Family*, for me the world had suddenly kind of become a great flower, everything began to co-relate – not completely, but it *began* to co-relate. It really wasn't until I was twenty-five or twenty-six that everything fell into position like the pieces of a jigsaw puzzle. Then I really began to think as a Marxist.

II

Life in our street was punctuated by all kinds of quite extraordinary events. For example, when a fellow from the bottom of the street cut his throat. All the kids were standing outside the house as the body was brought out by the police. I can remember Marsdon, who lived almost diagonally across from us. He was a carter for the railways, and treasurer of his union branch. His wife was known as 'Mrs John Bull' in the street, because she always displayed a Union Jack on fête days, Coronations or Silver Jubilees. My aunt had christened her 'Mrs John Bull'. She was an obsessive gambler and she found the union dues and put them on a horse and it lost. So he killed himself by attaching a rope round his neck to the mangle, and turned the handle till it broke his neck. I can remember the man at the bottom of the street, Houghton, being brought in with his lungs burnt out after he'd been in a rolling-mill explosion. It happened at Anaconda Copper.

And I can remember things like the great bonfire nights when the kids would organize in gangs and you'd raid each other's territory, and you'd tear each other's back-doors off their hinges. Our next-door neighbours, the Martins, would get pissed and bring out the bits of furniture they had and burn 'em rather than see the fire go out. Martin was a labourer in the Steel Works at Partington. And I can remember our house being raided, by the cops . . . coming home from school and not being able to get in because the house was surrounded by police. There was a fellow lodging with us who'd come down from Falkirk. He'd been one of my old man's apprentices, and was now wanted for incitement to mutiny – he'd been distributing the *Soldier's Voice* among the troops.

The kinds of things we used to do as small children! We'd make forays over to the docks which were one or two miles away. And we'd climb an eighteen-foot wall, and steal a barrel of apples, get it over the wall with ropes; I can remember going to the railway and actually digging up railway ties for bonfire night and being chased by the police. I remember, during the General Strike, spending days and days on the waste-tips of Agecroft and Pendleton pits, picking coal to take home, going out collecting wood; great heavy railway ties stacked along the canal-bank, they must have weighed a quarter of a ton and there'd be twenty kids dragging one of these through the streets on a rope. Or through the back streets, really, because if you were caught you were in trouble. You had to develop a sense of community, you had to develop loyalties, otherwise you just didn't survive, you couldn't survive. You were broken.

Of course there was tremendous entertainment in the streets,

tremendous theatre in the 1920s and 1930s. From way back I can
remember the streets having one long succession of performers.
This was particularly true during the period from 1929 to 1933,
when there was mass unemployment everywhere. In the summer
months, particularly in good weather, the street singers would
arrive at about 11 o'clock in the morning, and, you know, street
singers had the technique of making the verse of a song last all the
way from the bottom to the top of the street. The idea being that
you don't sing too fast, because if you do you can't catch the eye
of anybody who comes to the door. You catch the eye of somebody so that they'll feel embarrassed or ashamed if they don't give
you something, this is the theory of street-singing. So you'd get
street-singers, all kinds, soloists, groups of ten, twelve, fourteen,
fifteen Welsh miners singing things like 'David of the White Rock'.
You'd get choirs of fishermen from Grimsby and Hull. Because
there was tremendous unemployment among the trawlermen and
the fish-gutters, who worked on the docks. So they'd come, and
they'd sing songs, usually a mixture of tear-jerking parlour ballads
like 'Come into the Garden, Maud' or 'Just Plain Folk', you know,
that kind of thing, a mixed repertoire. Sometimes they'd have a
little placard which they'd carry with them saying 'We are Unemployed Welsh Miners', or 'Through no fault of our own we have
no jobs, can you help us?' These weren't professional street singers
– they were obviously men who felt embarrassed to be doing this,
because they were singing to people who were as poor as they
were. But it was only from the poor that they were going to get
any kind of help at all. So you had, as I say, choirs, soloists, blokes
who played the bones (rickers we used to call them; these were
two bones held between the fingers to make a noise like castanets,
sometimes they'd have a pair in each hand), fellows who played
spoons, barrel-organ players, you'd have instrumentalists, piano
accordionists, flute players, sometimes a small ensemble. I've even
known guys come round the streets with a piano on a hand-cart
and play that in the middle of the street. There were fellows who
did clog dancing. You had acrobats occasionally – escapologists
sometimes in groups of three or four; two of them would tie the
other two up in strait-jackets and chains and all the rest of it and
they'd be lying on the pavement often in the wet. They usually
got a fair amount of money – when I say a fair amount I mean
maybe 2 or 3 bob.

I've known groups of tumblers come round the streets; Punch and Judy men and fellows with displays. I remember a chap who used to come round with a display of butterflies mounted in a portable showcase that he would show for a ha'penny. I remember the songbook-sellers coming round the streets with the popular songs. A hundred or two or three hundred songs, very, very, poorly printed, all the latest songs. They would go down the streets singing a verse of each of the songs as though it was one continuous song! They sold them for a penny or twopence. And then the kids would sit round on the doorsteps and sing through the book. I can't remember if there was radio at that time – but somehow the songs got around, on gramophone records, I suppose. I learnt hundreds of songs in that way – I probably remember upwards of one hundred songs of that period, absolute trashy pop songs.

About the time I was due to leave school we were really on our beam ends. I'm not saying we were any different or any worse off than others. Perhaps a little worse off because my father was not just unemployed, he was on strike, and the strike pay had gone.

My old lady was going out to work. She left home at half-past four in the morning to clean offices, till 9, then she'd be off at 9 o'clock and go off to clean a big house till 1 o'clock. Occasionally they'd give her scraps of food, which would be our meals. I can't tell you the sense of shame with which one accepted scraps of left-over food. I remember once going to meet my mother and the lady of the house, who was very nice, invited me in – it was a rather posh place. Anyway this woman gave me an old jacket of her husband's and I can remember the feeling of hatred, a hatred so powerful that I was blind walking home along the street – just a red haze in front of me. It lasted for years, that feeling. It wasn't just that particular incident – a lot of things combined to produce that kind of response to society. I really did want to tear down the world in which I found myself, and build a new world, I really wanted to. And later, when I joined the Young Communist League, if I got criticized at meetings, I'd lie and weep at night because I thought I'd done something wrong. I couldn't understand what it was I'd done wrong, very often – often the criticism sessions were ridiculous because you were criticized for doing things in good faith, like bringing in people to join the YCL and later on being criticized by the people who are brought in because I've made them believe the revolution was nearer than it was.

I remember once getting blasted at a district conference of the YCL. A bloke that I'd brought into the branch stood up and really waded into me. He more or less accused me of bringing him into the YCL under false pretences by suggesting that the revolution was about to happen at any moment. I can still remember the sick feeling of betrayal I felt at the time.

When I left school I went to work in a wire factory, part of Anaconda. I was a labourer in the wire-drawing mill; was there for eight months, and then sacked, for cheeking the foreman. The annealing shop in Smith's had hellish conditions; they used to say that men were sent there to die, conditions were so bad. I wrote a couple of songs about it – no, they weren't songs, they were poems. I pinned them up on the notice board – I remember the title of one of 'em – 'The Hundred and Fifty-First Psalm'. It was a kind of cod-psalm, about the department. One of the typists from the office saw it and she typed a score more copies. She got the sack, too. All I can remember about her was that she was called Mabel. When she found out I'd written them, she came and complimented me.

I went on the dole, and I was sent after the odd job occasionally; we knew we hadn't got a chance. You'd turn up and there'd be 150 other blokes, or 200 or 300 or 1,000 or whatever. I remember once going to a cinema that had just been built in Eccles, I was sent there for a job as an usher; there were people who'd been there all night, and there were people who broke into the place so as to be in line for the office first thing Monday. It was one of the modern Odeons, and there were blokes who climbed those bloody great walls and got in the fanlights and crawled down the girders so they could be there in the morning. There was a couple of thousand people there. And I turned up in the morning! By this time it was fairly obvious that there weren't any jobs – or not many. I did get one after a time, a job on a journal called the *Textile Trader*. But it was a dying journal of a dying industry. My job consisted mostly of making innumerable cups of tea and waking up the editor when calls came on the telephone. I stuck that for about four months, then jacked it in.

Then I got a job as a motor mechanic's apprentice – I got fired from that, too, for being involved in a fist-fight with the shop foreman. At that time they didn't pay overtime to apprentices, so you were expected to work all the hours that God sent. You'd start work in the morning at 8 o'clock, and 5 o'clock or 6 o'clock would come, when you were supposed to knock off, and the journeymen would knock off, at least most of 'em would. Those that stayed on got paid for overtime. The apprentices were expected to work till 9 or 10 o'clock. Well I did this for a couple of weeks, and I was surprised to find there was no extra money in my hand, so I went round the other apprentices and tried to get them to sign a petition, and they refused. Well, word got to the shop manager, and one day I was working under a car taking the sump off, when suddenly somebody kicked me in the leg. I looked up and I saw the bottom of a white coat. It's the shop foreman, and he kicks me again. I say, 'Don't kick me'. He says, 'Listen, you little squirt', and starts calling me names. Well, I waded into him. I didn't get up actually. I got hold of his leg, and I pulled and his leg came against the running-board of the car, and he fell bang on his head. Name was Healey. I gave him a real bashing. I didn't only get sacked there, I was told if I showed my face again they'd have the police on me. But that was a rusty old job. After that I was unemployed for a long time. I did occasional jobs – like loading cabbages, did a stretch as a slater's labourer, and I did a bit as a grafter on Sheffield market. I was the guy who got the blankets from under the table and passed them to the punters.

III

Occasionally, when my father was unemployed for long periods, he'd spend time in the Workers' Arts Club. The Workers' Arts Club was in Hyndman Hall, Liverpool Street, Salford. Next to it was a cinder croft, and behind that the main gasworks for Salford. I wrote a song inspired by that scene when I worked in Theatre Workshop. It was called 'Dirty Old Town'.

The Workers' Arts Club was an extraordinary institution. I don't know how it got the name 'Arts Club', because there was very little in the way of arts; it was a three-storey building, with rat-infested cellars. The top floor was a boxing gym – where later a number of boxers were to be recruited into the Communist Party and the YCL. Some of them later went to fight in Spain, people like Joe and George Norman for example – the Norman brothers

– they went from there; they were two welter-weights who had been in the navy. On the floor underneath the gym there was a room that was kept for meetings, and on Saturday political groups would organize dances or socials there. The floor wasn't really fit for dancing – it was absolutely torn to ribbons by people's boots! It wasn't a very big room anyway. But there would be a little band – three or four instruments and people would dance. Downstairs, on the ground floor, there was a bar and a snooker table. There'd always be people playing snooker, and that's where the debates were held, in that room, to the click of snooker balls.

The old-timers would sit there on a Sunday evening. There was a fellow called Jimmy Tilbrook, a great mountain of a man. When I first heard about Dr Johnson I imagined he looked like Jimmy Tilbrook, and for God's sake, when I actually saw a picture of him, he did! A cross between G. K. Chesterton and Dr Johnson. He used to sit there in a special chair that had been made for him, one of those Windsor-type chairs, but about twice the normal size. And he'd sit there and pontificate, and the rest of the old fellows would sit round in a semi-circle and discuss and debate this or that topic. I can remember occasionally sitting on the edge of it and listening, when I was about fourteen, and thinking, 'What a lot of bloody nonsense'. They would discuss Edward Clodd's *History of Creation*, Volney's *Ruins of Empires*, Haeckel's *Riddle of the Universe*. And they'd have passionate debates on Dietzgen. Science and religion occupied a very important part of the talk. But also the mid-nineteenth- and late-nineteenth-century German philosophers would be discussed. The younger elements there, like George Poole for example, who was the son of a docker, would dismiss them as Utopians and not part of the century. And in a way he was right. They were the end of an epoch. Nevertheless it was a valuable atmosphere to grow up in.

George Poole was organizing discussions among his contemporaries, that is, kids from fourteen to eighteen. Among other things he ran a class on the history of philosophy and another on dialectical materialism. Poole lived in a two-up and two-down in West Park Street, Salford. His father had been caught between two shunting-waggons on the docks and his spine had been crushed. So they brought his bed down to the front room and he lay there for the rest of his life in that downstairs kitchen. And we would all go and sit round there, and we'd hear him coughing, we got so used to his coughing that you didn't hear it any more. While George and Larry Finlay tried to take us through the tortuous path towards an understanding of dialectical materialism.

From the time I was thirteen, I was no longer involved merely as the child of my parents, but involved in my own right. I was taking part in George Poole's group from the time I was about thirteen, or maybe from the time I was just turned twelve, no – about thirteen. I was getting interested in the idea of joining a political organization. And when I was fourteen I joined the Young Communist League.

I joined the YCL just after the Workers' Theatre Movement, strangely enough. There wasn't a Salford YCL. I was the first Salfordian to join the YCL – not strictly speaking, since part of the Cheetham ward of the Party and YCL was in Salford, but it was in the Jewish area of Salford, and they tended to go over the other side of the road into Manchester. So the first branch I was in was the Cheetham YCL. We used to meet in the room of the YCL secretary at the time, Mick Jenkins. And they lived below a *Schule* – and we used to meet on Friday evening so you'd see everybody going upstairs to the *Schule* with their kind of yamulkes on and all the rest of it. We'd be going in the back-door to a YCL meeting. And then after the meeting some of us would stay and we'd go in and eat *gefilte* fish – so in a way, those of us who weren't Jews were being initiated into the Jewish way of life as well. That part of it was very rich, it helped one overcome any residual feelings of hostility you might have for people who were in any way different from you. Not that I was ever aware of them.

Joining the YCL really took me away from the street, which was in some ways a bad thing. Before then, I'd lived my life in the street, I knew everybody, knew everybody's family, every door was open to you . . . and there wasn't anything that happened in the street that you weren't conscious of. If somebody had an abortion – you knew. By the time you were four you were able to carry the news. If a woman miscarried, you knew; if somebody died, as soon as you saw the two women going down the street to lay the corpse out, you knew before you'd been told there was a death – you'd recognized all the signs. You knew that you had to rely on yourself a great deal, but also that there was a group you could fall back on. Not your parents, but your contemporaries.

And then, suddenly, to move into a new area of activity, which meant an actual change of milieu, was in a way a traumatic experience. At the time, I didn't notice it. It was about six months after that that I began to notice that I'd lost all my friends. Of course, to some extent, it was because I'd left school – I left at fourteen – as they did. Now they were either working, or they were on the dole, so you wouldn't have seen so much of them anyway. Two or three of the lads I used to meet at the labour exchange when I was unemployed, and later on I managed to get them into the National Unemployed Workers' Movement. Some of them became militants. A guy called Teddy Howe became a local leader; a boy from just down the street who'd never shown any interest in politics all the time I'd known him: he came from a very reactionary Catholic family, but he turned out to be a good lad. So that when I joined the YCL I was suddenly in this new very small world, but learning about a whole lot of new things. I'd read things like *Ten Days that Shook the World* – my father had given me that, and I'd read one or two of Lenin's works at the philosophy class, and I'd read a bit of Marx, and a bit of Engels, but I hadn't experienced the cut-and-thrust of real political work, and real political debate – with people who were in pretty much the same boat that you yourself were in.

In the Manchester District of the Party there were two or three people who had been to the Lenin School in Moscow. You tended to take everything they said as gospel, even when it sounded ridiculous, because they knew, they'd been to a special university, our university, and of course it was everybody's dream to get there. And I remember when somebody was chosen to go, thinking, 'God, that could be me! Maybe it will be me next time . . .' This is how it would go on; everybody felt the same, I'm sure of it. I don't mean all the time, but occasionally. You'd feel that you wanted to get away from the depressing streets, from the greyness, from the unending monotony of unemployment, from the bad grub, from the staleness of life. At least I used to feel that, and I know my mate, Bob, did too.

The Party was growing, slowly, but nevertheless it was growing. It had premises in Great Ducie Street, Manchester, near the old London Road station. The party premises were old when Engels wrote *The Condition of the Working Class in England, 1844.* We had one room on the top of a four-storey flight of rickety stairs, and in this room there was a duplicating machine, a rickety desk, a wastepaper basket and a typewriter.

It was a poky little room, but all the work of the Party was done there and the work seemed to be endless. We were running factory newspapers, like the *Salford Docker*, for example, a duplicated news-sheet – one, two, three, four pages, sold outside the docks to blokes as they went on. At this time dockers went to work on spec. You stood in the quays which was just like a cattle market. And there were catwalks between the quays, and a ganger or 'bummer' would come out and say, 'You, you, you and you!' And there'd be five, ten or fifteen men selected out of several hundred, and the rest would go home. And it was like that every day. A number of strikes had developed, and one in Salford itself, a very successful strike, against this system. The demand was that men should be guaranteed work for a certain number of days each week.

During this period I used to be out at the docks maybe twice a week at the early morning shift – the 6 o'clock shift – and we'd sell papers there until they went in. And then I'd go off to the labour exchange, sign on, leave the exchange, and I'd meet Bob, my mate, and we'd maybe go to the party offices, and help with producing the *Crossley Motor*, which was the organ of the Crossley motor works. Sometimes I'd write little rhymed squibs about an unpopular foreman. Several of these would dot the page in between the more serious articles. I'd do the same for the *Ward and Goldstone's Spark* that was another duplicated news-sheet that was sold outside an electrical component factory in Lower Broughton. I used to write editorials for that as well, because it was reckoned that I lived near there and should therefore have contact with the workers inside. But as almost all the workers were girls, and mostly girls who were older than me, well, the chances of getting to know any of them weren't very good. So I used to go up and hang around outside the factory and chat girls up – and get them to tell me things about which department they worked in, what was the foreman's name, what were the management like, what was the grub like in the canteen; then I'd write an article and maybe make up a song and maybe three or four little lampoons, in rhyming couplets or in Alexandrines sometimes! I'd just learned about Alexandrine verse so I thought, 'All right, get the factory newspaper to print those!'

I must have written hundreds of these things, because I was writing for the *Salford Docker*, the *Ward and Goldstone's Spark*, the *Crossley Motor*. What else was I writing for? The British Dyestuffs Corporation factory at Blackley.

The Blackley division of the British Dyestuffs Corporation was the result of a takeover. It had previously been known as Levensteins, though the change of management didn't affect the hellish smells given off by the place. As a source of pollution, the place was hard to beat. The local kids had a rhyme about it:

> Down in Blackley stands the Dyestuffs
> Better known as Levensteins;
> O, it smells just like a carsey,
> Worse than working down a mine.
> Go to buggery, go to buggery,
> Go to buggery Levenstein!
> O, it smells just like a carsey,
> Worse than working down a mine.

I was doing about five factory papers every week, and helping to duplicate them, and sometimes helping to type them. We had a party typist, but she couldn't keep pace with all the things that had to be done.

In the factory papers there'd be a leading article written about, say, the state of the engineering industry, or some specific struggle that was going on inside the industry. And then the leader writer, if he was good, would relate this not only to the factory but to specific departments inside the factory. Some of this information he would arrive at intuitively or through his knowledge of the politics of the whole industry, some he would arrive at through consultation with whoever had been brought into the branch. Occasionally it would be someone from within the plant – that happened with the Salford Docker, where you got actual dockers writing the editorials. But at first it would be a party member who might be unemployed, who'd make it his business to find out as much as he could about that factory and to interpret it politically. Usually there was an attempt to write some kind of objective analysis of a specific situation. But there'd be all kinds of other pieces, of course, little satiric squibs, lampoons and verses and all the rest of it. These would deal with a little corner of the political picture. A foreman, for example, at Ward and Goldstones, had a reputation for trying 'to have it off' with the girls who worked under him – well, he was lampooned fantastically, and his position would be made very difficult. Suppose his missus got to hear of it! Well, you can imagine. And there were letters of course in the papers, usually phoney ones . . . not the information, just the signatures. You must remember you could be expelled from the AEU (Amalgamated Engineering Union) for being a Red at this time. The selling of the paper had to be done by people outside the factory, at the factory gate. I must have spent a fair amount of time selling at least half a dozen different factory newspapers, outside half a dozen different places of employment.

Now you can't write a four-line squib in formal English to workers who never use formal English; you have to use exactly their terms. Not just an approximation of their terms, but exactly their terms. I remember writing a little rhymed squib about the son of one of the bosses of Ward and Goldstone's who'd become a trainee manager.

I was selling the paper outside the gates when this guy rushed out and grabbed me, and pulled me into the factory yard, and gave me a going over. Well, I got away from him, and the girls were saying, 'What was he getting at you for? It isn't as if you wrote it. You couldn't have written that, you couldn't have known all those things.' That was great.

At lunch-time, me and my mate would make our way to Manchester to Yates's Wine Lodge, where you could get a small Hovis loaf, a bowl of soup and a mug of tea for tuppence. That was lunch, and it always felt great because you were starving by that time. We never took a tram or a bus anywhere, we walked everywhere. And looking back on it we must have covered anything from fifteen to twenty miles a day. Every day.

And in the evenings, rehearsing with the theatre two or three nights a week, or sometimes a district meeting, or a branch meeting, so you never had enough time. By the time I was making for home all the street lights would be out. At that period in the depression certain areas of the town had gone bankrupt, so street lights were out, people were running on paraffin in their homes. So I'd walk through the streets – through those miserable streets – seeing moonlight on the roofs of the factories and houses. Two o'clock in the morning . . . and feeling a fantastic sense of exhilaration, and hope. And saying, 'This is my world! When I grow up, I'm going to tear all this down, I'm going to make something so beautiful and so unobtrusive that men can become human.' I used to stay awake thinking like this – night after night.

Even when you went out with girls, most of your talk was political talk. Very often the girls weren't interested, and who could blame them? You were talking such fucking jargon! But the jargon meant something to you – it was a code that you'd cracked. Politics – there seemed to be nothing else in life, nothing else that was worth a damn.

All the time I was living on a thread of anger which was eating me away. Everything that happened contributed to that feeling of anger and of desperation. Every other Saturday night I used to go out and do my stint, selling the *Daily Worker* at the bottom of Oldham Street, as it comes into Piccadilly. I used to team up with a fellow called Seaman Morris, a quiet, diminutive Aberdeenshire seaman who was in the Salford branch of the Party, and who was unemployed. So we'd stand there shouting 'Read the *Daily Worker*, the only workers' newspaper, read the *Daily Worker*', then we'd walk back to Salford, from the bright lights of Piccadilly, to Salford. Seaman Morris was a kind of 'Jimmy Higgins', the sort of bloke who does all the menial day-to-day jobs, who is never on any committee, never in any position of authority. Once I asked him what it was like being at sea, and he said, 'It's just a floating factory', he says. 'But you canna get away from it at night,' he says. 'Dinna gang to sea, laddie, dinna gang to sea.' Later I went to a party meeting in Hanky Park which was where the Salford group was now meeting. That's the area that Green-wood wrote about in *Love on the Dole*. The party room was an abandoned stable in Hanky Park. And I remember going into that place, and there was a hell of a smell. Well, somebody climbed the ladder up into the straw loft above and found Seaman Morris dead; he'd been dead there for about ten days, he'd died of hunger. There was a kind of pride in him that wouldn't allow him to ask for food, not even his comrades.

IV

About 1929 I met a fellow called Stanley Harrison, an unemployed waterproof worker who came to lodge with us. I shared a bed with him for about a year. He had just become the organizer for an almost defunct Communist Party branch of about twelve people. He had three great passions – Shakespeare, the Communist Party, and *I Pagliacci* which he played on a portable gramophone every Saturday morning. He took me along to meet some friends of his who were in the Clarion Players.

They met in a house in Waterloo Road that belonged to a young couple who seemed very rich to me because they had a parlour. In actual fact they were ordinary working people. Their name was Helman. Both their parents had been Bundists in Russia, and were apparently caught up in that big cultural movement which was built around people like Ibsen and Shaw. They named all their children after characters out of Ibsen's plays. Anyway, it was at their house we used to meet. I can remember very, very, clearly the first time I went there because it was the first time I ever tasted coffee. It was very weak coffee, but it was a completely new taste. I thought, 'God! I'm really living it up now.' They were rehearsing a play called *Singing Jailbirds* by Upton Sinclair. And I was given a part. They said, 'Can you sing a tune?' I said, 'Yes', so they said, 'All right, sing this song.' So I sang:

> We speak to you from jail today,
> Six hundred union men.
> We're here because the bosses' laws
> Bring slavery again.
> > *Chorus*: In California's darkened dungeons
> > For the OBU,
> > Remember you're outside for us
> > While we're inside for you.
> We make the boast no tyrant host
> Can make us bend the knee,
> From coast to coast we make the boast
> of solidarity.
> > In California's . . . etc.

And so on, same chorus as before. It was a very simple play about the jailing of the IWW (Industrial Workers of the World) people in California when they refused to play ball, refused to answer any questions, because they took the line that this is a capitalist court and you can't expect justice in a capitalist court. Some of them were sentenced to four or five years' imprisonment, and the sheriff did all kinds of things like turning hoses of boiling water on them when they sang in the cells. Anyway, this was the theme of the piece.

The songs were an important part of the play. They were very much the type of things that Joe Hill and T-Bone Slim were writing at the time. In fact one of the songs was 'Long-haired Preachers Come out Every Night', Joe Hill's song:

> Long-haired preachers come out every night,
> Try to tell you what's wrong and what's right,
> But when asked how 'bout something to eat,
> They will answer with voices so sweet:
> 'You will eat, by and by,
> In that glorious land beyond the sky,
> Work and pray, live on hay,
> You'll get pie in the sky when you die.'

> Now my boss is a very good man,
> Tries to twist you as much as he can,
> When you go and you ask for a rise,
> He will answer with tears in his eyes:
> 'You'll get a rise, by and by,
> In that glorious land beyond the sky,
> Work and pray, live on hay,
> You'll get pie in the sky when you die.'

> Working men of all countries unite,
> Side by side we for freedom will fight,
> When this world ends, its wealth we have gained,
> To the boss we will sing this refrain:
> 'You will eat, in the street,
> When you've learnt how to cook and how to fry,
> Chop some wood, do you good,
> You will eat in the street by and by.'

I've missed a couple of lines but that was it roughly. It seemed to me that they waffled about an awful lot, rehearsals were social occasions, and here was I, a fourteen-year-old lad full of revolutionary feelings who didn't want to socialize, at least not during working time.

They staged *Singing Jailbirds* at a social organized by the Cheetham branch of the Communist Party. Everybody knew each other – it was an audience of maybe twenty, twenty-five people. And there was I wanting to see the revolution, not only in my lifetime, but before I was twenty! Anyway, I went along for maybe three or four months and then decided this wasn't the way to do it. So I got a couple of friends of mine to join me: two Salford lads. One, my mate Bob, was a young amateur boxer, and another chap, Jimmy Rigby. Jimmy was a fourteen-year-old kid who'd run away from an orphanage, and was dossing in Miles Platting. A quiet kind of bloke but very tough and well able to take it. I think he turned up at a fight at one of the boxing sessions at the Workers' Arts Club. I met Bob hiking – he was killed in Spain in 1938. Anyway they joined the WTM (Workers' Theatre Movement). We finished up with just the three of us being members of it. The original members of the group retired, and left it to the three of us.

We began to recruit. First a couple of girls came into the outfit. One was Grace Seden. She was a weaver from Swinton, and a girl called Blondie, a very good-looking blonde kid. A marvellous walker. She was a great asset. She had a beautiful soft Lancashire accent, spoke really classic dialect. Then another girl that we met hiking introduced her thirteen-year-old sister to us, and she joined as well.

Her name was Flo Clayton. Flo Clayton came from Redbank, which was the toughest area of Manchester. It was one of those areas where traditionally no policeman ever goes alone. It was the Lithuanian area of Manchester. And even when I was a boy, one could go round Redbank in the summer and see children playing naked on the streets, a thing you couldn't see in any other part. You'd see barefoot kids on the streets. She married a kind of middle-class guy who was an accountant, apparently, who did rather well for himself so I'm told. She met him hiking. She was a good-looking kid and he married her, but she stayed good solid working class, you know. She insisted that her sister should get into the struggle, and she more or less bulldozed her into it – this little kid.

Flo Clayton may have been in the Communist Party. At this time the Party was tiny and you could count it on two hands for the whole district, although there were three times as many people who had been expelled. The Party spent a lot of its time expelling people at that time, for all kinds of things. Trotskyism being the main thing, although very few of them had ever read anything about Trotsky.

So we now have five people. But Bob, my mate, didn't fancy theatre work because he wasn't particularly good at it. He was a boxer, with a bent nose and everything. This affected his speech. Very, very, bright, incredibly intelligent; the most voracious reader I've ever met, read everything by the time he was sixteen. But he didn't want to be in the group, so he left, and we got another lad to join who lived next door to George Poole, a guy called Alf Armitt. Alf was a jig-tool-maker's apprentice at Taylor Bros. In the course of time he got passionately involved in the whole thing and in the whole idea of the technique of theatre; he'd probably never been to a theatre. I'd not seen much, I'd seen a performance of that Dion Boucicault thing, *While London Sleeps*, at the Victoria Cinema. I'd also been to see a play when I was at school . . . the whole school had gone to see it . . . a terrible play, though I thought it was marvellous at the time, called *Monsieur Beaucaire*. All I can remember is the kind of lace jackets of the guys, and their swords. Looking back on it, I can't think of anything more inappropriate for kids. It was a kind of nineteenth-century imitation of Restoration comedy, heavily loaded with penny-novelette romance. So that was my experience. I had however been to variety shows. If the old fellow was in a job, we'd go to the Salford Hippodrome or the Palace, and see *Casey's Court*, a very funny show. Or we'd see George Elliot, the 'White-eyed Kaffir', or Nelly Wallace, one of the popular comediennes at that time. It cost ninepence to sit up in the gods. I used to enjoy that – made much more impression on me than *Monsieur Beaucaire*.

Now I saw the theatre simply as a new and exciting form of propaganda, a new and exciting way of giving voice to all your feelings, all your political feelings – all your political ideas. So that when I formed the group out of the old WTM – the group that was to be called Red Megaphones, I knew bugger all about theatre. But I knew a great deal, or rather I thought I knew a great deal, about politics. I knew I didn't know anything about theatre, except that I wasn't impressed with the theatre I'd seen. I thought there must be something better, and I thought that the theatre should become a weapon, it should be something that spoke for all the people like me, the people who'd gone through their childhood with a red haze in front of their eyes: the people who wanted to tear it all down, and make something better.

At that time, we could get out on a Sunday, we could take a

fourpenny bus ride to Hyde, and walk on the Derbyshire moors.
The contrast! The freedom of the moors! The purity and the
cleanliness of everything, including the air, compared with the
place you lived and moved through all your daily life! The contrast
was fantastic. So part of the revolutionary objective was to create
a world that would harmonize with that other one that you enjoyed
so much. And I'm sure this wasn't just true of me. It was probably
at the back of the minds of a lot of the lads and girls that went
walking. About 30,000 a week went out of Manchester and
Sheffield. That's a lot of people.

And it wasn't only the walks themselves, it was the people you
met on them. After a day's walk on the moors you'd come down
to the valley and make for a tea house and order a pot of tea: it
cost 4d. If you wanted a refill they'd refill it with hot water with
a pinch of soda in it to bring out the colour of the used tealeaves.
But it was hot. If it was a big place you'd maybe get as many as
seventy or eighty hikers: boys and girls from Salford, Manchester,
Sheffield, Macclesfield, Stockport, Oldham, from all these places.

They used to run cheap excursion trains to Glossop, and they
were always packed with young workers, many of them unemployed. You could go for 8d on the train, to Glossop or Hayfield.
That meant a day's outing for less than 1/9d. And no longer feeling
that you had to slink round back streets because you didn't have
clothes.

Because that was a problem, too. You were young, growing
up, but you were unemployed, and the nine bob you got on the
dole wouldn't feed you, let alone get you new clothes. It wasn't
like it is today, where a pair of jeans and a T-shirt is all you need.
At that time, a decent suit showed that you belonged to society.
A working fellow in a job would always have a good suit. It's
true he didn't use it except on Saturdays and Sundays, or at
weddings, at funerals, at Christmas and New Year, but he had
that good suit. But when he became unemployed, the suit went
to the pawn, and he finished up with anything he could get –
reach-me-downs from anywhere. I used to go around at this period
in a jacket which had been given to me by this lady my mother
worked for – it belonged to her man who was about six foot-
three! I was still a boy, and it came down to my knees; I was very
conscious of how absurd I looked, and I wore shoes that were size
10s and 11s. I know when I was an adolescent I had dreams of

finding a girl, but the girls laughed at you when you looked like the way we looked. So that after a time you began to keep to the back streets, you didn't like to be seen on the main streets. Perhaps I'm exaggerating a little, but I know that for many years I felt something like that.

In the country it didn't matter. All you wore was a khaki shirt and a pair of shorts. You bought your boots at an ex-army store. And you could live as you liked. You could thieve, as we used to. We learnt to poach grouse. We'd take the feathers off and gut it, mix it with salt and pepper, and bash it with a round stone into a paté. And it was gorgeous. And you suddenly felt, 'Christ! I'm master of my environment.' And at Easter we'd go out into the Derbyshire dales and we'd rob hen-cotes. We'd make pancakes, and if we had hundreds of eggs we'd make enough pancakes so that we could sell them by the roadside to other passing hikers for a penny each! Primitive capitalism at work! And it really was – the contrast was fierce. If the bourgeoisie had had any sense at all they would never have allowed the working-class youth into that kind of countryside. Because it bred a spirit of revolt.

Anyway, to go back, I formed this Agit-Prop group from the WTM. Very keen we were, very clear about what we wanted to do. I'd met somebody who'd been in Germany and seen the Blue Blouses there – a very big movement in Czechoslovakia. I can remember one of them was a Russian girl. All that I can remember about her is that she was known as 'Comrade Ludmilla'. And – this is almost unbelievable – she had been sent over by the Communist Youth International as a courier to make a report on the state of the peasant movements in Europe. And she came to – amongst other places – Manchester to study the peasant movement in Britain. And she came to Salford. I met her at a café – Lockhart's café. It was raided by the police the same night she was there – she escaped through a lavatory window . . . she was marvellous at escaping. The word had got through that she had no passport – or she had dozens of passports, I don't know which it was. Anyway she was there illegally. I remember her telling me about these groups that she'd seen in Germany and Czechoslovakia. She told me what they did, how they had megaphones and how they would appear on a street and do a very short political piece. This stuck in my mind as something absolutely marvellous. Comrade Ludmilla wasn't here to give instructions. She wasn't doing anything that was illegal, really. But she was here illegally. Relations with the Soviet Union were not good at that time. It was just after the Metropolitan Vickers engineers were tried as spies; the time of the Russian butter when they tried to break the Russian trading agreements by saying that the Russian butter was filled with needles and nails – all the rest of it.

Round about the same time I started to correspond with a YCLer in Leipzig. He used to send me newspapers – like the *Arbeiter Illustrierte Zeitung*. It was the time when John Heartfield was doing all those montages. Rudi Lehmann, that was the name of the guy I corresponded with, was the first to tell me in any detail about the Agit-Prop groups. He wrote to me about groups of people doing political theatre on the streets with megaphones, and that was it. I got him to tell me everything he could about them, and he did. I've still got things that he sent me – like a script by Bert Brecht and Hans Eisler called *Auf den Strassen zu singen*. I picked up a second-hand dictionary at Shudehill market in Manchester for a penny, and began to study German as best I could. I picked up enough to be able to struggle very, very, slowly through a simple article in the newspaper, no more than that. Captions I could read easily, and I learnt a lot of German songs. Rudi sent me records issued by the Volksbuehne, the federation of socialist theatre groups – so that I heard a lot of stuff that many people in better circumstances had not heard of at all.

Rudi was by this time on the central committee of the YCL of Saxony. He was murdered on the first month of Fascist takeover in Germany. He was a very lively lad. I learnt from him about the vaudeville movement – all kinds. He used to send me 20- and 30-page letters, you know. And they were fascinating to read – in English he wrote. I wish I had kept them. I remember him writing to me about the fantastic atmosphere, travelling across Germany in a train where everybody was singing *Auf, auf zum Kampf* – you know the song?

> Auf, auf zum Kampf, zum Kampf, zum Kampf
> Sind wir geboren.
> Auf, auf zum Kampf, zum Kampf, zum Kampf
> Sind wir bereit.
> Der Rosa Luxemburg reichen wir die Hand,
> Dem Karl Liebknecht haben wir's geschworen.

The song goes on to say that they can't be dismayed by the Fascists, by the Nazis. I remember Rudi telling me the train was filled with delegates going to this conference – a full train. And how one train was weeping as this song was being sung. Later on, David Ainley, who had been a delegate to the conference, told me exactly the same story. David said it was one of the most moving experiences he'd ever known.

When I heard about the Agit-Prop I thought it sounded great. You didn't need any special costumes or elaborate props, we could just wear bib-and-bob overalls. And most of us wore those anyway, when we were in jobs. So there was no expense there. Khaki shirts were part of the uniform of the unemployed of the time. They were very cheap, you know, you bought one for four bob, or two bob in some cases. You used them for hiking or for everyday wear.

So all we needed now was scripts. We started by attempting to write scripts collectively. We'd meet in the Workers' Arts Club, in a corner with the snooker players over there, and we'd be sitting on these horsehair benches trying to get ideas, and generally not getting them. Our first script was a burlesque piece about the Salford labour exchange. It was the only successful one that we ourselves wrote in that first period. It included parodies of popular songs, school songs like 'Billy Boy' and pop songs. I can't remember any of it though I believe I wrote most of it. It was very successful. We played it on the croft outside the Workers' Arts Club to a big meeting of unemployed one Sunday morning, and it went down a bomb!

We'd been functioning as a group for about 18 months when we discovered that there was in existence a national organization of groups who were doing a similar kind of work. So we wrote to them for scripts. The first sketch we got was called *Meerut*, an agitational piece about the Indian railway-workers' strike and the imprisoned leaders of the Gerni-Kamgar Union. It was a very simple and economical piece. It was an ideal script for street performance. The job was to get people to do it smartly, to be able to move into position, to perform it and be away before the cops got onto you. A gathering of any group of people attracts the police, even today. And it did then even perhaps more so, where every group of thirty people was a potential unemployment demonstration. For *Meerut* we had to drill ourselves as though we were drilling for an athletic event. Mass declamation demands great precision, and it was my job as producer to run the drill. And they got very good. Resentful but very good. I was the same age as everyone else in the group and I really knew no more than they did.

Perhaps I had more of a feeling for words than they did. And that, I would guess, came from my old man and my old woman. Because I'd grown up with this big body of traditional songs. My old man was a marvellous singer, he used to go out singing in pubs to earn a few bob. He had a huge repertoire of songs and ballads, many of which he used to sing on a Saturday afternoon when he'd come home from work. Y'know he'd had a few pints, and he'd sit by the fire with his feet up on the hob and just sing for a couple of hours till he'd sobered up. In a way that stood me in good stead, it gave me an understanding of the importance of words. I felt that we conducted our political work in a very slovenly way. I was determined that the Red Megaphones should be as smart and shining as a new pin. This was my simple production objective, to have everything clean and efficient. And ideas? Imagination? I was drowning in ideas. My idea of perfection was five voices all speaking the words at the same time.

We did another WTM script after that – *Their Theatre and Ours* – a take-off of some of the Hollywood films, and then we did a thing called *Rent, Interest and Profit*.

After a time we came to the conclusion that the WTM scripts we were getting weren't as good as they should be. We had a strong feeling that we were being written down to. Furthermore, we felt that the London groups were a bit out of touch with the problems that confronted us in the industrial North. We'd met one or two of them and they struck us as being somewhat middle class. The real fact of the matter was that we were beginning to doubt the efficacy of the endless sloganizing. I've noticed frequently among middle-class party people that I've worked with, over the years, that there's an idea that workers will accept anything, providing the message is OK. The quality doesn't matter, the form doesn't matter. All that matters is that we agree on the correct slogans.

About this time we were joined by a young weaver who'd just come back from the Lenin School, Nellie Wallace, the daughter of a coal miner from Pendlebury. Her stay at the school had left her rather disillusioned. She felt that the classes were all over her head and that money had been wasted on sending her there, merely because she'd taken part in a couple of successful strikes. The endless discussion of theory was really not what she expected of a revolutionary movement – and who could blame her, she was seventeen!

By this time we'd formed a slightly bigger group. In addition to the unemployed members, there were now two or three who had jobs and they were good for weekends. One of them was an industrial chemist employed by the British Dyestuffs Corporation.

Joe Davis was an extraordinary bloke – at least he seemed extraordinary to me at the time, and his influence on me was certainly a beneficial one. I think he was the first person I ever knew who had been educated beyond elementary-school level. He worked as a chemist in the labs at BDC and that in itself was enough to set him apart from the rest of us, who were either unemployed or doing unskilled jobs. What brought him close to us were his politics, his prowess as a moorland walker and his many passionate enthusiasms.

Geology, botany, palaeontology, languages, music and the twentieth-century novel were all grist to his mill. And he communicated his enthusiasms to all who came in contact with him. My reading until then had been almost exclusively in the area of European classical literature (up until, and including, Balzac) and nineteenth-century philosophy. Joe introduced me to writers like Joyce and Proust and Hermann Broch and Jakob Wassermann.

For a time he was an active member of our Agit-Prop group, but even at the time it was obvious that this kind of work was completely out of character. I think he was the first person to suggest that as a singer I might be worth listening to. He lived in a large, crumbling Victorian house at the bottom of Broughton Lane. The house had a sour old garden where even the weeds had a hard time trying to break through the poisonous black dirt. We used to go there after an evening's flyposting or chalking or sometimes we'd hold a branch meeting there and afterwards we'd sit and talk and Joe would attempt to explain the calculus to us or Einstein's relativity theory. He was the stuff of which great teachers were made.

Another came from a co-op drama group. He brought a couple of other people with him, but they didn't stay. But he stayed, for maybe a year and a half. And there was a young miner from Pendleton, and a girl who worked in the CWS biscuit factory, a big beautiful girl, who had the most horrifying hands I've ever seen on a human being, one of the spin-offs of her work. She was a packer, and biscuit-tins have sharp edges which would catch the flesh on the back of the hands and tear it down to the knuckles where it formed huge callouses. They were horrible to look at.

She was a kid who came to dance at the Workers' Arts Club because dances there were very cheap, cost thruppence to get in. And there were no fights at them, which was unique. There was a big dance-hall near by called 'The Jig', but the fights there were incredible. If you went there you took your partner with you. If you walked across the floor to ask a girl to dance and she was, say, a member of the Percy Street mob, a dozen blokes would converge on you. And you were lucky if you got out without being beaten up. The YCL dances, and the socials run by the Workers' Arts Club, were cheap and not very glamorous, but there were no fights.

Towards the end of 1931 we set about writing plays dealing with the cotton industry where a situation of acute crisis was developing, particularly in regard to the employers' attempts to introduce the eight-loom system in weaving. Now eight looms doesn't sound very many, particularly today when weavers often handle 13,000 looms at a time, but it was a great deal in Lancashire where most of the machines were antediluvian.

The struggle against the introduction of the eight-loom system in the weaving sheds of Lancashire and Yorkshire took place against a background of mass unemployment. The textile workers argued that the doubling up of the number of looms to be worked by a weaver would result in a 50 per cent cut in the labour force. Events proved them right. Another important factor was that most of the machinery in the Lancashire mills had been installed between the 1850s and the 1890s. It was cumbersome and grossly inefficient. The slightest inequalities in the yarn resulted in breakages. For workers employed on a piece-work basis, time spent on tying up ends was time without wages.

So we began, rather blithely, writing sketches about what the eight-loom system meant. What we hadn't realized was the way the industry was organized, and the state of the trade unions. We hadn't realized that the textile industry was the industry *par excel-*

lence of craft unions. There were unions with sometimes as few as twelve members in them. There were unions of little piecers, back-tenters, big piecers, card-room workers, combers. It seemed to us that there was a union for every single process in the cotton industry. So it wasn't a question of going to a factory and saying, 'Weavers, all out against the eight-loom!' One had to appeal specifically to card-room workers, back-tenters, little piecers, big piecers, combers, weavers, spinners, the lot. We just didn't have the knowledge. The acquiring of that knowledge had to be encompassed in a matter of days. You couldn't spend a year reading in a library and hope that the strike would hold off until you were ready. You had to cram it all into a very short space of time. It was our two weavers that made it possible.

It was arranged that we would accompany them 'Saturdaying', a traditional Lancashire cotton-mill practice. Technically the mills were closed on Saturday, but two or three workers from each department would spend the morning cleaning up and preparing the machines for Monday morning. The mill at such times had something of a holiday feeling, no clatter of looms, no whirling belts, just the girls talking.

The result of that visit was that eight workers from two mills attended a meeting with us the following week and explained their jobs to us. Blondie and Nelly, our two weavers, acted as interpreters – that is, they described technical processes and translated the specific terminologies of the different trades, the short-hand of factory workers for describing processes. By the end of that session we had a fairly good idea of how to go about writing our eight-looms script.

I think we produced either four or five different sketches about the eight-loom system, and each one of them was open-ended. Because in addition to the craft divisions inside the industry, there were also regional divisions inside the industry, this kind of thing. Generally speaking, in south-east Lancashire you got spinning exclusively, for instance, in Oldham, Delph, Waterford, Huddersfield. Now most spinners were men, and they were on male wage-rates. In north-east Lancashire you'd get towns where there was nothing but weaving, or a mill where there was nothing but weaving. Take a place like Skipton which is on the Yorkshire/Lancashire border. Strictly speaking it's in Yorkshire, but it's for textiles. Now, in the main mill there you got spinning, you got weaving, you got processing – that is bleaching – all in the one mill. Well, in the mill across the road you got nothing but back-tenting and weaving. So obviously you couldn't go with the same sketch to the two mills, because they would say, 'Oh, we don't want to listen to that!' So you had to be very genned up on what the organization of a specific mill was.

Wigan was mostly mixed textiles, with a lot of velvet weaving – Japhites – which was easy for them because that was also the same in most of the Salford mills, including the mill that Engels used to run. But you'd go into another place where it was completely different from Salford so you'd need a different sketch, so you had to inform yourself on the way.

We performed the first of the 'eight-loom' sketches outside Howard's Mill, Salford. Howard's was a fairly big mill that was weaving velvets amongst other things. We decided to launch the sketch outside the mill as operatives knocked off for the day. We assumed that that was our best chance of getting people to stop and listen. In actual fact it proved nonsense, because after a day's work everybody's keen to get away, and get the fluff out of their hair.

A few stayed to watch, and they appeared to like it. When we asked them 'What d'you think?', they said, 'Oh, it's great, love, it's great, you must do it again.' I would guess that maybe ten or fifteen people saw that performance. The sketch lasted about eight minutes. We felt it was too long, I remember, and reduced it to about five.

Two days later, we performed it again outside Elkemar Armitage's mill in Pendleton, and we really got a good response there. Except the police came and moved us on before we had time to talk to anybody afterwards. In fact we were gabbling the last few speeches because we could see the police coming, and there we were talking faster and faster and faster! But we got cheers and cries of encouragement, as well as a few raspberries, mostly from the men. The girls were much more prepared to accept us than the men were. Then the strike started and we went to Oldham, to present the sketch outside a spinning mill, where the workers were still undecided about joining the strike. As it happens, they voted to come out. I like to think that we played a part in that decision, but I doubt it. We were all youngsters – the oldest in our group was only seventeen.

From Oldham we went to Chorley, where we performed outside three mills, and from there we went on to Preston and performed outside a mill. We did four performances that day.

We came back to Salford that night, and the following day the strike had spread to Burnley, and then to Earby; no, Earby was the first lot to come out. They were out for fourteen weeks altogether.

We went to Wigan on the Saturday morning, and that was marvellous, because there was a market there and we just stepped into the middle of the market-place, near one of those big ornamental lamp standards. Some Wigan comrades had set up a coal-cart there, and we climbed onto it and went through our whole repertoire, every sketch we knew, starting off with *Billy Boy*. To our amazement a couple of hundred people gathered round us. We did our eight-loom sketch there, and it went down a bomb. And then we did a little sketch we had on mining, I forget what it was called. We'd learnt it specially for Wigan, because Wigan was a mining town. So we put that on, and got rapturous applause. Finally the stall-holders began to object because we were taking away their customers. Up till this time our audiences had never numbered more than fifteen or twenty. More often it was twelve or fifteen. And suddenly we found ourselves with this great audience, and we went through all our pieces, took about thirty-five minutes. The cops had always moved us on before. While we were performing, one of the blokes in the audience climbed the central lamp standard and tied a piece of red cloth to it. And a great roar went up from the crowd. When we'd finished, we said, 'Well, that's all we know.' And they said, 'Do it again,' so we did it again. We didn't actually get through it a second time because the police came. They were very polite on this occasion because the crowd was a big one; when there was only a few people around they would come up and say 'Piss off,' but here they were quite polite, just moved us on, it was a great day.

The following day was Sunday. We went to Rochdale and played in the streets. It was perfect conditions, everybody could see you, they only had to come and stand on their doorsteps, and you could bet your life that every family you were playing to had somebody working in the mill, or somebody who'd once worked in the mill and was now unemployed. That morning we gave about half a dozen performances in the Rochdale streets and in the afternoon we gave three performances in Bacup and about the same number in Haslingden. We must have given about twelve performances that day, and that's hard work. We didn't know how to use our voices properly, and pretty soon we were croaking like frogs.

But we were getting a fairly good response though occasionally we'd get blown a few raspberries, or somebody'd shout: 'You don't know what the bloody hell you're talking about, piss off,' that kind of thing. After all, we were strangers presuming to tell them about their jobs. Blondie and Nelly Wallace were towers of strength, as textile workers themselves they spoke with an authority that the rest of us didn't possess.

The songs were nearly all parodies, either parodies on songs that everybody knew, or on pop songs of the time. Often they'd consist of a verse and a chorus. They were almost always satirical. In that respect they were bang in the Great English tradition, and the great Scottish tradition too, since almost all the best of the English and Scots political songs have been satirical.

The strike gathered momentum. North-east Lancashire was the storm centre of the struggle against the eight looms, and Burnley was the heart of it. The authorities recognized this and the police, presumably under instructions, were given orders to seal off the town. The textile workers said things differently: their idea was that every single town in Lancashire would be represented in a giant assembly in Burnley. There they would make their demands known to the whole nation. By this time the whole of the organized working class of Britain were being appealed to for help, and those areas which were hardest hit were responding to these appeals. The first of the great food wagons to roll into Burnley came from Tonypandy – where two-thirds of the population were unemployed – where unemployment was endemic. Then Manchester, Salford, Liverpool, Glasgow, places like Hackney, Bethnal Green, West Ham. They were all sending food. It was magnificent to see the convoys rolling through the towns. We'd get notice that trucks would be coming through Manchester on Wednesday morning – and we'd be there, maybe fifty, sixty people to cheer it on; right through every town in the country this would be the case.

We were invited to Burnley by Jim Rushton – who was one of the strike leaders, a party bloke, for whom there was a warrant out by the police. We were invited to go up and perform there on the day of the big meeting. And we managed to get in, we slipped in in our food convoy that we'd picked up on the road coming from Liverpool actually – these great Pickford vans, huge things, absolutely filled with food. And when we got to Burnley the crowd was all through the whole centre of the city, it was just an occupied area. They just made way for the food convoys that came in and you just joined the ranks of these great trucks – and they stretched boards across a couple of them and we climbed up to the top of them and performed from the top there. There we were with our gleaming megaphones, and it was a lovely summer's day, I remember, the sun beating down and the stragglers kept getting in – the workers from Earby had come over the moors and actually had had to fight their way through columns of police when they came in – bloodily – and a great cheer went up when they came in, and it was a thrilling experience to stand on the top of that truck and sing and perform, for your own people – it really was the most magnificent experience, I never will forget it – it's what theatre should be. It was what it must have been like in the time of Aeschylus in great popular theatre. Crude? Yes, but as honest as we knew how to be, and we went on performing all through that period.

Shortly after that there was a by-election at Skipton, and the Party put up Jim Rushton as candidate even though there was a warrant out for his arrest, and he was sleeping in a different house every night so the cops couldn't get him and appearing on election platforms. We started doing a number of sketches for that election. The Skipton area was 140 square miles that we had to cover. It covered little mill villages like Grassington, where the owner of the mill lived in a kind of feudal hall and everybody else lived in company houses. Imagine performing in a place like that! And Skipton itself – up on the borders – and Oswaldtwistle. It included maybe twenty small towns, perhaps more than that even, as well as a lot of pastoral land. We were employed on that for something like three weeks and then we came back.

And then there were the hunger marches. There were regional hunger marches from Manchester to Lancaster: and of course national hunger marches; Lancashire to London; Glasgow to London; Tyneside to London . . . so we were performing for hunger marchers too. I wrote a fair number of songs for hunger marchers. They were all parodies of popular songs like:

Forward unemployed, forward unemployed,
Led by the NUWM★,
We fight against the cuts again.
From fighting Birkenhead, we've learnt our lesson well.
We'll send the National Government
And the means test all to Hell.

From Lancashire and down the Clyde,
From Birmingham, Yorkshire and Wales we stride,
We're marching south to London to open Parliament.

Forward unemployed, forward unemployed,
Led by the NUWM,
We fight against the cuts again,
From fighting Birkenhead, we've learnt our lesson well,
We'll send the National Government
And the means test all to Hell.

Songs like that.

I was also busy helping to organize the Ramblers' Rights movement and the mass trespass campaigns. I wrote songs about this
too. There was one to the tune of 'The Road to the Isles'. An old
friend reminded me of it recently when I was up in Manchester at
an Anti-Nazi rally:

We are young hikers who in search of healthy sport,
Leave Manchester each weekend for a hike,
Though the best moorlands and hills are closed to us,
We'll ramble anywhere we like.

For, by Kinder, and by Bleaklow and through the Goyt
  we'll go.
We'll ramble over mountain, moor and fen,
And we'll fight against the trespass laws
For every ramblers rights,
And trespass over Kinder Scout again.
For the mass trespass is the only way there is,
To gain access to mountains once again.

★ NUWM – National Unemployed Workers' Union.

A very awkward piece of writing, just doggerel. Another song I wrote at that time, 'The Manchester Rambler', is still fairly widely sung:

> I'm a rambler, I'm a rambler from Manchester way;
> I get all my pleasure the hard moorland way.
> I may be a wage slave on Monday,
> But I am a free man on Sunday.
>
> I've been over Snowdon, I've slept up on Crowden,
> I've camped by the Wain Stones as well,
> I've sunbathed on Kinder, been burnt to a cinder,
> And many more things I can tell.
> My rucksack has oft been my pillow,
> The heather has oft been my bed,
> And sooner than part from the mountains,
> I think I would rather be dead.
>
> I'm a rambler, I'm a rambler from Manchester way;
> I get all my pleasure the hard moorland way.
> I may be a wage slave on Monday,
> But I am a free man on Sunday.

That song now is almost part of the traditional repertoire of almost every town in the country. And it's not only here in Britain that it's known but in Belgium, Australia, Holland and Sweden as well.

The songs of the WTM sketches were too difficult to catch on, they were too clever, they were like Gilbert and Sullivan pieces in a way. We sang them as part of the sketches, but we always felt uncomfortable because they seemed to be written from outside. Saying things like 'the workers', but we *were* the workers. It seemed false for us to be standing there singing 'the workers'. Christ! We couldn't have been more the workers! We all worked at the same kind of job when we had a job, whereas when we made up our own songs we tried to make them from the inside, we sung about 'us' and 'we'.

V

Towards the end of 1933 we began to feel more and more dissatisfied with our work in the Red Megaphones. Apart from anything else, the continuous police harassment and endless fines meant we were spending more time on raising money to pay our fines than doing the political work we had set out to do. But this was by no means the only reason for our discontent.

Among other things we felt a perfectly natural desire to do things better, to do them more perfectly; as we gained more experience we became more ashamed of the quality of the work we were doing. We had a slogan at that time which we used to use rather cynically: 'Only the best is good enough for the workers,' meaning ourselves as well! So when we raided a gamekeeper's cabin on the moors just before the 12th, the slogan would be, 'Only the best is good enough for the workers.' And we'd sit there eating game pies and all the rest of it, and swigging the whisky we'd pinched.

But it was a very real thing too as far as the theatre and the group was concerned. We felt we were beginning to repeat everything, that we'd exhausted our very small repertoire of gestures and vocal ideas. Also a suspicion had grown in us that limitations in production ideas were an implicit feature of Agit-Prop theatre. We felt that just as we were becoming more mature politically, we needed a theatre which was sufficiently flexible to reflect the constantly changing twentieth-century political scene. We also felt we were being treated somewhat off-handedly by our comrades in the Party, who tended to see us as sugar to sweeten the political pill or as stand-bys who could be used to fill an awkward gap in a meeting or a social, who were there to provide breathing-space between more important activities. We didn't see ourselves like that at all.

We had been reading all the stuff we could get our hands on that was being put out by the Workers' Theatre Movement and the Red Stage, and we were not enormously impressed by some of it. Two or three of us hitched down to London determined to learn from the groups there, but it seemed to us they were no better than we were, and in some ways actually worse. We wanted our audience to be a working-class one, it was as simple as that, we weren't interested in anything else. But when we came to London to see – I think it was – Red Radio, our impression was that the audience was middle class. That was my first trip to London. I hitched down, and I was there for a weekend, and saw them at the Fred Talent Hall, Drummond Street. That was 1934.

We were bitterly disappointed. It struck us as the worst kind of amateur theatre; there was a painted backdrop of a battleship. They'd gone inside with a vengeance. 'Gone inside' was the phrase we used to describe the transition from street theatre to curtain theatre. In the process of moving on towards a better theatre they had, it seemed to us, abandoned completely everything they'd learned in the Agit-Prop theatre. The acting style of the new thing was amateur acting that was a shoddy imitation of the West End.

We came back from London very disillusioned. I remember very clearly the sense of outrage we felt at the way our attempts to engage in discussion were ignored. We felt we had been sold a pup. We had this northern chip on our shoulder, and we resented being talked down to. We also had this working-class thing. We felt we deserved only the best. We said, 'We've got to be better than the other side, better actors, better producers, better singers. We've got to do everything they can do but do it a hundred times better.' That was the end of our contact with the London WTM. From that time on we were going it alone. Our work in street theatre had taught us a lot and we had no intention of abandoning the things we had learned. The Agit-Prop techniques could be adapted and developed, and could form the base of a much more effective theatrical form.

Our aim, we said, was a theatre which would reflect the ideas and needs of the working class. In order to do this we would have to move on a series of different fronts simultaneously. It wasn't enough to keep the bourgeois forms and change the heroes. To change the costumes was not enough, to change the furniture was not enough, to present a play in the dead setting of the formal stage was not enough. A complete set of stylistic problems had to be solved while at the same time you were developing a new dramaturgy. Simultaneously we should be solving a whole lot of acting problems. We must, we said, create a theatre of synthesis in which the actors will be able to sing, dance and act with equal facility. Now none of these ideas was new.

Wagner had also called for a theatre of synthesis, Georg Kaiser, Toller and the Expressionists had attempted new theatrical forms. The constructivists had broken with old stage conventions in

Russia. Meyerhold and Vachtangov had explored uncharted areas of stage and audience relationships. Stanislavsky had found psychological solutions for the actors' problems, while Meyerhold had attempted to solve them in another way – via the circus and the Commedia dell'arte.

Biomechanics was an attempt to escape from naturalistic acting. After the Revolution in Russia there were great revolutionary movements in the arts, particularly in the theatre. They said, 'The theatre has not been a popular theatre in Russia since the time of the peasant theatres. Therefore we must try and create a theatre which makes the maximum use of all the technology at our disposal. Part of this technology is our understanding of the way the human body works. We must train our actors so that they can do all the things with their bodies that a conjurer can do, or an acrobat, or a dancer, that any athlete can do.' And they trained them like athletes. They even sent them to do theoretical work at the Pavlov laboratories. As a result, it was possible for Meyerhold, when he did plays like Ostrovsky's *The Forest*, to present it in the context of revolutionary society, with great constructivist sets – girders everywhere. At one point where the lover is bending down in a very exaggerated fashion before his lady-love, the husband shoots down a helter-skelter and gives the lover a tremendous kick up the arse as he lands at the bottom, a very difficult thing to do. It has a very obvious symbolical significance in the play, the way Meyerhold conceived it. We said, 'We can take some of these ideas.' In a way we were being very eclectic – testing things out, seeing if they worked. If they worked, fine, we'd keep them, if they don't, throw them away. This was not just true of us – the Workers' Laboratory Theatre were doing the same in New York – because they were also saying that a sophisticated political theory needs a sophisticated expertise.

We wanted a pliable theatre. We were closest – if we were close to anybody in the world of theatre – to Vachtangov. He seemed to us to have really found, created, a Marxist aesthetic of theatre. I can't remember specifically the source of our information about Vachtangov, but by this time some of us, certainly Alf Armitt and myself, were spending a fantastic amount of time in libraries, any spare moment that we had we'd be in the Manchester Reference Library, finding out what they had on theatre and, of course, being a kind of big city, they had a fairly good library of current theatre magazines and books about the theatre, theoretical works and technical works and all the rest of it. I think that it was that, plus the fact that there were write-ups about his productions and about his ideas in magazines like *Proletarian Literature* and in the Soviet theatre magazines and so on. But it seemed to us that he combined the best elements of, the most positive elements of Meyerhold, of Stanislavsky, and all the rest, you know.

The point is we'd become interested in Stanislavsky. Anybody who works in the theatre must ultimately become fascinated by the Stanislavsky theory of acting, of living the role, and from there to examining other theories of acting like the Cocolan theory of the French Representational Theatre of living the role at rehearsal but not living it on the stage. It wasn't merely that because one worked in the theatre, however crude that theatre was, that one's interest was exclusively about the theatre; it was the fact that the theatre that we saw around us, the theatre of the West End and to some extent the kind of theatre that was reflected in British films, for example, was so unreal, and the acting styles were so false, they typified what Stanislavsky called 'rubber-stamp' acting, a series of codified gestures, and codified grimaces, and to some extent codified dialogue. And we thought correctly that if the theatre is ever to become important, acting has got to get away completely from this concept. From that false diction, those false gestures and those false attitudes.

'An actor', we said, 'should be like an athlete, he should be in complete control of his body, he should be able to make his body do anything that he calls upon it to do. Thus far we agree with Meyerhold. On the other hand we don't want a theatre which is just a troupe of acrobats. Then again, we don't want a theatre like Stanislavsky's where everybody is so busy living the role that they cannot step out of the role and comment on it from time to time.'

Strange territory we were exploring – exploring is the right word. But we weren't like modern explorers who go out with botanists, biologists, radio engineers and all the rest of it – we were exploring from a position of ignorance. None of us could be said to have had any kind of education, we'd all left school when we were fourteen.

We weren't merely exploring the theories, we were having to learn the words that described the theories. When you went into the public library to read about something, you got the dictionary out automatically to help you over the hurdles of those big words. It was very exciting. We'd meet in the evenings and discuss all the things we'd found out that day, and we'd talk for hours and hours and hours after the work was finished, exchanging ideas. We were teaching each other. Alf, myself, Jimmy Rigby, we were all at it. In the end, of course, we divided up the formalized research, 'Right, you do this, and you do that, you read about this and tell us what you found out.' We were getting better at it all the time, and we were learning how to use libraries and books.

Our group were now in communication with the Workers' Laboratory Theatre in New York. We'd got their address through a Manchester guy called Lazar Copeland, who'd been in America as a garment worker. Lazar had gone with a fellow called Benny Segal, who'd led a strike over here, and then gone to America, and taken part in the famous Gastonia strike. They'd made contact, and apparently the Laboratory Theatre had written something about them, and performed it. So through them we got the address, wrote to them, and they sent us scripts, *Newsboy* for example. We'd also had contact with the Germans, right up until the coming of Hitler, and then after the coming of Hitler two guys turned up, representatives from the International Revolutionary Theatre Committee, a fellow called Otto, and one called Philip Minner. And Philip Minner had been a member of Kolonne Links – the troupe of the Left Column, one of the most highly praised of all of the German Agit-Prop groups. And he told us that they were having internal problems before Hitler came, a feeling that they should be moving to another area of work; and he put us in touch with a guy called Gustav Wangenheim.

Now the Wangenheim family were a kind of old Prussian nobility family. Gustav had been a theatre director, and his wife, Inge von Wangenheim, was an actress; they'd formed one of the best of all the transitional Agit-Prop groups that had existed. They were still a travelling group, very flexible, and could play in almost any conditions, but they weren't limited to five- or ten-minute sketches, but could put on a play that would last two and a half hours, in a hall, a theatre, a church, a covered market or in the open air. They'd been touring for several months before Hitler came to power with a play called *The Mousetrap*. It was about a group of travelling players with a repertoire of political sketches. They call at an inn and the innkeeper welcomes them. He allows

them to sleep in the barn in exchange for the promise of a performance of their play. He informs them that the people who live in
the village are weavers, whereupon they begin to act a scene from
Gerhard Hauptmann's play *The Weavers*. The innkeeper objects,
says that it will alienate his better-off customers. A spirited argument develops and the actors re-enact the scene in several different
ways using song, dance, burlesque, tragic theatre, the whole lot
in one single organism, absolutely beautiful, brilliant.

We got an American friend, who was living in Manchester at
the time, to translate part of it. He translated the first fourteen or
fifteen pages and then left. So we set about, with dictionaries,
trying to translate the rest. We managed to get to the end of the
second act, but it was very slow and laborious. Alf Armitt had a
girlfriend who knew some German, and she translated a bit more
of it and the rest we made up in our heads. We learnt a tremendous
lot about the theatre from that operation.

It was round about then that Joan Littlewood came to Manchester. She was a London working-class girl from Stockwell, who
managed to get a scholarship to the Royal Academy of Dramatic
Art; though she scooped the pool with every prize that was going
at RADA she couldn't get a job. So she went off to France to
work in the Pitoëff Theatre, and the day she arrived the Stavitsky
riots started, and the Government fell. So she came back home,
back to England, and decided to move north. She started walking
and collapsed at Stoke-on-Trent, and was taken into a pub and
given a job there, cleaning the place. She stood it for a week. In
the meantime she'd written to a guy in Manchester who was
working for the BBC, a bloke called Archie Harding. He put me
in touch with her, and she came to visit our group and discuss the
kind of things we'd been doing, and the things we wanted to do.
She joined us.

We never staged the Wangenheim play; it was too involved for
us at that stage. But in the meantime the Laboratory Theatre sent
us the *Newsboy* script and we decided to rehearse it. Joan had had
some movement training at the Royal Academy, and so we set
about a short training programme. We now had about twenty-
five people in the group. So we rehearsed a programme that could
be done under any circumstances, but which really needed a course
of spotlights, if you wanted to be extravagant. Well we had no

spotlights so Alf Armitt went out and pinched road-lamps, took the lenses out of them, and made spotlights out of biscuit-tins.

We had now changed our name to Theatre of Action and our first production was a mixed bag consisting of *Newsboy*, a short political dance-drama, a group declamation of a poem called *The Fire Sermon* by Sergei Funarov. Oh – and a short piece on the Chartists which I'd written – a mini-documentary linked together with Chartist songs set to music by a young Manchester composer. We also did a short piece which had been written by the group we'd seen in London. It ran for seventy-five minutes when we saw it there. I can't remember its title. We called it *John Bullion*. And we made it into a piece of pure constructivist theatre, after Meyerhold (running time eighteen minutes). And it got quite a good write-up in the *Guardian* from a drama critic called Teddy Thompson. It was probably very primitive, really, but at the time it seemed absolutely marvellous, a big leap forward, no question about that. And a bigger audience than we'd ever had except on the big demonstrations. We toured it around some of the textile towns – Bacup, Rochdale, Haslingden. And it played for two nights at the Round House in Ancoats, Manchester. It was a kind of Quaker Social Service Settlement; Mary Stocks was the director there at the time. The first time we'd ever done anything consecutively for two nights. Our first run!

We also took it to the Socialist Sunday School in Hyde, to the Clarion cyclists' place somewhere in Cheshire, I forget where . . . Kettleshulme was it? Somewhere like that. I remember it was a very wet day, and all the cyclists came in capes. It was good. And a very high level of technical efficiency, thanks to Alf Armitt.

We had no permanent premises of our own, but we moved into a slightly better rehearsal room. Our previous rehearsal room had been in the cellar of the Workers' Arts Club which had no lighting, only candles, rats and dirt. We moved to Grosvenor Street, Manchester, into a studio there, a long, narrow room which cost eight bob a week.

In the meantime Alf Armitt was pursuing his studies of stage lighting. If at this time anyone in the British theatre had done any serious thinking about the significance of electric light, then he had escaped our notice. The fact that you could throw light, that you could make parallel beams, or you could make arcs and circles of different sizes, that one could use light for the purpose of controlling space – for expanding and limiting space – that was a revelation to us. God knows there'd been enough written about it, but none of it translated into English.

Adolphe Appia was the great theorist and innovator in this field. He'd written the definitive work on the subject; it had been translated into German, Swedish, Russian and a host of other languages, but in England where they were still using electric light in the theatres as though it were candles, Appia was only a name. Alf determined that he would learn French, so that he could translate Adolphe Appia and he did. By the time he got through with it, he had plans for a portable lighting unit that could be rigged anywhere. He built it from components supplied by workers from a dozen different trades. Cable, switches, transformers, rheostats all came by the underground route. So there we were with lighting equipment which could be used anywhere, providing a power source was at hand.

At Haslingden we performed in a room that had no power source. Alf solved the problem by hanging out of a window and connecting our board to the electric trolley cable which supplied power for the trams! It's true the lights dimmed every time a tram passed, but apart from that it was perfectly effective.

In the Agit-Prop period we had struggled along with half a dozen people, all recruited from the militant Left. Now we were recruiting from outside the labour movement. On the strength of that first production, people were flocking in from all over the place.

The Agit-Prop basis of our work was still very obvious, particularly as acting was concerned, but now it had style, nuance. We were no longer deafening the audience with slogans, we were developing arguments in what we considered to be a new, exciting, theatrical language.

Our experience of working in confined spaces, such as on top of a coal-cart, had taught us to be economical with movement and gesture, and our work in the streets had taught us something about the use of the voice. That experience was to stand us in good stead for the next twenty years, including the first six years in the life of Theatre Workshop when we were constantly on the road playing in mission halls, miners' welfares, school halls, public parks and the national theatres of Stockholm and Prague.

We were now attracting lots of people with special skills and talents that they were prepared to share with us. Painters and sculptors were coming to us, engineers from Metro-Vickers who came along and said, 'Look, we'll build you back-projection equipment.' We were recruiting people like mad, it was very, very, exciting. I remember recruiting West Africans into the group at the time, to act in it. We did a thing on colonialism, a ten-minute sketch of colonialism, part dance, part song, part declamation. And we got two brothers who were very very black indeed, from Nigeria – they were Ibo people.

Joan was now working in the Rusholme Rep., and spending all her spare time with us. Round about this time the exiled German dramatist Ernst Toller came to Manchester, to supervise the production of his play *Draw the Fires*, a drama dealing with the revolt of the German navy during the Sparticist period in Germany. A good deal of the action took place in the stokehole of a battleship. Stokers, stripped to the waist, shovelled coal into the furnaces throughout several scenes. Well, the guys at the Rep. hadn't a clue; they looked ridiculous. And Toller couldn't stand it. Well, someone must have told him about Joan's connection with Theatre of Action and he asked her to bring us along to the theatre.

Half a dozen of us turned up, all mates, and he told us to strip to the waist and go through the motions of shovelling. Well, of course, we looked like people who'd done hard physical work, all of us had, and we were all in the pink of condition from hiking. 'Now, let's hear you talk, take some of the lines.' The lads, of course, belted 'em out, all the curses and everything. Christ! This was our natural speech. The leading actor there was a real nose-in-the-air bastard and he hated our guts. Nevertheless, we were hired for the run of the play, a fortnight I think it was. We went in because we felt it was a good revolutionary play, we were proud to be in it. That was the first time I'd ever been backstage in a professional theatre.

Theatre of Action lasted from about the end of 1933 to the end of 1934. It was during this period that we did Odets's *Waiting For Lefty*. We'd heard about the play from the Laboratory Theatre. I was in correspondence with the group that Odets had been in, and we sent across for it, got a copy by return and put it on within the month. For that we recruited a whole lot of people. It was a huge success – we played it for a week. That was the first time we'd ever done a full-length play. We played that at the Ancoats Settlement as well. I remember that it was a real *tour de force* for one of the actors in it – he was a market fellow, worked on the markets, a grafter; his name was Les Goldman; he was absolutely brilliant, completely authentic. He played the right-wing trade-union boss. Oh by God, he was good. He brought a lot of his friends in too, market grafters. They were all on the fringe of the political movement. They lived in that Jewish area of Strangeways, where politics was humming all the time.

We were also in touch with a group in Pennsylvania as well, who sent us a couple of scripts. There was a script that they did on an automobile strike, *The Sit-In*.

Theatre of Action now numbered about a hundred people in its ranks, people who could be called upon to act, build equipment, organize publicity, silk-screen posters, type scripts and all the rest of it. We really had a big outfit – all unpaid, of course, and many working at other jobs during the day. The bloke in charge of equipment was known as 'Stooge', because he looked like one of the Three Stooges. He was a steel erector named Gerard Davis, and he spent his boyhood in the next street to me. A real tough guy. His parents had spent a good part of their lives touring with fit-up companies. They had a large family, all conceived on the road, and named after the heroes and heroines of the plays currently on tour. Gerard Anthony Davis was born the year they were touring scenes from *Antony and Cleopatra* and *The Fortunes of Gerard*.

Alf Armitt was still in, now spending most of his time building better and better lighting units. He had left engineering and apprenticed himself in an optical lens factory. He said, 'There's no reason why we should have to pinch all our lenses. We can make them.'

The growing success of Theatre of Action was the cause of its sudden collapse. During the Agit-Prop period the Party had shown no interest at all in the way the theatre was run; that it was there on tap was sufficient. But now the party district committee began to question the wisdom of leaving an influential group in the hands of a couple of prima donnas. It wasn't that the Party objected to prima donnas as such but it wanted the prima donnas to be of its choosing. There wasn't enough democracy, it was argued, not enough committees; the casting of plays should be the work of a committee with strong party representation. Another argument was that too many people were spending too much time on the theatre. When we pointed out that most of them weren't party members we were told that they should have been recruited. There were those who were of the opinion that Theatre of Action's only important function was as a recruiting base for the Party. Others were suspicious of the whole idea of theatre work being a valid political function. Relations with the party district committee deteriorated to the point where Joan and I were called before the political leadership of the Party and presented with an ultimatum – we either accepted the recommendations of the DPC or faced expulsion from the Party. The recommendations would virtually have meant abandoning the theatre to the Agit-Prop department of the Party. Naturally we refused to see this happen. A special meeting of an extended DPC was called to thrash out the matter. It was one of those meetings when all the accumulated resentments of years boil to the surface. I must confess, also, that I was very brash and incredibly opinionated. It was my contention that the party line was completely opportunistic when it came to cultural affairs, and I set out to prove this in a rather unorthodox way. It was really rather stupid. I read out a statement by Trotsky, dealing with cultural work, but didn't name its author. I asked the party organizer to say whether he accepted it as a correct analysis of the problem. When he agreed that it was, I named its author. This juvenile trick produced pandemonium. It was as if I'd accused the pope of having an incestuous relationship. It certainly had the effect of hardening the opposition to us and alienating several people who up till then had been undecided. When the vote on our expulsion was taken, there were 21 votes for and 21 against. The chairman cast his vote in our favour. Though we escaped expulsion, it could hardly be described as a victory. The struggle had weakened the theatre, and the atmosphere was poisoned with mutual recriminations. Armitt and another survivor of the street theatre days left the group declaring that they would never again work with any outfit connected with the Communist Party. Several weeks prior to these events Joan and I had received an offer from the Soviet Academy of Theatre and Cinema offering us scholarships to study there. We had no intention of taking up the offer at the time, but now conditions had changed so we wrote accepting, and left Theatre of Action to those who had called for its 'democratization'. It continued in existence for three or four months and then fizzled out.

In London we hung around waiting for our visas to come through, but after a fortnight the £14 raised by our friends as a parting gift gave out. By an incredible stroke of luck, however, we got a job writing a film scenario based on a Christian Science novel. The lady who had written the novel gave us free lodgings in the basement flat of her Cheyne Walk apartment. And still there was no word of visas. Through friends in Manchester we made contact with a family in Battersea and discussed with them the idea of setting up a training-class for young working-class actors. They were enthusiastic and within a month we had set up a communal house on West Side, Clapham Common. There were eight of us, and for the next five months we discussed and analyzed and tried ideas in movement and voice and at the end of that period we had succeeded in formulating a training programme. There were lots of holes in it but it was the base on which our work was to develop over the next few years. Our visas didn't come through, and finally we were forced to give up the communal house as we had no job, no money and no prospect of any.

We were back in Manchester in the late spring of 1935. We set about forming a theatre immediately. It was the period of the United Front against Fascism, of the anti-war movement, the year before the beginning of the Spanish Civil War. We decided to bring together as many of the old Theatre of Action people as we could get hold of. About a dozen of us met and it was agreed that we should attempt to form a company to perform Hans Schlumberg's anti-war play *Miracle at Verdun*. It was an ambitious project, since the play called for fairly lavish sets and a cast of some eighty players. A friendly journalist organized a meeting of the drama critics of the *Guardian*, the *News Chronicle* and the *Daily Despatch*, and they wrote news items about the project and publicized the auditions that were planned. We approached all the progressive movements in the area.

The Quakers responded by providing us with rehearsal premises in central Manchester, the Peace Pledge Union undertook the booking of a hall and organized the sale of tickets, the Trades Council undertook financial backing and soon we were being bombarded with offers of help. Auditions were held during the lunch-hour and from 7 till 10 o'clock every evening for a whole week.

We rehearsed the show in shifts. I'd be rehearsing Act One, Scene One, in one room and next door Joan would be rehearsing Act One, Scene Two; then she'd take Scene Three and I'd take Scene Four, and so on, right through the play. It took three weeks from start to finish and it opened at the Lesser Free Trade Hall and played for six performances. It wasn't a particularly brilliant play, more of a spectacle, really, but it won us a great deal of support and out of it was born Theatre Union. This was the most significant of our pre-war theatre groups, for it incorporated all the most positive results of our previous experience. We were training a nucleus of actors and technicians now who were dedicated to the task of creating a revolutionary theatre.

When the Spanish Civil War began we immediately embarked upon a production of Lope de Vega's heroic play *Fuente Ovejuna* (*The Sheep Well*). We followed this with the Piscator/Brecht version of *The Good Soldier Schweik* and then with the *Lysistrata* of Aristophanes. In addition we were producing pageants and sketches at Aid for Spain meetings and at anti-Fascist demonstrations.

In 1939, after the war had started, we produced *Last Edition*, a living newspaper dealing with the events which had led up to the war. In it we used dance, song, mime, burlesque, mass declamation, parody . . . everything we had learned went into it. As with other shows, we opened at the Lesser Free Trade Hall and it was an immediate success. During the run Joan and I were arrested and charged with disturbing the peace. We were fined £20 each and bound over for two years. This brought nine years' work in revolutionary theatre to a close.

Our last task in Theatre Union was to draw up an advanced study syllabus before actors and technicians were called up for the services. Comprehensive reading lists were assembled covering every aspect of the theatre – history, theory and dramaturgy. Each member of the theatre nucleus undertook to study a different period or aspect of the theatre: one would study classical Greek theatre, another the Commedia dell'arte, another the Chinese theatre, another the Elizabethan and Jacobean theatre, and so on. At the same time, it was decided that each person would communicate his or her findings to the other members of the group. It didn't always work, but it gave us a sense of continuity, and when the war came to an end we were able to set up a full-time company (Theatre Workshop) almost immediately.

We learned a great deal from books and from each other, but mostly we learned by taking part in working-class struggle. We decided very early on that it was vital to know for whom you were playing, for whom you were writing, for whom you were acting. And for us, that was a working-class audience. They were our teachers and our inspiration. Nothing that has happened to me in the last fifty years has altered that belief.

From the very beginning I had worked on the assumption that what I had to say personally was not all that important unless it was informed with the experiences of other people who had similar problems. Their experiences would, I believed, reinforce and illuminate mine. When I was writing squibs for factory papers it would, I suppose, have been quite permissible to have written about a generalized employer, a generalized manager or a generalized foreman. But I could only see them in the terms of people who had big noses or freckles. The utterance had to be right, not almost right, but exactly right. My ideal was the anonymous author, the anonymous song-writer, and you only achieve anonymity by becoming part of the whole. When I write a song it is important that I make the people I am writing it for believe that I know as much as they do about the milieu that they live and work in. Only then will they accept it as a true record. If they feel for one moment that it is written from outside they will suspect its validity.

From the time I began to think – about the age of twelve or thirteen – I resented people who talked about us as 'you people', or 'you workers'. I felt reduced, as if my identity was being taken away. 'You people', you great enormous mass of nobodies who produce all the riches of the earth, you people, my people, me!

Of course, there's always a choice confronting everybody who works in the arts and escapes the factory, the shop, the mine – the choice is going over to the other side and beginning to think like the other side. Well, I have avoided that – I avoided it not because of any virtue on my part but because I recognized a long time ago that my only hope of survival as a human being lay in maintaining my relationship with the class that I came from. Not because that class is perfect – obviously if the working class was perfect there would be no need to dismember capitalism – but because that class at its best embodies all that is most positive in human beings, and because it has the historical function of changing the whole nature of society. That's the way I see it.

Those early songs I wrote for the mass trespass were written from inside the particular struggle. In everything I have done since I have made it a point to consult the people around me. They are my . . . I was going to say critics, but that isn't true – they are my co-workers. If I write a song about a fisherman and take it back to him and ask him what he thinks of it, and if he says 'Fine', well, that's good enough for me. If he says 'Lousy', I start again. We did that in the theatre, in the radio ballads. We've tried to do it in the folk revival. I say 'we'. It's not the royal 'We', it's just that I always feel embarrassed about suggesting that I am in any way special. Well, I suppose that I am special, but only in the sense that all human beings are special.

Part 7

The political stage in the United States

From Shock Troupe to Group Theatre
Stuart Cosgrove

I

The emergence of a Workers' Theatre Movement in Britain coincided with similar developments in the USA.[1] These similarities were not confined to historical trends but covered matters of theatrical form and prevailing ideology. A comparison of the two histories reveals certain similarities and numerous points of contact but ultimately gives way to two quite different approaches to political theatre which are themselves determined by the different socio-cultural characteristics of the British and American working classes.

The wider historical schema of the American Workers Theatre Movement is almost identical to its British counterpart: a diffuse beginning in workers' social clubs, a process of growth and consolidation during the 1920s, a logical zenith during the economic depression of the early years of the 1930s and an eventual resurgence during the period of 'New Left' activism in the late 1960s.

Within this historical structure the period of activism during the 1930s reveals a number of interesting parallels between the two movements. Both turned to Germany and, of course, the Soviet Union, for formal and even ideological guidance, and as a result a similarity in style and even in the final scripts performed by the various groups can be seen.[2] Both movements complied with a radical left shift in Communist International policy between 1928 and 1934 before reassessing their position to accommodate the ideas and strategies of the Popular Front. During the period 1928–34 Agit-Prop established itself as the main form for the Workers' Theatre on both sides of the Atlantic, but it was by no means the only form, nor did it achieve its status without considerable debate. Although the early years of the 1930s are seen in retrospect as a period of misplaced sectarianism, it was also a period of important theatrical experiment and interesting theoretical discussion. It was a period which exposed certain contradictions within capitalism but also within the positions adopted by the revolutionary groups opposed to capitalism, not least the Communist Party. To suggest that the international experience of different Workers' Theatre groups was uniform, and the result of workers uncritically accepting the cultural imperatives of the party and its functionaries, is a crude history to say the least. A close examination of the Workers Theatre in the USA exposes a number of these contradictions and immediately sets it apart from the British WTM. The two movements were as radically different as the cultural and sociological compositions of the countries themselves, and neither British nor American Workers' Theatre was a pale or diluted imitation of the more active and better known movements in Russia and Germany. The working classes of all countries are at various levels of class consciousness and are influenced by separate national and ethnic cultures. This will always lead to different, but not incommensurate, workers' cultures which in turn will produce varying approaches to Workers' Theatre.[3]

The American working class was, and to a lesser extent still is, composed of indigenous white workers, European immigrants and disinherited black workers whereas the British working class, during the 1920s and 1930s, was composed almost entirely of white indigenous workers. America's multi-racial society therefore generated a workers' culture which differed radically from that in Britain. Almost every ethnic minority in America had its own theatre group, whereas in Britain only the Jews were developed and numerous enough to create their own Workers' Theatre. In New York, on the other hand, the Jewish Artef group, the Hungarian Dramatic Circle and Uj Elöre group, the German Prolet Buehne and Die Natur Freunde, and numerous Negro groups, including the theatrical wing of the League of Struggle for Negro Rights, all mobilized to activate and entertain their own specific communities.

It is understandable, therefore, that the politics of racialism concerned the American worker more directly than it did the British working class and predictably this concern is reflected in American Workers Theatre. History, ideology and extant scripts all confirm that the American worker produced a potent and effective anti-racialist theatre.[4]

This anti-racialist stance was a reaction to two related reactionary trends which threatened to divide the American working class. The first trend tried to set up the emancipated black as a 'scapegoat' threat to traditional values whilst the other trend was an adaption of the perennial 'Conspiracy Theory'. The first accused blacks of being a sexual and moral threat, whilst the second accused immigrant workers of subversive and clandestine activities designed to promote international communism. Ironically both these anxieties came to their heads in the form of political trials – one in the 1920s and one in the 1930s. The first trial was the Sacco and Vanzetti controversy involving two immigrant anarchists accused of robbery and murder, and the second was the trial of the Scottsboro Boys, wrongly accused of multiple rape. Both trials were extensive in their repercussions – the first, set against a 1920s background of 'Red scare' xenophobia, and the second against a 1930s background of unemployment, rural poverty and Southern lynch law mentality. The trials became crucial landmarks in American working-class history and provided the Workers Theatre with ideal political material. It is one of the major consistencies of Workers' Theatre throughout the world that martyrdom makes good dramatic and propagandist theatre. The Workers' Theatre, by definition, has always apotheosized the workers' martyr.

In 1930, three years after the death of Sacco and Vanzetti and ten years after their alleged crime, they were still being commemorated by workers' groups. In Los Angeles the Rebel Players performed the play *Gods of the Lightning* in memory of the immigrants while in the same year, in New York, the Hungarian Workers' Dramatic Circle staged a Hungarian-language version of the same play to remind their militant workers of the excesses of xenophobia in the USA.

The Scottsboro case came at a very important time for the American Workers Theatre. It blew up against a background of violent anti-Negro activity which was being deliberately cultivated by proto-Fascist organizations like the Ku Klux Klan and the Black Legion. However, it was also a period in which the Workers Theatre was being encouraged to propagate for multi-racialism by way of black themes and plays and by the creation of Negro and multi-racial troupes. The Scottsboro case provided both material and opportunity. A plethora of sketches and plays emerged including the Prolet Buehne's *Scottsboro*, the Workers' Laboratory Theatre's *Lynch Law*, Langston Hughes's *Scottsboro Limited*, and the more social realist play *They Shall Not Die* by George Wexley, which was later produced by André van Gyseghem's Left Theatre in London.

The anti-racialist tenor of American Workers Theatre was only one strain in a whole series of differences which distinguished it from the British movement.

The attitude adopted by professionals from the legitimate stage to the Workers Theatre group throws interesting light on the British and American movements. In America there seems to have been a higher level of involvement by intellectuals and theatre experts in Workers Theatre than has ever been the case in Britain. As early as 1913 New York's intellectual élite were involved in Workers Theatre or Workers Singing Societies and by 1926 recognized professional playwrights like Mike Gold, John Howard Lawson and John Dos Passos of the New Playwrights Theatre helped form a militant amateur troupe, Workers Theater in New York.[5] This short-lived collaboration was only one event in a tradition which shaped the history of American Workers Theatre. The attention and support it received from bona fide theatre professionals continually influenced the organization, techniques and even the ideological stance of proletarian theatre in America. Prominent members of college and university theatres, the Little Theatre Movement and even Broadway companies offered their assistance or advice to the workers throughout the 1920s and 1930s. This assistance was often rejected, particularly during the most sectarian years of 'Third Period' strategy in the early 1930s, but more often than not it was accepted and absorbed. Whereas the British Workers' Theatre Movement appears to have been associated with professionals like W. H. Auden, who were at some distance from genuine working-class experience, the American workers were aided by individuals who shared working-class identity either by birth or by membership of workers' organizations and parties.

The campus theatres in America were particularly amenable to the workers' groups. Hallie Flanagan, a teacher and director at Vassar College and later the national director of the Federal Theatre Project, was the most sympathetic college director. In 1931 she wrote the first recognized article on Workers Theatre under the title 'A Theatre is Born' for the prestigious magazine *Theatre Arts Monthly*,[6] but more importantly she wrote and directed a Workers'

Agit-Prop for performance on Vassar's strictly middle-class campus. In 1931, with the help of Margaret Ellen Clifford, Hallie Flanagan co-wrote and staged a piece entitled *Can You Hear their Voices?* The play was adapted from a story by Whittaker Chambers and dwelt on the conflict between a rich congressman and the rural working class he represented. It was an appeal to American intellectuals to support the working class, and the appeal was presented in a style which was new and experimental by American college terms. *Can You Hear their Voices?* was a fusion of Agit-Prop and Living Newspaper forms which were already well established in the USSR and Germany but which were almost unknown in the USA outside the perimeters of the Workers Theatre Movement.[7] It is clear, therefore, that the influence professionals had on Workers Theatre was not a one-way process. The two parties certainly cross-referred and this cross-reference was just as valuable and just as advantageous to legitimate theatre as it was to the workers.

The Communist cell of the professional Group Theatre were the most ardent supporters of New-York-based Workers Theatre groups. Art Smith, Elia Kazan and Clifford Odets, all Group Theatre actors, were the most vociferous and active in their support. They arranged classes in acting and directing specifically for workers' groups and enlisted the support of less committed Group Theatre personnel, like Lee Strasberg and Harold Clurman, to give practical demonstrations. The involvement of Group Theatre sympathizers increased as 'Third Period' sectarianism thawed around 1934. Smith and Kazan wrote an anti-Nazi Agit-Prop entitled *Dimitroff* that year, and it was performed at Theatre Union's Civic Repertory Theatre by members of the cast of the Group Theatre's Broadway production of *Men in White*.[8] Although *Dimitroff* was never a popular play with the workers' groups it set a precedent for a much more important collaboration between the Group Theatre radicals and Workers' Theatre. On 6 January 1935, at a New Theatre Night, members of the Group Theatre, including Kazan and Smith, presented Clifford Odets's one-act agitational play, *Waiting For Lefty*.

Waiting For Lefty met with phenomenal audience reaction and soon became the most popular play in the American Workers Theatre canon. Set against a background of the 1934 taxi-drivers' strike in New York, the play was undoubtedly the most complete statement made by the militant Workers Theatre. It revealed the various ways in which the individual changes from apathy to commitment (a theme which fascinated the Workers Theatre) and did so within a framework which revealed corrupt unionism and violent anti-strike activity. *Waiting For Lefty* was therefore the most mature outcome of the collaboration of Workers Theatre and professional sympathizers and the most potent result of the fusion of Agit-Prop and social realism.

It is at this point in their historical development that the American and British Workers' Theatre Movements begin to diverge. The British movement did not receive the same support from sympathizers and never really produced a work of the vitality and importance of *Waiting For Lefty*. Historical events made the divergence even greater as the 1930s wore on. Roosevelt's New Deal Administration in America provided subsidy for the unemployed actor and designer under the Federal Theatre Project and this obviously affected the Workers Theatre Movement. As their British counterparts continued unaided and often badly supported, the American worker/actor was provided with a subsidized framework in which to work. Although the Federal Theatre Project did not replace Workers Theatre, it absorbed many of its participants and gave them a new opportunity to continue their experiment.

II

The history of the USA Workers Theatre during the 1920s and 1930s follows three distinct periods of development. The years between 1925 and 1932 marked the establishment and growth of the movement; the period between 1932 and 1935 saw a consolidation of the movement and an eventual progression towards an anti-Fascist ideology, and the final phase between 1935 and the Second World War saw the decline of Workers Theatre. These three phases correspond to similar developments in Britain and thus act as a useful historical framework in which to analyze the changes and developments in political culture during the 1930s. However, it should be borne in mind that these phases were not as conveniently defined as one might imagine. Workers Theatre responded to local and national political issues more than anything, and took its directives from the particular needs of the workers. A labour dispute, an extended picket-line, a sit-down strike, or a hunger march were likely to generate increased theatrical activity against the historical trends of development or decline.

7 June 1913 is probably the first significant date in the history of twentieth-century American Workers Theatre. The day marks the performance of the Industrial Workers of the World (IWW) pageant at Madison Square Garden. The pageant was part of an organized campaign supporting the Paterson silk strikers and recreated important events during the extensive strike including the death of Valentino Modestino at the hands of hired detectives, the resultant funeral, a mass meeting of 20,000 strikers, a May Day parade and the pathetic scenes of children being sent to 'strike' mothers in neighbouring cities to keep them away from the violent conflict. The pageant involved more than 1,000 performers, all workers from the Paterson, New Jersey, silk factories. It was directed by Jack Reed and supported by the IWW, but it seems that the pageant had adverse effects on the strike. No money from the performance ever reached the strike fund, the pageant effectively divided the workers and whilst activity centred on rehearsals, the strike itself was partly neglected allowing 'scabs' to break an almost foolproof picket.[9]

One positive result of the Paterson Silk Strike Pageant was the links it forged between the organized working class and New York's intellectual 'Bohemians'. This association of worker and intellectual became traditional and a crucial influence on subsequent Workers Theatre in America. In the early 1920s the links between workers and intellectuals were confused, primarily because the intellectuals were a strange mixture of anarchists, socialists, syndicalists and romantic idealists, and were generally unclear about their commitment to the working class. With the emergence of a Marxist vanguard within 'Greenwich Village intellectualism', the interaction between worker and intellectual became more clear and more productive. In 1926 Mike Gold and John Howard Lawson, both Marxist writers, formed the Workers' Drama League, which became the first sustained attempt to promote organized Workers Theatre in New York.

The Workers' Drama League was very European in its outlook and intention. It attempted to bring American workers up-to-date with cultural progress in Russia and Germany and establish a structure within which a native political culture could function. Mike Gold had previously visited Russia in his capacity as editor of *New Masses* and was keen to establish an American *Proletkult* along similar lines to those already mapped out in Moscow. The major work to emerge out of that short-lived experiment was a mass recitation written by Gold entitled *Strike!* In the Foreword to the recitation, written in 1926, he acknowledges its Soviet heritage and proposes certain approaches:[10]

> To begin with, no tinsel stage or stage settings are necessary; the rough bare platform of any ordinary union hall or meeting hall is enough, is the most fitting stage in fact.
>
> About thirty men and women are needed in the following Mass Recitation (*Strike!*). As indicated they are scattered in groups or as individuals through the audience. Except for those who take the parts of Capitalists, Police, etc., they are dressed in their usual street clothes; they have no make-up on, there is nothing to distinguish them from their fellow-workers in the audience.
>
> This is what makes a Mass Recitation so thrilling and real. The action in my recitation commences on the platform, with POVERTY speaking; suddenly from the midst of the audience a group of men workers chant; then a woman stands up and shouts something; then a group of girls in another part of the house . . .
>
> The audience is swept more and more into the excitement all around them; they become one with the actors, a real mass; before the recitation is over, everyone in the hall should be shouting: 'Strike! Strike!'

The Workers' Drama League's Soviet spirit paved the way for America's first known mobile theatre group, the Prolet Buehne, who broke away from their parent *Arbeiterbund* in 1929. The Prolet Buehne were a German-language group, directed by a Communist émigré John Bonn,[11] who specialized in a fast, visual and rhythmic style of recitation which owed much to the style of German worker's groups. The Prolet Buehne performed at meetings throughout New York, but were mostly to be found in the German immigrant areas around Yorkville and the Bronx, and at strikes or picket-lines in industries traditionally associated with German immigrant workers, particularly the waterfront docks and breweries. The Prolet Buehne soon became part of an activist vanguard which dictated the performance policy of American Workers Theatre until the mid-1930s. The other main group in this vanguard were the Workers' Laboratory Theatre – the most important English-speaking group in the history of American Workers Theatre.

By 1929 there were enough active workers' groups to form the Workers' Dramatic Council[12] which was based in New York but contacted groups in other industrial cities. Workers Theatre groups had by now emerged in Boston, Philadelphia, Chicago and Los Angeles.[13] The movement expanded rapidly over the next two years and in 1931 the Prolet Buehne and the Workers' Laboratory Theatre co-edited the first official organ of the Workers Theatre. The magazine, although at first limited to a few mimeographed sheets, soon became the united voice for a National Workers Movement – naturally the magazine was entitled *Workers Theatre*.[14]

As the early 1930s progressed, Workers Theatre became more organized and sought increased contact and co-operation. On 13 June 1931, a joint venture by the Marxist cultural magazine, *New Masses*, and the John Reed Club brought together delegates from 224 workers' cultural societies in New York and aimed to form a federation which would unite the various groups. The 1931 conference raised two particular issues which were crucial to the development of the first phase of the Workers Theatre Movement. The first issue was more or less confined to America but the second was a problem which confronted the organizers of Workers' Theatre throughout the world.

The American problem outlined the difficulties of formulating a united workers' culture in a country comprising numerous national cultures and ethnic minorities. The immigrant groups, of which there were many, were criticized for placing too great an emphasis on folklore and cultural nationalism, and ignoring the need for an international workers' culture. This criticism was clearly aimed at groups like the Bronx Hungarian Dramatic Circle, the Uj Elöre Dramatic Club and the Ukrainian Dramatic Circle which normally staged plays with an overtly Slavic atmosphere. Michael Gold urged that these groups reveal the problems of Slavic workers in America and unite with the indigenous workers' groups to form a unified political culture. The second problem was related to the first but was more international in its implications. It was a problem which was, and to some extent still is, fundamental to working-class culture. To what extent should the Workers Theatre associate itself with, and borrow from, the bourgeois stage?

The 'class antagonism' which characterized the first phase in the development of American Workers Theatre presupposed a rejection of bourgeois influence. John Bonn of the Prolet Buehne was adamant about the obvious antagonism between workers' culture and bourgeois culture.[15]

> We understand that aims, working conditions, players, directors, writers and audiences of the Workers Theatre are different from those of the bourgeois theatre, and at the same time, we try to find appropriate form for our theatre among the forms existing in bourgeois theatre. This is an obvious contradiction.

This hard-line, anti-bourgeois stance was at the backbone of the first phase. It certainly allowed Agit-Prop to establish itself as the main form for the mobile Workers Theatre, but at its most fanatical the anti-bourgeois line reduced the movement to sectarianism. The second phase (1932–5) allowed for a more tolerant attitude towards the bourgeois stage, partly because of the artistic failure of the first National Workers Theatre Spartakiade held in New York in 1932, and partly because of the interest being shown in the movement by prominent members of the social theatre, particularly the Communist cell of Group Theatre which included Elia Kazan and Clifford Odets.

As the second phase in the development of American Workers Theatre advanced, numerous improvements were made. The League of Workers Theatres (LOWT) had been formed in April 1932 and remained active until 1935. Theatre Collective was formed as an extension of the Workers' Laboratory Theatre late in 1932, and a year later the first professional Workers' Theatre group – Theatre Union – was formed.[16] By 1933 there were more than 250 Workers Theatre groups in the USA and a year later the number had risen to 400. The original *Workers Theatre* magazine was re-named *New Theatre* and, having dropped its 'class war' ideology, assumed a Popular Front stance 'dedicated to the struggle against war, Fascism and censorship'.[17] The circulation of *New Theatre*, which included articles by Piscator, Meyerhold and Romain Rolland, reached 10,000 copies a month, and in 1934

Waiting For Lefty, a product of the association of Agit-Prop and social realism, was produced. These developments were indicative of the success of the new movement which by this time was united under the New Theatre League, but the success in many ways obscured a sudden decline in Workers' Theatre. A decline that characterized the tragic third phase.

The year 1935 saw the establishment of the Government-sponsored Federal Theatre Project, a move which became one of the main factors in the decline of American Workers Theatre. By virtue of its twofold purpose of rehabilitating unemployed theatre personnel and creating a 'progressive people's theatre', the FTP attracted hundreds of actors who had previously been with Workers groups.[18] Meanwhile the Workers Theatre groups themselves were going through a radical change. The Workers' Laboratory Theatre changed its name to the Theatre of Action and aimed to produce full-length plays on a more firmly established, professional basis. This trend naturally forced the Workers groups to make the same artistic and financial compromises as legitimate theatre and for the first time made them financially responsible for a company and a theatre. This constriction, and the attraction of the FTP, proved too powerful for the US Workers Theatre Movement and it steadily declined.

The success of the movement had always been reflected in the circulation of its magazine. In December 1936 *New Theatre* ceased publication and a year later the alternative socialist magazine *Theatre Workshop* also capitulated. The movement continued for some years but as the war became imminent, the problems of Workers Theatre seemed redundant and were never really reassessed until 'New Left' theatre emerged in the 1960s.

III

American theatre during the depression was undeniably a social theatre. It dwelt upon political and sociological problems to an extent that had never been seen before and has yet to be repeated. The dialectics of the 1930s' socio-political culture were more evident in the social theatre movement than in any other area of cultural activity. These groups varied enormously and often only had one thing in common, a general dissatisfaction with Broadway's soporific and escapist naturalism. At one end of this social theatre spectrum was the reputable and professional Group Theatre[19] and at the other, the Shock Troupe faction of the Workers' Laboratory Theatre.

The Group Theatre and the Shock Troupe were in most respects antithetical. The former were the champions of social realism whilst the Shock Troupe were advocates of militant symbolism or Agit-Prop. The antithesis was based on radical differences in opinion about the function of theatre. The Group Theatre were concerned with the aesthetics of representing the social problems of the day whilst the Shock Troupe were committed to a theatre for workers' revolution and a theatre that was defined by its willingness to seek out an audience. The name Shock Troupe was indicative of their peripatetic nature and their organization was designed for street-corner propagation. They were the backbone of a mobile caucus, which consisted of the Prolet Buehne and the Hungarian Workers' Shock Brigade,[20] and which emerged as a direct response to the established principles of the mobile Workers Theatre:[21]

> Our task is to bring the message of the class struggle to as many workers as possible. When we want to reach the masses it is not enough to wait until they come to us or call for us. We have to go where the masses are: in meetings, in workers' affairs, on the streets, at factory gates, in parades, at picnics, in working-class neighbourhoods. That means we must be mobile.
>
> Our organizational structure, our plays, the form of our production must be such that we are able to travel with our production from one place to another, that we are able to give the same effective performance on a stage, or on a bare platform on the streets.

The Shock Troupe took this particular directive to its logical conclusion and established a living collective near the Communist Party headquarters in New York's lower east side. By living together, and in close proximity to the radical nerve centre of America, they were immediately available to the organized working class and could make an appearance at a picket-line with only very short notice. This particular interpretation of a collective mode of cultural production sets them apart from the Group

Theatre, who also believed in collective approaches but for purely aesthetic reasons. The Shock Troupe collective was mobile, utilitarian and was available to the working class, whereas the Group Theatre ensemble was detached, unavailable and were in existence to explore form with no real consistent concern for the ideological content of their work. At the theoretical base of the Shock Troupe's activities were the writings of Marx and the early Eisenstein, whilst the Group Theatre were informed primarily by Stanislavsky, and had only a vague, and at times inconsistent, commitment to social drama.

In an article which appeared in the American version of the *Daily Worker* in 1934, a Shock Troupe stalwart, Peter Martin, presented the collective's position within the diverse poles of American theatre:[22]

> As a whole the Shock Troupe constitutes a vital group developing along many lines which converge at the point of effective revolutionary activity, and unlike the actors of the bourgeois stage with a job and a career they have a grasp of the realities behind their theatre art which enables them to correlate their work to the broad historical process of which they are part.

At the base of their activities was a genuine concern for theoretical issues and the manner in which that theory could be put into meaningful revolutionary practice. They were the first American group to appropriate Eisenstein's writings on dialectical montage and apply those ideas to the theatre. By mixing native popular forms such as vaudeville and burlesque they created a theatre form which was essentially American but which had the same theoretical base as the Moscow *Proletkult*'s work during the 1920s. The point of contact was Eisenstein's seminal essay on 'montage of attractions'.

The Shock Troupe consisted of a core of around thirteen members, although the Workers' Laboratory Theatre had many more. Among the most active were Al Saxe, a mid-westerner who directed most of the troupe's plays, and Stephen Karnot, who had previously been a student of Meyerhold in Moscow, and brought a considerable expertise to group rehearsal. It was through these two members that the Shock Troupe built their considerable practical and theoretical awareness of Soviet revolutionary theatre. In addition to these two, another three members of the collective were Russian and at least two were black Americans. It was significant that, during a period in which the Communist Party had made very real advances within the black community, the Workers Theatre groups should have a sizeable number of black members. As far as the Shock Troupe were concerned, at least three of their most popular plays, *Newsboy*, *Lynch Law* and their own collectively written version of *Scottsboro*, embraced racial issues and many more involved the appearance of black workers.

By the end of 1932 the Shock Troupe had become one of America's most successful Workers Theatre groups. It was a success that can be measured by a number of different criteria. By 1934 they had built up a working repertoire of over eighty plays including Agit-Props, mass recitations and political vaudeville. An estimated 100,000 workers watched them perform at strike meetings, mass pickets or political rallies in 1934 alone, and prior to becoming Theatre of Action, they had appeared before approximately a quarter of a million people.

The qualitative achievements of the Shock Troupe can be measured by a study of extant scripts such as *Newsboy*, an analysis of their considerable theoretical influences, and by a close examination of the experimental and progressive work they included in a normal day. Fortunately several newspaper reports still exist which give some insight into the Shock Troupe's working methodology:[23]

They rise at eight, have breakfast, then clean the house, and arrive at the theatre at ten o'clock, where another half-hour is spent cleaning the theatre. Then daily classes begin: the subjects studied are current politics, dialectical materialism, make-up, techniques of acting and biomechanics, and are given by the comrades in the troupe most developed in the respective subjects. At one o'clock the daily rehearsal of material in repertory begins; new material is whipped into shape and the songs, skits and plays to be performed during the week are gone over and over in an attempt to achieve as perfect a performance as possible. Frequently the afternoon rehearsals may be suspended because of appearances at demonstrations and mass meetings. At four o'clock there is individual rehearsal wherein the comrades study their shortcomings.

We also have a schedule of a typical working day:[24]

11.00–11.15	Biomechanics – voice and body training.
11.15–12.00	Meeting – discussion of bookings, repertoire.
12.00– 2.00	Rehearsal of repertoire: *Newsboy*.
	Rest period.
3.00– 4.00	Rehearsal of satiric sketch: *Hollywood Goes Red*.
4.00– 5.00	Song practice.
	Dinner.
7.00– 8.00	Waterfront performance: *Dr Fixemup*.
9.00–10.00	Needle-Workers Industrial Hall: *Free Thaelmann*.

The extensive practical work, self-criticism and theoretical study which formed such a considerable part of a Shock Trouper's day help to explain their consistent ideological stance and the expertise they achieved in performance.

Newsboy is a suitable example of clear ideology and developed form. It was adapted from a poem by the Communist Party spokesman on culture, V. J. Jerome, and was first performed in 1933 but was later updated to coincide with Popular Front policy after 1935. In its original form as Agit-play, *Newsboy* dealt with the political conversion of an ordinary newsvendor from apathy to committed communism. It borrowed scenes and ideas from various diverse sources. Eisenstein's concept of dialectical montage provided a structural design which included excerpts from Claire and Paul Sifton's play *1931* and sequences from the ballets of Kurt Jooss. Obviously the Marxist principles of dialectical materialism provided *Newsboy*'s ideological base, and explain its conflict methodology. However, it should be borne in mind that *Newsboy* was a piece of theatre and not a piece of literature. Even a continual awareness of the fluency, structured stage patterns and precise lighting which characterized the Shock Troupe's performances cannot recreate *Newsboy*'s theatrical and propagandist quality.

Newsboy's basic plot involves the experiences of the young vendor on the streets of depression New York. Set against a background of poverty which was unknown in American history, and which led to phenomenal unemployment figures and suicide rates,

Newsboy was borrowing from contemporary reality. The vendor witnesses bread lines, street panhandlers, a fight over a dime and a racist attack on an innocent black. These realities conflict with the escapism and gratuitous wealth represented in the papers he is selling, and the newsboy comes to a clearer understanding of the class system. It is a simple political epiphany brought about by an uncomplicated dialectical process . . . poverty (thesis) conflicts with reports of wealth (antithesis) and the juxtaposition of both lead to a new concept, which is the Newsboy's political awareness (synthesis). He becomes aware of the inadequacies of capitalism and its subservient press, and the play finishes with the Newsboy selling the *Daily Worker*.

Newsboy soon became one of America's most popular Workers' plays, and the Shock Troupe's production easily won the award at the National Workers Theatre Festival in Chicago in 1934. On their way to the LOWT's Festival in Chicago, the Shock Troupe performed *Newsboy* over ten times in cities en route, and on their return to New York performed it regularly. Later in 1934 the Workers' Laboratory Theatre included *Newsboy* in their evening of revolutionary plays which was staged in a Broadway theatre, and within a few months it had been performed throughout America.

Newsboy remained popular with the Workers groups for years and was adapted and re-styled according to changing political strategy and ideology. The accompanying text of *Newsboy* was adapted by Gregory Novikov for the American League Against War and Fascism and differs considerably from the Shock Troupe's original. The League was established only in 1935 and was a Communist Party controlled, Popular Front organization. The adapted version of *Newsboy*, therefore, reflects the League's ideological stance and contemporary political concerns. The 1935 version of the play is more concerned with anti-war and anti-Fascist sentiments than the original. The shift in emphasis was achieved by one basic addition – the inclusion of three political speakers. The three speakers were all contemporary American politicians; the Southern demogogue Huey Long, the reactionary priest, Father Coughlin, and the newspaper magnate, William Randolph Hearst. All three were enemies of the League because they shared sympathies which were often Fascist either by statement or implication. Of the three, Hearst is the most important.

Unlike Long and Coughlin, he is speaking into a phone and not a microphone. Hearst is not making a public speech but is dictating policy and headlines to his newspaper editors. The inclusion of Hearst draws together the themes of escapist 'Red scare' journalese and proto-Fascist ideals, re-emphasizing *Newsboy*'s central critique that the media are controlled by an unfriendly ruling élite.

Despite the additional speeches by Long, Coughlin and Hearst, several changes in slogans and references and a more defined anti-Fascist stance, the 1935 version is similar to the Shock Troupe's *Newsboy* of 1933. A comparison of the two reconfirms Workers Theatre's response to changing political strategy and underlines Agit-Prop's adaptability. Both Agit-Prop and Living Newspaper styles were fundamental to Workers Theatre because they could be changed, reformed and reassessed. *Newsboy* manifests elements of both styles and emphasizes the American movement's commitment to utilitarian drama.

Although there is no clear indication that the Shock Troupe exerted much influence outside America, they were considered to be a very real influence on the Federal Theatre and on a number of other radical theatre ventures in the latter years of the 1930s. Ironically, their main influence on workers' culture outside America came about because of a visit abroad by one of the Shock Troupe's most active members, Will Lee. He spent a short time in Glasgow and was a close comrade of the Glasgow WTM. A considerable amount of their repertory material was borrowed from the USA and their Living Newspapers owed more to the Americans than they did to the Workers' Theatre groups in London. Within the Workers' Theatre Movement, international boundaries were crossed with phenomenal regularity and a veritable common market of playscripts, ideas and theoretical positions was in existence.

IV
A chronology of the Shock Troupe's activities

1928 The Workers' Laboratory Theatre formed in New York as a result of the cultural initiatives of European agencies such as Workers' International Relief.

1929   The Workers' Laboratory Theatre form the vanguard of the New York Drama Council and have an active membership of over fifty. They organize a 'Proletkult' centre in New York.

1930   An intensification of political activism in the USA and the socio-economic effects of the Wall Street crash begins to stretch the resources of the WLT. They perform several times a day in and around New York. The most popular plays include *Tempo! Tempo!*, *Vote Communist*, *Art is a Weapon* and *White Trash*.

1931   The Workers' Laboratory Theatre are forced, by the demand on their services, to create a special emergency theatre group called the Shock Troupe. The troupe live collectively in an apartment in the lower east side and make themselves available to strikers and workers' organizations. They have an active nucleus of thirteen members.
       The Shock Troupe write a short play in defence of the Scottsboro Boys, perform on behalf of the Communist Party in Union Square and appear at picnics in parks throughout New York.

1932   The Workers' Laboratory Theatre create yet another faction called Red Vaudeville who specialize in political comedy, magic and burlesque routines. One of Red Vaudeville's most popular sketches is an agitational comedy, *The Big Stiff*. They collaborate with the Shock Troupe on a political sideshow for outdoor performance.

1933   The Shock Troupe perform their summer extravaganza *World Fair* in opposition to the Chicago World Fair celebrating the progress of capitalism. The Theatre Collective faction of the WLT emerge as an active force within New York's radical theatre movement. Among the members of Theatre Collective are Joseph Losey, Nicholas Ray and Mordecai Gorelick. The Shock Troupe perform in front of an audience of 100,000 workers during the year.

1934   The Shock Troupe write a new Scottsboro play and perform the anti-Nazi satire *Who's Who in the Berlin Zoo*. In April they tour the industrial towns of Michigan en route to the annual Workers' Theatre Festival in Chicago. The Shock Troupe's festival entry, *Newsboy*, wins first prize. On returning from Chicago the troupe perform their summer extravaganza, *Chamber of Horrors*.

1934 The Shock Troupe begin to present theoretical writings in support of their dramatic productions. Al Saxe writes '*Newsboy*': *From Script to Performance* and Peter Martin writes *Montage*, which both display a grounding in dialectical materialism and an acquaintance with Eisenstein's early theoretical writings on dialectical montage.

The Workers' Laboratory Theatre form a separate puppet section and by the end of 1934 the troupe have performed to a total estimated audience of half a million people and now have a repertoire of eighty-three plays.

1935 The Shock Troupe perform productions of *Jews at the Crossroads* and *Daughter* but due to a policy shift within American Workers Theatre they were soon to be re-named Theatre of Action. The foundation of the Government's Federal Theatre Project in the autumn of 1935 radically changed the future of American Workers Theatre. Most groups subscribed to an unwritten policy of entryism and abandoned the mobile theatre to work inside the framework of the FTP.

Notes

1 For a more detailed study of American Workers Theatre see Malcolm Goldstein, *The Political Stage*, London, 1974.
2 Notice the similarity between Tom Thomas's *Their Theatre and Ours* and the League of Workers Theatres' play *Art is a Weapon* or the way in which the Prolet Buehne's sketch *Tempo! Tempo!* was used as a song ('Speed Up, Speed Up') in the British WTM *Rationalisation*.
3 The influence of national or ethnic cultures has always been of first-hand importance to political theatre. Even in Britain and America today 'cultural nationalism' is fundamental to political performance.

In Britain 7:84 (Scotland) relies heavily on the idiom and culture of the Scottish urban and rural working class, whereas in America the concerns and rituals of Chicano culture are central to the performance manifesto of El Teatro Campesino.

4 It should be borne in mind that the British WTM was more concerned with taking an anti-royalist position.

5 Goldstein, op. cit., p. 13.

6 Hallie Flanagan, 'A Theatre is Born', *Theatre Arts Monthly*, vol. 15, 1931, p. 908.

7 The Living Newspaper technique emerged out of the propagandist experimentation in post-Revolutionary Russia. It became a popular form with workers' groups throughout Europe and ultimately reached America. Flanagan had seen Living Newspaper productions in Russia and America and eventually adapted the style to suit the requirements of the Federal Theatre Project (FTP). The FTP Living Newspapers (1935–9) remain America's most valuable contribution to epic theatre and are clearly indebted to Workers Theatre.

8 Goldstein, op. cit., p. 50.

9 'Paterson Silk Strike Pageant', *Drama Review*, vol. 15, no. 3, summer 1971, p. 61.

10 Foreword to *Strike*, *New Masses*, July 1926, p. 19.

11 An *Arbeiterbund* was the name given to a workers' social club. John Bonn had previously worked with a number of important theatre practitioners in Germany, including Erwin Piscator. He arrived in the USA in 1929 as a Communist Party functionary and began to organize the German émigré community into a more coherent political and cultural force.

12 Within a year the Workers' Dramatic Council included twenty-one different Workers' Theatre groups including Germans, Lithuanians, Ukrainians, Russians, Hungarian and Jewish groups.

13 The most important groups performing outside New York seem to have been the Solidarity Players of Boston, the Vanguard Players of Philadelphia, the Rebel Players of Los Angeles and the Blue Blouses of Chicago. These groups were normally associated with more established workers' cultural organizations such as the John Reed Clubs.

14 Copies of the magazine *Workers Theatre* are almost impossible to locate. Cornell University Library, Ithaca, New York, have the complete set on microtext.

15 John E. Bonn, 'The Problem of Form', 1931. This essay originally appeared in *Workers Theatre* but is reprinted in *Guerilla Street Theatre*, ed. Henry Lesnick, Bard Avon, 1973.

16 Theatre Union remained in existence for four years. The company's most infamous production was the 1935 production of Brecht's *The*

Mother. Theatre Union did not fully understand Brecht's as yet uncodified propositions for an epic theatre style and as a result the production was a political, artistic and financial failure. The controversy caused by Brecht's and Eisler's attitude to the production left Brecht with very few admirers among New York's left-wing theatre circle and his work was partly ignored as a result. Only John Bonn and Mordecai Gorelick appeared to have any desire to understand Brechtian theory.

17 *New Theatre* magazine is equally difficult to locate, but copies still exist in New York Public Library.

18 John Bonn of the Prolet Buehne became director of the Federal Theatre German Unit, Stephen Karnot of the Workers' Laboratory Theatre became an FTP administrator, and Joe Losey of Theatre Collective became a director with the Living Newspaper Unit.

19 The professional Group Theatre was an offshoot of the establishment, the Theatre Guild, and was under the directorial control of Lee Strasberg, Harold Clurman and Cheryl Crawford. Group Theatre was reassessing the acting techniques of Stanislavsky and the Moscow Art Theatre and applying the principles of 'authentic emotion' and 'psychological realism' to the social concerns of depression America.

20 Hungarian workers were particularly adventurous in comparison to most other mobile troupes. In 1931 both the Hungarian Workers' Shock Brigade and the Uj Elöre group hired cars at weekends and drove away from New York to cities as far south as Baltimore to perform. They sought out Hungarian communities all over the eastern seaboard and used their performances as a means of advertising and selling the Hungarian Workers' daily paper *Uj Elöre*.

21 Bonn, op. cit.

22 Peter Martin, 'A Day with the Shock Troupe of the Workers' Laboratory Theatre', *Daily Worker* (New York), 23 May 1934, p. 5.

23 James Warren, 'How Members of the Shock Troupe Live and Work', *Daily Worker* (New York), 28 December 1934, p. 5.

24 Richard Pack, 'Shock Troupe in Action', *New Theatre*, November 1934, p. 13.

Documents

First National Workers Theatre Conference (1932)

The political, economic and cultural background

1 The first National Workers Theatre Conference takes place in a period of the most severe economic crisis that American capitalism has ever undergone. Thirteen million American workers are unemployed. Millions of small farmers are ruined. Production in every industry, except the war industry, is being sharply curtailed, in the face of the tremendous needs and growing misery of the workers and farmers. At the same time, American imperialism works imperialist powers to prepare an immediate war against the only country where the workers and farmers rule, the only country that steadily raises the economic and cultural level of its toilers – the Soviet Union!

2 In the present period, the bourgeois theatre (like all bourgeois culture) is also experiencing the sharpest crisis it has ever known. More than half of its actors, artists, and musicians are admitted to be unemployed. Wages of those still employed are being slashed. The bourgeois cinema has great mass influence, but the bourgeois theatre in the United States has never reached the great masses, except to a limited extent in a few big cities. And now all but a few theatres are unoccupied. Soup kitchens and the proceeds of charity concerts are all our American bourgeois society has to offer those theatre workers and artists who serve it. At the same time, the leaders of the Actors' Equity Association, affiliated with the American Federation of Labor, have not raised a finger to resist the worsening of the conditions of its members, but have gone ahead and increased the initiation fee and annual dues. The Little Theatre Movement, which under the false banner of 'Art for Art's Sake' set out to reform and rescue the bourgeois theatre, has collapsed under the strain of the economic and ideological crisis of capitalism.

3 At the same time, the reformist Socialist Party leadership suddenly sets up a so-called 'Workers Theatre' demagogically

repeating the revolutionary slogan of 'Art is a Weapon' and even speaking of 'Class War'. But its true nature came out in its very first production, which ends up with old unemployed workers finding their only way out by turning on the gas and committing suicide. As a further demagogic trick with the approach of the first National Workers Theatre Spartakiade and Conference, the 'socialist' fakers announce, on one day's notice in the bourgeois press, a 'First Workers Theatre Conference' to discuss forming a national organization. That this so-called conference was a dema-gogic stage trick is shown by the fact they had a total attendance of nine people, of whom some were paid functionaries of the Socialist Party Rand★ School.

This activity of the cultural fakers is a frantic attempt to coun-teract the rising influence of the revolutionary Workers Theatre.

4   The growth of the revolutionary Workers Theatre in America is an accompaniment of the intensifying crisis of capi-talism, which results on the one hand in a rising wave of revol-utionary struggle on all fronts by the workers and farmers, and on the other hand in the increasing radicalization of petty-bourg-eois theatre workers, artists, and students.

5   The rise of the revolutionary Workers Theatre, whose high spot in this country is marked by the present National Spartakiade and Conference, is an international phenomenon. Its increasing effectiveness as a weapon of the working class is shown by the attempts of the bourgeoisie and their 'socialist' henchmen to suppress the Agit-Prop theatre troupes in Germany, Japan, Czechoslovakia and other lands, attempts which will also be made soon in the United States. In fact, the police in Los Angeles, California, already seek to smash up all performances by the Rebel Players, a revolutionary Workers Theatre in that city.

6   The tremendous growth of the revolutionary Workers Theatre in the United States dates back a year and a half ago to the letter of the International Workers' Dramatic Union to the Cultural Department of the Workers' International Relief, to the establishment of the *Workers Theatre* magazine by the Workers' Laboratory Theatre of the Workers' International Relief in April 1931, and its rapid growth of influence under the joint editorship

---

★ Possibly a reference to a conservative faction within the American Socialist Party who took their name from the philosopher Rand. (S.C.]

of the Workers' Laboratory Theatre of the WIR and the Prolet Buehne, German Agit-Prop Troupe of New York.

Agit-Prop Theatre and stationary theatre

7 With the development of the Workers Theatre Movement, there is taking place a sharp turn towards Agit-Prop work. Workers Theatres in all languages in the United States are coming to realize more and more that this form of theatre, with its forcefulness, mobility, and political timeliness, is the basic form of Workers Theatre in the present stage of the class struggle. But we must be careful to see that our Agit-Prop plays have good entertainment value.

8 At the same time, there is a growing understanding of the proper role of the stationary Workers Theatre, which should be as highly political in content as the Agit-Prop type, but which has possibilities for more thorough and more impressive treatment of the most important subjects.

Basic tasks

9 The basic tasks of the Workers Theatre now are to spread the idea of the class struggle, to participate actively in the class struggle by raising funds for campaigns and for the revolutionary press, and by recruiting workers into the revolutionary unions and mass organizations, and especially to arouse the workers for the defense of the Soviet Union, against the coming Imperialist attack.

Shortcomings

10 The main shortcomings of the Workers Theatre in America today are
- that there are not enough contacts between groups.
- that there are not enough plays being written to meet the growing need.
- that the more developed groups outside New York City do not assist the weaker groups in their locality.
- that the groups underestimate the necessity for co-operation.
- that there is no systematic attempt to build theatre groups in the revolutionary unions and in most of the mass organizations.
- that international contacts are very weak.

Tasks – general

11   To overcome its weakness and to accomplish its important tasks, the Workers Theatre must undertake the systematic political and artistic training of its members. It must increase and improve its Agit-Prop work. It must go out to the masses – into the streets, to the factory gates, to the farms. It must reach the rank and file of the American Federation of Labor and the Socialist Party.

It must build and make use of the stationary Workers Theatre wherever there are possibilities for its effective utilization.

It must experiment with forms in order to find the most effective methods of presenting its subject matter. It must use music and the dance and all other cultural forms, in order to make its material more attractive. It must take over from the bourgeois theatre whatever can be used for revolutionary aims.

It must expose and fight anti-working-class propaganda of the bourgeois theatre and its 'socialist' stepchild. It must expose the deception of the slogan, 'Art for Art's Sake'.

It must draw in large numbers of workers and farmers. It must draw in sympathetic artists and intellectuals.

Tasks – repertory

12   It must more quickly catch up with, and dramatize, the day-to-day struggles of the American working class.

It must present the most important developments of the class struggle in other countries.

It must popularize the tremendous achievement of the workers and farmers of the Soviet Union.

It must make clear that the great vitality of the Soviet Theatre today was only made possible by the proletarian revolution in that country.

It must win workers and farmers, including those in the armed forces, for the tactic of turning the coming imperialist war against the Soviet Union into a civil war against the imperialists.

Tasks – organizational

13   To correct serious shortcomings in its organizational work
   – it must establish the closest contact with, and help build, Agit-Prop troupes in the revolutionary unions and mass organizations.

- it must stimulate the growth of the Workers Theatre in the important industrial sectors and in the rural districts.
- it must establish closer contact with the organizations of revolutionary writers, particularly to help solve the problem of adequate repertory.
- it must establish a national Workers Theatre organization as the United States section of the International Workers' Dramatic Union.

The national organization must include federations of all Workers Theatres in the various languages, building federations where they do not exist. The national Workers Theatre organization will be a tremendous stimulus to the further growth of the revolutionary Workers Theatre.

The 'Workers Theatre' magazine

14 All Workers Theatre groups should support and build the official organ of the national Workers Theatre organization. The *Workers Theatre* magazine is one of the most important instruments for the building of the revolutionary Workers Theatre movement.

Revolutionary competition

15 The experience of the Workers Theatres in other countries shows that one of the most effective methods of stimulating and improving the activities of the Workers Theatre group is the method of revolutionary competition. The Workers Theatre in the United States must adopt this method and must organize such competitions between the various groups and districts, including as an annual event the revolutionary competition of the National Workers Theatre Spartakiade.

Theatre and its relation to the general revolutionary movement
The workers

16 Every Workers Theatre group must realize that its existence is closely tied up with that of the entire revolutionary movement – that its aims are the same – that its slogans are the same – that only under the closest guidance of, and co-operation with, the revolutionary organizations of the Workers Theatre in the United States, as in other lands, can they march forward as an important

factor in the overthrow of the capitalist system, in the emancipation of the working class, to the glorious building of classless society.

(Source: *Workers Theatre*, May 1932, p. 5)

Terms for the National Workers Theatre Spartakiade (1932)

16 April 1932, at Manhattan Lyceum, 66 E.4th Street, New York City

Accepted at a general membership meeting of the New York Workers Theatres, 6 March 1932

1   The play to be performed must deal with problems of the working class.

2   The play must be one that has not yet been performed, or rehearsed, by the particular group.

3   The following plays, which have been performed too often, and a production of them will not show the ability of a group, are not to be used by the Workers Theatres of Greater New York and Newark, N.J.:

1 *Box, Nox, and Fox*	2 *Step on it!*
3 *Fight Against Starvation*	4 *It's Funny as Hell*
5 *Unemployed* (*Work or Wages*)	6 *Tempo! Tempo!*
7 *On the Belt*	8 Scottsboro Group Recitation
9 *Liberty in USA*	10 *Unite and Fight!* (Pantomime)
11 *ILD More Than Ever!*	12 *Lenin Calls* (Group Recitation)
13 *Fritz and Fedor*	14 *To Victory!*
15 *Help the Miners!*	

4   Each group is allowed
15 Minutes for the performance
5 Minutes to set up the stage
5 Minutes to clear the stage

5   Copies of the plays must be in the hands of the Dramburo by 1 April.

6   The stage consists of a plain gray back curtain and gray side hangers and will not be changed. Each group may put up the necessary props and scenery during the allotted time for preparation, five minutes. Five minutes after the performance, the neutral stage must be ready for the next group.

7   The order of the performances will be arranged at a meeting of representatives of all competing groups, on Monday, 4 April at 8.30 p.m. at the Workers Center, 35 East 12th Street, New York City.

8   Ten judges will be elected to judge the performances. Five will be taken from the Workers' Theatres and five from organizations not doing theatre work.

9   *How to judge the performances*

The performances will be judged by points.

Political value of play: perfect	50 points
Artistic value of play: perfect	50 points
Perfect score	100 points

Political

Best political content	20 points
Clarity of political content	20 points
Importance of subject	10 points
	50 points

Artistic

Entertainment value (effectiveness)	15 points
Technical execution of players	15 points
Use of technical means to express political content	5 points
Smoothness of performance	10 points
New ideas	5 points
	50 points

Minus Points

Points will be taken off for the following shortcomings

Overtime in preparing the stage

For each minute over the allotted time	1 point
For more than ten minutes' preparation	10 points

For non-political elements in the play, i.e., parts of the play that have no connection with the content of the play, parts that are only added, for example, to make the play 'pretty'

For slight mistakes	1 point
For medium mistakes	5 points
For serious mistakes	10 points

Besides the ten judges, the audience will also judge by question-naires, which will be distributed before the performances start.

(Source: *Workers Theatre*, March 1932)

'Newsboy': from Script to Performance (1934)

There has been much discussion pro and con about form in the Workers Theatre. Which is the real revolutionary form? Is it satire, realism, symbolism, etc.? Must we laugh in the revolutionary theatre or shall solemnity rule the day? In the Workers' Laboratory Theatre we have been producing various forms for the last four years. Patiently, diligently we have gone about dissecting the elements of various theatrical 'isms' looking for forms which will best solve the problems of the theatres of action – namely, to present a story dynamically, clearly, in terms of dramatic images within a time space of not more than forty minutes.

For four years we have been searching for forms pliable enough to fit any content, to be cast to any mould – any situation. By this time it is obvious that no one form will ever solve the problems of the Theatre of Action. To expect such is to narrow and simplify a problem which must of necessity – as a reflection of actual conditions – be as varied as these conditions. The more varied our approach to the present forms, the more critical and experimental our approach to these forms, the more quickly will new forms be added to the old.

Four years' work then have helped in the attempt at mastery of the old forms and, further, have already assisted in the development of a new form which to date shows great possibility for use in the Workers Theatre. One of the most pliable, dynamic theatre of action forms which has yet appeared is the technique utilized in *Newsboy*.

What are the elements of form and content which went into the construction of *Newsboy*? Groups facing similar problems throughout the country are to search for what – in the mastery of this technique?

Very sketchily I will attempt to draw a picture of the major element a director must be conscious of in approaching his problem. I boil it down to the essentials which make up *Newsboy* – conflict – mounting – economy – transition – timing.

Conflict is the basis, the root of all life movement. The Marxist who studies the dialectic forces, the scientist who analyses the struggle of plant and animal life – the molecular conflict of matter – understand very well the law of conflicting elements. The theatre long before the approach of materialism made use of conflict unconsciously as the basic factor in a play, without realizing its tremendous role in society. Today we have come to a historic period when this conflict has reached a higher level. Marxism has penetrated the entire economic and political thought. Industrialization has quickened the consciousness of this interplay of social forces on the minds of millions of workers. The crisis has torn down illusion after illusion and brought these conflicting forces more and more into the open. As a form *Newsboy* is a definite reflection of the quickening process of this conflict. It is pitched at the feverish tempo of industrialization gone mad. A scene comes and goes as swiftly as a machine. Push a lever and a character springs up like magic – press a button, he disappears, changes quickly to another character. What essentially makes *Newsboy* dynamic? It is the intensity, speed and conflict of present-day industrialized America. Nothing more. Here we must look for our answer to form such as *Newsboy*. The more deeply we go into the processes responsible for the growth of society and all its mainsprings; the more thoroughly we study the conflicts in today's

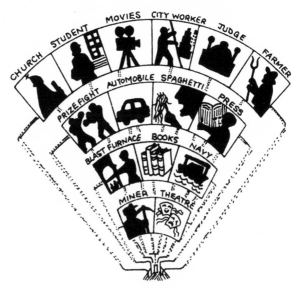

and tomorrow's events, the more capable we become of producing such dynamic material. Conflict is the first and primary factor. Conflict never leaves *Newsboy*. An analysis of any part of the script finds this clash – everywhere. In the opening scene, for example, playing time of sixty seconds, the conflicts illustrated opposite take place.

Within the space of sixty seconds four completely separate conflicts take place. We will find consistent conflict through the entire play. *Newsboy* is built around a series of conflicting images to the ideology of the newsboy and the attempt to draw him to a higher level of understanding. Every scene drips with this clash. The scene from *1931* is built on conflict. The third–degree scene is one of tightening tense conflict between the Negro and his torturers. Every available inch of space and time is taken up with the clash of two forces – the dialectical method is the manner of conceiving the things and beings of the universe as in the process of becoming, through the struggle of contradictory elements and their resolution. Thus with a thorough grasp of dialectics and its application, directors of the Workers' Theatre will be able to produce dramatic dynamic realities. . . .

The diagram opposite shows a series of seemingly unrelated incidents. Under capitalist society we are educated to believe that these incidents take place without rhyme or reason – that chaos bestrides the world like a colossus; that luck, opportunity, good fortune, chance and the roulette wheel make or break not only kings, queens and presidents but also, alack-a-day, the poor masses. The Marxist approach smashes this theory to bits. The Marxist interpretation of history clarifies and shows scientifically the relationship of the smallest details and incidents in every part of the world. The clash between the two dominating classes (historical materialism), the growth of this struggle leads today to a terrific heightening and quickening of the process of struggle throughout the world – and increase in the pitch, acceleration and rapidity with which the above events happen. *Newsboy* as a form is particularly suitable to throw into relief, to bring out the relationship of these incidents. Here is not the conventional two- or three-act production which requires an organic and intricate development of plot – a psychological analysis of characters – a growth of character to character and act to act. There is no plot, no relationship as we are acquainted with it in the ordinary theatre. Instead we take as our plot the line of Marxist thought of a particular poem, a short story, etc. (Note diagram – the thread which joins all.) Around this thread we are at liberty to choose any scene at random. In *Newsboy* for example the plot is as follows: to show the truth and strength of the revolutionary press in relationship to the working class and in opposition to this the hypocrisy of the capitalist controlled newspapers. This is what is expressed in poetic images in the poem 'Newsboy' by V. J. Jerome. Translating these poetic images into dramatic ones allows the liberty of choosing any one of hundreds of incidents, allows one to choose scenes from plays already written (scenes in *Newsboy* from Claire and Paul Sifton's *1931* and Maltz and Sklar's powerful *Merry Go Round*). Let us take for example the following line from the poem 'Newsboy':

'Seventeen million men and women.'

To dramatize this image we picked the scene from *1931*. Any number of other things could have been used. Evictions – men sleeping in subways, parks – death, misery, starvation in hundreds of forms happening in every section of the world . . . Having finished this scene we revert back to the poem carrying the thought of the poem further. Thus image after image is built and developed. Incident follows incident without the conventional continuity of conventional drama – street scene, bread-line, ballet – scenes which could just as easily be utilized in any other production.

These scenes, however, are built just as the conventional play is built – a logical climax, a growth of the idea to its completion. How these scenes are placed or mounted to allow for this development, both artistic and ideological, becomes highly important. Here one *must thoroughly plan, step by step, the process of development, allowing for both the social and artistic value of the play to grow up together.* Scenes must be mounted to build emotional and ideological climax organically to its finale. The pliability of this form – the fact that scenes may skip from coast to coast – from New York to San Francisco to Rome, utilizing the Marxist thread to keep them together, makes it possible for this form more so than any other to keep pace, to best reflect, to gather these incidents of seeming chaos and clarify them with scientific materialist understanding.

Economy – transition – timing. To carry through successfully such a form requires not alone the thorough study and application of dialectics and historical materialism – but, it goes without saying, theatrical knowledge; of problems of the theatre conquering all its forms (for such a form as *Newsboy* which is a composite and makes use of several forms in one – where the characters are at times symbols then real – where they jump from newsboy to thug to minister) and mastery of technique is essential. In *Newsboy* as in other plays of a similar character there are several outstanding technical problems which face director and actor. I choose at the present stage of theoretical development to touch on three elements. Economy – transition – timing. Here it is necessary to state that none of these elements is clear cut. Each overlaps into the other, each moulds and affects the other.

Here is a conversation which took place the other day after a particularly effective performance of *Newsboy*.

HE: I certainly enjoyed sweating through that performance.
I: Thank you.

(*Followed a discussion on the merits of collective work.*)

HE: By the way, how long does the performance run?
I: Twelve minutes.
HE: (*astonished*) What! You're kidding me.
I: Certainly not.
HE: You must be mistaken. I'm sure it takes at least a half-hour.
I: (*gently but firmly*) No. Exactly twelve minutes.

Here is the answer to the problem of economy. Every minute of a short production is highly important. Every minute of that twelve minutes is so full that the audience has lived through an entire evening. There is no waste. Every minute is filled with conflict, action, with theatrical pictures. Say what you have to say – and be done saying it. Thus scene by scene, point by point, idea following idea, each germinating to its emotional crisis, developing and growing minute by minute to a final great crash, the idea has crystallized – the play is finished.

I have seen many potentially good plays ruined because there was a lack of recognition of that essential element – economy of words and movement – no growth to new ideas but a constant repetition of the old ideas hiding in different words – prolonging a scene and dragging in ideas which are not important and in keeping with the sum total of the content. *To assist in achieving economy in production a clear and thoroughly planned script, step by step, from idea to idea, is highly important, with constant revision from rehearsal to rehearsal.*

Economy is closely tied up with the element of timing. Timing is a problem of every Workers Theatre production. In such a script as *Newsboy* timing becomes even more a part of the whole than in the conventional drama. Here we depend on speed and precision, one scene must dovetail into the next without a second's loss. A cross-section of events takes place – a bread-line – a street – a torture cell – never for a moment is the stage empty – as one actor leaves the other enters. Now, are we to know the proper moment when actions should begin – stop –? What is the basis for an understanding of the timing problems? Here we must understand the value and relationship of rhythm to the theatre. We find everything in life is rhythmic. The earth spins a rotating rhythm on its axis. The seasons come and go in rhythmic succession. All nature is rhythmically arranged. Our bodies work, play, walk in rhythm. Timing is the concrete application of these rhythms to the theatre. Timing is the coincidence in time of two or more actions. There are hundreds of variations in timing – some obvious, others highly subtle. The more conscious we become, the more keenly we adjust eye and ear to the rhythm and timings in realities around us, the more sensitive our reactions and our ability to transmit these rhythms to the stage. The director, let us say, is faced with the problem of bringing out competition under capitalism. He is given Capitalist A representing one trust, and B the other. The action is worked out as follows – at no time do A and B sit or stand together. When A sits – B is standing fully erect. And when B hits the chair we find A standing. If the scene is to be effective it depends on exact timing. *At exactly the point when A hits the chair B is standing.* Make use of musical time – four beats to a measure. At the end of the fourth beat A is standing, B sitting – at the end of the next measure the positions are exactly reversed. Simple enough in such an obvious problem in timing. *Newsboy* is filled with a series of subtle rhythms. The timing, the exact beat when one scene gives way to the next, one character enters, does his bit and makes way for a new character – a new scene – is what helps build the intense speed and excitement of the production.

Perhaps the most difficult task in evolving *Newsboy* and one
which is still far from clarified in its actual technical process of
growth is what we term 'transitions' – changes from scene to
scene. In a series of unrelated incidents as in *Newsboy* the task is
that of bridging the gap from realism to symbolism, from street
scene to home scene to bread-line and yet allowing your audience
to understand, to believe with the character in the illusion of this
change. Here the change will be dictated by the material – at times
soft, at times smooth, flowing easily into the next scene itself.
Timing plays an important role. Mechanically again let us do our
transition by means of beat. In three beats we shall change from
a street scene into a bread-line. As the street scene ends – Beat
One – the actors freeze – not a soul moves, *first movement* – preparation for the transition.

Beat Two – the actors make one movement which relates itself
to hungry men on the bread-line, for example – hunching over –
turning up collar, etc. Here the softness or strength of the movement is dictated by the content, i.e., if the content is weak the
transition movement will be weak and *vice versa*. *Second movement*
– transition half accomplished.

Beat Three – all actors turn on the third beat and to an increased
rhythm fall one behind the other to a steady hunger pace – *third
movement* – simple mechanical transition accomplished. Sometimes
these transitions are violent. In *Newsboy*, for example – a line of
the poem:

Two hundred white men take a black man for a ride and string
him up a tree and shoot his body full of holes because a white
woman said he smiled at her.

Action – Negro breaks from group back stage and runs forward
to audience. The position of the figures on the stage all grouped
at the back – the figure of the Negro worker at the front of the
stage makes it very difficult to change to the next scene, which is
from *Merry Go Round*. Four of the figures must leave the stage –
four others who are at the moment class-conscious workers must
become thugs. The position of Negro and white workers must be
completely reversed. The scene is a third degree. Very well. We
will make our transition violent. While the Negro worker has been
speaking, those not in the scene shuffle quietly and quickly off. At

the same time, the white men turn their back to the audience, and as the Negro finishes a white man grabs him and hurls him back. Crash – the Negro finds himself thrown to the floor into a frame-up scene – the backs of the white men loom ominously and obviously tell the story of the change. There are hundreds of transition methods. Many of them have not been touched at all – the actors' problem, of thought, imagery, concentration, etc., is a book in itself. I have merely attempted to open new avenues of thought and have tried to give a picture of the thorough study and concentration necessary to solving the vastness and scope of our problems. These problems will develop and grow with the development of Workers' Theatre. Every attempt must be made to clarify these problems. Groups and individuals can help by asking technical questions which will be answered here or analysing their own experiences for publication in *New Theatre*. In the meantime we must forge ahead. Our basis for development lies in an eagerness to delve into new fields, to learn from the theatre of the past – to draw in professionals and semi-professionals, to assist in this clarification, to gain strength in a new scientific Marxist understanding of life and its application to the artistic problems of the theatre.

(Source: *New Theatre*, July–August 1934)
ALFRED SAXE

Workers' art in summer camp (1930)

The scene is the social hall at Camp Nitgedaiget, a workers' summer camp at Beacon, N.Y. A drum beats out a rhythm and on the stage a group of workers go through staccato motions – slaves on the belt. A boss with a cigar in his mouth speeds up each worker while the drum beats faster. On the wall is a sign: $16. A worker drops out; from the unemployed workers who answer the 'Help Wanted' sign another takes his place at $14 a week. So it goes on – speed-up, wage-cuts, unemployment. And then the revolt. The mannequins spring to life. Strike! An A. F. of L. faker to the rescue. The boss and the faker embrace. But the Trade Union Unity League (TUUL) leads the workers, both employed and unemployed – The Trade Union Unity League and the Communist Party. The two moving groups of factory workers and unemployed workers join, and the boss and A. F. of L. fakers are crushed between them. The audience bursts forth in spontaneous applause while actors and audience join in singing 'Solidarity Forever' and 'The Internationale'. Out of the singing group of actors a speaker for the TUUL steps forth. Make-believe merges into reality and the speaker makes an appeal for the TUUL.

It is pantomime, simple, elemental, amazingly effective. The occasion was the beginning of the Trade Union Unity League week at Camp Nitgedaiget, for the benefit of the militant trade union center of the American working class. The pantomime, the central feature of the evening's program, was arranged by V. J. Jerome, educational director of the camp. The rhythms were the work of Lhan Adohmyan, a member of the John Reed Club, who is in charge of library and musical work. The actors were drawn from the campers. Among them were six hard proletarians from Seattle, who only a few hours before had driven into camp in their third-hand car on the way to the seventh National Convention of the Communist Party. They were tired and hadn't had a decent night's sleep for two weeks, but they were glad to take part in the pantomime. Later, one of them, a lean lumberjack with graying hair, addressed the crowd and told of conditions in Seattle.

There will be many more such evenings at Camp Nitgedaiget this summer. Cultural work is a regular part of the camp activities.

Artef, the remarkable Jewish workers' dramatic organization, is going to produce plays, and Fritz Brosius, another member of the John Reed Club, will do the scenery. And this year, more than ever before, cultural activities in the English language will occupy a leading place.

(*Source*: letter dated July 1930 to the editor of *New Masses*)
A. B. MAGIL
BEACON, N.Y.

The mill workers produce a play (1930)

Dear Comrades,

Members of the National Textile Workers Union in New Bedford planned a celebration for the second anniversary of the New Bedford Strike on 13 April 1930. The Union arranged for mass meetings all over the city. But the workers felt that they wanted something more in which they could express their fiery memories of the great struggle.

So a group of workers, most of them who had been among the best fighters in the strike and are still leading fighters in the New Bedford Mills, got together and informally wrote a play. The idea for it, and the play itself, came from Anton Ferrira. Manvel Perry, another mill worker gave a hand on it. Others suggested changes, worked out details. They called their play *The Life of a Worker*. In it they portrayed a typical worker developing through exploitation and struggle into a member of a revolutionary union.

The Life of a Worker is a crude and simple piece of work. This group of revolutionary textile workers, who wrote it without assistance, know nothing of 'literature' and have no conscious literary desires. Their only aim was to produce a dramatic utterance of their own class experience, in which as many workers as possible (as well as their worker-audience) could participate. They achieved this with a rough proletarian force and directness that proved more effective with the masses than any well-behaved and well-dressed 'literature' or 'drama' could have been.

I don't know how the group found time to rehearse and do all the other work involved in producing their play, for each of these workers is active day and night in his union. But they found the time. Between meetings, demonstrations, and the countless duties of the class struggle they rehearsed, built their own settings, made and distributed leaflets, sold tickets. (W. T. Murdoch, organizer, recounts that during the first rehearsals they used real clubs for nightsticks, and they took their parts so seriously, two of the actors were knocked cold.)

The play was a great success and was given before an enthusiastic overflow audience of New Bedford Mill Workers. The merriment was great when a worker like Neto, who was one of the leaders in the bloody clash of 5,000 workers with the police force at the Dartmouth Mill gates last January, was seen acting the part of a cop and quite realistically clubbing another union leader, Anton Ferrira, who took the part of the worker. The actors needed no coaching to act the part of: Scab, Picket Captain, Young Worker, Worker's Wife, Strikers, etc.

The play was often written only in outline. The speeches of the organizers, cops, judges and others were often left to the actors. They knew these parts well enough from life. A stage collection made in the play was continued through the audience by one of the actors while the play went on. The audience contributed as they never had before. The performance was splendid. Naïvely and unconsciously they brought to their little stage that evening a revelation of the New Workers' Art in creation.

For weeks afterwards the workers in New Bedford kept asking for another performance of *The Life of a Worker*. The play was given again on 23 August and the textile workers are planning to give it in Boston and perhaps elsewhere.

It must be stated in conclusion that *The Life of a Worker* as played in New Bedford was not written and performed through any motive or conception of Workers' Art but solely in order to raise funds for the defence of August Pinto, one of the bravest workers in the New Bedford strike, who has now been six months in prison for union activity and is in danger of deportation. Nevertheless, the whole affair revealed eloquently, if unconsciously, the deep hunger of the working class for expression in art and the great ability of the workers to create their own art, a Workers' Art – powerful and indispensable weapon in the class struggle.

(*Source*: letter dated September 1930 to the editor of *New Masses*)
MARTIN RUSSAK

Scripts

Art is a Weapon (1931)

(*Mass recitation*)
CAPITALIST:
Art is – between ourselves,
  quite confidentially . . .
Art is a weapon –
Art is a weapon in the fight for my interests.
That may sound strange coming from me,
However, it is a fact. And of course facts cannot be . . .
Oh yes they can.
One can deny facts
One can distort facts
One can juggle facts
One can do with facts whatever – I want.
That is, art is a weapon.
  Art is a weapon in the fight for my interests.

For example – in the US we produce yearly
  ten of thousands
  novels
  short stories
  poems
  plays
  shows
  movies
  concerts
  sculpture.
All non-political – presented thousands of times
  before:
  school children
  factory workers
  students
  housewives

teachers
office workers
soldiers
unemployed.

All these works of art
do not state
but imply,
and hammer and hammer away
as though it were a fact . . .

That the United States is the free-est country in the world,
That the laws of this country are made for benefit of the workers,
That the workers must fight and die for their country,
That every worker not born here is inferior and suspicious,
That every worker not born white is inferior and despicable
And so on and so forth . . .

Now then –
    ART
    is a weapon
    in the fight
    for my
    interests. Of course . . . quite confidentially . . . between
    ourselves . . .

(*The song 'Left' is heard off stage and a mass of workers march on
    singing*)

SONG: LEFT LEFT LEFT LEFT
        The bugles are calling to fight,
        Left, Left, Left, Left.
        We'll answer the call to unite.
        We're marching hand in hand with the mass,
        We dramatize the fight of the classes
        With powerful melody.
        Our work will weld our strength and might
        And what we play is dynamite
        To the culture of the bourgeosie.
        Hello comrades. We greet you comrades:
        We raise our fists to the fight.

Workers of the nation, build our federation,
For victory comes with might.
The bosses' onslaught is steady
And we are bearing the brunt.
PROLETARIANS, Let's get ready!
RED FRONT! RED FRONT!

CAPITALIST: Ladies and gentleman, how do you do . . .

GROUP: RED FRONT!

CAPITALIST: Pardon my curiosity – whom have I the honor?

ONE: United Workers' Theatres of New York.

TWO: Workers' Laboratory Theatre, New York.

THREE: Prolet Buehne, New York.

GROUP: Agit-Prop troupes in New York.

CAPITALIST: Agit-Prop? . . .

GROUP: Agitation and propaganda.

CAPITALIST: Agitation and propaganda – for what?

GROUP: For the class struggle.

CAPITALIST: Class struggle? Against whom?

GROUP: Against you (*all point*)

CAPITALIST: Ladies and gentlemen . . . there is some misunderstanding here. First you introduce yourselves as a theatre group . . . and now you talk about political propaganda. These are two distinctly different subjects. Art has nothing to do with politics. Art is free. Art for art's sake.

GROUP: Art is a weapon
 theatre is a weapon
 Workers' Theatre is a weapon
 Workers' Theatre is a weapon in the class struggle.
 A weapon in the class struggle.

CAPITALIST: Ladies and gentlemen, you are making an unfortunate mistake. Art soars miles above the common place of daily routine, above politics, above party strife. Art is the expression of our yearning for beauty and harmony.

GROUP: Art is the expression of our yearning –
 yearning of slaves (for) freedom
 yearning of the hungry for bread
 yearning of the homeless for shelter
 yearning of the persecuted for rest
 yearning of the unemployed for work

yearning of the victims of capitalist brutality for
justice
yearning of the mistreated negroes for equality
yearning of the suppressed class for the abolition
of all classes
yearning of the rebellious for the final conflict
art is a weapon
theatre is a weapon
theatre is a weapon in the class struggle.

CAPITALIST: False, false – one hundred per cent false. Art is
impartial. Art belongs to all. Art makes us forget.

WORKERS: It makes us forget that you are our oppressors and
exploiters
it makes us forget that we the producers of all
commodities are starving
it makes us forget that you enjoy the fruits of
our labors
it makes us forget that we sacrifice our strength,
health and time for your pleasure
it makes us forget that there's a way to freedom
it makes us forget that there is *one* way to
freedom – through fight.

CAPITALIST: This conception of yours contradicts the age-old
definition of art.

WORKER: This conception of ours contradicts the age-old
definition of BOURGEOIS art.

CAPITALIST: This means destruction of culture.

WORKER: This means the destruction of a decayed culture of
oppression and exploitation.

CAPITALIST: Destruction by means of the theatre?

WORKER: Destruction by all weapons – also theatre.

CAPITALIST: That is revolution.

WORKER: That *is* revolution
the theatre of the future is the theatre of revolution
we
awaken
enlighten
arouse
every working man
every working woman

every young worker
all proletarians
the masses
to action.
We do not play
for your and our entertainment
we play
because participation in the class struggle
is your
and our
duty.
We show
the exploitation of the workers.
We show
the way out.
We show the only way out –
mass organization
mass action
organized mass action.
That's what we pray for
and fight for
we

GROUP: United Workers' Theatres of New York.
          Workers' Laboratory Theatre, New York.
          Prolet Buehne, New York.
GROUP: Theatre of Revolution.
                    (Source: *Workers Theatre*, June 1931, pp. 15–17)

15-Minute Red Revue (1932)

An Agit-Prop play by John E. Bonn
Prolet Buehne, New York

Note on the direction: eleven players are needed. We will not give too many notes on how to direct the *15-Minute Red Revue* as we think that here is a good chance for the groups to create their own way of performing.

It is suggested that: the rhymes be spoken in a strong rhythmic way and that action be paced in the same manner.

Part 1, players line up, front stage, one by one, while saying their lines. (The numbers 1, 2, 3, etc., stand for 1st Worker, 2nd Worker, etc.)

Part II, players change their position so that at the end they stand in an angle (like an inverted W) pointing to the map of the Soviet Union at the back curtain.

Notes for the other parts are included in the script.

I Agit-Prop
1: Comrades, workers, listen, stop –
   Prolet Buehne Agit-Prop.
2: Agit-Prop – against hunger and destitution –
   Agit-Prop – theatre of revolution –
3: Agit-Prop – wakes the masses to fight –
   Agit-Prop – is the workers' light –
4: Agit-Prop – in streets and factory gates –
   Agit-Prop – all over the United States –
5: Agit-Prop – and the bosses quake with fear –
   Agit-Prop – for the workers' day is near –
6: Agit-Prop – against the yellow socialists –
   Agit-Prop – against the preachers and Fascists –
7: Agit-Prop – against police terror and exploitation –
   Agit-Prop – against the lying press and starvation –
8: Agit-Prop – is the cannon's roar –
   Agit-Prop – is class war –
9: Agit-Prop – bears the battle's brunt –
   Agit-Prop – builds the revolutionary front –

10: Agit-Prop – strikes the bosses' iron hand –
    Agit-Prop – defends the Soviet Union, the workers'
    fatherland!
10: The workers' news –
 9: The workers' views –
 8: Protest of masses –
 7: War of classes –
 6: Strong – unyielding –
 5: Victory wielding –
 4: Tempo – action –
 3: Fights reaction –
 2: In street and shop –
 1: We never stop!
ALL: AGIT-PROP!

II Fifteen Minutes
 5: Working women, working men.
 5: Attention. Our play begins.
 4: We are going to play for you
 7: A fifteen minute red revue.
 3: Fifteen minutes goes rapidly.
 8: Fifteen minutes is eternity.
 2: In 15 minutes a factory may be shut.
 9: In 15 minutes your wages may be cut.
 1: In 15 minutes you may be hired.
10: In 15 minutes you may be fired.
 5: In 15 minutes you may be in jail.
 6: In 15 minutes you may be out on bail.
 4: In 15 minutes see war of the classes.
 7: In 15 minutes learn the strength of the masses.
 3: In 15 minutes one question you must face.
 8: In 15 minutes you must choose your place.
 2: In 15 minutes we must definitely know.
 9: In 15 minutes, are you friend or are you foe.
 1: In 15 minutes
10: Say what you are
1, 2, 3, 4, 5: For
6, 7, 8, 9, 10: or against

THE SOVIET UNION

ALL: the USSR.

(*All except 9 off stage.*)

III What is the Soviet Union?
9: The Soviet Union!
      What is the Soviet Union?
       What is the Soviet Union to us?
        What is a country to us
          that is thousands of miles away –
          separated from us by two oceans –
          whose language we cannot understand –
          which the government of the United States does not
      recognize?
      What is the Soviet Union?
      What is the Soviet Union to us?
4: The Soviet Union!
      One-sixth of the earth –
      161,000,000 people
    The Soviet Union!
      the workers and peasants have driven out
        the profitmakers
        the landlords
        the exploiters.
    The workers and peasants
      have destroyed
        a system of profiteering and exploitation!
    The capitalist dictatorship of the bosses
      have been replaced
        by the Soviets of the workers and peasants.
    The chaos of capitalism
      has been replaced
        by socialist construction.
    The Soviet Union
    One-sixth of the earth
      belongs to the workers and peasants
      belongs to the producing masses
      belongs to the proletariat.
2: This is the death sentence of capitalism!
      If the workers and peasants of Russia

Could throw off the leeches and exploiters –
Then the proletariat of other lands
Can throw off their leeches and exploiters –
If the workers and peasants of Russia
Can rule themselves –
Then the proletariat of all other lands
Can rule themselves.
The success of socialist construction in the Soviet Union
Is the death blow to capitalism.
Will the capitalist willingly give up their rule?
Will the capitalist stand for that?

CAPITALIST: I will not stand for that.
I will not give up my power.
Above everything, I must have – my profit.
And don't forget
I'm not dead yet
Attention – Attention – to the attack!
Beat the Soviet Union back!

IV Capitalism and its servants

(*March in:* Press, Censor, Radio, Justice, Art, Church, Science, Police – *line up, bow to Capitalist during his next line*)

I've done all I'm able
To keep my rule stable
But that's not enough.
My slaves you must bluff,
You must show them the way
To work for less pay
And keep them afar
From the USSR.

CENSOR: We will not pause
JUSTICE: We'll twist the laws
CHURCH: We'll blindfold the eyes
PRESS: Of the workers with lies
POLICE: We'll keep them slaves
RADIO: With my radio waves
ART: We'll lull them to sleep
SCIENCE: Into slumbers deep.

CAPITALIST: Fine, gentlemen, fine.
                 The workers are mine
                 If you keep them afar
                 From the USSR.

WORKER: (*enters*) We, the workers and peasants of the capitalist countries have heard that our brothers in Russia have driven out the bosses, that our brothers in Russia have taken over for themselves the land and the factories, that our brothers in Russia are building a new classless, socialist society.

PRESS: This is the truth about the Soviet Union. Russia is terrorized by a minority, which refuses to pay the debts to the United States. We stand for honesty and reciprocity. We will not recognize the so-called government of Russia before she pays what she owes us.

SOVIET UNION: (*stands near map*) The revolutionary workers and peasants warned the United States government not to lend money to the Tsar or to Kerensky. The Soviet Union will not rob the proletariat of one cent to finance the tsarist and white terror. Workers and peasants of the world . . .

CENSOR: Halt – Enough – Bolshevist propaganda is censored – Films of Soviet Russia must be cut – Second class mailing rates denied – Importation of subversive literature prohibited.

RADIO: Stand by, ladies and gentlemen, and hear the real treat of the evening. This is station GOLD, of the Wall Street Broadcasting System. Ladies and gentlemen, I have the honor to present to you Mr Babbitt, who has just returned from a trip to Soviet Russia. Hear the truth about Soviet Russia. – Good evening my dear folks of the radio audience. Russia, one-sixth of the earth, is darkened by terroristic activities of the Bolshevist home police, the GPU. The prisons are overfilled, innocent blood flows in streams. The people of Russia are shivering in fear. Nobody knows who is next.

SOVIET UNION: The sabotageurs of socialist construction are trembling because the GPU guards the land of the workers and peasant against the counter-revolutionaries, because the GPU protects the freedom of the workers and peasants against the white terror, because the GPU strengthens the

step forward for the world revolution of the workers and
peasants. Workers and peasants of the world . . .

JUSTICE: Look out! There is still justice in America. Your interest
in the Soviet Union is suspicious. Propaganda for the Soviet
Union means treason. Militant workers are thrown into jail
if they are citizens, they are deported if they are foreign
born, they are lynched if they are Negroes. The fate of
Mooney and Billings, of Sacco and Vanzetti, of Harry
Sims, of the four workers shot in Detroit, of the nine Negro
boys in Scottsboro, serve as examples that justice still lives
in America.

ART: And also art, free of propaganda. Workers and peasants of
the world, there is something higher than the wage
problem, and that is love. There is something higher than
the defense of the Soviet Union – to fight and die for your
fatherland.

SOVIET UNION: The workers have only one fatherland, the Soviet
Union.

CHURCH: The fanatic Bolsheviks have no respect for the most
sacred sentiments. They have forbidden religion, they are
destroying the churches. In the name of all religions I call
upon you to join the holy crusade against these church
wreckers.

SOVIET UNION: Religion is not forbidden in the Soviet Union. But
the Soviet Union has no money to support fat and lazy
priests. The Soviet Union uses its unnecessary churches as
hospitals and rest centers for the workers and peasants.
Workers and peasants of the world . . .

SCIENCE: We still have science in the United States, that proves
to you that the capitalist system is the best and only correct
system, that proves it with figures –

SOVIET UNION: That's a lie.

SCIENCE: With facts –

SOVIET UNION: That are twisted.

SCIENCE: Worked up by official experts –

SOVIET UNION: Bribed by the bosses. Because press, radio, censor,
church, justice, art, science –

POLICE: And the police –

SOVIET UNION: And the police – are in the service of the ruling
class, are in the class struggle on the side of the bosses, the

exploiters, the profiteers. Workers and peasants of the world . . .

CAPITALIST: This is too much. Fight these Bolsheviks, with God, for business and fatherland.

(*Press, Radio, etc. shout to the Worker, each one his previous speech attacking the Soviet Union, while they crowd around the Worker. Then they go down from the stage and stand in front of the stage, pointing and hissing at the Soviet Union, while each repeats his verse from the rhymes that accompanied their entrance*)

CENSOR:	We will not pause
JUSTICE:	We'll twist the laws
CHURCH:	We'll blindfold the eyes
PRESS:	Of the workers with lies
POLICE:	We'll keep them slaves
RADIO:	With my radio waves
ART:	We'll lull them to sleep
SCIENCE:	Into slumber deep.
CAPITALIST:	Fine, gentlemen, fine.
	The workers are mine
	If you keep them afar
	From the USSR.

(*The Capitalist's servants rush behind the stage*)

CAPITALIST: Ha, ha, ha, ha. What do you say now? Who laughs best?

WORKER: Who laughs last. Ha, ha, ha, ha. You have most money, you tell the biggest lies. But the truth about the Soviet Union I can learn from there.

(*Points to left of stage, where enter Worker with sign Red Press, then other workers each with one of the following signs: Daily Worker, Young Worker, Working Woman, Liberator, New Pioneer, Moscow News, Soviet Russia Today. Each shouts the name of his paper as he faces the audience and lifts up his sign*)

SOVIET RUSSIA TODAY: Facts —
MOSCOW NEWS: Facts —
WORKING WOMAN: Facts —
YOUNG WORKER: Facts —
DAILY WORKER: About the —

ALL: Soviet Union!

SOVIET UNION: (*takes his place at end of workers' press line, next to Soviet Russia Today*) And this fact, the Five-Year Plan! The Five-Year Plan has created –

ALL: Factories, railroads, collective farms, electric power, new cities.

NEW PIONEER: The workers and peasants of the Soviet Union . . .

MOSCOW NEWS: Have gone ahead of their own plan . . .

SOVIET RUSSIA TODAY: The Five-Year Plan in four years.

(*All rise. AFL enters from left, Socialist from right*)

AFL: The Five-Year Plan?

SOCIALIST: In four years?

AFL: Socialization of industry?

SOCIALIST: Socialist construction?

AFL: That's bad for our reputation.

SOCIALIST: That's bad for our jobs.

BOTH: We've got to do something.

(*To audience*)

AFL: Forced Labor in Soviet Russia.

SOCIALIST: Dictatorship in Soviet Russia.

AFL: Friends.

SOCIALIST: Brothers.

AFL: Protect freedom.

SOCIALIST: Protect democracy.

AFL: Against forced labor.

SOCIALIST: Against dictatorship.

(*Both exit. Song behind stage:* 'We are the Builders . . .' *Seven Workers of the Soviet Union march on stage from left with signs, line up back stage. Five Workers (8–12) representing the USA with signs come slowly from right, lie down on floor front stage. All lift up signs with next slogans*)

8: Where is freedom?

1: Where is forced labor?

12: Where is the worker free?

7: Where is the worker oppressed?

10: In capitalist USA the worker is oppressed.

4: In the Soviet Union the worker is free.

9: In capitalist USA 15,000,000 unemployed are thrown out on the street.

2: In the Soviet Union is work for all.

11: In capitalist USA the workers are beaten up when they ask for social insurance.

5: In the Soviet Union the workers are protected by social laws: vacations without pay, free hospitals, free sanitoriums, free doctors, free medicine.

8: In capitalist USA the working time is lengthened.

1: In the Soviet Union the working time is shortened.

12: In capitalist USA wages are cut.

6: In the Soviet Union wages are rising.

10: In capitalist USA everything for the capitalists.

4: In the Soviet Union everything for the workers.

V For the Soviet Union

5: Fellow workers.

3: Comrades.

5: Where is your future?

6: In the capitalist decline of the USA

2: or in the socialist construction of the Soviet Union?

7: This is the question:

1: For or against?

5: The answer is clear:

(*The workers of the USA rush to sign 10 and tear it down, then all turn to sign 4, the Soviet Union, all pointing to Soviet Union*)

ALL: For the Soviet Union!

(*All turn to audience*)

8: Every step forward in the Soviet Union –

10: is a step forward –

11: toward the Soviet Union –

12: of the United States of North America!

(*All rush into one line, facing the audience*)

4: Therefore

ALL: For the Soviet Union!!

4: Every attack against the Soviet Union –

9: is an attack –

8: against –
ALL: (*pointing to audience*) YOU!
 4: Therefore fight
ALL: FOR THE SOVIET UNION!

(*with clenched fists*)

FOR THE SOVIET UNION!!!

(Source: Workers Theatre, June–July 1932)

Newsboy (1934)

(Adapted for American League against War and Fascism by Gregory Novikov from the poem by V. J. Jerome, as co-ordinated by the Workers' Laboratory Theatre)

The Scene.

The entire action takes place on the stage which has been draped in black so that we cannot distinguish its limitations. Before the black backdrop there are three 2-foot platforms, which serve as elevations for certain scenes and certain characters. However, these too must be covered with a black fabric, so that they are not seen by the audience. A street lamp is optional.

When the curtain rises, the stage is dark but the shuffling of many feet are heard. Slowly a light is thrown along the street surface which lights up only the feet of the passersby. We see all types of feet, well-shod, and poorly-shod, walking, strolling, and running back and forth. In the center stands the Newsboy, in the dark.

NEWSBOY: Extry, read all about it! Love nest raided on Park Avenue, Extry! Marlene Dietrich insures legs for fifty thousand dollars! Extry! Mrs Vanderbilt calls Mrs Whitney a liar! Read all about it! Babe Ruth joins Boston Braves . . . Extry . . . College student murders his professor's mistress. Get your papers. American, News and Mirror. Morning papers!

(*Slowly a spotlight creeps over the Newsboy's face and spreads until it covers the entire stage with a sickly amber glow. Now we see the crowd in full, passing back and forth in front of the newsboy. Occasionally someone stops to buy a newspaper. We see the following episodes as the newsboy continues his shouts.*)

1 An attractive girl, evidently a stenographer, walks across the stage, followed by a well-dressed man. She stops to buy a paper which the man pays for. They go off together.

2 A blind women comes tap, tap, tapping across the stage, wailing: 'Alms for the poor blind . . . Ain't no one goin' to help the blind . . . Alms for the blind!' A pompous man with a mustache

drops a coin in her cup, and then stops to enter an item in his budget book.

3 Two shabbily dressed radicals cross the stage talking earnestly.

4 A nice young girl walks tearfully across the stage followed by a pleading young man.

(*The murmuring of the crowd grows louder. The strollers now appear like some mad ballet, forming various patterns behind the newsboy as they buy their papers. The headlines of the newspapers scream out the words MURDER, SUICIDE, and DIVORCE. A piano has joined the medley of voices and the effect is of a discordant babble. Above it all we hear the newsboy.*)

NEWSBOY: Read all about it! Murder . . . Rape . . . Scandal . . .
   All the latest sports events . . . morning papers . . .

(*The crowd is chanting* Murder, Rape, Scandal, Suicide. *The symphony of sound reaches a climax when suddenly we hear the booming voice of the Black Man, as yet off-stage. At the first sound of his voice the murmur begins to die.*)

BLACK MAN: Hey, there, Newsboy, how long you goin' ter stand there under the 'L,' yellin' yer guts out? How long yer goin' to keep yellin' that workers should be murdered and strikes outlawed?

(*crowd continues soft chant.*)

BLACK MAN: Because somewheres in a hotel room in 'Frisco a Follies' girl shot the brains out of the old rip that kept her? Don't you ever get tired, Newsie, shoutin' about hold-ups, and murders, and raids on Love Nests? Come into the light, Newsboy, come into the light! . . .

(*As he speaks he advances into the sphere of light. The crowd pays no attention to him but the newsboy watches him carefully out of the corner of his eye, as if he senses a menace.*)

NEWSBOY: JAPAN WANTS WAR WITH THE UNITED STATES . . . SOVIET RUSSIA INSULTS UNITED STATES CONSUL . . . GERMAN OFFICIALS ATTACK AMERICAN GIRLS . . .

CROWD: (*as the chant changes in nature, their attitudes change from apathy to hatred*) Japan wants war . . . Soviet wants war . . .

Germany wants war . . . Down with the Soviet . . . Down
with the Soviet . . .

NEWSBOY: Eight thousand boys join CCC camps★ . . . Make
professors swear loyalty to government . . . Bill passed in
Congress to outlaw strikes . . . Japan prepares war . . .
Germany arms 100,000 men . . . Italy masses troops on her
border . . . attack on Abyssinia . . . Mrs Vanderbilt calls
Mrs Whitney a liar . . . Mary Pickford granted her final
decree . . . read all about it!

BLACK MAN: Why don't yer stop kiddin' yerself, Newboy? Don't
yer see yer drunk with the poison gin of lies? All this talk
of CCC camps and Boy Scout parades and International
insults . . . you've got poison in yer bellies and it's eatin'
yer guts and rottin' away yer minds. Yer linin' up fer war
. . . that's what! Yer gettin' ready to fight again and kill
again, and slaughter again . . .

CROWD: (*growing louder*) We need another war. War brings out
the best in men. We need another war. War is natural. We
need another war −

BLACK MAN: They're chloroforming yuh with lies, I tell yuh. Lies!

(*The noise grows again to a crescendo as the crowd repeats the last speech
and as the Black Man keeps shouting 'Lies'. The scene fades off. A corner
of the stage is brightened with a white spotlight, slightly above the level
of the crowd. In the spotlight we see a man at a telephone. Behind him
on the wall are the title streamers of the New York American, Mirror,
and Journal. It is William Randolph Hearst.*)

HEARST: (*into phone*) Rush through the following scare heads. Very
boldest type. 'Six Million Starve to Death in Soviet Russia.'
'Communism Must Go.' 'Down With American Reds.'
'USA Spends One Billion Dollars on Armaments to be
Vested as Airplane Bombers, Cannon, Gas Bombs . . .'

(*The voice fades with the spotlight. A light fades in on the other side of
the stage. We see a man making a speech before a mob of people. Behind
him is draped the bunting of Red, white, and blue. It is Huey Long.*)

★ Civilian Conservation Corps (CCC) were organizations of unemployed
youngsters formed into camp units under the jurisdiction of Roosevelt's
New Deal legislation to do socially useful work such as planting trees,
building, etc. [Ed.]

LONG: Every man is a king. That's my motto. Share the wealth.
Every man is entitled to his rights, but no man should
make over a million dollars. Every man a king, that's the
motto of the Kingfish. A war wouldn't be such a bad thing.
Boys, ha, ha, ha – every man a king . . .

(*The lights and voice fade. A light on center of stage shows a man behind
a microphone, in priest's clothes. It is Father Coughlin.*)

COUGHLIN: . . . But our country, right or wrong. Of course, I
am not a militarist . . . (*sweetly*) No man of Jesus can be a
militarist . . . Our Lord Jesus Christ teaches humility and
pacifism . . . BUT on the other hand, if our nation is in
danger of an attack by a foreign nation who is after our gold
– or, more particularly, our greatest asset, our silver supply
. . . it is the God-ordained duty of every American citizen
to fight and die for its protection. Our Government will
be only as safe from without her borders as she is from
within. Let us stamp out this ugly stain of communism
with its militant peace policies. I can only repeat the words
of that other great American, Chauncey Depew – 'Our
Country, right or wrong . . .'

(*The light and voice fade out, and again we see William Randolph Hearst
speaking.*)

HEARST: Our country right or wrong. Japan insults US envoy.
Russia plans to attack the USA. US steel up 40 points.
Anaconda copper up 23 points. Du Pont powder works rises
82 points . . . Soviet Union plans to attack . . .

(*Voice dies away and spot fades. Murmuring of the crowd has begun again
and grows louder. Sound of drums and martial music is heard in the
distance, growing louder. As the lights reveal them, the people in the
crowd line up in army formation, with rolled newspapers carried like
rifles. They march back and forth and finally march straight front, and
unroll their papers, revealing War Scare Headlines. The Black Man runs
up and down the line trying to make them listen to him. They pay no
attention; the Black Man is shouting over the music.*)

BLACK MAN: Come into the light, comrades, come into the light.
You're being chloroformed. Your heads are full of lies, and

you're gettin' ready to be killed. Cain't you see they're fixin'
you for the slaughter. Cain't you see . . .

(*They pay no attention. Black Man goes over and sits on the curb, his
head in his arms. An Unemployed Man in ragged clothes comes in and
stops a Well-dressed Man.*)

UNEMPLOYED MAN: How about a nickel for a cup of coffee, buddy?
WELL-DRESSED MAN: Why don't you get a job?
UNEMPLOYED MAN: Why don't I get a job? Ha, ha. That's rich.
    Why don't you get a job? Where do you suggest I look for
    one – in the *White House*?
WELL-DRESSED MAN: Why don't you go to a CCC Camp?
UNEMPLOYED MAN: Thanks, buddy, but I can starve here just as
    well as there.

(*The Well-dressed Man goes on, and the unemployed man approaches a
dignified Old Gentleman.*)

    Can you spare a nickel for a cup of coffee, sir. I've got to eat.
OLD GENTLEMAN: I don't believe in it.
UNEMPLOYED MAN: I don't get you.
OLD GENTLEMAN: I don't believe in charity. Why don't you join
    the army? It would make a new man of you. (*Feels his
    muscles*) A man with a body like yours should be in the
    service. It would build up your morale.
UNEMPLOYED MAN: I want to hang on to my arms and legs for a
    while, thanks. I'm not anxious to have them blown off in
    a war.

(*Old Gentleman goes on. Unemployed Man accosts a Kindly Old Lady.*)

UNEMPLOYED MAN: Lady, can you spare a nickel for a cup of
    coffee?
KINDLY OLD LADY: (*opening her purse*) Here you are, my good man.
    Always glad to help the unfortunate. But why don't you
    join the army? That would keep you off the streets.
UNEMPLOYED MAN: (*throwing nickel back at her*) Thanks for the
    charity.
KINDLY OLD LADY: It was only a suggestion.
OLD GENTLEMAN: A good suggestion. Why don't you join the
    army?
UNEMPLOYED MAN: And get blown to bits!

WELL-DRESSED MAN: (*coming back to him*) Or why don't you join
the CCC camps?

UNEMPLOYED MAN: And starve!

(*The cry of 'Why Don't you join the army?' and the answer, 'And get
blown to bits,' and the other cry of 'Why don't you join the CCC camps?'
'And starve,' are taken up by the crowd. They surge forward, and the
chant becomes rhythmic. The Black Man jumps to his feet. The left
entrance of the stage lights up. From off stage left is heard the voice of a
Second Newsboy, quieting the other sounds.*)

SECOND NEWSBOY: Fight against War and Fascism. Learn the truth
about the munitions racket.

(*He enters with a magazine bag at his side. He is holding aloft a handful
of papers, spread fanwise, so we cannot see their title.*)

Fight against War and Fascism. Fight NOW against that racket
of the death manufacturers. The CCC camps are preparing
men for war! Learn the truth!

(*The First Newsboy belligerently steps forward to bar his way, but the
Black Man and the Unemployed Man place themselves before the Second
Newsboy as a shield. They hoist him to the top of a box stage center,
and he gives them a stack of papers, which they distribute to the crowd.
The First Newsboy slinks away. The crowd reads.*)

MAN IN CROWD: (*as he reads*) Think of it. Eight and a half million
men killed in the last war.

GIRL IN CROWD: (*as she reads*) Ten million will probably die in the
next war.

ANOTHER MAN IN CROWD: (*as he reads*) Eight and a half million
men killed for the profits of the munition-makers.

CROWD: (*taking up cry*) Eight and a half million men. Eight and a
half million men. Killed – wounded – shell-shocked –
millions more. Eight and a half million men murdered in
war – murdered in war.

(*The crowd is huddled in the center, near the Second Newsboy, with their
backs to the audience, continuing this chant. The First Newsboy runs on
the stage, shouting his slogans, and wheeling each person of the crowd
around so they face the audience. He is faced by a solid wall of* Fight
(*the paper of the American League against War and Fascism), displayed*

to the audience. Above the wall, like a banner, the Second Newsboy waves his copy of Fight. *The First Newsboy runs up and down the line, shouting his slogans, but gets no response.*)

FIRST NEWSBOY: Japan insults the USA – Germany insults the USA – Soviet Russia insults the USA – William Randolph Hearst says – Marlene Dietrich insures her legs – Soviet Russia wants war with USA.

(*He runs angrily off the stage, having gotten no response. The crowd is still chanting* 'Eight and a half million men' *and so on. The tableau is something like the following:*)

Newsboy

Fight

Fight   Fight   Fight   Fight   Fight   Fight   Fight

Black Man   *Unemployed Man*

BLACK MAN: (*exultantly*) Get yourself a trumpet, buddy, a big red trumpet, and climb to the top of the Empire State building, and blare out the news . . . Now is the time to fight war and Fascism. (*Comes center and speaks to audience.*) Black men, white men, field men, shop men – it's time to fight war. It's time to fight Fascism . . . Get yourself a trumpet, buddy, a big red trumpet . . . and blare it out . . . time to fight war . . . time to fight Fascism . . .

CURTAIN

(*Source*: Karen Malpede Taylor, *People's Theatre in America*, Drama Book Specialists, New York, 1972.)

Waiting For Lefty (1935)
Introductory note

Waiting For Lefty was written some time during the latter months of 1934, whilst the playwright Clifford Odets was still a member of the Communist Party, and it was based on the New York taxi-drivers' strike of the previous February. Within the short space of one year the play had achieved considerable international recognition and had found its way into the repertoire of almost every Workers Theatre group in the USA and western Europe. Both *Waiting For Lefty*, and the strike on which it was based, were short, militant and politically effective.

At the time of writing, Clifford Odets was still an unknown actor with the Group Theatre, but he managed to convince several other Group members to assist with a performance of the play, in aid of the New Theatre League. Among the participants were Elia Kazan, Art Smith, Ruth Nelson, Phoebe Brand, Jules Garfield, Luther Adler and J. Edward Bromberg, all of whom were members of the cast of *Gold Eagle Guy* which was currently in performance on Broadway, and most of whom were members of the Group Theatre's highly influential Communist cell. The first performance of *Waiting For Lefty* took place on the evening of Sunday, 5 February, at the Civic Repertory Theatre, as part of a 'New Theatre Night' fund-raising event. Neither the organizers nor the cast were prepared for the phenomenal reception which greeted the play. As the final lines were being delivered from the stage the audience ran to the front and joined in with the ritual chants of 'Strike, Strike, Strike . . .' The publicity which surrounded the opening night served two purposes: it guaranteed the immediate playwriting future of Clifford Odets and pushed *Waiting For Lefty* to the forefront of the radical repertoire, where it remained for years to come.

By March 1935, the Group Theatre had included *Waiting For Lefty* in its own repertory as part of a double bill with Odets's anti-Nazi play *Till the Day I Die*. It ran on Broadway for 78 performances with Odets in his last acting role as the character of Dr Benjamin. Meanwhile, the reputation of *Waiting For Lefty* had spread throughout the United States. Almost every Workers

Theatre group affiliated to the New Theatre League applied for permission to stage the play and, as if gaining the establishment seal of approval, it became a popular play for student groups and even won the prestigious Yale Drama Tournament. Such were the contradictions of depression America that the play received numerous theatre awards but was simultaneously being suppressed by reactionary agencies in nearly every corner of the USA.

Within the short space of one week, in April 1935, the play was closed down in two American cities, Boston and New Haven. A month later, on 28 and 29 March, the Boston police intervened once again and stopped an amateur production of *Waiting For Lefty* which was due to be staged by the New Theatre Players at their Long Wharf theatre. As a result of that controversy yet another production scheduled for the Dudley Street Opera House had to be called off. According to the various authorities concerned, the play was under attack for *moral* and not for political reasons – they allegedly objected to the use of the words 'damn' and 'hell'. Despite threats from the police, fifteen members of the New Theatre Players decided to proceed with the play. At the end of the performance they were arrested and immediately charged with profanity. The arresting officers were not ordinary police recruits but were members of the Boston 'Red Squad', an élite core of officers specially trained to deal with political activists.

Unfortunately, the Boston incidents were not isolated cases but seemed to be symptomatic of a much wider policy of censorship; a policy that was always systematic and occasionally violent and disruptive. The worst chapter in the short history of *Waiting For Lefty* happened in close proximity to New York, across the river in Newark, New Jersey.

The Newark Collective Theatre planned to stage a double bill of *Waiting For Lefty* and the Scottsboro play *They Shall Not Die* but had their permit withdrawn by a local school board. Undeterred, they found alternative space, but this time the police intervened and stopped the performance because the seats were not bolted to the floor. The Collective found a third theatre and had their audience directed to it by sympathizers and a series of posters, but once again the police intervened and tried to end the performance. The cast and several union radicals stood up to protest and a riot broke out during which nine people were arrested including members of the cast and Joe Gilbert, of the Taxicab Drivers' Union and a leader of the New York taxi strike. It was a peculiar example of life almost imitating theatre: a union leader is arrested in the audience of a play which is based on events in his recent political past.

By the end of 1935 *Waiting For Lefty* was known in every country which had an active Workers' Theatre Movement. It was produced in Moscow by Joe Losey, in London by Herbert Marshall and in Glasgow by the Glasgow Workers' Theatre Group, but by 1940 it had virtually disappeared from the radical repertoire and only emerged periodically despite its very powerful dramatic and political appeal.

STUART COSGROVE

A Play in Six Scenes, Based on the New York City Taxi Strike of February 1934 by Clifford Odets

(As the curtain goes up we see a bare stage. On it are sitting six or seven men in a semi-circle. Lolling against the proscenium down left is a young man chewing a toothpick: a gunman. A fat man of porcine appearance is talking directly to the audience. In other words he is the head of a union and the men ranged behind him are a committee of workers. They are now seated in interesting different attitudes and present a wide diversity of type, as we shall soon see. The fat man is hot and heavy under the collar, near the end of a long talk, but not too hot: he is well fed and confident. His name is Harry Fatt.)

FATT: You're so wrong I ain't laughing. Any guy with eyes to read knows it. Look at the textile strike – out like lions and in like lambs. Take the San Francisco tie-up – starvation and broken heads. The steel boys wanted to walk out too, but they changed their minds. It's the trend of the times, that's what it is. All we workers got a good man behind us now. He's top man of the country – looking out for our interests – the man in the White House is the one I'm referrin' to. That's why the times ain't ripe for a strike. He's working day and night –

VOICE: *(from the audience)* For who? *(The gunman stirs himself.)*

FATT: For you! The records prove it. If this was the Hoover regime, would I say don't go out, boys? Not on your tintype! But things is different now. You read the papers as well as me. You know it. And that's why I'm against the strike. Because we gotta stand behind the man who's standin' behind us! The whole country –

ANOTHER VOICE: Is on the blink! *(The gunman looks grave.)*

FATT: Stand up and show yourself, you damn Red! Be a man, let's see what you look like! *(Waits in vain.)* Yellow from the word go! Red and yellow makes a dirty color, boys. I got my eyes on four or five of them in the union here. What the hell'll they do for you? Pull you out and run away when trouble starts. Give those birds a chance and they'll

have your sisters and wives in the whore houses, like they
done in Russia. They'll tear Christ off his bleeding cross.
They'll wreck your homes and throw your babies in the
river. You think that's bunk? Read the papers! Now listen,
we can't stay here all night. I gave you the facts in the case.
You boys got hot suppers to go to and –

ANOTHER VOICE: Says you!

GUNMAN: Sit down, Punk!

ANOTHER VOICE: Where's Lefty? (*Now this question is taken up by
the others in unison. Fatt pounds with gavel.*)

FATT: That's what I wanna know. Where's your pal, Lefty? You
elected him chairman – where the hell did he disappear?

VOICES: We want Lefty! Lefty! Lefty!

FATT: (*pounding*) What the hell is this – a circus? You got the
committee here. This bunch of cowboys you elected.
(*Pointing to a man on extreme right end*)

MANN: Benjamin.

FATT: Yeah, Doc Benjamin. (*Pointing to other men in circle in seated
order.*) Benjamin, Miller, Stein, Mitchell, Phillips, Keller. It
ain't my fault Lefty took a run-out powder. If you guys –

A GOOD VOICE: What's the committee say?

OTHERS: The committee! Let's hear from the committee!

(*Fatt tries to quiet the crowd, but one of the seated men suddenly comes
to the front. The gunman moves over to center stage, but Fatt says:*)

FATT: Sure, let him talk. Let's hear what the Red boy's gotta say!

(*Various shouts are coming from the audience. Fatt insolently goes back
to his seat in the middle of the circle. He sits on his raised platform and
re-lights his cigar. The gunman goes back to his post. Joe, the new
speaker, raises his hand for quiet. Gets it quickly. He is sore.*)

JOE: You boys know me. I ain't a Red boy one bit! Here I'm
carryin' a shrapnel that big I picked up in the war. And
maybe I don't know it when it rains! Don't tell me Red!
You know what we are? We're the black and blue boys!
We been kicked around so long we're black and blue from
head to toes. But I guess anyone who says straight out he
don't like it, he's a Red boy to the leaders of the union.
What's this crap about goin' home to hot suppers? I'm
asking to your faces how many's got hot suppers to go home

to? Anyone who's sure of his next meal, raise your hand!
A certain gent sitting behind me can raise them both. But
not in front here! And that's why we're talking strike – to
get a living wage!

VOICE: Where's Lefty?

JOE: I honest to God don't know, but he didn't take no run-out
powder. That Wop's got more guts than a slaughter house.
Maybe a traffic jam got him, but he'll be here. But don't let
this Red stuff scare you. Unless fighting for a living scares
you. We gotta make up our minds. My wife made up my
mind last week, if you want the truth. It's plain as the nose
on Sol Feinberg's face we need a strike. There's us comin'
home every night – eight, ten hours on the cab. 'God,' the
wife says, 'eighty cents ain't money – don't buy beans
almost. You're workin' for the company,' she says to me.
'Joe! you ain't workin' for me or the family no more!' She
says to me, 'If you don't start . . .'

(*The lights fade out and a white spot picks out the playing space within
the space of seated men. The seated men are very dimly visible in the
outer dark, but more prominent is Fatt smoking his cigar and often blowing
the smoke in the lighted circle.*

*A tired but attractive woman of thirty comes into the room, drying her
hands on an apron. She stands there sullenly as Joe comes in from the
other side, home from work. For a moment they stand and look at each
other in silence.*)

JOE: Where's all the furniture, honey?

EDNA: They took it away. No instalments paid.

JOE: When?

EDNA: Three o'clock.

JOE: They can't do that.

EDNA: Can't? They did it.

JOE: Why, the palookas, we paid three-quarters.

EDNA: The man said read the contract.

JOE: We must have signed a phoney . . .

EDNA: It's a regular contract and you signed it.

JOE: Don't be so sour, Edna . . . (*tries to embrace her*)

EDNA: Do it in the movies, Joe – they pay Clark Gable big money
for it.

JOE: This is a helluva house to come home to. Take my word!

EDNA: Take MY word! Whose fault is it?

JOE: Must you start that stuff again?

EDNA: Maybe you'd like to talk about books?

JOE: I'd like to slap you in the mouth!

EDNA: No you won't.

JOE: (*sheepish*) Jeez, Edna, you get me sore some time . . .

EDNA: But just look at me – I'm laughing all over!

JOE: Don't insult me. Can I help it if times are bad? What the hell do you want me to do, jump off a bridge or something?

EDNA: Don't yell. I just put the kids to bed so they won't know they missed a meal. If I don't have Emmy's shoes soled tomorrow, she can't go to school. In the meantime let her sleep.

JOE: Honey, I rode the wheels off the chariot today. I cruised around five hours without a call. It's conditions.

EDNA: Tell it to the A & P!

JOE: I booked two-twenty on the clock. A lady with a dog was lit . . . she gave me a quarter tip by mistake. If you'd only listen to me – we're rolling in wealth.

EDNA: Yeah? How much?

JOE: I had 'coffee and –' in a beanery. (*Hands her silver coins.*) A buck four.

EDNA: The second month's rent is due tomorrow.

JOE: Don't look at me that way, Edna.

EDNA: I'm looking thru' you, not at you . . . Everything was gonna be so ducky! A cottage by the waterfall, roses in Picardy. You're a four-star bust! If you think I'm standing for it much longer, you're crazy as a bedbug.

JOE: I'd get another job if I could. There's no work – you know it.

EDNA: I only know we're at the bottom of the ocean.

JOE: What can I do?

EDNA: Who's the man in the family, you or me?

JOE: That's no answer. Get down to brass tacks. Christ, gimme a break, too! A coffee cake and java all day. I'm hungry, too, Babe. I'd work my fingers to the bone if –

EDNA: I'll open a can of salmon.

JOE: Not now. Tell me what to do!

EDNA: I'm not God!

JOE: Jeez, I wish I was a kid again and didn't have to think about the next minute.

EDNA: But you're not a kid and you do have to think about the next minute. You got two blondie kids sleeping in the next room. They need food and clothes. I'm not mentioning anything else – But we're stalled like a flivver in the snow. For five years I laid awake at night listening to my heart pound. For God's sake, do something, Joe, get wise. Maybe get your buddies together, maybe go on strike for better money. Poppa did it during the war and they won out. I'm turning into a sour old nag.

JOE: (*defending himself*) Strikes don't work!

EDNA: Who told you?

JOE: Besides that means not a nickel a week while we're out. Then when it's over they don't take you back.

EDNA: Suppose they don't! What's to lose?

JOE: Well, we're averaging six–seven dollars a week now.

EDNA: That just pays for the rent.

JOE: That is something, Edna.

EDNA: It isn't. They'll push you down to three and four a week before you know it. Then you'll say, 'That's somethin',' too!

JOE: There's too many cabs on the street, that's the whole damn trouble.

EDNA: Let the company worry about that, you big fool! If their cabs didn't make a profit, they'd take them off the streets. Or maybe you think they're in business just to pay Joe Mitchell's rent!

JOE: You don't know a-b-c, Edna.

EDNA: I know this – your boss is making suckers outa you boys every minute. Yes, and suckers out of all the wives and the poor innocent kids who'll grow up with crooked spines and sick bones. Sure, I see it in the papers, how good orange juice is for kids. But dammit, our kids get colds one on top of the other. They look like little ghosts. Betty never saw a grapefruit. I took her to the store last week and she pointed to a stack of grapefruits. 'What's that?' she said. My God, Joe – the world is supposed to be for all of us.

JOE: You'll wake them up.

EDNA: I don't care, as long as I can maybe wake you up.

JOE: Don't insult me. One man can't make a strike.

EDNA: Who says one? You got hundreds in your rotten union!

JOE: The union ain't rotten.

EDNA: No? Then what are they doing? Collecting dues and patting your back?

JOE: They're making plans.

EDNA: What kind?

JOE: They don't tell us.

EDNA: It's too damn bad about you. They don't tell little Joey what's happening in his bitsie-witsie union. What do you think it is – a ping-pong game?

JOE: You know they're racketeers. The guys at the top would shoot you for a nickel.

EDNA: Why do you stand for that stuff?

JOE: Don't you wanna see me alive?

EDNA: (*after a deep pause*) No . . . I don't think I do, Joe. Not if you can lift a finger to do something about it, and don't. No, I don't care.

JOE: Honey, you don't understand what –

EDNA: And any other hackie that won't fight . . . let them all be ground to hamburger!

JOE: It's one thing to –

EDNA: Take your hand away! Only they don't grind me to little pieces! I got different plans. (*Starts to take off her apron*)

JOE: Where are you going?

EDNA: None of your business.

JOE: What's up your sleeve?

EDNA: My arm'd be up my sleeve, darling, if I had a sleeve to wear. (*Puts neatly folded apron on back of chair*)

JOE: Tell me!

EDNA: Tell you what?

JOE: Where are you going?

EDNA: Don't you remember my old boyfriend?

JOE: Who?

EDNA: Bud Haas. He still has my picture in his watch. He earns a living.

JOE: What the hell are you talking about?

EDNA: I heard worse than I'm talking about.

JOE: Have you seen Bud since we got married?

EDNA: Maybe.

JOE: If I thought . . . (*he stands looking at her*)

EDNA: See much? Listen, boyfriend, if you think I won't do this it just means you can't see straight.

JOE: Stop talking bull!

EDNA: This isn't five years ago, Joe.

JOE: You mean you'd leave me and the kids?

EDNA: I'd leave *you* like a shot!

JOE: No . . .

EDNA: Yes!

(*Joe turns away, sitting in a chair with his back to her. Outside the lighted circle of the playing stage we hear the other seated members of the strike committee. 'She will . . . She will . . . It happens that way,' etc. This group should be used thru'out for various comments, political, emotional and as general chorus. Whispering . . . The fat boss now blows a heavy cloud of smoke into the scene.*)

JOE: (*finally*) Well, I guess I ain't got a leg to stand on.

EDNA: No?

JOE: (*suddenly mad*) No, you lousy tart, no! Get the hell out of here. Go pick up that bull-thrower on the corner and stop at some cushy hotel downtown. He's probably been coming here every morning and laying you while I hacked my guts out!

EDNA: You're crawling like a worm!

JOE: You'll be crawling in a minute.

EDNA: You don't scare me that much! (*indicates ½ inch on her finger*)

JOE: This is what I slaved for!

EDNA: Tell it to your boss!

JOE: He don't give a damn for you or me!

EDNA: That's what I say.

JOE: Don't change the subject!

EDNA: This is the subject, the EXACT SUBJECT! Your boss makes this subject. I never saw him in my life, but he's putting ideas in my head a mile a minute. He's giving your kids that fancy disease called rickets. He's making a jelly-fish outa you and putting wrinkles in my face. This is the subject every inch of the way! He's throwing me into Bud Haas's lap. When in hell will you get wise –

JOE: I'm not so dumb as you think! But you are talking like a Red.

EDNA: I don't know what that means. But when a man knocks you down you get up and kiss his fist! You gutless piece of boloney.

JOE: One man can't –

EDNA: (*with great joy*) I don't say one man! I say a hundred, a thousand, a whole million, I say. But start in your own union. Get those hack boys together! Sweep out those racketeers like a pile of dirt! Stand up like men and fight for the crying kids and wives. Goddammit! I'm tired of slavery and sleepless nights.

JOE: (*with her*) Sure, sure! . . .

EDNA: Yes. Get brass toes on your shoes and know where to kick!

JOE: (*suddenly jumping up and kissing his wife full on the mouth*) Listen, Edna. I'm going down to 174th Street to look up Lefty Costello. Lefty was saying the other day . . . (*he suddenly stops*) How about this Haas guy?

EDNA: Get out of here!

JOE: I'll be back! (*Runs out*)

(*For a moment Edna stands triumphant.*)
(*There is a blackout, and when the regular lights come up, Joe Mitchell is concluding what he has been saying:*)

JOE: You guys know this stuff better than me. We gotta walk out!

(*Abruptly he turns and goes back to his seat.*)

BLACKOUT

The Young Hack and his Girl

(*Opens with girl and brother. Florence waiting for Sid to take her to a dance.*)

FLOR: I gotta right to have something out of life. I don't smoke, I don't drink. So if Sid wants to take me to a dance, I'll go. Maybe if you was in love you wouldn't talk so hard.

IRV: I'm saying it for your good.

FLOR: Don't be so good to me.

IRV: Mom's sick in bed and you'll be worryin' her to the grave.
She don't want that boy hanging around the house and she
don't want you meeting him in Crotona Park.

FLOR: I'll meet him anytime I like!

IRV: If you do, yours truly'll take care of it in his own way. With
just one hand, too!

FLOR: Why are you all so set against him?

IRV: Mom told you ten times – it ain't him. It's that he ain't got
nothing. Sure, we know he's serious, that he's stuck on
you. But that don't cut no ice.

FLOR: Taxi-drivers used to make good money.

IRV: Today they're makin' five and six dollars a week. Maybe
you wanta raise a family on that. Then you'll be back here
living with us again and I'll be supporting two families in
one. Well . . . over my dead body.

FLOR: Irv, I don't care – I love him!

IRV: You're a little kid with half-baked ideas!

FLOR: I stand there behind the counter the whole day. I think
about him –

IRV: If you thought more about Mom it would be better.

FLOR: Don't I take care of her every night when I come home?
Don't I cook supper and iron your shirts and . . . you give
me a pain in the neck, too. Don't try to shut me up! I bring
a few dollars in the house, too. Don't you see I want
something else out of life. Sure, I want romance, love,
babies. I want everything in life I can get.

IRV: You take care of Mom and watch your step!

FLOR: And if I don't?

IRV: Yours truly'll watch it for you!

FLOR: You can talk that way to a girl . . .

IRV: I'll talk that way to your boyfriend, too, and it won't be
with words! Florrie, if you had a pair of eyes you'd see it's
for your own good we're talking. This ain't no time to get
married. Maybe later –

FLOR: 'Maybe Later' never comes for me, tho'. Why don't we
send Mom to a hospital? She can die in peace there instead
of looking at the clock on the mantelpiece all day.

IRV: That needs money. Which we don't have!

FLOR: Money, Money, Money!

IRV: Don't change the subject.

FLOR: This is the subject!

IRV: You gonna stop seeing him? (*She turns away*) Jesus, kiddie,
I remember when you were a baby with curls down your
back. Now I gotta stand here yellin' at you like this.

FLOR: I'll talk to him, Irv.

IRV: When?

FLOR: I asked him to come here tonight. We'll talk it over.

IRV: Don't get soft with him. Nowadays is no time to be soft.
You gotta be hard as a rock or go under.

FLOR: I found that out. There's the bell. Take the egg off the
stove I boiled for Mom. Leave us alone, Irv.

(*Sid comes in – the two men look at each other for a second. Irv exits.*)

SID: (*enters*) Hello, Florrie.

FLOR: Hello, Honey. You're looking tired.

SID: Naw, I just need a shave.

FLOR: Well, draw your chair up to the fire and I'll ring for brandy
and soda . . . like in the movies.

SID: If this was the movies I'd bring a big bunch of roses.

FLOR: How big?

SID: Fifty or sixty dozen – the kind with long long stems – big
as that . . .

FLOR: You dope . . .

SID: Your Paris gown is beautiful.

FLOR: (*acting grandly*) Yes, Percy, velvet panels are coming back
again. Madame La Farge told me today that Queen Marie
herself designed it.

SID: Gee . . .!

FLOR: Every princess in the Balkans is wearing one like this. (*poses
grandly*)

SID: Hold it. (*Does a nose camera – thumbing nose and imitating
grinding of camera with other hand. Suddenly she falls out of the
posture and swiftly goes to him, to embrace him, to kiss him with
love. Finally:*)

SID: You look tired, Florrie.

FLOR: Naw, I just need a shave. (*She laughs tremorously*)

SID: You worried about your mother?

FLOR: No.

SID: What's on your mind?

FLOR: The French and Indian War.

SID: What's on your mind?

FLOR: I got us on my mind, Sid. Night and day, Sid!

SID: I smacked a beer truck today. Did I get hell! I was driving along thinking of US, too. You don't have to say it – I know what's on your mind. I'm rat poison around here.

FLOR: Not to me . . .

SID: I know to who . . . and I know why. I don't blame them. We're engaged now for three years . . .

FLOR: That's a long time . . .

SID: My brother Sam joined the Navy this morning – get a break that way. They'll send him down to Cuba with the hootchy-kootchy girls. He don't know nothing, that dumb basketball player!

FLOR: Don't you do that.

SID: Don't you worry, I'm not the kind who runs away. But I'm so tired of being a dog, Baby, I could choke. I don't even have to ask what's going on in your mind. I know from the word go, 'cause I'm thinking the same things, too.

FLOR: It's yes or no – nothing in between.

SID: The answer is no – a big electric sign looking down on Broadway!

FLOR: We wanted to have kids . . .

SID: But that sort of life ain't for the dogs which is us. Christ, Baby! I get like thunder in my chest when we're together. If we went off together I could maybe look the world straight in the face, spit in its eye like a man should do. Goddammit, it's trying to be a man on the earth. Two in life together.

FLOR: But something wants us to be lonely like that – crawling alone in the dark. Or they want us trapped.

SID: Sure, the big shot money men want us like that –

FLOR: Highly insulting us –

SID: Keeping us in the dark about what is wrong with us in the money sense. They got the power an' mean to be damn sure they keep it. They know if they give in just an inch, all the dogs like us will be down on them together – an ocean knocking them to hell and back and each singing cuckoo with stars coming from their nose and ears. I'm not raving, Florrie –

FLOR: I know you're not, I know.

SID: I don't have the words to tell you what I feel. I never finished school. . . .

FLOR: I know . . .

SID: But it's relative, like the professors say. We worked like hell to send him to college – my kid brother Sam, I mean – and look what he done – joined the navy! The damn fool don't see the cards is stacked for all of us. The money man dealing himself a hot royal flush. Then giving you and me a phoney hand like a pairs of tens or something. Then keep on losing the pots 'cause the cards is stacked against you. Then he says, what's the matter you can't win – no stuff on the ball, he says to you. And kids like my brother believe it 'cause they don't know better. For all their education, they don't know from nothing.

But wait a minute! Don't he come around and say to you – this millionaire with a jazz band – listen Sam or Sid or-what's-your-name, you're no good, but here's a chance. The whole world'll know who you are. Yes sir, he says, get up on that ship and fight those bastards who's making the world a lousy place to live in. The Japs, the Turks, the Greeks. Take this gun – kill the slobs like a real hero, he says, a real American. Be a hero!

And the guy you're poking at? A real louse, just like you, 'cause they don't let him catch more than a pair of tens, too. On that foreign soil he's a guy like me and Sam, a guy who wants his baby like you and hot sun on his face! They'll teach Sam to point the guns the wrong way, that dumb basketball player!

FLOR: I got a lump in my throat, Honey.

SID: You and me – we never even had a room to sit in somewhere.

FLOR: The park was nice . . .

SID: In winter? The hallways . . . I'm glad we never got together. This way we don't know what we missed.

FLOR: (*in a burst*) Sid, I'll go with you – we'll get a room somewhere.

SID: Naw . . . they're right. If we can't climb higher than this together – we better stay apart.

FLOR: I swear to God I wouldn't care.

SID: You would, you would – in a year, two years, you'd curse the day. I seen it happen.

FLOR: Oh, Sid . . .

SID: Sure, I know. We got the blues. Babe – the 1935 blues. I'm talkin' this way 'cause I love you. If I didn't, I wouldn't care . . .

FLOR: We'll work together, we'll –

SID: How about the backwash? Your family needs your nine bucks. My family –

FLOR: I don't care for them!

SID: You're making it up, Florrie. Little Florrie Canary in a cage.

FLOR: Don't make fun of me.

SID: I'm not, Baby.

FLOR: Yes, you're laughing at me.

SID: I'm not.

(They stand looking at each other, unable to speak. Finally, he turns to a small portable phonograph and plays a cheap, sad, dance tune. He makes a motion with his hand; she comes to him. They begin to dance slowly. They hold each other tightly, almost as tho they would merge into each other. The music stops, but the scratching record continues to the end of the scene. They stop dancing. He finally unlooses her clutch and seats her on the couch, where she sits, tense and expectant.)

SID: Hello, Babe.

FLOR: Hello. *(For a brief time they stand as tho' in a dream.)*

SID: *(finally):* Good-bye Babe. *(He waits for an answer, but she is silent. They look at each other.)*

SID: Did you ever see my Pat Rooney imitation? *(He whistles 'Rosy O'Grady' and soft shoes to it. Stops.)* He asks:

SID: Don't you like it?

FLOR: *(finally)* No. *(And buries her face in her hands.)*

   (Suddenly he falls on his knees and buries his face in her lap.)

BLACKOUT

Labor Spy Episode

FATT: You don't know how we work for you. Shooting off your mouth won't help. Hell, don't you guys ever look at the records like me? Look in your own industry. See what happened when the hacks walked out in Philly three months

ago! Where's Philly? A thousand miles away? An hour's ride
on the train.

VOICE: Two hours!!

FATT: Two hours . . . what the hell's the difference. Let's hear
from someone who's got the practical experience to back
him up. Fellas, there's a man here who's seen the whole
parade in Philly, walked out with his pals, got knocked
down like the rest – and blacklisted after they went back.
That's why he's here. He's got a mighty interestin' word
to say. (*Announces*) TOM CLAYTON!

(*As Clayton starts up from the audience, Fatt gives him a hand which is
sparsely followed in the audience. Clayton comes forward.*)

Fellers, this is a man with practical strike experience – Tom
Clayton from little ole Philly.

CLAYTON: (*a thin, modest individual*) Fellers, I don't mind your
booing. If I thought it would help us hacks get better living
conditions, I'd let you walk all over me, cut me up to little
pieces. I'm one of you myself. But what I wanna say is
that Harry Fatt's right. I only been working here in the big
town five weeks, but I know conditions just like the rest
of you. You know how it is – don't take long to feel the
sore spots, no matter where you park.

CLEAR VOICE: (*from audience*) Sit down!

CLAYTON: But Fatt's right. Our officers is right. The time ain't
ripe. Like a fruit don't fall off the tree until it's ripe.

CLEAR VOICE: Sit down, you fruit!

FATT: (*on his feet*) Take care of him, boys.

VOICE: (*in audience, struggling*) No one takes care of me.

(*Struggle in house and finally the owner of the voice runs up on stage,
says to speaker*)

CLAYTON: Where the hell did you pick up that name! Clayton!
This rat's name is Clancy, from the old Clancys, way back!
Fruit! I almost wet myself listening to that one!

FATT: (*gunman with him*) This ain't a barn! What the hell do you
think you're doing here!

VOICE: Exposing a rat!

FATT: You can't get away with this. Throw him the hell outa
here.

VOICE: (*preparing to stand his ground*) Try it yourself. . . . When this bozo throws that slop around. You know who he is? That's a company spy.

FATT: Who the hell are you to make –

VOICE: I paid dues in this union for four years, that's who's me! I gotta right and this pussy-footed rat ain't coming in here with ideas like that. You know his record. Lemme say it out –

FATT: You'll prove all this or I'll bust you in every hack outfit in town!

VOICE: I gotta right. I gotta right. Looka *him*, he don't say boo!

CLAYTON: You're a liar and I never seen you before in my life!

VOICE: Boys, he spent two years in the coal fields breaking up any organization he touched. Fifty guys he put in jail. He's ranged up and down the east coast – shipping, textiles, steel – he's been in everything you can name. Right now –

CLAYTON: That's a lie!

VOICE: Right now he's working for that Bergman outfit on Columbus Circle who furnishes rats for any outfit in the country before, during, and after strikes.

(*The man who is the hero of the next episode goes down to his side with other committee men*)

CLAYTON: He's trying to break up the meeting, fellers!

VOICE: We won't search you for credentials . . .

CLAYTON: I got nothing to hide. Your own secretary knows I'm straight –

VOICE: Sure. Boys, you know who this sonovabitch is?

CLAYTON: I never seen you before in my life!!

VOICE: Boys, I slept with him in the same bed sixteen years. HE'S MY OWN LOUSY BROTHER!!

FATT: (*After pause*) Is this true? (*No answer from Clayton*)

VOICE: (*to Clayton*) Scram, before I break your neck!

(*Clayton scrams down center aisle. Voice says, watching him*)

Remember his map – he can't change that – Clancy!

(*Standing in his place, says:*)

Too bad you didn't know about this, Fatt! (*After a pause*) The Clancy family tree is bearing nuts!

(*Standing isolated clear on the stage is the hero of the next episode.*)

BLACKOUT

The Young Actor

(*A New York theatrical producer's office. Present are a stenographer and a young actor. She is busy typing; he, waiting with card in hand.*)

STEN: He's taking a hot bath . . . says you should wait.

PHILIPS: (*the actor*) A bath did you say? Where?

STEN: See that door? Right thru' there – leads to his apartment.

PHIL: Thru' there?

STEN: Mister, he's laying there in a hot perfumed bath. Don't say I said it.

PHIL: You don't say!

STEN: An oriental den he's got. Can you just see this big Irishman burning chinese punk in the bedroom? And a big old rose canopy over his casting couch. . . .

PHIL: What's that – casting couch?

STEN: What's that? You from the sticks?

PHIL: I beg your pardon?

STEN: (*rolls up her sleeves, makes elaborate deaf and dumb signs*) No from side walkies of New Yorkie . . . savee?

PHIL: Oh, you're right. Two years of dramatic stock out of town. One in Chicago.

STEN: Don't tell him, Baby Face. He wouldn't know a good actor if he fell over him in the dark. Say you had two years with the Group, two with the Guild.

PHIL: I'd like to get with the Guild. They say –

STEN: He won't know the difference. Don't say I said it!

PHIL: I really did play with Watson Findlay in *Early Birds*.

STEN: (*withering him*) Don't tell him!

PHIL: He's a big producer, Mr Grady. I wish I had his money. Don't you?

STEN: Say, I got a clean heart, Mister. I love my fellow man! (*About to exit with typed letters.*) Stick around – Mr Philips. You might be the type. If you were a woman –

PHIL: Please. Just a minute . . . please . . . I need the job.

STEN: Look at him!

PHIL: I mean . . . I don't know what buttons to push, and you
do. What my father used to say – we had a gas station in
Cleveland before the crash – 'Know what buttons to push,'
Dad used to say, 'And you'll go far.'

STEN: You can't push me, Mister! I don't ring right these last few
years!

PHIL: We don't know where the next meal's coming from. We –

STEN: Maybe . . . I'll lend you a dollar?

PHIL: Thanks very much: it won't help.

STEN: One of the old families of Virgina? Proud?

PHIL: Oh not that. You see, I have a wife. We'll have our first
baby next month . . . so . . . a dollar isn't much help.

STEN: Roped in?

PHIL: I love my wife!

STEN: Okay, you love her! Excuse me! You married her. Can't
support her. No . . . not blaming you. But you're fools,
all you actors. Old and young! Watch you parade in an' out
all day. You still got apples in your cheeks and pins for
buttons. But in six months you'll be like them – putting on
an act: Phoney strutting 'pishers' – that's French for dead
codfish! It's not their fault. Here you get like that or go
under. What kind of job is this for an adult man!

PHIL: When you have to make a living –

STEN: I know, but –

PHIL: Nothing else to do. If I could get something else –

STEN: You'd take it!

PHIL: Anything!

STEN: Telling me! With two brothers in my hair!

(*Mr Grady now enters; played by Fatt*)

Mr Brown sent this young man over.

GRADY: Call the hospital: see how Boris is. (*She assents and exits*)

PHIL: Good morning, Mr Grady . . .

GRADY: The morning is lousy!

PHIL: Mr Brown sent me . . . (*Hands over card*)

GRADY: I heard that once already.

PHIL: Excuse me . . .

GRADY: What experience?

PHIL: Oh, yes . . .

GRADY: Where?

PHIL: Two years in stock, sir. A year with the Goodman Theatre in Chicago . . .

GRADY: That all?

PHIL: (*abashed*) Why no . . . with the Theatre Guild . . . I was there . . .

GRADY: Never saw you in a Guild show!

PHIL: On the road, I mean . . . understudying Mr Lunt . . .

GRADY: What part? (*Philips cannot answer*) You're a lousy liar, son.

PHIL: I did . . .

GRADY: You don't look like what I want. Can't understand that Brown. Need a big man to play a soldier. Not a lousy soldier left on Broadway! All in pictures, and we get the nances! (*Turns to work on desk*)

PHIL: (*immediately playing the soldier*) I was in the ROTC in college . . . Reserve Officers' Training Corps. We trained twice a week . . .

GRADY: Won't help.

PHIL: With real rifles. (*waits*) Mr Grady, I weigh a hundred and fifty-five!

GRADY: How many years back? Been eating regular since you left college?

PHIL: (*very earnestly*) Mr Grady, I could act this soldier part. I could build it up and act it. Make it up –

GRADY: Think I run a lousy acting school around here?

PHIL: Honest to God I could! I need the job – that's why I could do it! I'm strong. I know my business! YOU'll get an A1 performance. Because I need this job! My wife's having a baby in a few weeks. We need the money. Give me a chance!

GRADY: What do I care if you can act it! I'm sorry about your baby. Use your head, son. Tank Town stock is different. Here we got investments to be protected. When I sink fifteen thousand in a show I don't take chances on some youngster. We cast to type!

PHIL: I'm an artist! I can –

GRADY: That's your headache. Nobody interested in artists here. Get a big bunch for a nickel on any corner. Two flops in a row on this lousy street nobody loves you – only God, and he don't count. We protect investments: we cast to type. Your face and height we want, not your soul, son.

And Jesus Christ himself couldn't play a soldier in this show . . . with all his talent. (*Crosses himself in quick repentance for this remark.*)

PHIL: Anything . . . a bit, a walk-on?

GRADY: Sorry: small cast. (*Looking at papers on his desk*) You try Russia, son. I hear it's hot stuff over there.

PHIL: Stage manager? Assistant?

GRADY: All filled, sonny. (*Stands up; crumples several papers from the desk*) Better luck next time.

PHIL: Thanks . . .

GRADY: Drop in from time to time. (*Crosses and about to exit*) You never know when something –

(*The Stenographer enters with papers to put on desk*)

What did the hospital say?

STEN: He's much better, Mr Grady.

GRADY: Resting easy?

STEN: Dr Martel said Boris is doing even better than he expected.

GRADY: A damn lousy operation!

STEN: Yes . . .

GRADY: (*belching*) Tell the nigger boy to send up a bromo seltzer.

STEN: Yes, Mr Grady. (*He exits*) Boris wanted lady friends.

PHIL: What?

STEN: So they operated . . . poor dog!

PHIL: A dog?

STEN: His Russian wolf hound! They do the same to you, but you don't know it! (*Suddenly*) Want advice? In the next office, don't let them see you down in the mouth. They don't like it – makes them shiver.

PHIL: You treat me like a human being. Thanks . . .

STEN: You're human!

PHIL: I used to think so.

STEN: He wants a bromo for his hangover. (*Goes to door*) Want that dollar?

PHIL: It won't help much.

STEN: One dollar buys ten loaves of bread, Mister. Or one dollar buys nine loaves of bread and one copy of *The Communist Manifesto*. Learn while you eat. Read while you run . . .

PHIL: Manifesto? What's that? (*takes dollar*) What is that, what you said . . . Manifesto?

STEN: Stop off on your way out – I'll give you a copy. From
   Genesis to Revelation, Comrade Philips! 'And I saw a new
   earth and a new heaven; for the first earth and the first heaven
   were passed away; and there was no more sea.'
PHIL: I don't understand that . . .
STEN: I'm saying the meek shall not inherit the earth!
PHIL: No?
STEN: The MILITANT! Come out in the light, Comrade.
   BLACKOUT

Interne Episode

(*Dr Barnes, an elderly distinguished man, is speaking on the telephone.
He wears a white coat.*)

DR BARNES: No, I gave you my opinion twice. You out-voted
   me. You did this to Dr Benjamin yourself. That is why
   you can tell him yourself.

(*Hangs up phone, angrily. As he is about to pour himself a drink from
a bottle on the table, a knock is heard*)

BARNES: Who is it?
BENJAMIN: (*without*) Can I see you a minute please?
BARNES: (*hiding the bottle*) Come in, Dr Benjamin, come in.
BENJ: It's important – excuse me – they've got Leeds up there in
   my place – He's operating on Mrs Lewis – the hysterectomy
   – it's my job. I washed up, prepared . . . they told me at the
   last minute. I don't mind being replaced, Doctor, but Leeds
   is a damn fool! He shouldn't be permitted –
BARNES: (*dryly*) Leeds is the nephew of Senator Leeds.
BENJ: He's incompetent as hell!
BARNES: (*obviously changing subject, picks up lab. jar*) They're doing
   splendid work in brain surgery these days. This is a very
   fine specimen . . .
BENJ: I'm sorry. I thought you might be interested.
BARNES: (*still examining jar*) Well, I am, young man, I am! Only
   remember it's a charity case!
BENJ: Of course. They wouldn't allow it for a second, otherwise.
BARNES: Her life is in danger?

BENJ: Of course! You know how serious the case is!

BARNES: Turn your gimlet eyes elsewhere, Doctor. Jigging around like a cricket on a hot grill won't help. Doctors don't run these hospitals. He's the Senator's nephew and there he stays.

BENJ: It's too bad.

BARNES: I'm not calling you down either. (*Plopping down jar suddenly*) Goddamit, do you think it's my fault?

BENJ: (*about to leave*) I know . . . I'm sorry.

BARNES: Just a minute. Sit down.

BENJ: Sorry, I can't sit.

BARNES: Stand then!

BENJ: (*sits*) Understand, Dr Barnes, I don't mind being replaced at the last minute this way, but . . . well, this flagrant bit of class distinction – because she's poor –

BARNES: Be careful of words like that – 'class distinction'. Don't belong here. Lots of energy, you brilliant young men, but idiots. Discretion! Ever hear that word?

BENJ: Too radical?

BARNES: Precisely. And some day like in Germany, it might cost you your head.

BENJ: Not to mention my job.

BARNES: So they told you?

BENJ: Told me what?

BARNES: They're closing Ward C next month. I don't have to tell you the hospital isn't self supporting. Until last year that board of trustees met deficits . . . You can guess the rest. At a board meeting Tuesday, our fine feathered friends discovered they couldn't meet the last quarter's deficit – a neat little sum well over $100,000. If the hospital is to continue at all, its damn –

BENJ: Necessary to close another charity ward!

BARNES: So they say . . . (*a wait*)

BENJ: But that's not all?

BARNES: (*ashamed*) Have to cut down on staff too . . .

BENJ: That's too bad. Does it touch me?

BARNES: Afraid it does.

BENJ: But after all I'm top man here. I don't mean I'm better than others, but I've worked harder –

BARNES: And shown more promise . . .

BENJ: I always supposed they'd cut from the bottom first.

BARNES: Usually.

BENJ: But in this case?

BARNES: Complications.

BENJ: For instance? (*Barnes hesitant*)

BARNES: I like you, Benjamin. It's one ripping shame –

BENJ: I'm no sensitive plant – what's the answer?

BARNES: An old disease, malignant tumescent. We need an anti-toxin for it.

BENJ: I see.

BARNES: What?

BENJ: I met that disease before – at Harvard first.

BARNES: You have seniority here, Benjamin.

BENJ: But I'm a Jew!

(*Barnes nods his head in agreement. Benj stands there a moment and blows his nose.*)

BARNES: (*blows his nose*) Microbes!

BENJ: Pressure from above?

BARNES: Don't think Kennedy and I didn't fight for you!

BENJ: Such discrimination, with all those wealthy brother Jews on the board?

BARNES: I've remarked before – doesn't seem to be much difference between wealthy Jews and rich Gentiles. Cut from the same piece!

BENJ: For myself I don't feel sorry. My parents gave up an awful lot to get me this far. They ran a little dry goods shop in the Bronx until their pitiful savings went in the crash last year. Poppa's peddling neckties . . . Saul Ezra Benjamin – a man who's read Spinoza all his life.

BARNES: Doctors don't run medicine in this country. The men who know their jobs don't run anything here, except the motormen on trolley cars. I've seen medicine change – plenty – anaesthesia, sterilization – but not because of rich men – in *spite* of them! In a rich man's country your true self's buried deep. Microbes! Less . . . Vermin! See this ankle, this delicate sensitive hand? Four hundred years to breed that. Out of a revolutionary background! Spirit of '76! Ancestors froze at Valley Forge! What's it all mean! Slops! The honest workers were sold out then, in '76. The

Constitution's for rich men then and now. Slops! (*the phone rings*)

BARNES: (*angrily*) Dr Barnes. (*Listens a moment, looks at Benjamin*) I see. (*Hangs up, turns slowly to the younger doctor*) They lost your patient.

(*Benj stands solid with the shock of this news but finally hurls his operation gloves to the floor*)

BARNES: That's right . . . that's right. Young, hot, go and do it! I'm very ancient, fossil, but life's ahead of you, Dr Benjamin, and when you fire the first shot say, 'This one's for old Doc Barnes!' Too much dignity – bullets. Don't shoot vermin! Step on them! If I didn't have an invalid daughter – (*goes back to his seat, blows his nose in silence*) I have said my piece, Benjamin.

BENJ: Lots of things I wasn't certain of. Many things these radicals say . . . you don't believe theories until they happen to you.

BARNES: You lost a lot today, but you won a great point.

BENJ: Yes, to know I'm right? To really begin believing in something? Not to say, 'What a world!', but to say, 'Change the world!' I wanted to go to Russia. Last week I was thinking about it – the wonderful opportunity to do good work in their socialized medicine –

BARNES: Beautiful! Beautiful!

BENJ: To be able to work –

BARNES: Why don't you go? I might be able –

BENJ: Nothing's nearer what I'd like to do!

BARNES: Do it!

BENJ: No! Our work's here – America! I'm scared . . . What future's ahead I don't know. Get some job to keep alive – maybe drive a cab – and study and work and learn my place –

BARNES: And step down hard!

BENJ: Fight! Maybe get killed, but goddam! We'll go ahead!

(*Benjamin stands with clenched fist raised high*)

BLACKOUT

AGATE: LADIES AND GENTLEMEN, and don't let anyone tell

you we ain't got some ladies in this sea of upturned faces!
Only they're wearin' pants. Well, maybe I don't know a
thing; maybe I fell outa the cradle when I was a kid and
ain't been right since – you can't tell!

VOICE: Sit down, cockeye!

AGATE: Who's paying you for those remarks, Buddy? – Moscow
Gold? Maybe I got a *glass eye*, but it come from working
in a factory at the age of eleven. They hooked it out because
they didn't have a shield on the works. But I wear it like
a medal 'cause it tells the world where I belong – deep down
in the working class! We had delegates in the union there
– all kinds of secretaries and treasurers . . . walkin' delegates,
but not with blisters on their feet! Oh no! On their fat little
ass from sitting on cushions and raking in mazuma.

(*Secretary and Gunman remonstrate in words and actions here.*)

Sit down boys. I'm just sayin' that about unions in general. I
know it ain't true here! Why no, our officers is all aces.
Why, I seen our own secretary Fatt walk outa his way not
to step on a cockroach. No boys, don't think –

FATT: (*breaking in*) You're out of order!

AGATE: (*to audience*) Am I outa order?

ALL: No, no. Speak. Go on, etc.

AGATE: Yes, our officers is all aces. But I'm a member here – and
no experience in Philly either! Today I couldn't wear my
union button. The damnest thing happened. When I take the
old coat off the wall, I see she's smoking. I'm a sonofagun
if the old union button isn't on fire! Yep, the old celluloid
was makin' the most god-awful stink: the landlady come up
and give me hell! You know what happened? – that old
union button just blushed itself to death! Ashamed! Can
you beat it?

FATT: Sit down, Keller! Nobody's interested!

AGATE: Yes, they are!

GUNMAN: Sit down like he tells you!

AGATE: (*continuing to audience*) And when I finish –

(*His speech is broken by Fatt and Gunman who physically handle him.
He breaks away and gets to other side of stage. The two are about to*

make for him when some of the committee men come forward and get in between the struggling parties. Agate's shirt has been torn)

AGATE: *(to audience)* What's the answer, boys? The answer is, if we're Reds because we wanna strike, then we take over their salute too! An uppercut! The good old uppercut to the chin! Hell, some of us boys ain't even got a shirt to our backs. What's the boss class tryin' to do – make a nudist colony outa us?

(The audience laughs and suddenly Agate comes to the middle of the stage so that the other cabmen back him up in a strong clump.)

AGATE: Don't laugh! Nothing's funny! This is your life and mine! It's skull and bones every incha the road! Christ, we're dyin' by inches! For what? For the debutant-ees to have their sweet comin' out parties in the Ritz! Poppa's got a daughter she's gotta get her picture in the papers. Christ, they make 'em with our blood. Joe said it. Slow death or fight. It's war!

(Throughout this whole speech Agate is backed up by the other six workers, so that from their activity it is plain that the whole group of them are saying these things. Several of them may take alternate lines out of this long last speech.)

You, Edna, God love your mouth! Sid and Florrie, the other boys, old Doc Barnes – fight with us for right! It's war! Working class, unite and fight! Tear down the slaughter-house of our old lives! Let freedom really ring!

These slick slobs stand here telling us about bogey men. That's a new one for the kids – the Reds is bogeymen! But the man who got me food in 1932 he called me Comrade! The one who picked me up where I bled – he called me Comrade too! What are we waiting for . . . Don't wait for Lefty! He might never come. Every minute –

(This is broken into by a man who has dashed up the centre aisle from the back of the house. He runs up on stage, says:)

MAN: Boys, they just found Lefty!
OTHERS: What? What? What?
SOME: Shhh . . . Shhhh . . .

MAN: They found Lefty . . .

AGATE: Where?

MAN: Behind the carbarns with a bullet in his head!

AGATE: (*crying*) Hear it, boys, hear it? Hell, listen to me! Coast to
coast! HELLO AMERICA! HELLO. WE'RE
STORMBIRDS OF THE WORKING CLASS. WORKERS
OF THE WORLD . . . OUR BONES AND BLOOD!
And when we die they'll know what we did to make a new
world! Christ, cut us up to little pieces. We'll die for what
is right!, put fruit trees where our ashes are! (*to audience*)
Well, what's the answer?

ALL: STRIKE!

AGATE: LOUDER!

ALL: STRIKE!

AGATE: (*and others on stage*) AGAIN!

ALL: STRIKE, STRIKE, STRIKE!!!

THE END

Notes for production of 'Waiting For Lefty'

Note: Copyright 1935 by the author.

For the immediate present no production of this play may be
presented without permission of the author, who may be reached
c/o NEW THEATRE, 114 West 14th Street, N.Y.C.

The background of the episodes, a strike meeting, is not an
excuse. Each of the committeemen shows in his episode the crucial
moment of his life which brought him to this very platform. The
dramatic structure on which the play has been built is simple but
highly effective. The form used is the old black-face minstrel form
of chorus, end men, specialty men and interlocutor.

In Fatt's scenes before the 'Spy Exposé,' mention should again
be made of Lefty's tardiness. Sitting next to Fatt in the center of
the circle is a little henchman who sits with his back to the audience. On the other side of Fatt is Lefty's empty chair. This is
so indicated by Fatt when he himself asks: 'Yeah, where's your
chairman?'

Fatt, of course, represents the capitalist system throughout the
play. The audience should constantly be kept aware of him, the

ugly menace which hangs over the lives of all the people who act out their own dramas. Perhaps he puffs smoke into the spotted playing space; perhaps during the action of a playlet he might insolently walk in and around the unseeing players. It is possible that some highly gratifying results can be achieved by the imaginative use of this character.

The strike committee on the platform during the acting out of the playlets should be used as chorus. Emotional, political, musical, they have in them possibilities of various comments on the scenes. This has been indicated once in the script in the place where Joe's wife is about to leave him. In the climaxes of each scene, slogans might very effectively be used – a voice coming out of the dark. Such a voice might announce at the appropriate moments in the 'Young Interne's' scene that the USSR is the only country in the world where Anti-Semitism is a crime against the State.

Do not hesitate to use music wherever possible. It is very valuable in emotionally stirring an audience.

Index